Balkan Dance

ALSO BY ANTHONY SHAY

*Choreographing Identities: Folk Dance,
Ethnicity and Festival in the United States
and Canada* (McFarland, 2006)

Balkan Dance

*Essays on Characteristics,
Performance and Teaching*

Edited by
ANTHONY SHAY

McFarland & Company, Inc., Publishers
Jefferson, North Carolina, and London

LIBRARY OF CONGRESS CATALOGUING-IN-PUBLICATION DATA

Balkan dance : essays on characteristics, performance and teaching / [edited by] Anthony Shay.
    p.   cm.
Includes bibliographical references and index.

ISBN 978-0-7864-3228-8
softcover : 50# alkaline paper ∞

1. Folk dancing, Balkan. 2. Folk dancing, Balkan—Study and teaching. I. Shay, Anthony, 1936– II. Title.
GV1679 B35   2007
793.3'1496—dc22   2007048717

British Library cataloguing data are available

©2008 Anthony Shay. All rights reserved

No part of this book may be reproduced or transmitted in any form or by any means, electronic or mechanical, including photocopying or recording, or by any information storage and retrieval system, without permission in writing from the publisher.

On the cover: Dancers of Posavina, Croatia (photograph by D. Young)

Manufactured in the United States of America

McFarland & Company, Inc., Publishers
  Box 611, Jefferson, North Carolina 28640
    www.mcfarlandpub.com

To the many dancers and musicians
of the UCLA Village Dancers, the Aman Folk Ensemble,
and the AVAZ International Dance Theatre
for giving me the joy
of choreographing the Balkans for them

Acknowledgments

The essays in this volume both honor and address many of the intellectual interests and concerns that interested Dick Crum during his life and teaching career. This volume is akin to a *Festschrift* in that many of the contributors to the volume perceived Dick Crum as a mentor; his strength as a towering figure in the International Recreational Folk Dance Movement was multi-layered. He was a pioneer teacher of Balkan dance and devised effective teaching techniques that many have tried, and largely failed, to emulate. Hundreds of thousands of individuals who participated in the International Recreational Folk Dance Movement participated in his classes. He was an indefatigable researcher. He constantly followed a quest for the historical, ethnographical, and sociological issues that underpinned the teaching which he so successfully undertook, and in so doing, he amassed what is probably the single largest collection of books, recordings, and research materials on Balkan music, dance, costume, ethnography, and history ever assembled in a private collection.

Many of those who contributed to this collection, as well as many other scholars, owe an intellectual debt to Dick Crum. He always made time to open his collection to interested students and to hold lengthy discussions with them concerning their research interests. In addition, I would like to mention those like John Filcich, Michael and Maryann Herman, and Mario Casetta, who each supported Dick Crum's efforts in his teaching endeavors.

In the preparation of this volume, I wish to thank Ann Howe, who first suggested this project. I owe an intellectual debt to Barbara Sellers-Young, as well as the debt of friendship, for invaluable suggestions in the writing of the Introduction. In addition, I am grateful to Robert Henry Leibman and Larry Weiner, trustees of Dick Crum's estate, for their support in this project.

Table of Contents

Acknowledgments   vii
Preface   1

1. Richard George "Dick" Crum: A Life
   ROBERT HENRY LEIBMAN   5
2. Introduction: Choreographing the Balkans
   ANTHONY SHAY   12

Nationalism, Ethnicity, and Performance

3. Transnational Čoček: Gender and the Politics of Balkan Romani Dance
   CAROL SILVERMAN   37
4. Dance and Place: The Case of a Roma Community in Northern Greece
   CHRISTOS PAPAKOSTAS   69
5. Dance as Propaganda: The Metaxas Regime's Stadium Ceremonies, 1937–1940
   IRENE LOUTZAKI   89

6. Nationalism and Scholarship in Transylvanian Ethnochoreology
   COLIN QUIGLEY   116

7. Bulgarian Dance Culture: From Censorship to Chalga
   ERICA NIELSEN   130

8. Clapping for Serbs: Nationalism and Performance in Bosnia and Herzegovina
   LYNN D. MANERS   145

9. Choreographing the Other: The Serbian State Folk Dance Ensemble, Gypsies, Muslims, and Albanians
   ANTHONY SHAY   161

Balkan Dance in America

10. "Inside, Outside, Upside-Down": The Role of Mainstream Society Participants in the Ethnic Dance Movement
    ROBIN J. EVANCHUK   179

11. Balkan Tradition, American Alternative: Dance, Community, and the People of the Pines
    JUNE ADLER VAIL   195

Morphology of Balkan Dance and Music

12. Hai la Joc! Periodicity at Play in Romanian Dance Music
    JAMIE L. WEBSTER   213

13. *Dvoransko Kolo*: From the 1840s to the Twentieth Century
    NANCY LEE CHALFA RUYTER   239

14. Dance Structure and Its Application to the Understanding of Macedonian "Cross" Dances
    ROBERT HENRY LEIBMAN   250

About the Contributors   271
Index   275

Preface

Balkan dancing was, and continues to be, one of the most popular activities for thousands of young Americans, including me. It was an activity that consumed every waking spare minute in our lives. We attended classes where we learned the songs and dances, and we also attended large festivals and folk dance camps that specialized in Balkan dances.

Many of us joined performing groups that sometimes numbered almost 100 individuals, dancers, singers and musicians. I founded and directed two of those groups, the Aman Folk Ensemble and the AVAZ International Dance Theatre and the participation in those groups can be accurately described as a sub-culture, often hidden from the eyes of most other Americans. Most dance groups were smaller, but they proliferated throughout the United States, from small communities in New England to large urban centers, and in many college and university communities. Those of us who participated in those groups spent countless hours learning embroidery patterns, sewing costumes, learning how to speak Serbian, Croatian, Macedonian, Rumanian, Greek, and Bulgarian, and mastering Balkan cooking.

At the height of this period, 1955–1980, cities like Los Angeles and San Francisco boasted several performing companies and many coffeehouses catered to those who were interested in dances of the Balkans. They were packed with excited Balkan dancers night after night. Many of us spent every dollar and available time to travel to the various countries in the Balkans to attend folk dance festivals, classes, and concerts and conduct field research. Sometimes just being at the source of those wonderful dances was all we desired.

Dick Crum was one of the most important and iconic figures in teaching, choreographing, and researching dance of the Balkans. When Dick passed away in 2005, people in the world of Balkan dance were devastated, and we looked for a way to memorialize his enormous contributions to the field. Knowing Dick was a bibliophile who had amassed what is probably the largest private collection of books and other research materials about every aspect of the cultures — music, dances, costumes — of the Balkan nations and societies, I decided to edit a volume that would be dedicated to his memory.

As I began the project, I was surprised to realize that there were no general works published in English about the dances of the Balkans. In part, the reason for this is that most research concerning Balkan dances is published in the languages of the related culture. The governments of the Balkan nations were very generous in funding folklore research, since folklore is a core subject that, in the minds of many individuals, studies the "primordial" origins of the various peoples of that region and therefore has nationalist implications, as several articles in this volume address. Thus, many native dance researchers in the Balkan nations have produced many important works on the topic, and so for many American individuals who are intensely interested in the subject, until recently, it appeared that the research in the field was being adequately covered by those researchers who lived and worked in the Balkans.

Now, after the first enthusiasm for the learning of the dances has passed, many of us who became scholars are taking a fresh look at many aspects of Balkan dance that native scholars, who frequently have different goals and viewpoints, have not addressed. Thus, this collection fulfills our commitment to honor the memory of Dick Crum, and also provides original research on a variety of topics in the field of Balkan dance studies that have not been addressed elsewhere.

The articles in the book address three general aspects of Balkan dance that have interested Balkan dance enthusiasts and researchers (most of us belong to both of these groups) alike. The first aspect of several of the essays addresses the issue of how folklore, especially dance, as the most embodied form of cultural production, takes on political and nationalistic meaning in the context of the societies of the Balkans, especially after World War II (Loutzaki, Maners, Neilson, Papacostas, Quigley, Shay, Silverman). The costumed dancing body constitutes an iconic marker of ethnic identity, and this is one of the principal reasons that governments in the Balkans spent considerable funding for large scale, state supported national folk dance ensembles to represent their nations and cultures on world stages. Many of us in America modeled our performances after those of the national companies of Eastern Europe.

The second aspect of the essays in this volume addresses the topic of how and why so many thousands of Americans became so engrossed with and enthusiastic about the learning and performing of Balkan dance and music. Mirjana Laušević has recently produced a magisterial ethnomusicological study of Americans involved in the performing and playing of Balkan music (*Balkan Fascination: Creating an Alternative Music Culture in America*). Three of the articles (Shay in the Introduction, Evanchuk, and Vail) address the way in which Balkan dance consumed and inspired thousands of young Americans, and in many ways they complement Laušević's important study.

Finally, many American enthusiasts in the field of Balkan dance became fascinated with the minute details of dance performance for purposes of learning Balkan dance and music. Three of the articles (Leibman, Ruyter, and Webster) demonstrate the unique ways in which Americans approach the study and learning of Balkan dance and music, in some cases creating unique models to analyze performance practices.

These essays constitute a wide array of topics and research that are imbued with the passion that Balkan dancing inspired in so many of us, and thus, they make a fitting tribute to the memory of Dick Crum, one of the pioneers in this field, who inspired and engaged so many of us and whose wit and wisdom we sorely miss.

1

Richard George "Dick" Crum: A Life

ROBERT HENRY LEIBMAN

Dick Crum was born on December 8, 1928, and grew up in a Romanian immigrant neighborhood in Minneapolis, Minnesota. As a young child he learned to speak Romanian and attended many cultural events at the Romanian Hall across the street from his home. It was there that he learned his first folk dances; in these Romanian social events he learned the seven or eight circle and couple dances that the community performed in both social and festive contexts. As a child, he regularly appeared with the Romanian community's dance group in the St. Paul Festival of Nations folk dance festival, sponsored to this day by the International Institute. Together these early events inaugurated his life-long passion for and engagement with dance and foreign languages.

While in high school, Crum took lessons in ballroom dancing at Arthur Murray's Dance Studio. He proved to have an outstanding talent for both performing and teaching dance, and soon he was earning money teaching ballroom dances. After graduating high school as valedictorian at the age of sixteen, during the next four years he enrolled in Latin American Studies at the University of Minnesota. During this period, he began attending recreational folk dance groups, learning Latin American dances from classmates, and dancing in various ethnic performing groups. He became part of the leadership of the St. Paul Festival of Nations and became intimately involved with its teaching and preparation, as well as dancing with several of the community groups that participated in the festival.

In 1949, Crum traveled to Mexico where he was able to study with Dr. Marcelo Torreblanco, the foremost authority on Mexican dance at that time. He remained there for nine months and was able to accompany his mentor on field trips to Vera Cruz and Jalisco. He cited this as the time when he learned how to take careful field notes on the dances he observed. As a budding researcher, he crucially realized that in the village context, individuals were each doing their own version of the dance and that individual improvisation and certain types of innovation constituted important elements of traditional dance. He found that there was no absolute normative style that all the village population performed, but just as with the Lindy Hop and Jitterbug that he knew from his own dance experiences, individuals constantly created new variations, movements, and stylistic elements. This concept was a new one to the vast majority of individuals who participated in the burgeoning recreational folk dance movement.

Portrait of Dick Crum from 1978 by Eliot Khumer. We thank the Richard George Crum Estate for permission to reproduce the photograph.

In 1951, Crum won a scholarship to Duquesne University to become a member of their well-known touring and performing ensemble, the Duquesne University Tamburitzans. Becoming a member of the Tamburitzans provided each member with a full-paid scholarship to attend Duquesne University, somewhat like the athletic scholarships provided by many American colleges. He was a member of the company for one year, studying sociology as his major, when the Duquesne University Tamburitzans were invited to tour Yugoslavia. It was during this trip that he discovered the rich variety of dance to be found in Yugoslavia. He expressed his excitement at finding a trove of dances in Yugoslavia that were so much more varied than the limited set of *kolos* that he had learned from Yugoslav Americans in the United States, who formed the principal audience for the Duquesne Tamburitzan concerts.

This journey to Yugoslavia sparked Crum's interest in dance ethnography. He began to spend his free time meeting dance scholars and choreographers and notating dance wherever he found it. It was at this time that Crum began teaching Balkan dances to recreational folk dancers, an activity that he continued until near the end of his life. He taught several workshops and camps, the first in 1953 at Michael and Maryann Herman's Maine Camp, one of the most prestigious dance camps in the United States even today.

In 1954, Crum undertook a Duquesne University-sponsored research trip to Yugoslavia, the first of many, to gather raw ethnographic music and dance materials for adaptation to stage and recreational dance. From 1955 through 1959 he lived in Pittsburgh where he worked as choreographer and technical advisor for the Tamburitzans. He also attended the University of Pittsburgh from which he earned a BA in French in 1958.

In 1959, Crum moved to Cambridge, Massachusetts, where he began his graduate studies in Slavic languages and literature at Harvard University. During his graduate years he retained his ties to the Tamburitzans, creating choreographies and training the company performers at their camp in Lake Nebagamon, Wisconsin, where the company trained and prepared the concert programs for their annual touring activities. During this period, he earned an MA in Slavic Languages and Literature in 1961 and remained at Harvard until 1966, where he completed his coursework towards a Ph.D.

From 1956 to 1971, he held the position of associate professor of humanities at Robert Morris College in Pittsburgh, teaching courses in beginning and intermediate French, German, and Spanish. In the summer of 1968, he toured Latin America as part of a United States State Department People-to-People tour, interpreting for touring American performers and giving lectures in Spanish on American folk music and dance.

By the time he moved to Los Angeles in 1971, Crum had been researching, teaching and choreographing the dances of the Balkans for more than 20 years and he had become the premier teacher of Balkan dance in this country. He had been one of the first Americans to go to the Balkans to see, record, and bring back the rich diversity of dance traditions that still existed in the Balkans at that time. It was Crum, more than anyone, through his ability to teach in a warm, engaging, humorous way who helped move Balkan dance to the center of the recreational folk dance movement. In the 1950s, when he began, recreational folk dancing focused primarily on the dances of Western

Europe, mostly done in couples, although the repertoire did include some simple line and circle dances from Yugoslavia, Romania, and Greece. While most of the Western European dances had long since ceased to be a part of the living dance tradition of their respective populations, except perhaps as symbolic performances of a specific people's past, many of the Balkan dances that Crum learned and taught constituted a living tradition that the rural, and even urban, populations still danced at social events in Yugoslavia, as well as in the corresponding immigrant communities in the United States.

By the early 1970s in the United States, the profile of a typical folk dance evening had changed: it included fewer dances from the older Western European corpus and many more dances from the Balkans. At the same time, there was a drastic expansion in the number, type, and complexity of Balkan dances that were being taught and performed by recreational folk dance groups. This new corpus of dances reflected the rich, diverse, living dance traditions which had so intrigued Crum on that first trip in 1952 and involved rhythms, meters, and choreographic patterns which presented exciting new challenges for recreational folk dancers.

Dick Crum lived in the same three-bedroom apartment in Santa Monica from August 1974 until his death 31 years later. Many of those who shared this apartment with him were young folk dancers who were attending UCLA and majoring in folklore, ethnomusicology, and particularly the dance ethnology program, through which Dick maintained an active involvement with the more intellectual, ethnographic approaches to dance. He was stimulated by these young students who offered him an alternative intellectual appreciation than he experienced from the majority of folk dancers who were interested in folk dance purely as a source of recreation and entertainment. Crum was widely read in all aspects of dance and its history and during his lifetime he amassed an extraordinary library of research materials on the topics of dance, music, costume, languages, and ethnography. Because of his linguistic abilities, he had much greater access to original ethnographic and theoretical works about traditional dance, so that his apartment-mates gained as much from their discussions on dance with him as they did from any of their UCLA professors.

Until health problems affected him in the late 1990s, Dick Crum continued to teach workshops at least once a month throughout the country, and he always received many more requests than he could fulfill. He also continued to create occasional choreographies for different performing groups about the country, especially for the Aman Folk Ensemble of Los Angeles where he briefly served as Artistic Director.

As more Americans began to travel to the Balkans and bring back dances which they taught and, more importantly, dance teachers from the Balkans (often former members of major state-sponsored performing ensembles) began coming to the United States to teach dances, the Balkan dance repertoire within the recreational folk dance grew rapidly and became more and more dominated by multi-figured choreographies that crowded out the simpler immigrant *kolos* and village dances that characterized the recreational folk dance repertoire of the 1950s and 1960s. While Crum had taught many of these more complex, excitingly challenging dances, by the mid–1970s, he began to focus his workshop teaching on simpler, less choreographed dances, often going back and reviewing material that he had introduced years earlier. While interested in recreational folk dancing and its repertoire as a subject of study, he explicitly rejected judgments of value based on "authenticity." Increasingly he found that choreographically created dances were of less interest to him than those dances which had been performed as part of living traditions.

As part of his teaching technique he had always tried to include ethnographic and cultural information about the dances and the people who performed the dances natively, both while he was teaching the dances and in a shorter separate session that came to be called the "culture corner." As people grew to know more and more about the basic geographic and demographic facts of the Balkans, in these sessions Crum spent more time discussing the cultural settings for the dances. Beginning in the 1970s, he developed one such session which he entitled "Naški" = "Ours" (the villagers' reference to their own dance) in which he tried to explain how and why a village dance changed in dynamics, or possibly even in some minor choreographic details, when it was performed by the villagers in a stage performance, how additional changes might occur as the same group of villagers began to perform these dances at festivals in which other similar groups from other regions were also performing—and in a sense competing—and finally, as the dance might be performed as part of a state ensemble's choreography. Unlike other culture corner topics, this was not simply a lecture but involved the participation of the listeners in a dramatic performance of these events.

Two other themes that Crum frequently talked about during these cultural sessions were the history of U.S. recreational folk dancing and old-time *kolos*, the 31 Yugoslav circle dances that he had documented as having made up the basic repertoire for most Yugoslavs in this country from the time of their immigration, between 1885 and 1920, through the 1950s. Though he presented these and other topics in these lectures and talked about writing a book about them — as early as the mid–1950s he mentioned a soon-to-be-published book on Yugoslav dances in his correspondence with Yugoslav dance scholars — his only actual publication on dance was a small book, *Old Tyme Kolos*, published by Festival Records in 1993 for the Tamburitza Extravaganza held in Los Angeles. In this book he describes and discusses the 31 *kolos* done by the earlier Yugoslav immigrants, although he did not include all of the ethnographic data that he had accumulated on this material. Crum also wrote a song book, *The Dick Crum Book: Vranjanka and other Jugoslav Songs and Dances*, and a few articles in folk dance magazines, as well as hundreds of dance descriptions for workshop syllabi. However, his principal impact on the world of folk dance and beyond was made not through print so much as through public teaching and personal interaction with those he taught.

In the end, Dick Crum was a teacher — a man with a great breadth of knowledge about dance generally and folk or ethnic dance in particular — who had a special gift for presenting the material in a simple, entertaining way that made it available and understandable to all without in any way deforming or distorting it. As a pioneer, directly or indirectly he played a major role in creating the great interest in Balkan folk dance and folklore that developed in the United States.

His second passion was the learning, teaching and translation of foreign languages. By the fifth grade, Crum had begun teaching himself German, French, and Spanish. He was also interested in cryptography and created all sorts of codes. At age thirteen, he was writing a diary using Latin, French, Spanish, Romanian, and Egyptian hieroglyphs. He also created an entirely new imagined language from scratch, creating a textbook describing its vocabulary and grammar as well as offering exercises intended for the learner. He taught languages in several institutions of higher learning as was mentioned earlier.

From 1973 until 2002 he served as the senior multi-lingual editor for a translation firm that changed ownership several times, including Berlitz. With his knowledge of multiple languages, Crum was an invaluable professional translator and oversaw translations into English from a wide group of languages including Bulgarian, Macedonian, Bosnian, Croatian, Serbian, Serbo-Croatian, Slovenian, Czech, Slovak, Polish, Russian, Danish, Norwegian, Swedish, Dutch, German, French, Italian, Portuguese, Romanian, and Spanish. He also trained new translators. In addition to the languages listed above, Crum also had knowledge of several other languages including Greek, Albanian, Yiddish, and Tagalog.

Dick Crum also developed a deep interest in genealogy. At some point early in his time at Harvard, he discovered that a the Rev. Winston Crum was living across the hall from him in his dormitory. The Rev. Crum was in the process of preparing a revised edition of his book on his branch of the

Crum family tree. Crum became interested in the project and offered to help by beginning to gather information on his own branch of the Crum family. This was the beginning of his involvement with Crum family genealogy, an interest which he pursued with fervor, particularly in the latter years of his life. Through his research, he became an expert in genealogy, one to whom others would turn for help, particularly on methodology. In 2006, only months after his death on December 12, 2005, a book on Crum genealogy, to which he was a major contributor, was published.

In addition to languages and dance, he was a man with an overpowering curiosity about a variety of topics ranging from cuisine to genealogy. Although he loved history, he never wanted to become out of touch with what was currently happening. Everyone who knew him regarded him as a natural teacher; he enjoyed sharing his knowledge, which was encyclopedic, with all and did so in ways which made it accessible to almost everyone, a hallmark of his teaching method. Crum once said: "My highest happiness is teaching whether it's foreign languages, folk dance, or how to make lasagna.... What I find I enjoy most in life... If I had my druthers, I'd be teaching twenty-four hours a day, and I find I have energy and apparently I'm effective because I see results.... Primary in my life is being a teacher."

This *Festschrift* has been gathered to honor Dick Crum and his work, which directly or indirectly led to the several authors' interest and involvement in the field of Balkan dance and culture.

2

Introduction: Choreographing the Balkans

ANTHONY SHAY

For more than two centuries people in the West, that is those few who had ever heard of the Balkans, regarded those regions as sites of primitiveness, wildness, and mystery. Before the nineteenth century most of the Balkans were either backward outposts of the Hapsburg or Ottoman Empires, and as such attracted no particular attention. But, in the early nineteenth-century as revolutionaries in Serbia, Greece, Romania, and Montenegro established tiny, impoverished kingdoms, their presence intruded, often annoyingly, into the arena of great power politics. The only bare knowledge of these remote regions came from little-known travel journals of a few intrepid travelers and adventurers, often on their way to Istanbul; their destination was not the Balkans. That all changed when Lord Byron, the infamous British poet ("mad, bad, and dangerous to know")[1], traveled to Greece in the 1820s and championed the cause of the Greeks against the Ottoman Turks. His contemporary, the poet Shelley, said "We are all Greeks" in imagining the inheritors of the glories of ancient Greece struggling against the oriental Ottomans in his poem "Hellas" (Crompton 1985, 86). In this essay I will lay out both the ways in which the Balkans came to be imagined and perceived in the West and how the various peoples in the Balkans came to imagine and perceive one another to establish the context for the chapters in this volume that honors the memory of Dick Crum.[2]

The nineteenth-century reality of the Balkans appalled Byron and a multitude of other literary figures after him, who at first looked to find in Greece

2. Introduction

the descendents of the glory of Classic Greece. Instead, they found impoverished peasants and discovered that the highly vaunted local *hajduks* and *klephts* were not the brave mountain revolutionaries of local epic poetry, but rather common, vicious bandits who fought both Turks and plundered and victimized their own ethnic kinsmen indiscriminately. As historian Maria Todorova points out: "In practically every description, the standard Balkan male is uncivilized, primitive, crude, cruel, and without exception, disheveled" (1997, 14), thus establishing the Balkans as another region over which the superior West might establish intellectual and political dominion. Another Byron contemporary, the French viscount Chateaubriand, quipped, "Never see Greece, Monsieur, except in Homer. It is the best way" (quoted in Todorova 1997, 94). In the late nineteenth and early twentieth centuries a kind of orientalizing literary trend established the Balkans as a site for comic opera settings for novels, operettas, and poetry. Historian Larry Wolff comments: "One might describe the invention of Eastern Europe as an intellectual project of demi-Orientalization" (1994, 7). By the second half of the twentieth century the Balkans metamorphosed into a gritty Cold War battleground, a fertile site for adventure and spy novels by British authors such as Eric Ambler and John Le Carré.

Since the 1950s, especially after the 1956 appearances of Tanec, the Macedonian State Folk Dance Ensemble, followed in a few months by a major tour of Kolo, the Serbian State Folk Dance Ensemble, the first national folk ensembles from the Iron Curtain countries to perform regularly in the United States, hundreds and later thousands of young mainstream Americans discovered Balkan music and dance.[3] In the wake of the appearances of the state-supported dance ensembles, in Los Angeles, San Francisco, New York, Boston, Seattle, Minneapolis, and other cities several mainstream Americans founded large-scale performing dance ensembles, singing groups, and orchestras further popularizing the dances and music of Croatia, Bulgaria, Serbia, Macedonia, Greece, Slovenia, Romania, and Albania. These performances provided many of the young Americans, experiencing a lack of ethnicity and roots in the mass post–World War II move to the suburbs, with their own "Different Village," in ethnomusicologist Mirjana Laušević's terms (1998). Performing in these ensembles was a life-changing experience for many of the participants, leading some of them into careers of teaching, performing, and scholarship.

Dick Crum was one of the pioneer teachers of Balkan dances, and throughout his fifty-year teaching career, which included numerous research trips to the Balkans,[4] he became pre-eminent in the large international recreational folk dance movement as a teacher and as a major source of knowledge and information about Balkan dances.[5] Although his encyclopedic knowledge of folk dance from other areas such as Mexico and Eastern Europe was in fact much broader than most people realized, he became nationally famous among folk dancers and musicians primarily for his knowledge of Balkan dance and music. Large-scale classes in which Crum, as well as many others, taught proliferated throughout the United States, including summer camps devoted to the teaching of folk dance, which became the emotional life blood of many of the participants (see Laušević 1998, 336–456). Dick Crum influenced the lives of many people thirsty for knowledge about these new and exciting dance genres, and although he produced but a few short, popular articles for folk dance magazines, he was particularly supportive of individuals who undertook the study of music and dance of the Balkans as a scholarly pursuit.

It therefore seems strange, given the intense interest and popularity in the dances of the various Balkan peoples, that to date, while several books about the music of various areas of the Balkans have been recently published, with one exception on Romanian dance (Giurchescu with Bloland 1995), no single book devoted to the study of Balkan dance has appeared in the English language. It is most appropriate that this collection of essays, devoted to aspects of dance and music of the Balkans, should be devoted to the memory of Dick Crum.

This volume contains a variety of essays about Balkan dance and music, and for all of their differences, they focus on some of the most salient aspects of these forms of cultural expression. These essays address (1) the ways in which ethnic and national identities constitute an important aspect of Balkan music and dance performances, whether by state folk dance ensembles, peasants in local and national festivals, immigrant groups in the United States, or mainstream American participants. Crucial elements of ethnicity and nationalism are profoundly complicit in and serve as a nexus in the way in which folkloric dances, music, and costumes constitute ethnic and national icons of identity in these small nation states. As an important element of identity it is important to grasp the ways in which the Balkans have constituted a site of phantasmic images, both among Balkan peoples' images of themselves and their neighbors, as well as the way in which the Balkan peoples appear in the imaginary of the West. This volume also covers (2) the unique phenomenon of thousands of Americans, from the late 1950s on, seeking new identities through the performance of exotic music and dance genres, of which Balkan dances and music were among the most popular; and (3) descriptions and analyses of the formal morphological properties that characterize the dances and music of the Balkans.

Ethnicity and Nationalism

Identity issues have recently occupied many folkloric and anthropological studies, as well as engaging the philosophical and ethical issues of how the scholar frames issues of identity, ethnicity, and nationalism within their studies. As folklorist Barbara Kirshenblatt-Gimblett observes:

Difference does make a difference. This is the basis for multiculturalism in its many forms, affirmative racialism, and the biologizing of difference, most recently in the form of the gay gene. This is also the arena in which folklorists operate, particularly in public folklore... Underlying much celebratory diversity is an affirmative racialism coded in terms of culture. It reveals itself in the privileging of origins and originality, true character, precedence, preeminence, uniqueness, and authenticity, especially when linked to primordial claims [emphasis in the original, 1994, 236].

Folklore, the "true" and "authentic" expression of the "people," became a major cornerstone in the production of nationalist mythologies of ethnic origins and their accompanying historical and territorial entitlements. This late eighteenth-century romantic concept, most forcefully enunciated by Johann Gottfried Herder, and felt to our day, endorsed the study of folklore as the means for understanding the basic ethos of each specific ethnic group. In this concept the peasantry constituted the true, uncontaminated source of knowledge of a nation's history and origins, a continuation of romantic thought. This inspired the massive collection of tales, songs, beliefs, music, and, lastly, dance throughout Central and Eastern Europe that continues unabated today.[6] Governments — national, regional, and local — throughout the Balkans and on both sides of the Iron Curtain established national dance companies, following the Moiseyev model of the USSR, and supported massive amateur dance and music activities and festivals to demonstrate folklore. The national companies of all of these countries, under the careful guidance of the state apparatus, produced sanitized picture postcard choreographies that underscored the positive image of each titular national group, while frequently suppressing or distorting the images of undesirable minorities (see Rice 1994; Shay 2002).

Clearly, the performance of folk songs and dances, whether by a professional national state ensemble or by peasants in regional folk dance festivals, takes on the characteristics described by Kirshenblatt-Gimblett. These expressive forms serve to underline the unique ethnic character of particular ethnic communities, justifying their right to occupy the "original" homeland in which these are widely perceived as unique, primordial, and unique to a specific ethnic group.

Identity, in the form of ethnicity and nationalism, quickly assumes an important sociological and historical dimension in any study of Balkan folklore. Ethnicity and nationalism infuse the performance of Balkan dance and music because folk dance and music in the minds of many observers constitute primordial aspects of ethnic identity. No one interested in the Balkans can long escape the large role that ethnicity and nationalism play in Balkan cultural expression. Sometimes the performance of music and dance, in specific regional costumes, attains an iconic status of ethnicity, and sometimes it can assume the representation of the nation state.

Such displays of folklore were not limited to local and national venues. Most of the governments supported international touring as well, sending their finest performing groups to sites like world fairs. As late as 1992 at the International Exhibition in Seville:

> The national state was produced as a territorial unit with key symbolic (flags, capital cities, anthems) and a quantifiable citizenship. These symbolic identifiers were most clearly visible on National Day, allocated to each participant, when official ceremonies, street parades and folkloric performances encourage the display of national dress and national dance [Harvey 1996, 54].

Nationalism, the sometimes dark side of ethnicity in this region, also plays a role in the performance of music and dance. This becomes clear in the founding of and state support for both professional and amateur performance groups from urban areas, and the encouragement of regional festivals to showcase peasant dance and music groups.

Ethnicity

Nationalism and ethnicity, while intertwined, are, in fact, different phenomena. Ethnicity differs from nationalism, although also linked, in that ethnicity occurs frequently within states and across national borders. Ethnicity predates nationalism. Before a sense of nationhood occurs, a consciousness of a modern ethnic identity must pre-exist. In the Balkans this is frequently inextricably intertwined with religion, which, to some degree, results as a legacy of the Ottoman millet system under which individuals were identified by their religious affiliations rather than by modern ethnic markers such as folklore and language. For example, a Serb is an individual who is born into the Serbian Orthodox faith, or at least his or her parents were, and speaks Serbo-Croatian (now designated as Serbian, Croatian, Bosnian, but still 95 percent the same language), no matter where he or she was born. Thus, Serbs can live in any state: Serbia, Bulgaria, Croatia, Bosnia, Macedonia, and they will always be Serbs. Roma, Moslem Slavs (speakers of Serbo-Croatian), Albanians, and Hungarians are significant minorities that live in Serbia, but they are not regarded as Serbs by the majority Serb population. "For the nationalists, the continuous presence of Islamic populations among the Balkan Christians is a sign of the latter's shameful backwardness" (Longinović 2002, 45).

Ethnicity, in the sense that we currently use it — a cluster of elements defining a collectivity of individuals such as, but not limited to, a specific name and identity recognized by both insiders and outsiders, specific languages, a common ancestry (usually mythological), a common historical territory, and shared folkloric expressions of tales, music, dance, and costumes — is new. According to historians of nationalism John Hutchinson and Anthony D. Smith the modern concept of ethnicity is recent and only "first recorded in the Oxford English Dictionary in 1953" (1996, 5), although the concept of "us and them" certainly existed in the antique world in which Greeks and other peoples conceived of the world as Hellene and barbarian, Roman and barbarian, Egyptian and barbarian, etc. Herodotus and other ancient historians and observers devoted much of their writing to descriptions of the "Other."

Especially under the Ottoman Empire (1390–1918), in which the millet system, based largely on religious affiliation, determined identity, ethnic consciousness, based not only on religious confession but also on language and a perceived common heritage came late to some groups.[7] Ottoman historian Fikret Adanir claims that "only at the turn of the twentieth [century] did a distinct Macedonian consciousness begin to develop" (1992, 170). As late as 1891, members of a small elite were attempting to develop a Macedonian literary language and "folklore and a literary language were important aspects of the national question also for Macedonian students in Russia" (1992, 179).

The Nation and Nationalism

Nationalism in the Balkans frequently descends to jingoism and murderous chauvinism, as the recent breakup of the former Yugoslavia demonstrates. Patrick Geary, historian of medieval history, observes:

> A historian of the early Middle Ages, who observes this problem first hand, who listens to the rhetoric of nationalist leaders, and who reads the scholarship produced by official or quasi-official historians, is immediately struck by how central the interpretation of the period from circa 400–1000 is to this debate. Suddenly, the history of Europe over a millennium ago is anything but academic: The interpretation of the period of the dissolution of the Roman Empire and the barbarian migration has become the fulcrum of political discourse across much of Europe [2002, 7].

These ideologies appropriate and pervert history as their justification. This pseudo-history assumes, first, that the peoples of Europe are distinct, stable and objectively identifiable social and cultural units, and that they are distinguished by language, religion, custom, and national character, which are unambiguous and immutable [2002, 11].

It is important to cite Geary at length for such claims dominate the national discourses of many regions of the Balkans, and certainly laid the basis for the shrill nationalist claims that constituted the raison d'être for the violent dismemberment of the former Yugoslavia. Geary observes, "Surely, if Lithuanians and Croats have their own language, their own music, their own dress, they have a right to their own parliament and their own army." But, as he concludes: "There is nothing particularly ancient about either the peoples of Europe or their supposed right to political autonomy" (2002, 12).

Yet, we see, through mutual antagonism, and as justification for the establishment of separate states, the Bosnian Muslims, Croats, and Serbs attempted to establish separate languages. Linguist Thomas Magner states:

> The designation of a speech variant as a distinct language can be the result of a *political* decision and not necessarily a *linguistic* judgment. There is a greater difference between British English and American English than between Croatian and Serbian... The correspondence of Croatian and Serbian sounds, vocabulary, nominal declensions, verb declensions, and syntactic formations ranges from 95 percent to 100 percent [emphases in the original, 2003, ix].

Nationalism constitutes a stage beyond ethnic consciousness — a demand for territory with all of the panoply of the nation-state: armed forces, state-controlled educational systems, national languages, as well as less attractive characteristics of obedience to the state such as forced adherence to a state-sponsored religion, banning linguistic use of other than officially approved languages, wearing special clothing, etc.

I suggest that the nationalism found in many small states, especially recently established ones (as opposed to older established states like Luxembourg and Lichtenstein), can become very defensive: a sort of barrier mentality. Raftis Alkis, the director of the Dora Stratou Greek Folk Dances Theatre, stated: "Greek identity must be understood in terms of the fortress mentality to which this small nation feels the urge to protect its boundaries, mental and ethnic" (personal interview, February 16, 2000).

In the Balkans the establishment of nation states came late compared to Western Europe. Fikret Adnan notes that "recognition of a Macedonian nationality is of relatively recent date, being connected with the formation of a Macedonian republic in the framework of the Yugoslav Federation after the Second World War" (1992, 161). While Romania, Greece, and Serbia grew incrementally around tiny kingdoms throughout the nineteenth century, Croatia did not attain full statehood until 1992, after the breakup of the former Yugoslavia.[8]

Thus, for people in the Balkans, as in many areas of the world, the research through dances and music, costumes and folk tales, establishes a patrimony, a primordial link with the "original" settlers of their land, which establishes their authentic claim to the territory they inhabit: a nation of their own. Cultural historian Alexander Kiossev says of folklore studies: "It was taken for granted that the spatial span of the national 'fruits' coincided in a natural way with the boundaries of the imagined homeland. Thus these academic disciplines in fact reaffirmed the national mapping (and the official national identity) and were even used to justify territorial claims" (2002, 176). The search for the historic moment that a particular ethnic group put its collective feet on the national territory constitutes a major aim of historic and folkloric research — the basis for national identity — and occupies much of the scholarly output from the various Balkan countries.

The Balkans: Orientalism and Balkanism

Edward Said (1979) and Michel Foucault (1972) exposed the construction of the imaginary, for example the western imaginary of "The Orient," as a systematic means of knowing, a means of establishing a sense of superiority and dominating the "Other." The western imaginary of the Balkans, less well known than that of the Orient, has taken two distinct forms: what I will call the "comic opera" and the "noble (savage) warrior peasant" who will commit violence only in defense of his nation and his hearth. They both stem from the Romantic images of the Balkans created by Western travelers and writers and both images feature singing, dancing peasantries. These two threads occasionally meet. The origins of this romantic turn can be traced to the career of George Gordon, Lord Byron, who literary scholar Vesna Goldsworthy characterized as "by far the most important figure in the Romantic discovery of the Balkans in English literature" (1998, 16).

It has become fashionable for some scholars to characterize the western perception of the Balkans as a sort of orientalism known as "balkanism." While sharing some of the characteristics of orientalism, such as essentializing the Balkans so that, Agatha Christie, for example, could create the tongue-in-cheek, comic opera Kingdom of Herzoslovakia (1987) and Anthony Hope's mythical Ruritania became shorthand for the comic opera Balkan state.

Nevertheless, there is a major difference between orientalism and balkanism: The Orient is a feminized place, epitomized by veiled women and the harem. The Orient is fecund and sexually available, largely created through the male gaze of such authors as Gustave Flaubert (see Karayanni 2004). By contrast, the Balkans is a masculinized place, peopled in Byronian terms by brave and true (preferably mountain-dwelling) warriors, as venerated and largely created by Rebecca West, Olivia Manning, and Edith Durham through what I suggest we may characterize as the "female gaze." Women hardly appear in their accounts; it is a man's world.

Another crucial difference exists: Major artists went in great numbers to North Africa, Egypt, the Holy Land, and Turkey and painted a vast array of romantic paintings, followed by Broadway and Hollywood orientalist productions like *Kismet* and *The Sheik*, from which westerners could construct orientalist views. No such corpus of works exists for the Balkans, thus creating an empty space for the construction of fantasies and images.

The comic opera image of the Balkans has been an enduring aspect of adventure novels like Agatha Christie's *Secret of Chimneys*, modeled loosely after the lurid events of 1903 in Serbia, during which the Obrenović dynasty was literally thrown out of the palace window by members of the Black Hand (the Red Hand in Christie's oeuvre), who hacked the king and his commoner wife, Draga, to pieces in a sensational *coup d'etat*. It is not only contemporary Eastern European scholars who object to this orientalist approach to depicting the Balkans and reducing its inhabitants to quaint peasants. In 1913, when Franz Lehar used Montenegro as a "model for the comic Ruritanian-style kingdom of Pontevedro" in "The Merry Widow," Montenegrin students in Vienna angrily demonstrated at its premiere in Vienna (Ash 2006, B11).

The other literary line of the Balkan imaginary is best characterized by the novels of Eric Ambler: the cold, skulking, lurid world of spies. In these novels, Sofia, the Bulgarian capital, frequently serves as the model for the typical Eastern European/Balkan sinister locale for the gray world of Cold War espionage and treachery. Goldsworthy points out that the famous writer Lawrence Durrell demeaned the Balkans with the creation of Vulgaria, which he describes as "an unspeakable place full of unspeakable people" (1998, 142), and that "Durrell's stories are, in fact, fairly ruthless in exploiting a multitude of prejudices about the Balkans" (1998, 143). Needless to say, this aspect of Balkan life was of little interest to the majority of young Americans who were enthralled with Balkan dance and music.

Victims and Violence

Victimization constitutes a striking trope of Balkan existence. Many of the Balkan peoples feel that they are victims of others: the Ottoman Empire providing the most fodder for historical victimization, but also the immediate neighboring ethnic groups with whom each of the fledgling Balkan states struggled to obtain territory, and the Big Powers like Russia, France, the Hapsburg Empire, and Great Britain whose interference in the destinies of Balkan borders remains notorious. "Hence each people was perpetually making charges of inhumanity against all its neighbors. The Serb, for example, raised his bitterest complaint against the Turk, but was also ready to accuse the Greeks, the Bulgarians the Vlachs, and the Albanians of every crime under the sun" (West 1966, 20).

It is common to hear in Serbia that everything that goes wrong can be laid at the door of "*pet stotina godina pod Turcima*" (five-hundred years under the Turks).[9] Such an imaginary of the perpetual victim, never the aggressor, which looms large in the lives of many of the peoples of the Balkans, is based only partly on reality since in reality no one's hands are clean. Victimization at the hands of others is a common theme that frequently is sounded in conversations with potentially sympathetic foreigners. Even before World War II, Rebecca West noted:

> English persons, therefore, of humanitarian and reformist disposition constantly went out to the Balkan Peninsula to see who was in fact ill-treating whom, and being by the very nature of their perfectionist faith unable to accept the horrid hypothesis that everybody was ill-treating everybody else, all came back with a pet Balkan people established in their hearts as suffering and innocent, eternally the massacree and never the massacrer [*sic*] [1966, 20].

Victimization is not merely an historical aspect of how the people in the Balkans view the past, but as travel writer Susan Spano notes of a recent afternoon spent in Beograd among several Serbs discussing the events in Bosnia and Kosovo: "Unlike others his age who justify Serbian aggression in the 1990s by citing the ethnic Serbs' history of victimization, he has no illusions about the recent past" (2006 E8).

A striking aspect among many individuals in the Balkans is the almost desperate need they have for approval from westerners. Anthropologist Ivaylo Ditchev adds that this need for western approval comes from "... what we might call the Byronic complex: the predominant role of foreign gaze and approval in the construction of identities" (2002, 241). Thus, one finds among many people in the Balkans, because of bad press and negative images of unruliness and violence held in the West, that the Balkans frequently begins just east of wherever one is. Croats and Slovenes, in particular, frequently distance themselves from any association as a Balkan state. Typical of both current and historical western reactions to the Balkans is Rebecca West's observation: "Violence was, indeed, all I knew of the Balkans; all I knew of the South Slavs" (1966, 21).

Balkan Music and Dance

The third group of essays largely addresses the formal musical and choreographic properties of the dances and music of specific Balkan regions. These formal properties engage the interested reader as well as the performer with the intricacy and uniqueness of these genres of cultural expression.

It would be difficult to characterize the dazzling variety of choreographic and musical diversity found throughout the Balkans from Slovenia in the northwest to Turkey in the southeast and Romania to the north and the Greek Islands in the southwest. While solo forms of music and dance exist, these forms and music dance are overwhelmingly communal. It is the great variety of these forms found in a comparatively small area that many observers and participants find so compelling.

The most widespread choreographic form throughout the Balkans are group dances characterized morphologically by closed and open circle dances and line dances, mostly featuring short choreographic footwork sequences. These are called *kolo* or *horo(a)* in most of these regions. In some areas such as Croatia, Slovenia, the Greek Islands, and Romania couple dances are also popular. These latter forms tend to be historically newer forms, including polkas and waltzes, but many indigenous forms are also found throughout the Greek and Croatian coastal regions and islands, for example. Solo forms such as the *çiftetelli* (Turkish), *tsiftetelli* (Greek), and *čoček* or *kyuchek* (Serbia, Macedonia, Bulgaria) constitute a popular urban genre of solo improvised dance, and a musical genre, a legacy of Ottoman culture, that many subsume under the belly dance genre (Shay and Sellers-Young 2005, 2). This solo improvised dance form's association with the Turkish and Ottoman past and its contemporary association with the Roma (Gypsies) create ethnic and generational tensions in the Balkans, especially since young people are frequently rebelliously attracted to these solo dance genres because of their negative erotic and ethnic connotations. Alexander Kiossev notes: "In the last decade... a new mass taste for the old belly dance developed, new-old small taverns and kafanas opened, a new type of arrogant Balkan intimacy haunted the air. The most important symptom of this process was the lack of popular will to be Westernlike" (2002, 184).

Of great musical and choreographic interest and excitement for many in the West is the spectacular proliferation of asymmetric rhythms: 5/4, 5/8, 7/8, 9/8, 11/16, 13/16, among others, that characterize many dance and music genres of the Balkans. While largely associated with East and South Serbia, Macedonia, Greece, and Bulgaria, they can also be found in Croatia.

Musically, in addition to the rhythmic varieties, unique harmonies in non-tempered scales have created world-wide interest, especially with the information age popularization of the "Voix Bulgares" Bulgarian female vocal ensemble through numerous live concerts throughout the world and CDs. Unique harmonies not familiar to most Westerners can be found in Croatia, Bosnia, Bulgaria, and Macedonia, among other regions. Familiar western harmonic forms are also found in those coastal regions of Greece such as the island of Corfu, where the men perform a vocal genre known as *cantadhda* and Croatian Dalmatia where men's groups perform vocal *klapa* music, both Italian-derived musical forms that show the centuries-long political domination of Venice in these areas. Many solo forms, such as the musically sophisticated urban *sevdah* genre of urban Bosnia, with its complex melismas, show Turkish influences, as well as natively developed solo vocal and instrumental genres.

The unusual rhythmic construction of various Balkan musical and choreographic forms attracted many young American dancers with backgrounds in mathematics and engineering. Lauševic found that 43 percent of the men in her statistical cohort had science/engineering/computer professional backgrounds (1998, 372). I remember vividly listening to the lively discussions among dancers, especially males, who listened with fascination to the newest recordings and attempted to parse the rhythmic breakdown of a new Bulgarian or Macedonian dance melody. Robert Henry Leibman's article in this volume vividly demonstrates this interest and the combination of mathematics and dance that still attract the interest of mainstream Americans, though in fewer numbers than in the 1960s and 1970s.

Research in Balkan Dance and Music

While little scholarly literature about Balkan dance and music has appeared in English, research and publication in the Balkans in the Serbian, Croatian, Slovene, Macedonian, Romanian, Greek, Bulgarian, and Albanian languages has been prolific and intense. All of the socialist states supported folklore research as a means of establishing political legal rights to the territories that they held that were frequently contested by neighboring political entities and populated with sizeable irredentist populations. The 1912 and 1913 Balkan wars, and World War I, particularly vicious in atrocities for which the Balkans became infamous, in which many of these ethnic groups fought and vied for territories held by the dwindling Ottoman Empire, were still fresh in the memories of many of the founding politicians of the socialist states following World War II. With this bloodshed of the Balkan wars (1912, 1913) and World War I (1914–1918), exacerbated by the bitter interethnic strife and hideous massacres that occurred on the soil of the former Yugoslavia during World War II, Josip Broz Tito, in particular, forbade frank discussions of ethnicity. Such discussions might have had a psychologically cleansing effect for the inhabitants of the multi-ethnic Yugoslav state, but instead Tito idealistically opted for projects such as those involving multiethnic youth brigades to construct the "Highway of Brotherhood and Unity" between Zagreb and Beograd, that was largely destroyed in the war between Serbia and Croatia in 1992–1995.[10]

In Serbia, the Janković sisters, Danica and Ljubica, conducted the first serious, systematic folk dance research which they published in their seminal *Narodne Igre* (Folk Dances), an eight-volume study of the dances of the Eastern (Serbian and Macedonian) Orthodox peoples of the former Yugoslavia (1929–1964). Their work, which can give the reader an idea of the diversity of dance and musical traditions among the Serbs and Macedonians, began in the 1920s and continued for four more decades. Other researchers began their work after World War II when a new generation of professionally trained folklorists appeared in all of the Balkan states, established a wide variety of journals and published voluminous scholarly monographs and articles. For example, the annual yearbooks of the Yugoslav Union of Folklorists published the research findings of folklorists from all over the former Yugoslav republics and in addition each republic had its own journals devoted to the research of the specific republic, like *Narodna Umjetnost* for Croatia.

Balkan Music and Dance in America

Thousands of young Americans not only undertook learning the dances and songs that were performed by national dance and musical ensembles of the Balkans, they sometimes eagerly embraced learning the languages, embroidery patterns, cuisines and other pleasurable aspects of Balkan life as well.[11] They frequently fantasized being Balkan peasants, whom many Americans imagined to be near kin to Rousseau's "noble savage." During the Age of Aquarius, which *Wikipedia* characterizes as "the Heyday of the Hippie and

New Age "movement" of the 1960s and 1970s" epitomized by the anthem-like song "The Age of Aquarius" from the 1967 blockbuster *Hair*, many young people faced a Brave New World, rejecting what they regarded as the repressive, antiseptic 1950s. Balkan peasants appeared to many disaffected young Americans as an alternative to a gray existence: noble, stoic agriculturalists, primitively attired in stunningly colorful costumes and dancing and singing their lives away in quaint villages to celebrate bountiful harvests and fruitful weddings, in other words "real people," untainted by the city, an image promoted by the national dance ensembles.

This period was the inception of the "New Age" and one could conveniently forget about the unpleasant and insalubrious sanitary arrangements, backbreaking field work, and the bitter poverty that was the lot of many of the actual Balkan peasants. The imaginary, as portrayed on the stages on which the national ensembles performed, trumped reality. After all, it was well known that Americans were notoriously ignorant of geography, and courses in Balkan history and geography were only rarely taught even in graduate programs in American educational institutions, and thus the "empty space" of the Balkans provided many individuals a site onto which they could inscribe their own fantasies and images.[12] This was a time when many middle-class youth sought alternative life styles, founded communes (in total ignorance of agricultural science), and thus "village life" was celebrated for its simplicity, its pristine innocence, its avoidance of empty materialism, and, above all, its connections to the soil.[13] It is important to note, as Robin Evanchuk does in her essay in this collection, that in the beginning of the period in the late 1950s and early 1960s, Balkan dance was an essentialized dance genre with "Croatian" or "Macedonian" variants for many eager young hobbyists. This concept was made manifest in a film, *Balkan Dancing*, created by dance teacher Mario Casetta, in which the young narrator talks about "Balkan" dancing throughout the documentary.

One informant declared that: "I envied the closeness and warmth of the Greeks" (Louise Anderson-Bilman, January 26, 2003). This sentiment was echoed by many individuals involved in learning and performing Balkan dances, and the students eagerly embraced an exotic form of cultural expression in an effort to obtain that warmth. Ethnomusicologist Mirjana Laušević documents many of her American informants involved in the performance of Balkan dance and music expressing a sense of anomie and searching for a more colorful and "authentic" way of life filled with warmth, and exciting music, dances, and costumes twenty-five and thirty years after my similar experiences (Laušević 1998).

Even Rebecca West, before World War II, wrote that for her the Balkans represented "a mode of life [that] was so honest" that it impelled her to undertake the journey that was to inspire the writing of her famous *Black Lamb and Grey Falcon*, one of the most brilliantly written travel journals of the Balkans ever published and still widely read (1966, 1).

By the 1960s an explosion of recordings by the Philip Koutev Ensemble of Bulgaria and LADO, the Ensemble of Folk Songs and Dances of Croatia, among a myriad variety of performances by Eastern European dance and music ensembles, increased the visibility and popularity of folk dances and music of the Balkans to the point that many college and university campuses and civic locations throughout America became performance sites. Enthusiastic individuals in some large cities founded coffee houses devoted to teaching dance, particularly to Balkan dances, but also featuring related forms of circle and line dances such as Greek and Israeli dances. My own experiences in the Bay area and Southern California showed that hundreds of young men and women pursued this passion for Balkan dance night after night in these venues and other locales.[14]

While many young American men, who were frequently peace activists, were overwhelmingly attracted to the machismo of the showier men's dances in a Walter Mitty fashion, young women, occasionally frustrated by the secondary role of women in many dances, carved a feminist niche in the vocal production of many Balkan musical genres such as Bulgarian and Croatian songs, which featured unique harmonic and rhythmic elements that were popularized by the performances of the Koutev ensemble and LADO. The recordings of these ensembles inspired the founding of many women's singing groups specializing in Balkan musical genres in America over the past half century. As ethnomusicologist Timothy Rice eloquently wrote of his own early experiences of Balkan music and dance:

> In this world [the world of "international folk dancing"] we manipulated Bulgarian music, and particularly our dancing to it, as symbols that helped us establish new friendships, demonstrate our attractiveness and attractions to others, enjoy the physical and mental exertion of maintaining repeated aesthetic patterns in the body, and create a sense of small-scale community within the vastness of American society [1994, 4].

Thus, through the various images of the Balkans, many young mainstream Americans sought through Balkan music and dance a means of acquiring, if only temporarily, new and exotic identities. This ability of inscribing new identities, as Rice points out, was facilitated by the very lack of knowledge that most Americans had of Balkan peoples and their history.

2. Introduction

Nationalism, Ethnicity, and Performance

This section of essays covers a wide range of geographical areas: Macedonia, Greece, Bulgaria, Bosnia, Serbia and the many minority groups that inhabit these regions, sometimes uneasily. Silverman and Papakostas focus on the dance practices of the Roma populations of Macedonia: Silverman addresses the Roma of the former Yugoslav republic, while Papakostas addresses Roma ethnicity in Greece. The difference between the two areas, separated by no more than 20 to 30 miles, demonstrates the complexity of Balkan history. After the First World War, the Muslim population of what became Macedonia after World War II remained largely in place, although some left for Turkey rather than live under a Christian regime, while the Muslim population of Greece was exchanged for Christian Greeks in the large, difficult population exchange between Greece and Turkey in 1922–23. This created two very different social and ethnic environments in these two neighboring regions.

Carol Silverman uses the site of the solo improvised dance genre *čoček*, considered to be a form of belly dance, to fuel the discourse of ethnicity, nationalism, and gender in the Balkans. The čoček is associated with all that is perceived as negative in the Balkans: Roma, Ottoman Turks, Muslims, and wanton, out-of-control sexuality. Silverman describes and analyzes the ways in which Roma negotiate their ethnic identity through the performances. She underscores that the čoček has both domestic and professional poles, but may best be conceptualized as a continuum between the two poles.

Chris Papakostas's essay analyzes how the Roma (Gypsy) population of Northern Greece (Macedonia) negotiates identity in the larger Greek world through music and dance. Papakostas shows how the Roma rely on the Greeks' "essentialist" imaginary of Gypsies as "natural-born" musicians to increase their community's status, highly reminiscent of how white Americans viewed, and in some cases continue to view, African Americans as having "natural rhythm" or "natural athletic capacities." As linguistic director of the Romani archives at the University of Texas, Austin Ian Hancock points out: "Making music for the non–Roma is, after all, a traditional means of livelihood and one that carries some status both within and outside of the Romani world" (2002, xxiii).

Irene Loutzaki's essay amply demonstrates the ways in which non-representative governments, fascists, communists (and in the past, absolute monarchies like that of Louis XIV) can utilize the primordial forms of folk dance and music as a means of aggrandizing the themes upon which their regimes are constructed. These governments utilize large-scale extravaganzas peopled with thousands of colorfully costumed participants to suggest the population's support of the regime. Loutzaki describes and analyzes the nationalist underpinnings and xenophobia that characterized the fascist Metaxas regime of Greece (1936–1940), and the many facets of how the use of folk dance can further nationalistic political agendas. Especially telling, as was the case of Bulgaria under the socialist regime (1945–1989), was how any non–Bulgarian element such as Turkish musical instruments, song texts, or Roma performers were eschewed as "unpure."

Dance research in the Balkan countries was mostly conducted by individuals who were professional folklorists or ethnologists. These individuals frequently wielded enormous authority in deciding which dances were "authentic" and which village groups were eligible to participate in local, national, and international folk dance festivals. These decisions were crucial for the villagers because their performances, besides bringing prestige to the community, often resulted in having their village electrified, a new road built, or some other desirable civic project carried out. Colin Quigley's essay "Nationalism and Scholarship in Transylvanian Ethnochoreology" charts the course of dance scholarship in the communist period and the post-communist era in the ethnically contested region of Transylvania among scholars of Romanian, Hungarian, and Roma dance and music traditions. The music and dance studies form the nexus of nationalism, ethnicity, and a new questioning generation of scholars who contest past nationalistic practices of scholarship required by the state. He analyzes and describes the new generation's response to older studies and the problems encountered in establishing new standards of scholarship in a region where nationalism and ethnicity still have strong roots, and in which dance and music still occupy the role of primordial ethnic and nationalist identity markers.

Erica Neilsen describes and analyzes how the demise of state-supported styles of folk dance performance in Bulgaria after the fall of communism, and the current embracing of Turkish and Gypsy dance genres, especially forms of solo improvised dance known as belly dancing in the West, has given rise to intergenerational anxieties over the perceived erosion of Bulgarian identity. Neilsen explores the issues of nationalism and ethnicity that are manifest in different dance genres in Bulgaria. Her observations have resonance in other areas of the Balkans like Romania, Turkey, and Serbia in which youth culture is abandoning what they perceive as sanitized and outdated forms of folklore which no longer have relevance in their lives.

Lynn Maners's and Anthony Shay's essays show how nationalism and ethnicity inhabit and sometimes haunt performances of folk dance. Maners's article, "Clapping for Serbs," describes and analyzes how the various Bosnian ethnic groups (Serbs, Croats, and Muslims) showed increasing separation through demonstrating support only for the performances of their own ethnic groups in concerts which featured the dances of all the ethnic groups in Bosnia, foreshadowing the civil war and ethnic cleansing that occurred shortly after the performance he describes.

Shay describes and analyzes the way in which the Serbian State Folk Dance Ensemble, Kolo, choreographically depicts its three major ethnic groups — Roma, Slavic Muslims, and Albanians (Šiptari) — by utilizing popular preexisting negative images in contrast to the way the majority Serb population is depicted in Kolo's repertoire. Shay argues that such depictions help to create the dismissive attitudes that, at their most extreme, can reinforce the kind of attitudes that can lead to the ethnic cleansing that occurred in Serbian-occupied Bosnia and Kosovo.

Balkan Dance in America

Robin Evanchuk in her essay "Inside, Outside, Upside Down" recalls the beginnings of the "kolomania" that enveloped many young people of the mid–1950s. She details and analyzes the impulses that propelled so many individuals to adopt an exotic culture. Her essay depicts the beginnings of the mass interest in Balkan dance in the 1950s.

June Adler Vail recalls in her essay on a personal level what participating in one of the myriad American dance companies devoted to the performance of Balkan dances was like for a participant twenty years after the period described by Evanchuk. Vail also analyzes how different the meanings of these performances were for Americans than the cultural meanings that the performances of these same dances convey to the peoples of the Balkans.

Morphology of Balkan Dance and Music

In this volume Jamie Webster's essay, using an example of dance music from the Romanian population of Transylvania, shows how the Romanian word *joc*, noun, and *joaca*, verb, means both "play" and "dance" (like its Serbian counterpart *irga* and *igrati*). This indicates how improvisation constitutes an important element for the musicians, dancers, and vocalists to "play" within the framework of a single dance melody.

Nancy Lee Chalfa Ruyter documents Dick Crum's reconstruction of *Dvoransko* or *Salonsko Kolo*, a Croatian ballroom dance created for the urban elite of Zagreb in the 1840s. Following a common choreographic maneuver by Eastern and Central European nationalists in the romantic period, dance masters created ballroom dances like the polonaise and mazurka in Poland, the *csardas* in Hungary, and the Czech, Moravian, Slovak *beseda*, in which elements, real or imagined, of the dances of actual peasants, who were believed to be the carriers of authentic national culture, were included. No member of the urban elite wanted to perform actual peasant dances in their elegant salons (see Shay 2006). Thus, the dance masters mediated between the rural and urban to create new dances to represent the nation. Ruyter describes the many permutations the dance passed through and the final reconstruction of the dance as taught by Pietro Coronelli, a dance master resident in Zagreb in 1860s, taught to Crum by the daughters of Coronelli in the 1950s, and then taught to the students of the dance department of the University of California, Irvine.

Robert Henry Leibman constructs an elegant model for the structural analysis of the morphological aspects of dances from the Southeastern Balkans (Macedonia, South Serbia, Northern Greece, and Bulgaria). His enthusiasm for discovering important structural aspects of dance led him to develop a mathematically based formula for analyzing the way in which individuals improvise within a particular choreographic pattern. These patterns are frequently described as a "set" manner of performing the dance in books such as those by the Jankovic sisters (1929–1964). Thus, Leibman's essay provides a model for future researchers to understand and analyze the process of improvisation and variation in Balkan dances, and to detect underlying aesthetic elements that many individuals find so compelling.

Notes

1. This characterization of Byron was famously made by Lady Caroline Lamb, who was madly in love with the bisexual Byron. As his biographer Louis Crompton remarked (1985, 197), it actually applied more to Lamb because of her relentless pursuit of Byron, which ultimately, through her exposures of his unorthodox sexual activities, forced him to flee England and return to Greece, where he died while attempting to organize the Greeks to fight the Turkish army.

2. For the interested reader, Maria Todorova's outstanding book *Imagining the Balkans* (1997) analyzes in great detail how the Balkans were and are imagined, not only in various nations in the West, but also from other points of view, such as those of the Russians, who were searching for their own Slavic origins during the nineteenth century. As Todorova cautions us, both the West and the Balkans are not essentialized places, not a simple binary but rather highly differentiated.

Another work of importance to the reader who wishes to understand not only how images of the Balkans, and more generally Eastern Europe, came to be accepted in the West is Larry Wolff's *Inventing Eastern Europe* (1994).

3. These state-supported ensembles were established right after World War II in imitation of the Moiseyev Dance Company, which enjoyed immense popularity in the West. In keeping with the Socialist/Communist principle of exalting "the people," the Moiseyev Dance

Company was known in the USSR as the People's Ensemble of Folk Dances of the USSR, while Kolo, Lado, and Tanec traveled outside of the former Yugoslavia, as the Yugoslav State Folk Ballet, and the Koutev Ensemble was known in Bulgaria as the Bulgarian State Ensemble of Folk Dances and Songs (see Shay 2002). Technically speaking, by the time the Yugoslav companies toured America, Yugoslavia was no longer behind the Iron Curtain, but most Americans remained ignorant of that fact and went to see "the Communists" dance.

4. Other early teachers of Balkan dance genres included Michel Cartier, John Filcich and Vilma Matchette.

5. For information on the development of the recreational international folk dance movement see Casey (1981), Laušević (1998), Shay (2006), and Tomko (1999). Unfortunately, no single scholarly history of this movement has appeared. Tomko's work covers the early origins of the use of international folk dances as part of appropriate physical education activities for young girls at the end of the nineteenth and early twentieth centuries. Casey gives a popular, but fragmented account of the years of the 1930s and 1940s (and beyond) in which the recreational movement of international folk dance clubs for adults was established. Shay and Laušević each fill in other information, but this remains an area for a major study of a dance phenomenon that attracted thousands of mainstream Americans.

6. The detailing of the history of folklore studies is beyond the scope of this essay. Those interested in a fine, detailed study of the development of folklore studies in Europe may consult Cocchiara (1981 [1952]).

7. The famous Battle of Kosovo Polje in which the Ottoman army defeated the Serbian medieval empire was in 1389, so I use that as a convenient date. Different parts of the Balkans fell under Ottoman rule at different dates. The farthest reach of the Ottoman Empire was reached in the last years of the 16th century when the Ottoman territories included Hungary and Croatia, which were later retaken by the Hapsburgs. The decline of the Ottoman Empire was also a piecemeal disintegrating process, beginning with the establishment of the tiny, semi-independent states of Serbia, Romania, and Greece in the early nineteenth century, and the dismemberment of the Ottoman Empire continued until the end of World War I.

8. An Axis-sponsored "Independent Croatia" was formed from parts of Croatia and Bosnia from 1941 to 1945, although Italy retained control of the Adriatic Coast and Germany "supervised" the Ustaša state. This terrorist state did not receive universal support among the Croatian population, especially in the capital, Zagreb, which grew increasingly disenchanted with the brutal ethnic cleansing of Serbs, Jews, and Gypsies (see Tanner 2001, 154–155).

9. Upon frequently hearing about downtrodden Balkan peasant masses as victims of the Turks, a Turkish friend declared that he was going to claim all of the problems of backwardness in Turkey were due to spending five-hundred years in the Balkans.

10. My geography professor at UCLA, Hugh Kostinick, reminded our class in 1958: "Any time that a Highway for Brotherhood and Unity replaces Highway One, there is bound to be trouble." And, forty years later his prescient remark came to pass in the dismemberment of the former Yugoslavia.

11. The embracing of group line and circle dances constituted a major break with the practice of dancing a repertoire overwhelmingly comprised of couple dances from Northwestern and Central Europe that characterized the international recreational folk dance hobby movement until that time. It was also a generational break as younger dancers attracted to the newly introduced line and circle dances formed new groups and venues like coffee houses, as opposed to gymnasiums and civic recreational centers, to pursue their interests in these new music and dance genres and frequently caused many hard feelings among the older, couple dance–oriented folk dancers.

12. Americans largely still remain ignorant of geography. A recent survey by the National Geographic Education Foundation and Roper Public Affairs found that half the population could not locate the state of Mississippi on a map. "Three quarters of young Americans polled could not find Indonesia on a map. And half or fewer could pick out New York or Ohio on a map of the United States" (Stall 2006, B19). Imagine, then, the chances of Americans, even many Balkan enthusiasts, locating Croatia, Serbia, or Montenegro in their atlases. Many of my acquaintances confuse the Balkan states with the Baltic republics.

13. Mirjana Lauševič has caught much of this anomie in her Ph.D. dissertation, but her study took place two decades after the peak of the Balkan dance movement. During this time period, I was the artistic director of the Aman Folk Ensemble, one of the foremost Balkan performing groups in the United States, and the experience of living in this period, still vivid in my memory, took on a sharp focus because the nearly 100 performers in the ensemble frequently voiced their passion for participating in this genre of dance and music and why they were willing to spend the time commitment of a second job in pursuing this passion.

At one time in Los Angeles there were seven coffee houses devoted to folk dance, in addition to recreational, performance, and campus activities. Only one of these remains.

Bibliography

Adanir, Fikret. 1992. "Macedonians in the Ottoman Empire, 1978–1912." In, *Formation of National Elites: Comparative Studies on Governments and Non-Dominant Ethnic Groups in Europe, 1850–1940*, ed. Andreas Kappeler. Volume VI. New York: New York University Press, 161–191.
Ambler, Eric. 1989 [1951]. *Judgment on Deltchev*. London: Fontana.
_____. 1966 [1951]. *Mask of Dimitrios*. London: Fontana.
Ash, Timothy Garton. June 1, 2006. "There she is, Miss Montenegro." *Los Angeles Times*, p. B11.
Balkan Dancing. 1964. A film by Mario Casetta. Los Angeles: Film Associates.
Casey, Betty. 1981. *International Folk Dancing U.S.A.* New York: Doubleday.
Chianis, Sam. 1967. "Vocal and Instrumental Tsamiko of Roumeli and the Peloponnesus." Unpublished Ph.D. dissertation, UCLA.
Christie, Agatha. 1987 [1925]. *Secret of Chimneys*. New York: Bantam Books.
_____. 1983 [1934]. *Murder on the Orient Express*. New York: Bantam Books.
Cocchiara, Giuseppe. 1981 [1952]. *History of Folklore in Europe*. Translated from the Italian by John N. McDaniel. Philadelphia: Institute for the Study of Human Issues.
Crompton, Louis. 1985. *Byron and Greek Love: Homophobia in 19th-Century England*. Berkeley: University of California Press.
Ditchev, Ivaylo. 2002. "Eros of Identity." In *Balkan as Metaphor: Between Globalization and Fragmentation*, ed. Dušan I. Bjelić and Obrad Savić. Cambridge, MA: MIT Press, 235–250.
Foucault, Michel. 1972. *The Archaeology of Knowledge*. London: Tavistock.
Geary, Patrick J. 2002. *Myth of Nations: The Medieval Origins of Europe*. Princeton, NJ: Princeton University Press.
Giurchescu, Anca, with Sunni Bloland. 1995. *Romanian Traditional Dance*. Mill Valley, CA: Wild Flower Press.
Goldsworthy, Vesna. 1998. *Inventing Ruritania: The Imperialism of the Imagination*. New Haven, CT: Yale University Press.
Hancock, Ian. 2002. "Foreword." In *Bright Balkan Morning: Romani Lives and the Power of Music in Greek Macedonia,* by Charles Keil and Angeliki Vellou Keil. Middletown, CT: Wesleyan University Press.
Harvey, Penelope. 1996. *Hybrids of Modernity: Anthropology, the Nation State and the Universal Exhibition*. London: Routledge.
Hope, Anthony. 1894. *Prisoner of Zenda*. London: J. W. Arrowsmith.
Hutchinson, John, and Anthony D. Smith. 1996. "Introduction." In *Ethnicity*, ed. John Hutchinson and Anthony D. Smith. New York: Oxford University Press, 3–14.
Janković, Danica S., and Ljubica S. Janković. 1934, 1937, 1939. *Narodne Igre* (Folk Dances). Volumes 1, 2, Beograd: Srpske Kraljevske Adakemije Nauka.
_____. 1948–1962. *Narodne Igre*. Volumes 3–8. Beograd: Prosveta.
Karayanni, Stavros Stavrou. 2004. *Dancing Fear & Desire: Race, Sexuality, and Imperial Politics in Middle Eastern Dance*. Waterloo, ON: Wilfrid Laurier University Press.

Kiossev, Alexander. 2002. "Dark Intimacy: Maps, Identities, Acts of Identification." In *Balkan as Metaphor: Between Globalization and Fragmentation,* ed. Dušan I. Bjelić and Obrad Savić. Cambridge, MA: MIT Press, 165–190.

Kirshenblatt-Gimblett, Barbara. 1994. "On Difference." *American Journal of Folklore,* 107 (424), 233–238.

Laušević, Mirjana. 1998. "Different Village: International Folk Dance and Balkan Music and Dance in the United States." Unpublished Ph.D. dissertation. Middletown, CT: Wesleyan University.

Longinović, Tomislav Z. 2002. "Vampires Like Us: Gothic Imaginary and 'the Serbs.'" In *Balkan as Metaphor: Between Globalization and Fragmentation,* ed. Dušan I. Bjelić and Obrad Savić. Cambridge, MA: MIT Press, 39–59.

Magner, Thomas F. 2003. *Introduction to the Croatian and Serbian Language.* Revised Edition. University Park: University of Pennsylvania Press.

Rice, Timothy. 1994. *May It Fill Your Soul: Experiencing Bulgarian Music.* Chicago: University of Chicago Press.

Said, Edward W. 1979. *Orientalism.* New York: Vintage Books.

Shay, Anthony. 2002. *Choreographic Politics: State Folk Dance Companies, Representation, and Power.* Middletown, CT: Wesleyan University Press.

_____. 2006. *Choreographing Identities: Folk Dance, Ethnicity, and Festival in the United States and Canada.* Jefferson, NC: McFarland.

_____, and Barbara Sellers-Young. 2005. "Introduction." In *Belly Dance: Orientalism, Transnationalism, and Harem Fantasy,* by Anthony Shay and Barbara Sellers-Young. Costa Mesa, CA: Mazda Publishers, 1–27.

Spano, Susan. June 11, 2006. "So ... This Is Serbia?" *Los Angeles Times,* pp. E1, E8.

Stall, Bill. May 27, 2006. "Where's Tannu Tuva?" *Los Angeles Times,* p. B19.

Tanner, Marcus. 2001. *Croatia: A Nation Forged in War.* New Haven: Nota Bene Press.

Todorova, Maria. 1997. *Imagining the Balkans.* New York: Oxford University Press.

Tomko, Linda. 1999. *Dancing Class: Gender, Ethnicity, and Social Divides in American Dance, 1890–1920.* Bloomfield: Indiana University Press.

West, Rebecca. 1966 [1940, 1941]. *Black Lamb and Grey Falcon: A Journey Through Yugoslavia.* New York: Viking.

Wolff, Larry. 1994. *Inventing Eastern Europe: The Map of Civilization on the Mind of the Enlightenment.* Stanford, CA: Stanford University Press.

Nationalism, Ethnicity, and Performance

3

Transnational Čoček: Gender and the Politics of Balkan Romani Dance

Carol Silverman

Among Roma in Macedonia and Bulgaria, dance is closely embedded in the social life of the community and is especially tied to gender and status. *čoček* (or *kyuchek*) as a form of solo dance, has a long history rooted in Ottoman professional genres. Although today it is associated with women, in the Ottoman era young men were also regular performers. In contemporary Romani life, dance mediates female sexuality and reputation and its practice is governed by community ideas of propriety, context, and talent. In the last fifty years čoček has been appropriated into many new settings, including Yugoslav professional and amateur ensembles, Romani music festivals, world music events, and Slavic, Albanian, and Romanian community dance events. It has also traveled in the Balkan Romani diaspora to Western Europe and the United States. This article compares and discusses the dance genre čoček in these numerous locations, emphasizing its stylistic, social, and power dimensions in relation to the marginality of Roma in the wider society and the ambivalent position of women.[1]

Who Are Roma?

Linguistic evidence reveals that Roma[2] are originally from India and that they migrated out of the area sometime around 1100 A.D. According to linguists the Romani language is descended from Sanskrit and exists in several dialects (Matras 2002; Hancock 2002). Roma were established in large numbers throughout Eastern Europe by the fourteenth century, some settling and others following a nomadic way of life. To non–Roma, Roma have been indispensable suppliers of diverse services, such as music, dance, animal training, fortune-telling, metal working, horse dealing, wood working, sieve making, basket weaving, comb making, and seasonal agricultural work.

Initial curiosity about Roma by European peoples and rulers quickly gave way to discrimination, a legacy that has continued until today. In the southern Romanian principalities of Wallachia and Moldavia, Roma were slaves from the fourteenth to the nineteenth centuries. Despite their small numbers, Roma inspired fear and mistrust and were expelled from virtually every western European territory. Assimilation was attempted in the Austro-Hungarian Empire by forcibly removing children from their parents and outlawing nomadism, traditional occupations and Romani language, music, and dress. Similar assimilationist legislation was enacted in Spain after 1499 (Hancock 1997, 2002; Petrova 2003). The policy of the Ottoman Empire towards Roma was in general more lenient than in Western Europe, at least from the sixteenth to the eighteenth centuries (Marushiakova and Popov 2000); many Balkan Roma converted to Islam in the sixteenth to eighteenth centuries in order to pay lower taxes and to move up the Ottoman ranks. In the Balkans today approximately half of the Roma are Muslim. In practice, the religion of Muslim Balkan Roma is quite syncretic. Approximately half of Balkan Roma have lost the Romani language; in the southern Balkans many of those who have lost the Romani language speak Turkish as their first language, but, in general, multilingualism is the norm.

Perhaps the most tragic period of Romani history was World War II when Roma faced an extermination campaign in which from 500,000 to 1.5 million were murdered, representing between one-fourth and one-fifth of their total population at the time (Hancock 2002). The post–World War II communist regimes in Eastern Europe officially downplayed ethnicity but nevertheless defined Roma as a social problem. Roma were targeted for integration into the planned economy, forced to give up their traditional occupations, and assigned to the lowest skilled and lowest paid industrial and agricultural state jobs (e.g., street cleaners). Nomadic Roma were forcibly settled, settled Roma were sometimes forcibly moved, and sometimes aspects of their culture, such as music, were outlawed (such as in Bulgaria, see below). Cheap housing was provided by the state but ghetto-like segregated neighborhoods were commonplace. Specific policies varied by country and by decade, with forced sterilization common in Czechoslovakia and the forced changing of Muslim names to Slavic names in Bulgaria. On the positive side, during socialism Romani school attendance grew (despite inferior segregated schools), violence was rare, and Roma held steady employment and received the benefits of the paternalistic state.

In the postsocialist period, harassment and violence towards the Roma of Eastern Europe have increased, along with marginalization and poverty. They are the largest minority in Europe (8–12 million) and have a very low standard of living in every country, with unemployment reaching 80 percent in some East European regions. Today East European Roma face inferior and segregated housing and education, including tracking of children into special schools for the disabled. Poor health conditions, specifically higher infant mortality and morbidity, shorter life expectancy, and higher frequency of chronic diseases all plague Roma. Discrimination is widespread in employment and the legal system, and even educated people routinely express disdain for Gypsies. Hate speech and racial profiling are common in the media. Perhaps most troubling are the hundreds of incidences of physical violence against Roma perpetrated by ordinary citizens and also by the police. In response to historic discrimination and recent abuses, a Romani human rights movement has mobilized in the last fifteen years via a network of activists and NGOs.[3] Considering the above history, Romani migrants and refugees can now be found in every western European nation and in the United States and Canada.

The fact that music is one of the oldest Romani occupations may be one reason why it has a deep symbolic connection for Roma and why the terms music and Roma are almost synonymous for non–Roma. For centuries, some Roma in Eastern Europe have been professional musicians, playing for Romani communities and for non–Romani peasants and city dwellers for remuneration in cafes and taverns and at events such as weddings, baptisms, circumcisions, fairs, and village dances. This professional niche, primarily male and instrumental, requires Roma to know expertly the co-territorial repertoire and interact with it in a creative manner. A nomadic way of life, often enforced upon Roma due to harassment and prejudice, gave them opportunity to enlarge their repertoires and become multi-musical as well as multi-lingual (Silverman 1999). Thus music has been a viable occupation for professional Romani men for over six hundred years; furthermore, in the current period of crisis, it still remains viable. In fact, Romani music has become a valuable commodity in the world music economy. Since the 1990s a plethora of Gypsy music festivals has been organized and Gypsy fusion genres have emerged (Silverman 2007).

Professional Dancers of the Balkans: Ottoman Roots

According to Ottoman sources, in the eighteenth, nineteenth and early twentieth centuries Romani women and men were professional dancers, hired in aristocratic, courtly, and military as well as tavern settings (And 1963–4, 26–28). An 1804 observation, for example, counted 600 dancing boys in the taverns of Constantinople (And 1976, 140). Sugarman, in her excellent summary of Ottoman solo dance, claims that in the early period, most performers were non–Turks (and non–Muslims) from a variety of ethnic backgrounds (for example, Greeks, Jews, Armenians, Roma, and Caucasians), but by the nineteenth century they were primarily Roma (2003, 94, 98). Turks did not dance professionally because it was deemed degrading; this comes from the Islamic association of music with immorality (Nieuwkerk 1995, 2003). Seeman similarly observes that *čalgija* musicians (who played a Turkish-derived repertoire) in Skopje in the post–World War II war period did not include Turks because of the stigma of the profession (1990).[4]

Professional male dancers in the Ottoman era were known as *köçeks* (or *raqqas*) and the females were known as *çengis*, although both sexes were often called çengis (And 1976, 138). The appellation "köçek" also became associated with the style of music played for accompaniment and later for the sensuous solo dance form known all over the Balkans today as *čoček* (see below). Dancers were organized into guilds (*kols*) that were divided by sex and sometimes by ethnicity and served as training grounds for dance instruction (Seeman 1998, 4).[5]

Ottoman performances were not solely composed of dances. As court entertainers, köçeks and çengis sang, played daires, enacted theatrical skits (often comic), did acrobatics, and balanced swords, plates, and steaming kettles. The show was also a visual spectacle of velvet, brocade and billowing silk costumes. But their striking solo dances received the most attention from their chroniclers, who were composed of European travelers and local observers.[6] In interpreting these Ottoman materials we must be wary of the Orientalist tone of many writers. Çengi dances were described by European travelers as sexually revealing and erotic.[7] Brandl wisely remarks, "Concerning these reports, one should not forget that, leaving aside the prejudice against the Roma that they brought with them from their homelands, most travelers had before their eyes the court-bourgeoisie dances such as the minuet, contradances, etc. The erotic gestures and body movements of the *tsifeteli* (hip dance) and other Oriental dances must have therefore been shocking to them, above all, when these dances took place on the stages of coffee houses"

(1996, 26–27). The western gaze, then, produced a judgmental commentary that was simultaneously drawn in by the exoticism of the dance and at the same repelled by its wantonness.[8]

Ottoman male audiences, however, likely viewed dancers of both sexes less sexually and more aesthetically "as objects of beauty and desire" (Sugarman 2003, 96). Anthony Shay, in his detailed chronicle of male dancing in the Middle East, points out that "The professional male dancer in many ways, was, and is an embodiment of the Persian, Arabic, and Turkish poetic ideal" (2005, 61).[9] European writers have tended to assume these male dancers were homosexual. It is true that many of the boys had feminine appearances, and indeed, they often grew their hair long, dressed like girls, cultivated a girlish grace, and mimicked the provocative postures of women.[10] However, we should be wary of applying modern concepts to previous eras. "Within Ottoman constructions of sexuality ... a man might feel erotic attraction to both women and young men without being seen as something that would translate as 'homosexual,' and being an object of male desire as a young man did not preclude marriage at a later date" (Sugarman 2003, 96).

Trangendered mimicry occurred among çengis as well as köçeks; females dressed as and impersonated males in their suites and enacted fighting scenarios (And 1976, 142, 144). But male dancers could also be super masculine and female dancers could be super feminine. Judith Butler's ideal of the performativity of gender is useful here — it seems that gender was playful and fluid, an arena of conscious artful enactment (1993).[11] Despite their ill repute in mainstream society, professional dancers were so loved and so admired that respectable poets sang their praises, aristocratic tavern-goers fought over them, and courts adopted them (And 1976, 141, 145). Tipping was not only expected but accomplished in a direct and provocative manner.[12] At various times, local laws were enacted to regulate dancers, or more precisely to regulate the monetary outlay of their patrons.[13] Sugarman claims that females filled the void after the ban on males dancers and that their performances became more eroticized for western visitors (2003, 96–97).

Sugarman suggests that by "the nineteenth and early twentieth centuries, women had moved into more public and less elite settings," and that accounts from this period are invariably of Roma (2003, 95).[14] By this time the professional female dancer had entered the realm of theater and the popular stage. Seeman writes that in urban Turkish theaters, singers of popular songs (*kantocu*) also performed çengi movements (1998, 5). The čoček dancer became an almost iconic figure in literary works such as *Koštana*, a Serbian play written in 1902 by Borislav Stanković.[15] In the 1930s the pioneering dance researchers Ljubica and Danica Janković wrote about a specific Romani dance called čoček in Gostivar, Macedonia, involving movement of the hips, abdomen, and shoulders. They also describe pantomimes where a pair of same sex dancers mimic a hunt. In addition, the Janković sisters notated urban Muslim line dances (many of which were shared by Turks, Roma and Albanians) and these became the basis of Yugoslav ensemble choreographies (1939 and see below).

Hasluck notes that by the twentieth century, professionals often worked in families, and gender performance roles were sometimes flexible due to patron needs: "Among sedentary Albanian [Gypsy] musician families, both men and women are professionals. They go generally in family parties, the men to play for the men guests and their wives for the women; in Christian households in south Albania I have sometimes seen men admitted with their wives to the women's quarters, and at Mohammedan weddings I have found female Gypsies playing for men" (1938, 27).[16] These descriptions illustrate that Romani women have historically worked outside the home alongside Romani men among non–Romani women and men. Economic imperatives directly loosened sexual segregation, although ideals remained conservative.

The legacy of professional Ottoman dance in the current Balkans is quite complex. There is definitely an overlap between the professional realm and the realm of social and ritual dance in Romani communities (see below). In Turkey, there are still male köçeks who perform in villages in female style and with elements of female costume.[17] It is obvious that older çengi dancing informs contemporary female professional oriental dance, "belly dancing," *çiftetelli* in Turkey, *tsifeteli* in Greece, and solo čoček dancing in various Balkan communities. In Turkey, Seeman reports that professional çengis adopted Egyptian style movements and tighter choreographies, resulting in a style known as "oriental." In Romani neighborhoods of Istanbul such as Sulukule, çengis were and still are hired for weddings and for tourist shows (1998, 3–5). Seeman reports that in the 1980s there was one professional Romani dancer in Skopje who was hired for men's celebrations (personal communication). Pettan remarks that in Kosovo in the early 1980s, "in the area of Peč it is customary that female musicians perform for a short while for male guests, and one of the musicians even dances" (1996, 317). In Bulgaria the budget for a *panair* (fair) in 1884 included income from the kyucheks of female performers (Peicheva 1999:41). And more recently, in the early 1970s, Bulgarian Turkish-speaking Romani clarinetist Ivo Papazov partnered with Zvezda Salieva, a professional Romani dancer who performed at weddings. She and her sisters were part of a "dance dynasty" (Peicheva 1999, 214 and 247).

Çengis, on the one hand, were admired for their musicality and beauty, while on the other hand, they were criticized for their licentiousness and abandon, and many were assumed to be prostitutes. In the early years of the Turkish Republic (1920s), belly dancing was "a despised genre," associated with "fallen women." It was rehabilitated in 1980 when it was featured on television for the first time. Now belly dancers regularly grace tourist brochures and provide a steady income for restaurants and cafes (Öztürkmen 2001, 143).

Sugarman points out that the late nineteenth-century nationalist movements of the Eastern Orthodox Southern Slavs mobilized specifically against the perceived decadence of Muslim culture (as symbolized by çengis) (2003, 101–2). In this emerging nationalist discourse, Roma had two strikes against them: they were Muslim and they were Gypsy. According to Sugarman:

> Their identity as Roma was yet another factor contributing to their poor reputation, leading to a highly ironic situation for them: having taken up the role of entertainer in part because it was one of the few economic niches available to them as a marginal social group, they were then further marginalized by the profession itself. Their perceived indecency could then be ascribed by non–Roma to the moral character of their ethnic groups, rather than to the particular social and economic conditions and gender arrangements that prevailed within late Ottoman society [2003, 101].

Below I will explore how the market has been a constant factor in determining the place of professional dance, but first we need to examine čoček in Romani communities and the historical/religious/cultural baggage of ambivalence that surrounds it.

Sexuality and Dance

The condemnation of sensuous dancing voiced above is grounded in an ideology of female modesty and decorum that was historically shared by all Balkans groups regardless of religion; today this ideology appears stronger among Muslims. Based on Greek Macedonian materials Cowan writes: "Dance is a problem for women because in the dance site ... ambivalent attitudes about female sexuality as both pleasurable and threatening are juxtaposed" (1990, 190). Among all Balkan groups, the embodied nature of dance highlights its association with female sexuality. For Muslims "the female body is the embodiment of seductive power and its open expression is therefore strongly condemned in moral-religious discourses" (Nieuwkerk 2003, 268).

The literature on honor and shame in the Mediterranean region is useful in that it identifies the honor of the family with the proper control of female sexuality. But this literature must be criticized for reducing complex and variable systems to a rigid dichotomy. Various authors have shown that the supposed pan-Mediterranean concept of honor means different things to different cultural groups (Magrini 2003). The Balkan Romani moral system contrasts *pativ* (or *pačiv* or *pakiv*, Romani, respect) with *ladž* (Romani, shame). In the South Slavic languages, Roma speak of these concepts as *čest* (honesty) and *sram* (shame). A bride who is a virgin is *čestna* (honest, pure). A professional belly dancer *nema sram* (has no shame). A family's reputation is expressed by offering hospitality to guests, respecting elders, and caring for family members in gender-specific ways. A man works and provides for his family; women work too, but they also cook, clean, and take care of children, and serve men. In public, women are expected to cater to and to defer to men, as the latter are nominally "heads of households."

This association of women with sexuality bears directly on the stigma of the female professional dancer for it is both the commercial relationship with a paying audience and the display of the body to strange males which threaten female modesty. For this reason dancing professionally is regarded as far more immoral than singing professionally (Silverman 2003). Yuri Yunakov, a Bulgarian Muslim Romani musician, remarked that he would never let his daughter (who is a very talented dancer) become a professional dancer, as it was a degrading profession. Dancing for money involves performing for strange men, selling one's sexuality and thereby devaluing it. Dancing non-professionally in the Romani community also has its dangers (see below), although they are mitigated by the high value on dance as a female art form.

These are the ideals, but they are contradicted by realms of female power and influence. The female role in income-producing activities, in budget decisions, in marriage decisions, in information networks, and in ritual all mitigate her subordination (Silverman 1996b). In the realm of sexuality, however, women theoretically must conform most to ideal behavior precisely because sexuality poses the greatest danger of ladž or sram. Women are scrutinized by other women as to their bodily appearance and deportment. Clothing (especially hem lines and bodices), make-up, eye contact, socializing patterns, company kept, time spent outdoors — all are noted and evaluated for violations of modesty. The most highly charged symbol of the proper deportment of female sexuality is the test for the virginity of the bride, still performed today in many Muslim Romani families in the Balkans and in the diaspora.[18]

The common social structural argument explaining the potency of female sexuality argues that in patrilineal patrilocal societies the possibility of a woman having a child with a man who isn't her husband disrupts the patriarchal system and poses a problem of affiliation of the child. Other views argue that it is the female body itself that is inherently sexual, in contrast to the "productive" body of men (Nieuwkerk 1995, 154). A third view interprets Islam as conceiving of women as more sexual than men, thus needing to be constrained (Mernissi 1975). These views are somewhat relevant for the Romani case, but they are insufficient explanations. Balkan Roma talk constantly about the problems of a child who is not rightfully attached to an extended family; children conceived in adulterous relationships are pitied and their mothers are rebuked. But a woman's deviant sexual behavior is seen as part of her intrinsic immoral character. Roma seem to view sexuality as inherent to females but not in contrast to the "productive bodies" of males. True, males have to worry less about public scrutiny of sexuality, but on the other hand, Roma also view females as productive bodies. In fact women are often viewed as more productive than men. Most Roma agree that women hold the family together emotionally and culturally, and, in addition, many families survive on women's incomes.

An important manifestation of the proper deportment of sexuality is monitoring where and among whom dance is performed. Because dance is so sexual, it should, ideally, only be performed among one's own sex. According to Dunin's research in Macedonian Romani communities, segregated male and female dancing was the norm until the 1970s. Women danced in private home settings to the accompaniment of a female daire player and women's singing; to dance for men was considered crude (1971, 324–325; 1973, 195). Note, however, that this was also true for Christians and for non–Romani Muslims of the Balkans (Rice 1994; Sugarman 1997). Esma Redžepova, speaking of her childhood in the 1950s, remembered: "Women used to be in a separate room, men separate, and they used to celebrate segregated at weddings." During the women-only bathing-the-bride ritual at Esma's wedding in 1968, there was a female orchestra composed of one violin and two daires (Teodosievski and Redžepova 1984, 108).

Some women conceived of the wedding as two simultaneous events: a women's party and a men's party. An elder woman remembered a 1950s ceremony as follows: "During the Saturday celebration of the wedding at the bride's house, there would be a professional female orchestra — two violins, a daire player, and the singer, usually the daire player." Esma similarly recalled, "Among us, for example, there was one female violinist, and there were two female daire players — my sister at one time played the daire and the tarabuka and sang at weddings. But this was only for women, not for men. It wasn't shameful because they sang for women, they were, in fact, very popular" (personal interview, 1996).

The spatial segregation during celebrations was often described in terms of the "inside" women's world and the "outside" men's world. This concept of space is shared with non–Romani Muslims of the region (Sugarman 1997). In the henna ceremony, for example, Esma recalls that "the women were inside, the men were outside with the *zurlas* (double reed aerophones) and *tapans* [two-headed drums]." Pettan reminds us not to take the words "outside" and "inside" too literally. In the Balkans many courtyards have high walls, thus a women's courtyard performance is outside but not as public as the street. The courtyard is sharply distinguished from the street, where men perform (Pettan 1996, 316 and 2003). Henna celebrations in Šuto Orizari, Macedonia, for example, take place either "inside" the house or "inside the courtyard" of the bride. Women from the groom's family dance through the streets with trays of henna and clothing, accompanied by male musicians. When they reach the house of the bride, they are either led inside or they make the courtyard area women's space. Here they enact the required rituals; if men are present, they look on from the periphery.[19]

The descriptions above may wrongly imply that Romani women are confined to the domestic sphere. While they are associated with the domestic, both historical references and ethnographic observations show that Romani women regularly venture into the public sphere, primarily for economic activities such as music, dance, seasonal agricultural work, and selling at markets. Pettan observes a greater freedom of movement of Romani women in comparison to other non–Romani Muslims of Kosovo: "Their private domain, is however, extended in comparison to most non–Gypsy women" (1996, 316). Pettan further explains that while the above is true for sedentary Roma, nomadic Romani women are even more exposed in the public realm, through fortune-telling, selling herbal medicines and begging (1996, 316). Unlike upper class non–Romani Muslims, Romani women have historically worked outside the home with men among non–Romani women and men.[20]

To return to the theme of propriety, Dunin's Macedonian research in the 1970s shows that line dancing was sexually integrated while solo dancing (which is coded as more sexual) was segregated. Dunin remarks that "whenever the dancing began during segregated parties, the curtains or drapes were secured so that no one could look indoors. If a child playfully pulled the curtains from outside, he was sent scurrying for fear of being punished.... This dance was meant to be performed by women for women and not in mixed situations" (Dunin 1973, 195). By the 1980s, however, due to Westernization and the relaxation of gender divisions in many areas of life, solo dances could be found in mixed company. In banquet halls, on the street at weddings, and at home parties, women now dance solo in the presence of men; women also continue to dance in sexually segregated events such as henna parties. How women negotiate these contexts is discussed below.

Čoček at Romani Family Events in the Balkans and the Diaspora

The most characteristic Romani dance form is the solo dance known today as *čoček* or *čuček* in Macedonia and Kosovo and *kyuchek* in Bulgaria. Note that čoček also refers to the musical genre used for this dance which is often marked by Turkish-derived scales and by *mane*, or *taksim*, a highly improvised exploration of the scale or *makam*, using stock motives and figures, played over a metric ostinato. The term thus serves a double function as indicating both a dance and a music genre. The rhythms typically associated with čoček are variants of 2/4, 4/4, 7/8, and 9/8 (see accompanying figure). Actually there are many variations on these rhythms, each imparting a distinct style and sometimes indicating to dancers what should be danced. Also note that Roma (especially in Macedonia) do line dances to čoček music that vary in step and style by region, age, and sub-group of Roma. Finally note that in addition to čoček, Balkan Roma have always danced at least some of the line-dance repertoire of the non–Roma in their region; for example, Roma from the southern Macedonian city of Bitola regularly dance *Beranče* (sometimes in 12/8, 3-2-2-3-2) (see Leibman, this volume), and Bulgarian Roma dance *pravo horo* (in 2/4). In contemporary communities, elder Roma are often called upon to lead the slow, heavy, older line dances that young people do not know.

As a solo dance, čoček is improvised, utilizing hand movements, contractions of the abdomen and pelvis, shoulder shakes, movement of isolated body parts (such as hips and head), and small footwork patterns. Men as well as women perform it but it is overwhelmingly associated with women. Čoček is clearly an heir to the dances of the Ottoman çengis but in Romani communities its subtlety and restraint distinguish it from contemporary belly dancing (see Shay and Sellers-Young 2005). I conceive of solo čoček dancing on a continuum, with subtlety and a covered body (as found at Romani community events) on one end and belly dancing and exposed skin on the other end. I will develop this point below.

Both solo čoček and line dances are typically combined at ritual events, which are numerous and obligatory in Romani communities. Dunin's research describes ordinary Romani women looking "very comfortable and confident of their movements probably due to the frequency of dancing, which occurs almost every week" (1971, 323–24; also see 1973, 1977, 1985, 1998). Indeed, from

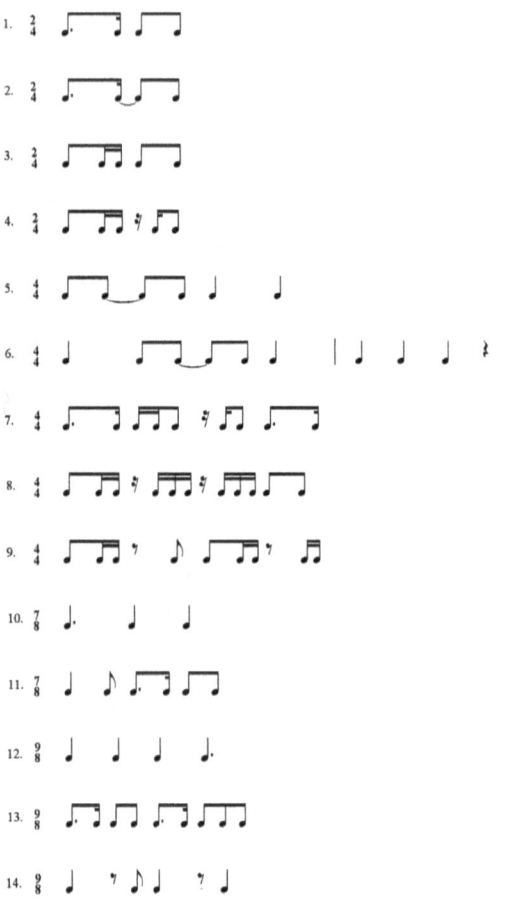

Typical rhythmic variants of čoček.

June to September in Šuto Orizari, Macedonia, on any weekend evening one can find from five to ten weddings on the streets. The outdoor dance portions of the weddings are regularly viewed by scores of uninvited onlookers, and there are times when uninvited people may dance. Dance-crazy Šutka teenagers regularly make the rounds looking for the best music for dancing!

It is not surprising to find so much music and dance in Šutka, for it is perhaps the largest Romani settlement in Europe (40,000 people with very few non-Roma), and music and dance are the community's expressive focus (Silverman 1996b). In smaller neighborhoods, Balkan Romani weddings are less numerous but can be found practically every summer weekend, although in the post-socialist period the size and duration of celebrations have declined due to economic constraints (Silverman forthcoming). Besides weddings, dance events include circumcisions (for Muslims), baptisms (for Eastern Orthodox Christians), house-warmings, soldier-send-off celebrations and calendrical celebrations, the most important of which is the spring holiday of Erdelezi (Dunin 1998). In the North American diaspora, dance events also include New Year's Eve, graduations and birthday parties.

Participants structure events through dance, which enacts some of the most important rituals in the wedding (Sugarman 1997; Cowan 1990). In Macedonia, for example, the *igranka* (dance) is held for the bride's relatives on Saturday. The first dance of the event is led by the most respected female elder who holds a sieve decorated with a grain product, greenery, and a red scarf. The sieve symbolically links the fertility of the land (wheat and flour) to the fertility of the bride. At Silvana Mahmud's igranka, the bride's mother Altana led the first dance, followed by Silvana's brother's wife, followed by Altana's sisters; eventually Silvana led, dressed in the clothes she had received at the henna party a few days earlier (wide billowing trousers typically called *šalvari*, *čintijani*, or *dimije* in Romani). Women were called up to lead the line one by one, in the order of age and closeness to the sponsoring family, by the "speaker," a man who has a flair with words, is a good organizer, and knows the proper order. He must not insult people by omitting them; the sequence must be *ko redo* (in order, Romani). Dance, then, is a performative display of social structure. One common speaker's formula is *Akana ka khela...* (Romani, now so-and-so will dance). I have been at several weddings where people were furious at the order. Often a speaker is instructed in the proper order by knowledgeable females.

The igranka is a decidedly female event even though men are present, and the dance lines are usually led by women. As the family goes up to the front of the dance line, someone requests a tune from the musicians and a male tips them. Knowing they are on display, females dress up for the event and sometimes young unmarried women change their clothes several times (borrowing their friends' and relatives' outfits). This is an occasion for parents to scrutinize potential spouses for their children. People discuss who is wearing what and who is dancing next to whom; most important, parents of marriageable children ask *kaske* (whose, Romani) is that son or daughter, meaning to what family does he or she belong. Because dance lines are now integrated sexually, they serve as meeting places for young people. Since dating is not practiced and arranged marriages are still the ideal (although they are declining in number), youths of the opposite sex look each other over on the dance line and exchange glances. Young men and women sometimes dance next to each other (as long as friends or relatives are close by watching) and conversations are initiated. Future matches, then, are planned at ritual celebrations (Silverman forthcoming).

Close kin women are expected, even obliged, to dance for hours at weddings, sometimes for three or four days in a row, no matter how hot and how tired they are. The only excuse not to dance is illness or mourning. Women who do not dance well or are mentally or physically disabled also dance and even lead dance lines. Because women have so many obligations, such as ritual enactments, food preparation, and dancing, men end up taking care of children, something that rarely happens outside of rituals. Male dancing is more optional than female dancing. There are some moments where male dancing is required such as when their families are called up to lead the dance line. The males of the bride's family must also solemnly dance with her just before she is transferred to the groom's family. Men dance for entertainment too, and some men dance a great deal, but they are not obliged to dance as much as women.

On the dance floor one finds both children learning by immersion and from seasoned elders. A typical wedding dance line, whether located in the Balkans or in the diaspora, has a ratio of approximately three women to one man. Men often dance together, put a great deal of energy into the dance for a short while, and then sit down. In the diaspora, I have noticed groups of young men who always dance together; they look for each other at celebrations and try out complicated steps. Whenever their favorite dance is played, these boys will appear. In fact, men seem to demonstrate their masculinity more in line dances rather than in solo čočeks. Women and girls also tend to dance with their relatives and friends; they too join the dance line in pairs or groups, rarely alone. But unlike men, women and girls are on the dance floor for practically the whole event.

Čoček as a female solo dance also has an important place in ritual. It is danced in the middle of the dance floor near the front of the dance line; simultaneously, the line snakes around. For example, in Šutka, at an igranka, the bride's close female kin will dance čoček in the center as relatives are called up to lead the dance line. A few female members of the beckoned relatives (rarely men) will join the bride's women in the center to dance čoček. The style changes as new tunes are played and new family members are summoned. Even though women may be ostensibly doing the same dance for hours, its texture migrates, for example, from fast and bouncy to slow and heavy. While ritual contexts of čoček are obligatory, dancing čoček for entertainment is also common, for example, during the less ritualized parts of dance events.

A good čoček dancer has the admiration of the entire community, and her family will show off her talents. At a wedding in Šutka the father of an excellent teenage dancer was very angry with her because she was nowhere to be found when the family was called up to lead the dance line. His family's artistic competence depended partly on his daughter, who possessed a valuable female asset. Women and girls squarely take center stage as excellent dancers, and people crowd around them to watch. Esma Redžepova remarked, "That was the most beautiful, to show dignity. A mother-in-law might say to another mother-in-law, 'my daughter-in-law raises her hand while dancing, as if she could take everyone's life!' This would show how delicately she danced; this was the realization of Romani tradition." Girls are coached by family members to dance while boys are not. At home, taped music is played as experienced female dancers demonstrate moves and technique. At dance events, mothers "put up" their daughters to dance on tables.

The female art of dancing čoček is chronicled and admired in hundreds of songs. For example, Macedonian Romani singer Džansever recorded the following song (on the cassette *Kemano Bašal/Violino Sviri* [The Violin Plays], Sokoj 21102; Text: Džansever; music and arrangement: Ferus Mustafov):

E davulja e zurle bašalen	The drums and the zurlas play
Amaro kefi ola keren	They create our pleasure
Tikne, bare, terne, phure	Small, big, young, and old
Sarine čučeko džanen te khelen	Everyone knows how to dance chuchek
O davuli kuvel man vikinel	The drum calls me to dance
Čučeko te khelav ov mangel	It wants me to dance čuček
Ko bijav me aljum te khelav	I went to the wedding to dance
Mo baro gyubeko me te furdav	To throw my big stomach
Romani čhai sijum, Romale	Hey Roma, I am a Romani girl
Čučeko me džanav te khelav	I know how to dance čuček

Note that Džansever sings of "throwing" the stomach, implying that the movement is quite sharp and rhythmic; this is a characteristic move for Balkan Roma. When asked about kyuchek, many of Peicheva's Bulgarian Romani informants speak of the stomach flick as an essential component (1999, 244–245).

Although family members seek to show off the dancing of unmarried girls, they must delicately negotiate the propriety of the display. Some displays are crass and transgressive while others are appropriate, depending on context and audience. At a wedding banquet in Šutka, for example, a mother put her sixteen-year-old daughter on a table to dance while the mother, her sister, her husband, the dancer's sister, and the dancer's brother all danced in front of her (on the floor), encouraging her with shouts of appreciation and even with monetary tips. Similarly, female relatives of good dancers often stop dancing and instead clap for the talented performer. In spatial terms, the closest audience for proper female čoček dancers is composed of relatives. Strangers, however, do watch from afar. Ironically, it is precisely for strangers that the girl's talent needs to be shown (for marriage purposes). The physical proximity of relatives is not only a permeable wall—a shield of protection against claims of sexual immorality—but also a transparent screen through which to view female bodily displays.

While most of my above observations are taken from fieldwork in the Balkans, the same may be said of dancing in the Romani diaspora. During virtually all line dances during rituals in New York, several female relatives dance solo in the center of the curve of the line. Dancing remains a vital part of celebrations whether they are at home or in a banquet hall. As part of Samir and Lebadet's wedding in New York in 2004, the groom's parents sponsored a large henna party with live music for women only in the courtyard of their apartment building. Lebadet led the first dance with a lacy handkerchief (not a decorated sieve, as in Macedonia). One by one, her female family members, as well as the groom's female relatives, led the line. Before each woman led, she (not a man) tipped the musicians. Lebadet wore a gown, then *šalvari*, then another gown. Shalvari are infrequently worn in the United States but a few elders insist that brides wear them at ritual moments such as these. As this was a female-centered party, men were absent or stayed on the sidelines, except for the male musicians. The dancing became more bawdy as the women loosened up, and the mothers of the bride and groom climbed on chairs and mimed sexually suggestive movements in a humorous way. In terms of the intense female presence, this event resembled the henna parties I had attended in Macedonia despite the absence of some of the specific customs.

In the diaspora, weddings have been condensed in time due to work schedules. As in the Balkans, women are the primary dancers; they dance for hours while men dance sporadically. There are several older women in the New York community who are excellent dancers and they tend to request *Pharol Teško* (heavy, slow dance; Romani/Macedonian) in 2/4 or 7/8 that displays their mastery of grace and style. An exceptional dancer can even receive *bakšiš* (tips) on her forehead. The New York Macedonian Romani repertoire of line dances includes *Bugarsko, Ibrjam Odža (Berance), Lesno, Pharol/Teško, Čačak, Bitolska Gaida, Eleno, Jeni Jol*, and several 9/8 dances (including *Afe Dude*), as well as the ubiquitous line čoček, which they sometimes call oro[21] or specify by the name of a tune such as *Čuperlika*. Rhythms such as 9/8 and 7/8 are less common than 2/4 rhythms, and often 9/8 tunes are played later in the evening and induce increased intensity.[22]

As in the Balkans, the solo čoček is considered a female specialty, and talented women are surrounded and encouraged by their relatives. Towards the end of a New York wedding, when everyone had loosened up, the bridal couple danced solo čoček standing on chairs. At one wedding in 2004, the sponsoring family innovated by hiring a non–Romani American belly dancer. Note that, as mentioned above, while a Romani čoček shares some movements with belly dancing, the latter is more overtly sexual, is costumed with naked flesh showing, and is danced by professionals for strangers for money. Wedding guests had mixed reactions to the belly dancer; elders for the most part did not like it (because it was not part of their tradition), and younger guests either liked the novelty or criticized the focus it took off the couple.

Čoček as Social Dance among Non-Roma in the Balkans and the Diaspora

Today the solo čoček can be found at community events not only among Roma but also among Bulgarians, Albanians, Macedonians, Serbs, Romanian, Greeks, and Turks, that is, among virtually all the ethnic groups of the Balkans. The line version of čoček known among Roma in Macedonia is found among Macedonians and Albanians from Macedonia but not among the other Balkan groups. As a variant of the six-measure *lesno/pravo/oro*, it probably disseminated from Šuto Orizari and was picked up by Macedonians and Albanians in the 1970s; by the 1980s it had spread to Albanians in the Prespa region of Macedonia, and by the 1990s to Albanians in the North American diaspora, according to Sugarman (2003 and personal communication).

As a solo dance, čoček encodes various meanings for non–Roma, who to varying degrees may be aware of its sexual associations and its ties to Roma. Sugarman thoughtfully explores how contemporary Muslim Albanian young women from Macedonia redefine aspects of their sexuality and their modernity when they dance čoček with other women. While they still condemn professional female dancers, "the genres once associated with them have been adopted by 'respectable' women and even men" (Sugarman 2003, 112). Furthermore, they relate čoček to Turkish urban culture, thereby placing it in the realm of art and "civilization."

For Bulgarian non–Roma, however, I posit that something else is at work. I observed Bulgarians dancing solo kyuchek at community events in the 1970s when wedding bands included them in their repertoires (despite prohibitions against them). The typical pattern among Bulgarians is for guests to dance kyuchek when they are at least slightly drunk — at the end of a wedding — at a moment of abandon and release. This is a time for enacting the perceived freedom and unbridled sexuality of "the other" in the form of the internal Muslim (Roma, Turks). For Bulgarians, who are eastern Orthodox Christians (unlike Albanians who are Muslims), Turkish and Romani cultures are coded as less bounded by the constraints of civilization. Although I do not have the space to explore this in depth, I note that the Muslim issue has a long history and is still sensitive in Bulgaria today (Neuburger 2004). For example, the pop/folk genre *chalga* is criticized by many Bulgarians because it is too Muslim and too Gypsy (see below; Buchanan 2007; Rice 2002; Statelova 2005).

Van de Port reports a similar phenomenon among Serbs who frequent cafés with Romani music in Novi Sad, Vojvodina (1998). Neither these Serbs nor the Romani musicians who play for them are Muslims (both are Eastern Orthodox), but nevertheless, Roma function as the internal uncivilized "other." In the cafés Serbs dress like Gypsies, dance čoček, and drink with abandon, as if enacting what they perceive as the culture of Roma. "Within the Gypsy bar the door is opened to all those forbidden and hidden things which were deposited in the figure of the Gypsy.... As would-be Gypsies the visitors gain access to what is labeled as primitive and Balkan in the civilization debate" (1998, 188).

Finally, in Romania since the 1989 revolution, a form of solo čoček known as *mahala* or *manele* has been appropriated into popular culture. This is an import from the southern Balkans (Serbia and Bulgaria), although it has roots in *manea*, the urban Romani dance of the Ottoman period (Garfias 1984).[23] Critics associate it with commercialism, sex, and Roma, all marks of the uncivilized. Like čoček in the southern Balkans, It is danced primarily by women while men are the instrumentalists and most of the singers. Despite public condemnation by intellectuals, folk music scholars and folk musicians, it has a growing fan base among Romanians as well as Roma (Beissinger 2007). In addition, the Romani brass band Fanfare Ciocarlia from the northern Romanian region of Moldavia currently tours with two female solo manele dancers with bare midriffs. Upholding the tradition of performing with family members, these women are the Romani wives of the German managers of the band.[24] Thus this popular dance form has entered the professional realm.

Čoček as Professional Dance: Ensembles, Festivals, and Music Videos

Since World War II čoček has found a place in professional and amateur Balkan ensemble choreographies, some of which incorporate romantic and orientalist images of Roma. According to Shay and Sellers-Young, "Belly dance contexts ... negotiate a transnational discourse of exoticism" (2005, 14). Similarly, in her research on tango, Savigliano notes that "exoticism is a way of establishing order in an unknown world through fantasy" (1995, 169). Dance choreographies also are effective visual communications about what constitutes civilization, the nation, and the folk vs. "others" (Shay 2002).

Based on Tito's ideal of "brotherhood and unity" of all the ethnicities of the nation/state, Yugoslav national ensembles often incorporated Gypsy suites into their repertoires. Note, however, that actual Roma did not typically dance in these companies. Shay describes one of two of Kolo's (Serbian State Folk Dance Ensemble's) Gypsy suites as depicting "Gypsies as childlike, irresponsible, sexually lax individuals who dance, sing and fornicate the night away.... All the visual clues — the campfire, the gypsy wagon, the false mustaches are present" (2002, 8). The men pull knives and carry the women off, and the women wear costumes revealing their legs and breasts, uncharacteristic of Serbia's Romani communities (Shay 2002, 8). I viewed a suite with similar images in 1989 at the Ohrid Folk Festival in Macedonia, performed by a visiting Dutch group. The men were bare-chested and had whips and the women had flared skirts and off-the-shoulder blouses. While I was offended at the stereotypification, a Romani journalist clapped wildly. When I asked him how he could approve, he answered that it was wonderful that the Dutch performers sang in Romani. Below I will discuss the implications of stereotyping for marginal minorities.

Shay describes a second Kolo suite depicting Gypsies from Sandžak, South Serbia, a Muslim region: "The women wear costumes right out of the Broadway musical *Kismet*, with see-through gauze veils never seen in the clothing of the Balkans but immediately recognizable to viewers of Hollywood film depictions of *A Thousand and One Nights*. Thus the Slavic Muslims and the Gypsies constitute the Other by which the Serbian nation is defined" (2002, 8–9). This resonates with my earlier point about how Slavs define themselves in opposition to an internal Muslim other.

The Serbian dance company Frula (which broke off from Kolo) has an entire show *Tzigane*, whose 1986 press release states:

> Lacking any national folk heritage of their own, the Gypsies have adopted the cultural traits of the localities in which they have settled ... and have mysteriously made it their own. In addition to the many songs and dances, the program will feature performances of hitherto secret tribal rites celebrating marriage, birth, and death, as they have been practiced since time immemorial in Gypsy encampments all over the world. For centuries Gypsies have been the objects of curiosity, fascination and persecution among the world's people. Their carefree, nomadic life style has inspired envy in the hearts of some, suspicion and disgust in the hearts of others. Their caravans and campfires have sung of the open road. Their flashing eyes, unbridled zest for living, and their passion for singing and dancing have made them popular attractions wherever they have settled or roamed. Though often identified with the supernatural and the occult, Gypsies generally will adapt to their environment and are happy carefree people.

Although I do not have the space to analyze all the implications of this text, note that the major Gypsy fantasy themes are present: mystery, secrecy, the occult, rootlessness, freedom, music, wildness, passion, and sex. The message is these are people NOT like us, thus the alternation of the dual polarities of fascination and repulsion (Silverman 2007).

Not all Yugoslav ensembles, however, utilized stereotypic imagery. Up until 1960, Tanec, the Macedonian State Folk Dance Ensemble, included one traditional Romani line dance in its repertoire, Čuperlika, mentioned above in relation to its melody. The 1950 Tanec program lists Čuperlika as a Turkish women's dance, but it is also still widely done among Macedonian Roma. The dance was collected by the Janković sisters in 1939 in Skopje (1939, 75–77). Tanec's first 1950s line dance choreography was changed to add a solo čoček, and, for the 1956 United States tour, "costumes were changed from Turkish style šalvare to translucent and narrower type pantaloons because Americans like to see more of the legs" (Višinski and Dunin 1995, 127).

When ensemble performers are Romani, they too must constantly negotiate what to present as Gypsy dance. For example, government-sponsored amateur Romani ensembles (composed of Roma) in the former Yugoslavia were encouraged to present their folklore and that of neighboring ethnicities at festivals. The first Romani KUD (*Kulturno Umjetničko Društvo*, Cultural Artistic Group) in Serbia was founded in Priština, Kosovo, in 1969 (Dunin 1977, 14). In the mid–1970s a festival for Romani KUDs from all over Serbia was organized that was an exciting moment in the non–Romani public's recognition of Romani musical talent. Not surprisingly, the festival followed the typical model of presenting complicated choreographies unknown in Romani communities. Although subtle čoček s were danced in many of the Romani KUDs, some KUDs imitated the gross erotic movements done in non–Romani KUDs in their "Gypsy suites" (Dunin 1977, 15). This brings up the question of self-stereotyping, which I discuss below.

Known as *Phralipe* (brotherhood), the Macedonian Romani KUD founded in 1949 was very popular, won prizes at Yugoslav folk festivals, and even traveled outside the country (Džimrevski 1983, 216).[25] As was common for all KUDs, the group performed non–Romani dances from all over Yugoslavia, but did include one "Gypsy suite." Dunin noted in the 1960s that most of the group's repertoire consisted of Macedonian line dances. Dunin was told by members "that it was difficult to maintain a repertoire of Rom dances, because the girls did not continue in the group beyond marriage (usually between the ages fourteen and seventeen)" (1977, 13). Similarly, I learned that the group had problems recruiting girls and eventually had to disband in the 1980s. As sites of male/female socializing, ensembles might compromise the morals of unprotected females. Pettan writes of Kosovo Roma: "Engagement of Gypsies with music and dance within the school or amateur ensembles ends with marriage.

This is more strict with the female part of the Gypsy population than with its male counterpart" (1996, 316). This very same problem of female reputation plagued Severdžan Azirov in New York City in the 1990s when he tried to start a Romani performing group (Silverman forthcoming).

The performance of Romani dance by ensembles in Yugoslavia can be contrasted sharply to its virtual absence in Bulgaria during the socialist period. From the 1970s to 1989 the entire genre of kyuchek (both dance and music) was prohibited in the official media because the state claimed it was Turkish and Romani, thus not "purely Bulgarian." Fines were levied and jail sentences were imposed on musicians who played kyuchetsi and weddings were closed down if guests danced kyuchetsi.[26] Of course, Roma, Turks, and Bulgarians found ways to resist and the genre thrived in private settings (note Zvezda Salieva above) and eventually emerged in vital form after 1989. During post-socialism Bulgarian kyuchek became more "orientalized" and was influenced by trends in Turkey and Yugoslavia.

During the 1980s and early 1990s, for example, in Yugoslavia, television programs for New Year's Eve regularly featured Romani musicians with a bevy of writhing, scantily clad belly dancers. When watching these programs with Romani friends the musicians remarked how these women had virtually nothing in common with Romani čoček dancers, plus they gave Romani women a bad name. One of Ferus Mustafov's [a Macedonian Romani musician] videos from the 1990s features him as a doctor in uniform playing to his bed-ridden female patients who shed their hospital sheets and emerge as belly dancers. Singer Esma Redzepova commented:

> In recent times, ... there has appeared ... with Ferus Mustafov a Macedonian woman (she isn't Romani) who does belly dance — and they show this as if it were Romani. This isn't Romani, it is Turkish. That is Ferus' mistake. He makes a profit — money — from this.... A Romani woman would never be undressed to show her belly button.... Women used to be in a separate room, men separate, and they used to celebrate segregated at weddings. At our weddings our women used to be dressed in beautiful dimiya, beautiful shoes ... nothing at all bare — beautiful vests, underdresses, handkerchiefs at their hands, blouses with handmade lace. When they got up to dance, two-by-two ... all of the elders ... would cheer whomever danced better. Among us, we didn't do any mixed [sex] dances — we only danced čoček. You dance čoček with your stomach, you don't dance (with your hips) in a circle, you don't dance it with moans; we didn't have any of the new things with which people now deceive people [personal interview, 1996].

Esma's sensibility prevailed at Šutkafest, the 1993 Romani-sponsored festival in Skopje: the performers were fully clothed in šalvari and danced modest solos or line čočeks.

It is clear that newer commercial dance images are directly related to the high market value of the hyper-sexualized female Gypsy body. A cursory glance at the graphic designs of cassettes, CDs, videos and DVDs with Romani music produced in Macedonia and Bulgaria since 1990 reveals that many of them feature semi-nude belly dancers, and some are pornographic.[27] In Bulgaria the genre *chalga* (a fusion of pop and folk with predominantly kyuchek rhythms), which arose in the 1990s, capitalizes on the association of kyuchek with erotic belly dance (Buchanan 2007; Rice 2002; Statelova 2005). In the early 1990s chalga music videos often depicted eastern themes (e.g., sheiks with dancing harems) intertwined with texts about themes in contemporary life such as inflation, drugs, and gambling. In the last fifteen years a virtual media frenzy[28] has fueled the growth of chalga as it has become more pop, slick, and pornographic while the technical and production values have increased. The oriental/Romani elements are still visible and audible but they have become more stylized and abstract and have been absorbed into formulaic narratives enacted by larger casts of dancers and actors. The 2005 song *Zabravi* (Forget), for example, from the singer Emilia[29] features a text about failed love and a visual display that includes a bare-chested man striking a gong (engraved with E for Emilia) and a harem-like group of women in sheer veils dancing synchronous steps that are closer to Bollywood than belly dance. The dancers are then transformed into hip hop performers with a DJ, but the video concludes with the gong.

The kyuchek rhythm is still very common in chalga but male musicians are no longer depicted, rather the emphasis is on the star. And the typical female chalga star is a non–Romani bombshell with fair skin and often blonde hair. Sofi Marinova, the only female chalga star who is Romani, has been marginalized by the media; a scandal erupted in 2005 when her entry to the Eurovision competition (a duet with Slavi Trifonov, a popular television show host) did not win due to the alleged fixing of votes (Silverman forthcoming). Many Bulgarians were outraged that a Gypsy might represent Bulgaria at Eurovision. In sum, it is clear that Romani dance and music had been appropriated into chalga without the visible participation of Roma.

The one exception to the above observation is Azis, who has emerged as a mega-star in the last five years. A Romani male who is bisexual, transgendered, and transvestite, he breaks every Balkan gender code of behavior. In his videos, he dances erotic kyucheks, loves fancy gowns and high heeled boots, has sex with men, women, himself, or several people at once. He can be super macho or super feminine, reminiscent of the Ottoman köçeks. The public fascination with him draws on his transgressive behavior which is tolerable and even expected because he is Romani; if he were a Bulgarian man he would be despised (Silverman forthcoming).

While we may view most of the examples above as the product of non–Roma marketing, Roma themselves are not immune to these stereotypes. While activists condemn these images, entertainers often capitalize on them (Silverman 2007). For example, even Esma Redžepova, who eloquently protested against belly dancing above, was featured in videos in the 1970s with veiled belly dancers, although no flesh was shown.[30] She explained to me that the scenarios were staged beautifully even though she knew they were not representative of her culture. Similarly, Alaina Lemon's research shows how, on a documentary film shoot in a Russian Kelderara Romani neighborhood, the crew insisted on building a campfire in the snow and ordering all the young girls to dance simultaneously, behaviors which were totally foreign to the Roma; yet she learned that "the Kelderara did not criticize how they had been filmed.... In fact, ... Kelderara themselves shared and valued some of the same forms of stereotypic representation valued by the crew" (2000, 156–157).

The postsocialist mania for belly dancing in Bulgaria illustrates the interplay of stereotype, history, and politics. In 1990, at one of the first public concerts to be labeled with the words *Tsiganska Muzika* (Gypsy Music), the all-Romani audience was ecstatic to hear and see the formerly prohibited kyuchek. The dancing, however, was not the subtle kyuchek which Roma do at their in-group events, but rather belly dancing with bare midriffs and gross bodily contortions. Belly dancers (some non–Romani, some Romani) now regularly appear on videos of Romani singers in romanticized stagings. Furthermore, since the early 1990s in Bulgaria, belly dancers have been appearing with bands at Romani music festivals, creating a virtual craze. At the 1995 Romani Music Festival in Stara Zagora, the winning band Džipsi Aver (Gypsy Friend) appeared with five *kyuchekinyas* (kyuchek dancers) and the thousands of audience members went wild. All five dancers had bare midriffs; one wore an oriental style outfit and the other four wore Russian-influenced costumes. Since 2000, the Russian Romani costume (flair skirts and shawls for women, wide shirts and boots for men) is emerging as standard attire (Peicheva and Dimov 2005, 21). In 2000 a new award category, best dance ensemble, was created, and as a result, many new Romani dance groups have been created which have wide repertoires and serve as community centers (Peicheva and Dimov 2005, 10).

In Bulgaria, the belly dance craze has complex connotations embedded in the ethnic politics of the postsocialist period. First, it is a youth phenomenon. The annual Stara Zagora festival, for example, has grown tremendously since its inception in 1993 and regularly attracts several thousand Roma and increasing numbers of non–Roma, mostly under thirty years of age, who actively dance while watching the performances. There is a party atmosphere, and it is one of the places where Roma feel safe congregating. Second, the festival is tied to the cultural and political mobilization of Roma in a society that actively discriminates against them. Romani festivals often feature speeches by politicians and are sponsored by political organizations or non-governmental organizations (Georgieva 2006; Peicheva and Dimov 2005). This is also true in Macedonia, where (less frequent) Romani festivals are sponsored by television or radio stations which have political ties. Romani beauty contests in Macedonia are another forum for music, dance, and costume display, and sometimes music and dance contests are piggybacked onto these contests. Thus the professionalization of čoček into belly dance is embedded in economic and political projects, all propelled by the precarious position of Roma in Balkan society.

Conclusion

How can we begin to tackle the thorny question of why professional Romani productions of čoček now resemble non–Romani productions? Indeed, with the orientalization of čoček, it is sometimes hard to distinguish what is produced by Roma anymore. Roma engage in self-stereotypification (or mimesis of other's projections of them) in part because it is economically profitable. "Self-orientalizing" moves, however, should not be taken at face value but should be examined within the webs of power in which they are located. "Self-orientalization" displays the predicaments of marginal "others," but also points to their "agency to maneuver and manipulate meanings within different power domains" (Ong 1997, 195). Savigliano coins the term "autoexoticism," defined as "exotic others laboriously cultivat[ing] passionate-ness in order to be desired, and thus recognized" (1995, 212). Romani dancers, who have never been in control of their own imagery and reputations, are quite used to being made into and making themselves into "exotic others."

We must also remember that the commercial success of belly dance performances and videos among non–Romani and Romani audiences is one of the only positive economic niches in an otherwise bleak economy. And yet here too Roma remain marginal — they do not profit nearly as much as non–Romani performers, managers, and producers. Now that Romani music and dance have been appropriated, Roma are not needed any more for the enactment of their cultural symbols. Furthermore, they are a liability in the growing atmosphere of nationalism and xenophobia.

Throughout history Roma have had to rely on outside patrons and the trade in outsider imagery for work. Some observers, even Romani activists, have criticized Roma for "cashing in" on outsider stereotypes. This position ignores the tremendous power inequalities between Roma and the non–Romani world of promoters and media producers. In truth, Roma have historically had few choices about their work and their images and even today they lack access to image-creating mechanisms (Hancock 1997). Few Roma produce their own music and dance and most are subject to the marketing decisions of others.

Female belly dance performances sell precisely because they fit the image non–Roma have of Romani women — sexually alluring, promiscuous, dangerous, provocative, and musically talented. The historical information about çengis can be interpreted from this angle: çengis were selling not only their musicality but also their perceived (and often actual) sexuality. This is in contrast to Romani community čoček performance which has a muted sexuality. A community čoček dancer must be monitored for modesty, but must also display the potentially sensual fluidity of body movement that defines a talented dancer. Traditional social arrangements, such as where and when she dances, shield the čoček dancer from criticism, but the embedded ambivalence about the female dancer remains. For Roma, female Romani professionals are suspect but necessary. Because they embody the selling of sexuality, they can disrupt the social system from the inside. On the other hand, their performances in the marketplace foreground the paradox of economic necessity vs. ideal modesty.

Notes

1. Materials for this article are drawn from fieldwork with Roma (1980–2006) in Bulgaria, Macedonia (specifically Shuto Orizari, known as Shutka, the largest Romani neighborhood of Skopje) and New York City. Some ideas appeared in Silverman 2003. Research was supported by the International Research and Exchanges Board, the Open Society Institute, and the University of Oregon (Summer Research Award, Oregon Humanities Center Research Fellowship, and Research Grant from the Center for the Study of Women in Society). I have benefited from conversations with Kalin Kirilov, Jane Sugarman, and Mark Levy. Note that I have used Croatian-type orthography in this article when the original language is Macedonian, Serbian, or Romani.

2. I use the appellation Roma (singular Rom, adjective Romani) instead of Gypsies because it has emerged as a unifying term in the last decade as political consciousness has been mobilized (Petrova 2003:111–12). In this article I use Gypsy as an outsider term, although I acknowledge that it is sometimes used as an insider term. Along with its cognates *Gitan* (French), *Gitano* (Spanish), *Yiftos* (Greek), and *Gjupci* (Macedonian, plural), Gypsy connotes faulty history (i.e., Egyptian origins) and usually has strong negative connotations. Some groups, however, willingly embrace the term, such as the *Gitanos* in Spain and the *Egjupkjani* in Macedonia and Kosovo. Another common outsider term, *tsigan* (and its cognates such as the German *Zigueneur*, Italian *Zingaro*, Turkish *Çingene*) derives from the Greek *atsingani*, a heretical sect in the Byzantine period (Soulis 1961:145). Other groups, such as the *Sinti* in Germany, the

Rudari and *Beyashi* in Hungary, and the *Ashkalia* of Kosovo also distinguish themselves from Roma (Hancock 2002:34).

  3. NGOs include the European Roma Rights Center (errc.org), the European Roma Information Office (erio.net), the International Romani Union, and the Roma National Congress. European organizations such as the European Union, the Council of Europe, and the Organization for Security and Cooperation in Europe also deal with Roma (Kilmova-Alexander 2005; Petrova 2003; Barany 2002; Guy 2001). For detailed information on these topics see the World Bank Reports by Ringold 2000 and Ringold, Orenstein, and Williams 2004, and issues of *Roma Rights*, the journal of the European Roma Rights Center.

  4. Both early Christians and early Muslims "took a negative stance toward dance in an attempt to separate their austere and simple religious practices from those of previous groups that combined dance and worship" (Shay and Sellers-Young 2005).

  5. An account from 1638 describes 3000 male dancers in twelve guilds (And 1976, 141). Some female guilds consisted of the leader and her assistant, four musicians (usually violin, drum, and two daires), and twelve dancers (each having an age limit of thirty to thirty-five years). A famous guild leader in the nineteenth century was a *zurla* (double reed aerophone) player, quite unusual for a woman. Her performance site was a public bath for women in Istanbul (And 1976:143). Buonaventura remarks: "The çengis of Turkey were well organized in this respect, with an older member of the troupe acting as a business manager for the entire company. In this way they managed a degree of protection enjoyed by few independent female entertainers" (1994:49). Oldenburg (1990), writing about courtesans (female entertainers) in India, raises the question of whether they were resisting male domination through their independent and often opulent lifestyle. Ottoman materials about çengis, however, are too fragmentary to support Oldenburg's model.

  6. Seeman describes a four-part çengi suite consisting of a unison entrance, a raks dance section emphasizing the stomach and upper torso, a rabbit imitation, and songs (Seeman 1998:4). Chroniclers consistently noted the raised arm and hand movements (as opposed to an emphasis on footwork in line dances) and the torso undulations, shoulder shimmies and head and eye movements (Sugarman 2003:92). Traveler accounts are, then, the origin of the English term "belly dancing" (French, *dance du ventre*). Turkish dance historian Metin And comments: "Their dancing consisted of suggestive contortions, a good deal of stomach play and twisting the body, falling upon the knees with the trunk held back until the head nearly touched the floor behind (a position which usually encouraged the enthusiastic spectator to put a coin on the forehead), writhing, swaying the body with a side twist. Every muscle and both shoulders were made to quiver, and all this was alternated with postures mimicking grace and affections" (And 1976, 142).

  7. A British traveling woman wrote in 1767: "This dance was very different from what I had seen before. Nothing could be more artful, or more proper to raise *certain ideas*. The tunes so soft! The motions so languishing! accompanied with pauses and dying eyes; half-falling back and then recovering themselves in so artful a manner; that I am very positive, the coldest and most rigid prude upon earth, could not have looked upon them without thinking of *something not to be spoken of*" (And 1976:142).

  8. And points out that "Turkish sources offer little information with regard to dancing boys and girls. This is because dancing was regarded ... as an improper and wicked sport.... On the other hand, foreign travelers have given much attention to this topic..., and, although they emphasize the slack morality and obscene character of the dancing, they cannot hide from their descriptions the breathless interest they took in these performances" (1959:24).

  9. Shay further explicates that köçek is derived from the Persian root for small, and that male professional dancers began their careers at a young age (2005). Sugarman (2003:96), drawing from And (1976:141–143) notes two Ottoman compilations of love poems dedicated to dancing boys, one specifically to the dancer Çingene Ismail (Gypsy Ismail).

  10. Clownish scenarios of the abduction and debauchery of women were enacted (And 1976:139–140). "The boys danced along as they preserved their good looks and could conceal their beards" (And 1976, 139).

3. *Transnational Čoček*   63

11. For women, hyper-erotic scenarios might involve disrobing. And states "If they were encouraged by their admiring spectators, they would make themselves more sensual and tantalizing by displaying their breasts in a most daring manner" (1976: 144). Accompanying musicians, if they were male, were sometimes blindfolded, supposedly so they would not witness the nudity of the women. Accusations of prostitution pepper traveler accounts, but again, this may be a result of the Orientalist gaze (Brandl 1996:27).

12. British traveler Gilliat-Smith claims he had no choice but to tip when "the two *cheia* [unmarried Romani girls] threw themselves on their knees in front of me, and continued to dance with the upper part of their bodies and arms and fingers" (1910–11, 79). Similarly, Hasluck remarks for Albania of the 1930s: "If a Gypsy girl dances for male guests, one may spring to his feet in the middle of the dance, wet a coin with spittle, and so stick it on the dancer's perspiring forehead (coins are sometimes stuck in the same way on the foreheads of musicians). At the end of her dance ... the guest produces a number of coins, wets them in the usual way, and plasters them all over the Gypsy's face. When he has finished, he gives the back of her head a slight push to indicate she must go.... If he is a merry fellow or knows his duty to fellow guests, he will, after tipping the Gypsies, keep them in his knees and make them sing together" (Hasluck 1938:28).

13. "The popularity of the dancing boys led to so much trouble and quarreling among the Janissaries that, finally, to preserve order in his army, Sultan Mahmud forbade their appearances. Many of them fled to Egypt ... Finally, so as to put an end to the riots, there was a law passed in 1857 which outlawed köçeks, prohibiting their performances" (And 1976:141).

14. On the other hand, Dzimrevski describes several troupes of Greek Jewish female tavern dancers in Macedonia in the 1920s whom he calls chocheks (1985: 36; discussed in Sugarman 2003:102). Dordevic's 1903 accounts from Serbia describe Romani professionals performing in private lodgings and inns: "One or two Gypsy women dance, bending and turning with the greatest of elegance and lightness and with castanets [finger cymbals] attached to their fingers" (quoted in Sugarman 2003:99). Sugarman translates a landowner's description of an Albanian men's gathering: "Four Rom beauties ... radiant in multi-colored, gold-covered velvet and silk clothing ... stood up to sing and dance, accompanying themselves with the def.... At other times they exchanged the def for the çampara [metal finger cymbals].... The çingis are also masters of the Oriental belly dance ... within which they incorporate several feats. So, for example, Shahe placed a full glass of water on her head, and then isolated all the various parts of her body in trembling movements without spilling even one drop of water. Dife ... threw a jatagan on the floor, and, following the beat of the music, bent over completely backwards until she could grab the blade with her teeth and pick up the weapon from the floor.... Each round of applause ... produced a storm of lovely fairies, who fell back [into the lap of their] admirer; so that he, depending on his financial capabilities, would place a larger or smaller amount of change on their forehead or cheek" (2003:99). Describing the monetary outlay, Hasluck reports for 1930s Albania that "The average tip given a Gypsy nowadays amounts to only a few pence. But formerly, when there were neither cinemas nor cabarets to provide rival distractions, vast sums were squandered by the young and foolish on dancing girls. One guest at a party would seek to outdo another.... The evil grew so great that about fifteen years ago the Albanian government forbade Gypsies to dance in public places of entertainment. In 1934, rival distractions having multiplied, the rule was relaxed.... For Gypsies engaged to dance in private houses, no tax need be paid. Much the same regulations were in effect in Turkish times" (Hasluck 1938:28). Similarly, Bernatzik wrote in 1930, regarding Albanian Roma: "Their women can dance like masters, but the authorities have forbidden their dances because the officials take advantage of this opportunity to spend large amounts of money, with which they can cover their grabbing into the public coffers. In honor of my presence, the proscription on dancing was lifted for one day in Elbassan. The female Gypsies dance as though possessed, some even performed the old Turkish belly dance" (quoted in Brandl 1996:26).

15. In this play, Kostana, the daring Romani dancer, drives a respectable Serbian man to ruin because of love. Thus the dangerous, sexual, and predatory nature of Romani dancers is dramatized. An excerpt of one film version of *Kostana* is featured in the documentary film

Whose Is This Song? by Adela Peeva (2003). The play appeared in several versions throughout the twentieth century with the part of Kostana being played mostly by non–Romani women; there is one 1992 film version featuring Romani singer Usnija Redzepova as Kostana.

16. Hasluck continues, "In a northern village, where manners are freer than elsewhere, I once saw a none too modest dance between an Albanian man and a Gypsy woman. He advanced now timidly, now boldly, she retreated now coyly now, now invitingly, the whole so beautifully done that the grossness was all but lost in the artistry. Only the most abandoned Albanian women would have danced such a dance" (1938:27).

17. Shay documented the broader framework of male dance in the wider Middle East and Central Asian regions (2005). Yvonne Hunt (1995) described a carnival dance in Greek Macedonia performed by young boys called *kechekides*, who accompany themselves with finger cymbals, frame drums, the *lyra* (a vertically held stringed instrument), and singing.

18. The bridal sheet is examined for virginal blood, and if the "news is good," the sheet is sent to the bride's mother and displayed for the guests. Note, however, that there is an activist movement to abolish this custom (Silverman forthcoming).

19. In North America, henna ceremonies take place in urban apartments in a room designated for women. At a 1996 New York ceremony that took place in a three room apartment, approximately 25 women occupied the living room and the few men were relegated to the kitchen.

20. In the 1930s the freedom of movement of Romani women was noted by Catherine Brown, a British traveler: "One of the most striking features of these gypsy women is their great freedom and independence of bearing as compared with other Mohamedan women in Macedonia. Although among orthodox Mohamedans [non–Romani] one may occasionally see on feast days groups of men strolling about the village together, tinkling gently and rather half-heartedly on small stringed instruments, no women are ever to be seen with them, the women's festivities being invariably quite separate and confined to the harem. Here [among the Roma] men and women joined freely together in whole-hearted enjoyment. The whole scene resembled an enormous ballet..." (1937, 307).

21. Most community members do not know the names of these dances, and the names are not standardized. When a leader requests a song or dance, there is sometimes miscommunication, and the leader will refuse to dance until the musicians get it right. From the point of view of musicians, this can be very frustrating because they sometimes have to guess several times what the leader wants.

22. For example, at New Year's dances, $9/8$ tunes are played exactly at midnight.

23. *Mahala* means neighborhood in Turkish and the Balkan languages, but its use implies that it is a low-class Turkish or Romani neighborhood. *Manele* (plural of *manea*) from the Turkish *amane* means an instrumental or vocal-free rhythm improvisation. These terms are also used for the accompanying music, which may be referred to as *musica orientala* (oriental music).

24. The film *Iag Bari: Brass on Fire* (by Ralf Marschalleck, HS Media Consult, 2002) features several performances of these female dancers.

25. Phralipe traveled to France, Poland, Bulgaria, Italy, and other locations.

26. The prohibitions were related to the broad anti–Muslim campaigns of the 1970s and 1980s that included name changing (see Silverman 1996a, Buchanan 1996, and Neuburger 2004).

27. For example, the Bulgarian Romani wedding band Trustenik's cassettes are titled *Gol Kyuchek* (Naked Kyuchek) 1 and 2 and feature bare breasted women. Clearly the rise of this music/dance imagery is related to the spread of pornography throughout Bulgaria after the fall of socialism, which is, in turn, related to the reconfiguration of female roles and the economic crisis. See Daskalova 2000.

28. Aside from a constant stream of new CDs and DVDs featuring female stars, there are now cable television stations, radio stations, calendars, magazines, contests, mega-concerts, tours, and merchandise devoted to chalga. Payner is the largest company producing chalga; see www.payner.bg.

29. Featured on *Hitove na Planeta Payner 3* (2005).

30. Esma claims that the dancers in her videos are Macedonian, not Romani. Actually, she did not have full artistic control over the staging. Her videos also feature campfires, tents, and other stereotypic symbols which have nothing to do with the actual history of Esma's urban-based music (Silverman forthcoming). For example, see videos MP 31003: *Volim Te/U Zemlji Baro-Than* (I Love You/In the Great Land); MP 31005 *Romano Horo/Chaje Sukarije* (Romani Dance/Beautiful Girl).

Bibliography

And, Metin. 1959. *Dances of Anatolian Turkey.* New York: Dance Perspectives 3.
_____. 1963–64. *A History of Theatre and Popular Entertainment in Turkey.* Ankara: Forum Yayinlari.
_____. 1976. *A Pictorial History of Turkish Dancing.* Ankara: Dost Yayinlari.
Barany, Zoltan. 2002. *The East European Gypsies: Regime Change, Marginality, and Ethnopolitics.* Cambridge: Cambridge University Press.
Beissinger, Margaret. 2007. "Musicá Orientalá: Identity and Popular Culture in Post-Communist Romania." In *Balkan Popular Culture and the Balkan Ecumene: Music Image and Regional Political Discourse,* ed. Donna Buchanan. Lanham, MD: Scarecrow Press, 91–141.
Brandl, Rudolf. 1996. "The 'Yiftoi' and the Music of Greece, Role and Function." *The World of Music* 38(1), 7–32.
Brown, Catherine. 1937. "Gypsy Wedding at Skoplje." *Folk-Lore* 48, 305–309.
Buchanan, Donna. 1996. "Wedding Musicians, Political Transition and National Consciousness in Bulgaria." In *Retuning Culture: Musical Change in Eastern Europe,* ed. Mark Slobin. Durham, NC: Duke University Press, 200–230.
_____. 2007. "Bulgarian Ethnopop along the Old Via Militaris: Ottomanism, Orientalism, or Balkan Cosmopolitanism?" In *Balkan Popular Culture and the Balkan Ecumene: Music Image and Regional Political Discourse,* ed. Donna Buchanan. Lanham, MD: Scarecrow Press, 225–267.
Buonaventura, Wendy. 1994. *Serpent of the Nile: Women and Dance in the Arab World.* New York: Interlink Books.
Butler, Judith. 1993. *Bodies That Matter: On the Discursive Limits of "Sex."* New York: Routledge.
Cowan, Jane. 1990. *Dance and the Body Politic in Northern Greece.* Princeton: Princeton University Press.
Daskalova, Krassimira. 2000. "Women's Problems, Women's Discourses in Bulgaria." In *Reproducing Gender: Politics, Publics, and Everyday Life After Socialism,* ed. Susan Gal and Gail Kligman. Princeton: Princeton University Press, 337–369.
Dunin, Elsie. 1971. "Gypsy Wedding: Dance and Customs." *Makedonski Folklor* IV (7–8), 317–26.
_____. 1973. "Cocek as a Ritual Dance Among Gypsy Women." *Makedonski Folklor* VI (12), 193–197.
_____. 1977. "The Newest Changes in Rom Dance (Serbia and Macedonia)." *Journal of the Association of Graduate Dance Ethnologists* 1(Spring), 12–17.
_____. 1985. "Dance Change in the Context of the Gypsy St. George's Day, Skopje, Yugoslavia, 1967–1977." In *Papers from the Fourth and Fifth Annual Meetings, Gypsy Lore Society, North American Chapter,* ed. Joanne Grumet. New York: Gypsy Lore Society, 110–120.
_____. 1998. *Gypsy St. George's Day — Coming of Summer: Romski Gjurgjovden, Romano Gjurgjovdani — Erdelezi, Skopje, Macedonia 1967–1997.* Skopje: Association of Admirers of Rom Folklore Art: Gypsy Heart.
Dzimrevski, Borovoje. 1983. *Vie se Oro Makedonsko* (The Macedonian Dance Line Winds Around). Skopje: Nova Makedonia.

———. 1985. *Chalgiskata Traditsiya vo Makedonija* (The Chalgiya Tradition in Macedonia). Skopje: Makedonska Kniga.
Garfias, Robert. 1984. "Dance among the Urban Gypsies of Romania." *Yearbook for Traditional Music* 16, 84–96.
Georgieva, Nadezhda. 2006. "Contesetation and Negotiation of Romani Identity and Nationalism through Musical Standardization." *Romani Studies*, ser. 6, 16(1), 1–30.
Gilliat-Smith, Bernard. 1910–11. "The Fate of Kasim Pasha." *Journal of the Gypsy Lore Society*, n.s.(4), 79–80.
Guy, Will. 2001. *Between Past and Future: The Roma of Central and Eastern Europe*. Hatfield: University of Hertfordshire Press.
Hancock, Ian. 1997. "The Struggle for the Control of Identity." *Transitions* 4(4), 36–44.
———. 2002. *We Are the Romani People: Ame Sam e Rromani Dzene*. Hatfield: University of Hertfordshire Press.
Hasluck, Margaret. 1938. "The Gypsies of Albania." *Journal of the Gypsy Lore Society*, ser. 3, 17, 20–30.
Hunt, Yvonne. 1995. "Ta Kechekia — A Greek Gypsy Carnival Event." In *Dance Ritual and Music: Proceedings of the 18th Symposium of the Study Group on Ethnochoreogology*. Skierniewice: Polish Society for Ethnochoreology, Warsaw, 97–103.
———. 1996. *Traditional Dance in Greek Culture*. Athens: Center for Asia Minor Studies.
Janković, Ljubica, and Danica Janković. 1939. *Narodne Igre* (Folk Dances), vol. 3. Beograd: Štamparija Drag. Gregorića.
Kilmova-Alexander, Ilona. 2005. *The Romani Voice in World Politics: The United Nations and Non-State Actors*. London: Ashgate Publishers.
Lemon, Alaina. 2000. *Between Two Fires: Gypsy Performance and Romani Memory from Pushkin to Postsocialism*. Durham, NC: Duke University Press.
Magrini, Tullia. 2003. "Introduction: Studying Gender in Mediterranean Musical Cultures." In *Music and Gender: Perspectives from the Mediterranean*, ed. Tullia Magrini. Chicago: University of Chicago Press, 1–32.
Marushiakova, Elena, and Veselin Popov. 2000. *Tsiganite v Osmanskata Imperia* (Gypsies in the Ottoman Empire). Sofia: Litavra.
Matras, Yaron. 2002. *Romani: A Linguistic Introduction*. Cambridge: Cambridge University Press.
Mernissi, Fatima. 1975. *Beyond the Veil: Male-Female Dynamics in a Modern Muslim Society*. Cambridge: Schenkman.
Neuburger, Mary. 2004. *The Orient Within: Muslim Minorities and the Negotiation of Nationhood in Modern Bulgaria*. Ithaca: Cornell University Press.
Nieuwkerk, Karin van. 1995. *"A Trade Like Any Other": Female Singers and Dancers in Egypt*. Austin: University of Texas Press.
———. 2003. "On Religion, Gender and Performing: Female Performers and Repentance in Egypt." In *Music and Gender: Perspectives from the Mediterranean*, ed. Tullia Magrini. Chicago: University of Chicago Press, 267–286.
Oldenburg, Veena Talwar. 1990. "Lifestyle as Resistance: The Case of the Courtesans of Lucknow, India." *Feminist Studies* 16(2), 259–287.
Ong, Aihwa. 1997. "Chinese Modernities: Narratives of Nation and of Capitalism." In *Ungrounded Empires: The Cultural Politics of Modern Chinese Transnationalism*, ed. Aihwa Ong and Donald Nonini. London: Routledge, 171–202.
Öztürkmen, Arzu. 2001. "Politics of National Dance in Turkey: A Historical Appraisal." *Yearbook for Traditional Music* 33, 139–143.
Peicheva, Lozanka. 1999. *Dushata Plache — Pesen Izliza* (The Soul Cries and a Song Comes Out). Sofia: Terart.
Peicheva, Lozanka, and Ventsislav Dimov. 2005. *Muzika, Romi, Medii* (Music, Roma, Media). Sofia: Zvezdan.
Petrova, Dimitrina. 2003. "The Roma: Between a Myth and a Future." *Social Research* 70(1), 111–161.
Pettan, Svainbor. 1996. "Female to Male — Male to Female: Third Gender in the Musical Life of the Gypsies in Kosovo." *Narodna Umjetnost* 33(2), 311–324.

_____. 2003. "Male, Female and Beyond in the Culture and Music of Roma in Kosovo." In *Music and Gender: Perspectives from the Mediterranean*, ed. Tullia Magrini. Chicago: University of Chicago Press, 287–305.
Rice, Timothy. 1994. *May It Fill Your Soul: Experiencing Bulgarian Music*. Chicago: University of Chicago Press.
_____. 2002. "Bulgaria or Chagaria: The Attenuation of Bulgarian Nationalism in Mass-Mediated Popular Music." *Yearbook for Traditional Music* 34, 25–47.
Ringold, Dena. 2000. *Roma and the Transition in Central and Eastern Europe: Trends and Challenges*. New York: The World Bank.
Ringold, Dena, Mitchell Orenstein, and Erika Williams. 2004. *Roma in an Expanding Europe: Breaking the Poverty Cycle*. New York: The World Bank.
Savigliano, Marta. 1995. *Tango and the Political Economy of Passion*. Boulder, CO: Westview.
Seeman, Sonia Tamar. 1990. "Continuity and Transformation in the Macedonian Genre of Chalgija: Past Perfect and Present Imperfective." M.A. thesis, University of Washington.
_____. 1998. Notes to *Sulukule: Rom Music of Istanbul*. Traditional Crossroads CD 4289.
Shay, Anthony. 2002. *Choreographic Politics: State Folk Dance Companies, Representation, and Power*. Middletown, CT: Wesleyan University Press.
_____. 2006. "The Male Dancer in the Middle East and Central Asia." In *Belly Dance: Orientalism, Transnationalism and Harem Fantasy*, ed. Anthony Shay and Barbara Sellers-Young. Costa Mesa, CA: Mazda Publishers, 51–84.
Shay, Anthony, and Barbara Sellers-Young. 2005. "Belly Dance: An Introduction." In *Belly Dance: Orientalism, Transnationalism and Harem Fantasy*, ed. Anthony Shay and Barbara Sellers-Young. Costa Mesa, CA: Mazda Publishers, 1–27.
Silverman, Carol. 1996a. "Music and Marginality: The Roma (Gypsies) of Bulgaria and Macedonia." In *Retuning Culture: Musical Change in Eastern Europe*, ed. Mark Slobin. Durham, NC: Duke University Press, 231–253.
_____. 1996b. "Music and Power: Gender and Performance Among Roma (Gypsies) of Skopje, Macedonia." *The World of Music* 38(1), 63–76.
_____. 1999. Rom (Gypsy) Music. In *The Garland Encyclopedia of World Music*, ed. Timothy Rice, James Porter, and C. Goertzen. Europe volume. New York: Garland, 270–293.
_____. 2003. "The Gender of the Profession: Music, Dance, and Reputation among Balkan Muslim Rom Women." In *Music and Gender: Perspectives from the Mediterranean*, ed. Tullia Magrini. Chicago: University of Chicago Press, 119–145.
_____. 2007. "Trafficking in the Exotic with 'Gypsy' Music: Balkan Roma, Cosmopolitanism, and 'World Music' Festivals. " "In *Balkan Popular Culture and the Balkan Ecumene: Music Image and Regional Political Discourse*, ed. Donna Buchanan. Lanham, MD: Scarecrow Press, 335–361.
_____. forthcoming. *Performing Diaspora: Cultural Politics of Balkan Romani Music*. New York: Oxford University Press.
Soulis, George. 1961. *The Gypsies in the Byzantine Empire and the Balkans in the Late Middle Ages*. Washington, DC: Dumbarton Oak Papers No. 161.
Statelova, Rosemary. 2005. *The Seven Sins of Chalga: Toward an Anthropology of Ethnopop Music*. Sofia: Prosveta.
Sugarman, Jane. 1997. *Engendering Song: Singing and Subjectivity at Prespa Albanian Weddings*. Chicago: University of Chicago Press.
_____. 2003. "Those 'Other Women': Dance and Femininity among Prespa Albanians." In *Music and Gender: Perspectives from the Mediterranean*, ed. Tullia Magrini. Chicago: University of Chicago Press, 87–118.
Teodosievski, Stevo, and Esma Redžepova. 1984. *On the Wings of Song*. Kochani: Dom Kulture Beli Mugri.
Trumpener, Katie. 1992. "The Time of the Gypsies: A 'People Without History' in the Narratives of the West." *Critical Inquiry* 18(Summer), 843–884.
Van de Port, Mattijs. 1998. *Gypsies, Wars, and Other Instances of the Wild: Civilisation and its Discontents in a Serbian Town*. Amsterdam: Amsterdam University Press.

Višinski, Stanimir, and Elsie Dunin. 1995. *Dances in Macedonia: Performance, Genre, Tanec.* Prilep: 11 Oktomvri.

Vukanović, Tatomir. 1962. "Musical Culture Among the Gypsies of Yugoslavia." *Journal of the Gypsy Lore Society,* ser. 3, 41, 41–61.

4

Dance and Place: The Case of a Roma Community in Northern Greece

CHRISTOS PAPAKOSTAS

Irakleia, 17–7–2001... interview in the mahala *(neighbourhood):*[1]

QUESTION: Were you born in Irakleia?

INFORMANT: Not in Irakleia, a little further down. There in the *paranges* [shanties]. You won't find where we come from easily, because we were all in the shanties, we're from Irakleia, we don't know anywhere else. We were born here but where we came from, I don't know. Nobody knows. Look, I don't remember them saying anything about where we came from. We're *dopioi* [locals], that's it.

QUESTION: How did you learn to dance?

INFORMANT: Our family danced a lot, my father, my mother, all our *milet* dances.

QUESTION: What do you mean by *milet*?

INFORMANT: The *ratsa* [race]. Our race dances everywhere, we dance everywhere, we're *glentzedes* [merrymakers, good-timers]. If you'd been born earlier... How old are you?... Thirty?... If you're thirty years old, you know nothing about Irakleia. This settlement was alpha, number one. Here in the *mahala* even the pots and pans danced. There were *zournades* [shawms] in all five coffee shops. The whole *mahala* danced the same songs, because they don't dance our songs in any village, you won't find them anywhere.

QUESTION: What other *ratses* where there in Irakleia?

INFORMANT: All the races. Our race, *tsinganiki* race, *yuftiki* race, Rom race as they call it. In the *Agora* [marketplace] there were Vlachs and *Entopioi*. The *Entopioi* are remnants of Bulgaria.

QUESTION: Did you sing at all?

Informant: In the past, *entopia* [local songs]. During the Occupation we mostly lived here, we were singing Bulgarian songs.

QUESTION: What did you dance?

INFORMANT: Lots of songs, *gerika* (of the old folks), but we don't know them. The old men used to dance them and we'd follow. No. Only when they joined hands. Here we had 400 years of occupation, Turkey, 120 years ago. They were Turkish songs. The Bulgarian ones under Bulgaria. We learned them all under occupation. Look, when you're enslaved, you'll flow with the tide. Because it was forbidden to sing Greek songs. We didn't play Greek [music] here. There were no Greek songs here. As soon as you heard a song, they'd call you to the police station. There were Bulgarians here, we learned Bulgarian, the Turkish [songs] were from our parents.

QUESTION: In the *mahala* you danced dances from all the *ratses*, didn't you?

INFORMANT: There isn't a dance that the *mahala* doesn't know. We learned from our parents. What man sees he learns. What he lives he learns.

QUESTION: Are there many variations of the *prastaimnaski*?[2]

INFORMANT: There's the Bulgarian, there's also the Greek, and there's the Turkish too.

QUESTION: Isn't there a Rom, a Romany *prastaimnaski*?

INFORMANT: In Romany, no there isn't.

QUESTION: The *sahai si varo ninai*?[3]

INFORMANT: It's Bulgarian. *Sahai si varo ninai*, it's Bulgarian. We transformed it. From Bulgarian, we made it *yuftiko* [Gypsy]. And the *Eleno mome*'s Bulgarian too, and we made it *yuftiko*.

QUESTION: What was the first [lead] dancer called?

Informant: *Bashi*. *Bashi*'s what the Turks call it and the *Yufti* [Gypsies] call it *bashi* too. It's the same word, first. Whoever wanted to could dance, but we had a fixed time. That is, you danced five minutes, we leave you to dance, so that I can enter. Yes, wherever you were from, if you wanted to take the lead, you waited for the dance going on to come, you sat at one edge, as soon as the first [dancer] comes, the dance comes close to you, you'll take first place. It wasn't like that, to run and join in.

QUESTION: Were there dances that you dance in couples, in twos?

INFORMANT: Tango in couples, only European [dances].

QUESTION: *Tsifteteli* and *karsilamas*?

INFORMANT: Alone. All together.

QUESTION: Could you dance with your friend's wife?
INFORMANT: Yes, here there's no ... here there's solidarity. There's no jealousy here, nothing. We all dance in each other's arms, that's why we're poor. Because we didn't keep a rearguard, as we say. Here, from my work, let's say, if I were a bit thrifty, if I weren't a *glentzes*, I'd have loads of money. If I were economical, like the Vlachs are.
QUESTION: Don't the Vlachs spend money?
INFORMANT: The Vlachs in the *Agora* are another kettle of fish. They're tight-fisted, they hoard, they don't spend. The Vlachs are types who only save money, they don't give. Jumaya was destroyed by the Vlachs, I say that for everyone to hear. These people are only out for their race, for their own arse, as we say. They're not out for me and you, they're only interested in what they can take from you, how they can harm you.

The above excerpt and the others which follow are the translation of an interview with an elderly Rom man, an expert dancer of the region, taken at Irakleia, Serres, in the summer of 2001. The above excerpt is cited verbatim so that the local Rom voice, its opinions, its interpretations, can "be heard" and, in the end, contribute to the writing of the text. At the same time, this view from within indicates the fluidity of concepts, with their parallel, successive and even contradictory meanings.

Beyond the settlement function of space (*mahala/Agora*, for example), people attributed to space a set of meanings and qualities which are linked together by symbolic and practical representations (Koumarianou 2000: 236). Space functions also through the representations and the ideas that people have of it, through the conception and the lived experience of the limits and the borders, of here and elsewhere, of near and far (Lafazani 1997: 101). Dance, like every cultural phenomenon, refers to localness, to a local scale of cultural expression and to belongingness[4] (*entopiotita*) — that is, the sense and the consciousness of a particular origin and identity that corresponds to one place (Nitsiakos 2001: 23).

We could argue that dance practices constitute cultural practices (Bourdieu 1977). Through these the community manages its past and present, is reformed at a symbolic level and incorporates elements of contemporary developments dynamically in its tradition (Nitsiakos 2003).[5] In the wider region of Macedonia, localness as a concept appears more neutral. On the contrary, belongingness is ideologically charged, since it embodies opposing and conflicting meanings which are heightened in the context of forming a single nation state (Papakostas 2001: 267). This becomes readily comprehensible on studying the multi-dimensional usages and interpretations of the term *entopiotita* (belongingness) in the so-called mixed communities,[6] that is, communities in which two or more ethno-cultural groups coexist.

The groups are distinguished, according to various criteria, hierarchically among themselves. That is, there is a relationship of dominant group(s) and dominated group(s). It would be interesting, I believe, for us to see how many categories or aspects of belongingness are encountered in the wider area of Serres. In the view of Lafazani,[7] "A first distinction gives two main categories that are concerned with immediately visible diacritica and which refer us to Goffman's (Goffman 1963) study of the visible character of belonging and otherness, and their potential function as stigmas. Nonetheless, the most refined, painless and relatively free of ideological or axial content local terminology in use, even today distinguishes the locals racially into 'whites' and 'blacks'" (Lafazani 1997: 97). By extending the above viewpoint, we can distinguish the group of local "whites" into two sub-categories: "Bulgarian" locals (stigmatized) and "Greek" locals (non-stigmatized). The young Greek state in the early twentieth century was formed on the basis of a central ideological construct: Greekness. Any deviations from the structural components of Greekness (religion, doctrine, language) were deemed problematic. Consequently, the linguistic otherness of the "Bulgarian" Greeks casts doubts on their Greekness.[8] The "Bulgarian Greeks" live mainly in the Serres plain, but also in highland communities (Oreini, Xirotopos).

The "Greek" locals are to be found in the villages of Mt. Pangaion (Proti, Kormista), the Darnachoria (Neo Souli, Pentapoli) and the area around these (Nea Zichni). With the settling of the refugees from Asia Minor, after 1922, the sub-category was augmented. Through state practices, both the refugees and the transhumant populations (Vlachs, Sarakatsans) have been included in the "Greek" locals and subsequently in the autochthons (including also the "Bulgarian" locals).[9] In the majority of the mixed communities in the region the "black" and "Bulgarian" locals form the base of the social hierarchy.[10]

In the case of Irakleia, where Vlachs,[11] refugees, "Bulgarian" locals and Roma coexist, the Vlachs are at the top of the hierarchy and the refugees in the middle. The principal trait of the Rom identity was related to their definition as a stigmatized ethnic group (Eriksen 1993: 30). Two further components have contributed to constructing the Rom identity: (1) the space (town/village) in which the Roma live, (2) the cohabitant group with which the Roma share the space (Vlachs, "Greek" or "Bulgarian" locals). On account of this situation, we can speak of a "borrowed" or rather a "reflected" identity. This distinction is eloquently imprinted in the village of Pontismeno, a nearby community just five kilometers from Irakleia, inhabited in the majority by Roma and "Bulgarian" locals. At certain moments in history this population synthesis has resulted in the Roma of Pontismenos being doubly stigmatized *vis-à-vis* Greekness, "racially" and ethnically. This is in contrast to the case of the Roma in Irakleia, where the coexistence with the dominant cohabitant group (Vlachs) takes place in a semi-urban milieu of markedly commercial character.

The relationship of dominant and dominated groups is the nucleus around which centrifugal and centripetal forces are developed, which ultimately organize and structure the individual ethnic identities of a mixed community. One such case, with its singularities, is Irakleia (formerly Jumaya) a town of 4,000 people, in the prefecture of Serres. Irakleia was built in the Serres Plain close to the River Strymon, some 20 kilometers from the Greek-Bulgarian border.

My work focuses on the "Gypsy" space, the *mahala*,[12] which is home to about 800 Roma. The *mahala* can be characterized as "other," as "stigmatized" space, because of the group that lives there. Concurrently, however, the *mahala* is part of the wider Irakleian space and inseparably linked to it. It is a "sub-space" that exists in direct dependence on and conflict with the *Agora* (marketplace), the space of the "others," the Vlachs. Through this study of the official and the oral history of Irakleia, everyday reality is more easily understood. That is, how and under what circumstances Roma cultural identity, and consequently dance identity, was structured in space and time.

Yorgos Kaftantzis, an author of Vlach origin, in his book entitled *The History of Irakleia* (in Greek), ignores a whole group of people by making only minimal references to the Roma. Indeed, when he does mention them he uses the term *Gyftoi'* (Gypsies). In contrast, he devotes an entire chapter to the Vlachs, a fact that puzzled the ethnomusicologists Charles and Angeliki Keil. When the author was asked why he had done this, he simply replied: "I was not interested." Although the Roma are defined as "of/from Irakleia," they do not appear in its formal history.

Kaftantzis notes that the Roma are among the first inhabitants of Irakleia and associates their presence with the job opportunities that the *Agora* of Jumaya offered. The town was a large commercial center in the late nineteenth and early twentieth centuries, since "it always had a petty bourgeois character. It was ... a large centre of mainly export trade of the produce of the plain, with a long mercantile tradition. The professionals of Jumaya, merchants and manufacturers, were all Christians, organized in guilds (*isnafia*), each one dedicated to a patron saint. The Turks were involved solely with agriculture or were petty tradesmen (coffee shop owners, barbers, ferriers etc.)" (1973: 26–28).

There is reference to the economic heyday of Jumaya, to which its renowned bazaar contributed as well as the annual fair, held each August and famed throughout Balkan Turkey. "Peasants and middlemen gathered in the bazaar, not only from the surrounding villages but also from centers further afield: Poroia, Vetrina, Demir-isar, Serres, Nigrita, Thessaloniki, Meleniko. They arrived here by all means of transport in those days, from Thursday evening, lodging in the inns, and departed to return at daybreak on Saturday. At the fair, which was held every 15th of August [feast of the Dormition of the Virgin] and lasted several days, large-scale trade of livestock, large and small, was conducted. Large caravans of livestock dealers gathered, especially Circassians, Vlachs and Sarakatsans, from all parts of Turkey. In general the commercial importance of Jumaya, with its significant transactions, was so well known that the Turks dubbed it characteristically Kutchuk Istambul (Little Istanbul)."

Last, Kaftantzis provides typical information on the spatial otherness[13] of Irakleia in the early twentieth century: "Before the destruction in 1916, Irakleia had five neighborhoods. Two Greek, one Gypsy (*Tsegene maalesi*), one Turkish and one Turkogypsy. The Greek neighborhoods were in the north of the town, numbering some 1200 households in all. They were divided internally into eastern (known as Nea or Vlach) and western (Slavianiki). The Greek cemetery included the Gypsy burial ground too, which was separate" (1973: 16).

Within this *status quo*, the Rom economy was based on occupations such as livestock-trading, loading and unloading (porters), and fiber crafts (making mats, baskets, ropes and nets).[14] However, the Roma were precluded from selling their products in the Friday bazaar. They were only allowed to sell them to *balamoi* (a Roma term for non–Roma) merchants (Blau, Keil, and Feld 2002: 130). Also, Rom musicians (Christians and Muslims) played as the caravans unloaded their wares. The arrival of the caravans assumed a ceremonial character and the marketplace a "cosmopolitan" air (129).

Under the Ottoman Empire religion was the basic factor for the distinction of population groups into administrative units and the most important aspect of identity for most inhabitants of the region.[15] At the level of religion too, the Roma are treated as another class of Christians.

By the early twentieth century the gradual break-up of the Ottoman Empire was underway and the more intensive rivalries in the Balkans for the formation of strong nation states had emerged. The end of the Balkan War (1913) found the Roma inside the frontiers of the Greek state. Even so, nothing seems to have affected their everyday life. They continued to work as farmhands and in the marketplace. In this hybrid fabrication of Greekness, the Roma were landless, illiterate, devoid of central political guidance and without a myth of origin, affinal to the newly instituted Greek state (Blau, Keil, and Feld 2002: 133). The year 1916 was a landmark date in the oral and official history of Irakleia. The First World War was already in full swing and the town was at the center of martial conflicts between the British-French and the German-Bulgarian armies. It was razed to the ground and the Bulgarians deported its inhabitants via Bulgaria to Pazarewitz in Serbia (a town near Belgrade). In 1918 half the population of Irakleia returned. Some 3000 people died as a result of privations, hunger and epidemics (Tzemailas 1973; Kaftantzis 1973; Aslanidis 1997).

At first those who returned settled about one kilometer west of the site of their former town, initially in tents, subsequently in wooden huts put up by the state.[16] Despite many efforts, plans to rebuild the town were thwarted by the catastrophic Asia Minor Campaign and the various political changes that intervened. This was finally achieved in 1930, in conjunction with the redistribution of landholdings. After various political ploys, the Roma were given smaller houses and reduced landholdings (Blau, Keil, and Feld 2002: 135; Kafkoula 1990: 137–144).[17]

It is from this point that the modern history of the Gypsy space (the *mahala*) and the space of the "others" (the *Agora*) essentially commences. In this new reality the Roma continued to be another class of Christians and to be considered as not engaged in honest trades, but in those which we would today class in the non-mainstream or the black economy (Vaxevanoglou 2001: 112). In the long course of their history the Roma were obliged to fill in "empty" professional and social spaces.[18] As Okely maintains, Roma employment opportunities lie in those jobs which others are less able or less willing to undertake (1983: 49).

Roma involvement with music, which was a vital and attractive social space but professionally "empty," is consistent with this logic.[19] Indicative is the fact that in many areas the term *Gyftos* is synonymous with musician (Mazaraki 1984: 50–52). This assessment contradicts and cancels the myth that "music is in their blood" (Blau, Keil, and Feld 2002: 134). This is a stereotype which in essence constructs a "genetic," "inborn" relationship of the Roma with music.[20] This essentialist position draws on the works of classical Tsiganology (see e.g., Webb 1975; Clebert 1967), which constructs a series of stereotypes for "Gypsy culture."[21] A consequence of this viewpoint is that Roma professional involvement with music (to a greater degree than with other occupations) has acquired a mythical dimension. The Roma themselves are aware of this mythical dimension of their musical ability — as well as of other myths of Tsiganology, such as their origin. They cultivate it and in the end utilize it through their contact with the dominant group. In this process the Rom community does not participate as a spectator in a work written about it, without it. It critically processes the data and tries to locate the fields of possible convergences (music) and to equalize or even interpolate negative stereotypes.[22] The exploitation of the myth on the part of the Roma of Irakleia is a negotiating tool and consolidates, in themselves and in the others,[23] a sense of musical, artistic and potentially cultural superiority. Music, like belongingness, is enhanced as a solid platform of strategy by the Roma[24] for taking an equal place in the Irakleian identity (Lafazani 1997: 106; Avdikos 1996: 43). Thus Roma define themselves (as well as are defined by others) as locals and as "musicians."

Could someone claim the same for dance too? In this particular case there is an essential contradiction between dance and music. Significantly the professional involvement of the Roma with music starts off from the fluid conventions: I play for the others the music of the others, "there" and not "here," outside the spatial and cultural boundaries. According to this version, music does not function only "in the context" but also sets the context itself of conversation between different personal and collective types of identity.[25] At the other end, dance takes place inside the *mahala*, it is not interwoven with economic or professional practice and symbolically reforms the community in a sentiment "of loneliness." The conventions now are virtually dissolved: "here" we play for our own people to dance our own dances, without the others. Ostensibly the quality of dance as a medium of negotiating strategy is annulled.[26]

Nevertheless, marginalization, social and ethnic stigmatization, and common origin and fate form and forge the idea of a common identity, albeit from the inside. Consequently, dance represents the sense of common origin and reforms symbolically the community, albeit in the absence of the cultural other.[27] In practice, however, some fields of communication through dance — of limited extent — between the marketplace and the *mahala* are identified.[28] Here we shall consider an incomplete form of communication, which is based only on the one-dimensional relationship between dancer/Rom and spectator or guest/*balamos*. This occurs during the celebration of the climactic event in the *mahala*, the wedding. The *balamoi* are around and a short distance away from the locus of the wedding feast, in this case the square of the *mahala*. The wedding and its music and dance are pretexts for transcending the boundaries of the *mahala*, a not very common event for the *balamoi*. The motive for this action is founded in exoticism, that is, the axiomatic conceptualization of the other as intrinsically different (e.g., given, static, without history, etc., Herzfeld 1987).[29] "Let's see the Gypsy kids dancing"; "They sure dance well, the blighters"; "We don't dance like that." In this way the dance/cultural difference is transformed into an element of impression-making (Herzfeld 1987).[30] Considering that the others consider the Roma more "con-

Loading and "dancing" the *roumba* (dowry) from the bride's house. Photograph by Christos Papakostas.

servative" with regard to customs, music and dance, we could formulate a hypothesis. This exoticism possibly stems from the different conceptualization of the term tradition. The rhetoric on tradition is embodied in the discourse and the practice of the *Agora* (Vlachs, refugees and others) with a clearly romantic and static gravitas. The Roma have nothing to do with the above rhetoric, because they are inside it and, to the degree that they partake in such a discussion do so because the other group, of the Vlachs, imposes it (cf. Nitsiakos 2003).[31]

The unilateral discussion on tradition — the recognition of prowess in dancing, the exoticism and the response to this — mobilizes the *mahala* in a process of negotiation of identity, with dance as spearhead. Dance as a representational practice helps us to understand how a group gives meaning to, signals, forms and negotiates its cultural identity (Desmond 1997: 29). Hall comments that "cultural identity ... is not something which already exists, transcending place, time, history and culture. But, like everything which is historical they undergo constant transformation ... and should be seen as a dialectical relationship ... between two axes or vectors simultaneously operative: the vector of similarity and continuity, and the vector of difference and rupture" (1990: 225–226). According to this version, dance, as cultural praxis, not only represents but also contributes to the formation of identity (Koutsouba 1999: 207). We note that dance — like music — is simultaneously product and process (Cowan 1990: 25–32). Both dance and music define a space without boundaries, they are a game without frontiers (Frith 1996: 125). Consequently, the Roma of Irakleia are able to be the "same" and "different," depending on what the reference point is. With dance as criterion, they appear generally the "same" as the *balamoi* with regard to "what they dance" and different with regard to "how they dance it." Fieldwork pre-empts such a position, since the Roma handle and manage the total of dance forms that we encounter in the Irakleia area.

As in the case of Thrace (see Rombou-Levidi 1999), so in the case of Irakleia, two common points are identified: (1) dance in the wider area clearly bears the signs of a particular localness which is formed by the historical course of the space and its populations, and (2) this localness expresses concurrently a wider space that transcends today's conventional frontiers imposed by the existence of the nation states. The dance experience in the *mahala* is distinguished by great fluidity, both at the level of the nomenclature of the dance and in the process of its "classification" in "local taxonomic categories." The local "classificatory logic" is governed by extremely elastic and loose principles. Thus, for the Roma the terms depict and/or denote moments and functions, and have no fixed and permanent character:

"Ah! Don't ask me about the names. I see and I dance. The men know the names. Very often not even they.... But we have the musicians, whatever they play we'll latch onto. If we see an old man dancing, we hold hands behind. One, two, we get into it. That's our race... The *voulgarika* [Bulgarian dances], the women know, they know them all ... The *gerika* [old men's dances] are under Turkey, we don't know them so well. But if we see them, we'll be able to dance them."

In the nomenclature as well as in the classification, the historical past of Irakleia and of the Roma is inscribed. The "*gerika*" (old men's dances) as a local analytical category embody the Ottoman past of Irakleia, before the Balkan Wars, and function as the "old dances." Some names of dances and tunes are *mangoustar chavasi, karanta vasi, drama vasi*, etc. From the point of view of rhythm, they are characterized as slower than the "*voulgarika*." The "*voulgarika*" include the dances *Leno mome, tsourapia, paitouska*, and *rando mirtsou*.[32] Many of these are known throughout Greek Macedonia and were adopted during the period of the Bulgarian Occupation (1940–1944). In the same way, the Greek state imposed, primarily through the educational system, some other dances. Defined as "Greek," but without being named, are the *syrta, kalamatiana* and *tsamika* (which, as they say, they learned from the Sarakatsans). The dance puzzle is completed by the use of the so-called European dances, the waltz and tango. It is worth noting that very often these are played on *zournades* (shawms) and *daoulia* (drums). The "Bulgarian" dances are danced by almost all the ethnic groups in Irakleia. The "old men's dances" are beginning to be forgotten. In addition to these major categories, some Pontic, Thracian and Asia Minor dances are particularly popular in the *mahala* and in the *Agora*. All this reality is epitomized eloquently in the informant's expression: "Look, when you're enslaved, you'll flow with the tide." Perhaps here, however, "enslavement" contains, in addition to the literal meaning also a metaphorical one. That is, it is meant as a synonym of marginality. Clearly, however, it represents dance as a process that contributes to the Roma adaptation to diverse historical and cultural environments. The above "taxonomic categories" overlap and intersect among themselves. It is possible for a dance to be classed in one or the other category, or even both, depending on the context.

One such case is the dance *prastaimnaski* (or *tafterimnaski*), which in Romany means "running." It is the most widespread kinetic form, not only in the *mahala* but also in the wider region of Serres. In terms of origin and form it is included, always in accordance with local logic, among the *gerika*. Whereas in terms of the tune and the song that accompany it, it can be characterized as *voulgariko*. To the locals the same dance is called *nastritzini*, which means to slide, to scrape fish. So, both names denote the way in which the dance is danced. Frequently, however, the Roma subsume the *voulgarika* under the *gerika*, which as a category is considered more general. So, by definition we realize that the quest for pure forms of dance praxis is a utopia, which eventually becomes problematical, during the phase of analyzing the data. For example, in the dance *striptsko*, which means Serbian, is inscribed the collective experience of the Irakleians (Roma and *balamoi*) during a three-year forced absence in Serbia. Through empirical observation and from the rudimentary knowledge of Balkan dances, it seems that the motif of the dance resembles that of the Serbian circular dance *kolo*. This dance is encountered in various forms throughout Serbia and could perhaps be considered as something analogous to the *syrtos* in Greece. The strange thing is that the dance is danced to the familiar music of the Cretan dance *pentozali* "*mes stou Mayou tis myrodies*" (the perfumes in the month of May).[33] The example speaks for itself as far as the nomenclature and the classification of the dances are concerned on a local scale and the terms with which these are negotiated.

A special case of dance form for the Roma is the *tsifteteli (belly dance)*.[34] It is neither *geriko*, nor *voulgariko*, nor Greek. No historical and ethnic origin, at least recent, can be inscribed in it. Yet the *tsifteteli* is an organic part of the dance events in the *mahala*. The Roma themselves declare emphatically "it is our food, our bread. You can't have a wedding without *tsifteteli*." They themselves, however, debunk the myth of origin and the romantic

Bringing the dowry to the groom's house. Photograph by Christos Papakostas.

stereotype of the Gypsy *tsifteteli*, which too is attributed to "inborn" Rom traits. "It is not just ours, the Gypsies dance it and the *balamoi* dance it. We dance it differently."

Contrary to the prevailing view, the Roma of Irakleia define the *tsifteteli* as a group dance, not an individual dance. For them the fact that there is no holding does not constitute individualism. The hold between the dancers is not visible, rather it is symbolic. "It is inconceivable that anyone would dance alone. There is freedom of movements, but also a relationship of responsibility between dancers. They do not so much dance 'one with the other' as 'one for the other'" (Giurchescu 2000: 327). Frequently the *tsifteteli* is presented as untidy in the space, because the members break away from the group and dance, not so much individually as "separately, but together." This manner of executing the dance reinforces the solidarity and the unity of the group. "We dance the *tsifteteli* '*koupa*.' We'll all get up together. We'll form our company. We'll fling the '*kioubekia*' (belly shakes)... Then we'll dance with others. But always together... What are we? Like the *Tsinganoi* or like *Allibekioi*?[35] It's a *parangelia* (commissioned dance), he'll say. No one else will dance. What does it mean *parangelia*? Why? Does it spoil the dance? Ah! There's no such thing in the *mahala*. No one is alone."

The above words show that the *tsifteteli* displays a singularity that is not related only to the dance as dance praxis but also to its use as an index of cultural convergence or divergence. Depending on the circumstances, it represents identity and otherness. It is included in a wider network of practices

Bringing the dowry to the groom's house. Photograph by Christos Papakostas.

aimed at transmitting the stigma and the negative stereotypes, at constructing lower strata in the social hierarchy and at putting up resistance to arbitrary homogenization (*Gyftoi/Tsinganoi*, they're all the same). Apart from the other differences that the Roma invoke in relation to the *Tsinganoi*, such as non-belongingness, a nomadic existence, the way of life, dance and tradition generally, are utilized as fields of opposition. Essentially, they try to construct even lower ranks in the social pyramid (Lafazani 1997: 105). So the *Tsinganos* becomes the "other's other," the "other other."

"Don't mention them, they brought them in '74 for votes, and they stayed. We don't want them. They come into the *mahala* and steal ... We don't have Datsuns ... they're always on the move and yet they come back ... they dance a *tsifteteli* and that ... maybe also a *karsilamas* and *syrtos*. Do they know '*gerika*'? Bah! Not likely! They don't even know where to hold from ... all they do is make trouble."

Thus dance represents social distinction too (Desmond 1997: 33). Another picture exists in the case of the *balamoi* of the *Agora*. Knowledge and use of the totality of dance idioms in the region is an advantage for the Roma, whose prowess at dancing is acknowledged by all. Frequent improvisations, embellishments, syncopations, and counter-beats would be some of the terms we would use to describe — fully aware of the pitfalls — the Rom mode, the Rom style. It is no accident that all the above are also musical terms. At the risk of oversimplifying the issue, we could say schematically that "they dance in the same way as they play music." To a fixed music or dance phrase they add their own special personality. Essentially this element is the Roma contribution, their own brushstroke, to the dance of the region. It is perhaps the most serious parameter of their dance, and consequently of their cultural, identity. Desmond (1997: 31) analyzes the concept of style — in analogy with the way Bourdieu speaks of taste — and notes that the style, the dance style in this case, which is learned actively or absorbed passively at home or in the community constitutes an important way of discriminating between social groups. Let us follow the informant's word in his attempt to represent the dance style for the *tsifteteli*:

QUESTION: What is the difference between your *tsifteteli* and the *balamoi's*?

INFORMANT: They dance a little more calmly. They are more educated, we are a bit uneducated. Everything has to do with education. Every word that a man utters, if he isn't educated, it doesn't come out well. Dance is a word too, everywhere. Everything comes from there. If you don't know, if you haven't got good pronunciation, you can't speak about anything. You've to know what you're going to say, you can't just come out with it willy-nilly.

QUESTION: Do you mean that because the *balamoi* are better educated they dance better *tsifteteli*?

INFORMANT: Not better. They dance in a more educated way, more reservedly. We've all got the same madness.

QUESTION: Sometimes it seems to me that you dance more reservedly than they do.

INFORMANT: Not more sedately, more pleasingly. More enthusiastically, how can I say! We are people who get enthusiastic more easily, they don't get enthusiastic easily.

On the pretext of dance the informant had the chance to speak about what were for him serious issues and to put them at the epicenter of a discussion about the "other." Taking as the starting point the Word (the dance) and its pronunciation (style) he develops the bipolar distinctions educated/uneducated (in dancing), reserved/enthusiastic, *Agora/mahala* and, in the end, we/the others, representing in parallel the ambitions and objectives between the two groups (Eriksen 1993: 74, 142)[36] in the specific space and time.

I would say that the kinetic management and negotiation of "Romness" or "Gypsyness" by the Roma of Irakleia has synchronic and spatial application. This case study enhances the particularity of the example and is contrary to "self-evident" research findings of the axiomatic type, which have pretensions of being of universal application, that is for Rom communities as a whole. I have tried to show that through a series of complicated but conventional interpretations the local dance in its Rom version represents the current as well as the potential local Rom identity.[37] It is an identity that tries to balance on brinks and boundaries (spatial and cultural) which, in the end, the others place. All these make up a fluid reality in which the certainties about Rom culture are refuted and the definitions by self and the definitions by other are placed under constant conditionality and negotiability.[38]

QUESTION: The *Agora* is one thing and the *mahala* another, isn't it?

INFORMANT: Yes, those living here in the *mahala* are called *yufti*, because if you go to get information from there [the *Agora*] the Vlachs will tell you: 'If you want Yannis you'll find him in the *yuftiko mahala*.' They're the ones who destroyed us here, they're the ones who gave us a bad reputation.

QUESTION: If I ask you what you are, what will you tell me?

INFORMANT: I'll tell you the truth, no one else will. I'm a Gypsy. No, I, if I were in another village, I wouldn't be a Gypsy. Just like you're a gentleman, we'd be gentlemen. They wouldn't know me. Our race wouldn't be known.

QUESTION: In your language, if I ask you what you are, would you say Rom or *gyftos*?

INFORMANT: I'd say Rom, that I'm *yuftos*; *yuftos* means Rom.

Notes

1. The ethnographic material presented in the text was collected in the course of fieldwork in Irakleia (1999–2001), in the framework of preparing my doctoral thesis. A preliminary version of the text was presented in Athens, 25-2-2002, in the series of lectures organized by the Hellenic Ethnological Society on the theme "Anthropological Approaches to Dance." I wish to express my warm thanks to Vangelis Avdikos, Vasilis Nitsiakos, Maria Papapavlou, Jane Cowan and Irene Loutzaki for their pertinent and substantial remarks.

2. The *prastaimnaski* or *tafterimnaski* is perhaps the favourite and most familiar dance form in the *mahala*, which is accompanied by various tones, which differ in style, intensity and rhythm.

3. One of the rare cases of tune/dance with Rom verse.

4. "Of this place."

5. Nitsiakos (2003) adopts the concept of cultural practice in order to overcome both the impediment of the substantivization of the place-community relationship and the problem of the structure-action relationship. Cf. Hall (1990, 222).

6. For a definition of mixed villages see Lafazani (1997, 96).

7. Lafazani's study is of the community of Maratho as well as other communities in the area of the Lower Strymon in the prefecture of Serres. In this study the *Tsinganoi* (Gypsies) are included in the "black" locals.

8. It should be noted that the Roma at this time were polyglot (Rom, Greek, "Bulgarian" local and Turkish).

9. Lafazani (1997, 107) considers this incorporation abusive.

10. See also Boeschoten (2000, 32).

11. The term Vlachs (Vlahoi), in contemporary Greek context, refers in an ethnic group which in the past considered as transhumant nomad and bilingual (a Latin idiom). According to Keil (Blau, Keil, and Feld 2002, 124): "Even before the creation of the Greek state, Vlachs as Rigas Fereos provided crucial leadership in the development of the Greek national idea, fusing the models of the Byzantine Empire and the Ottoman *millet* system with new European concepts of state. Vlachs have made and continue to make direct commitments — financial, military, educational and governmental — to the major institutions of Greece, finding no apparent contradiction between Vlach and Greek identity. " For the Vlachs see Balamaci (1995, 50–53) and for the Vlachs in Greece, Papathanasiou (1994).

12. For the *mahala* as boundary see Avdikos (2002, 185–220).

13. The otherness that is not confined to the space of the living but of the dead too (cemetery). Cf. Alexakis (1992, 73).

14. Teneketzis mentions that Christian tenant-farmers, Bulgarians, Gypsies and very few Greeks, worked "extensively" on çifliks. He also stresses that the shepherds, the swineherds and those employed in the lowest tasks were Slavophone or Gypsies (1973, 250).

15. See Mazower (2000) and Matalas (2002).

16. These huts were known as *b/paranges*.

17. Ploys and "regulations" of this kind had preceded at the level of political rights. In the Community Charter of 1924, the Roma were excluded from the right to vote — which all other Christians over 30 had — on the grounds that they were not engaged in an honest trade. See Kaftantzis (1973, 80).

18. As we saw above, Teneketzis calls these "empty" professional spaces "lowest tasks." Cf. Damianakos (1985, 30).

19. In particular after the Exchange of Populations in 1923, the Roma' professional field in relation to music widened considerably. This is due to the fact that the Muslim Roma (*magoustarides*), who were expert musicians, were judged "exchangeable" and sent from Irakleia to Turkey. See Keil and Vellou-Keil (2002, 133).

20. H. Rasmussen (1996, 251) calls it "innate."

21. 'Tsiganology' has also been criticized abroad (see Okely 1983; Sutherland 1975; Willems 1997) in recent years, as well as in Greece (Vaxevanoglou 2001, 33–60; Papapavlou 2002, 9–24; Gotovos 2001, 115–135; Politou 2001, 89–140).

22. Very often this results in 'Tsiganology' re-collecting its "cultivated" theories, this time through the mouths of its research subjects. See also Okely (1983, 11).

23. The Vlachs of the marketplace acknowledge and respect the musical dexterity of the musicians from the *mahala* and this is perhaps one of the very few points regarding the Roma that they promote outside the community. It is one of the cases in which the *mahala* gains essential "visibility" in the everyday discourse of the marketplace.

24. See also Theodosiou (1998, 10).

25. For the relations of power between musicians and clients in Soho, see Cowan (1990, 126–130).

26. This is quite the opposite of the case analyzed by Alexakis (1992, 71–86).

27. See also Royce (1977, 164).

28. One example of such a field is the wedding. Especially the sub-case in which a *balamos* is guest or *koumbaros* (best man) and is at the center of attention, not so much because of a certain proficiency at dance but because his presence of itself enhances the social status of the head of the house. The patronal feast of Irakleia, which is held on the first Thursday after August 15, is inseparably linked with the history of Irakleian space. In the course of its long history it was very commercial in character — a fair. In recent years it tends to have only commercial and entertainment character. On this occasion, indeed, a community dance for all is held, in which the individual ethnic groups or some of them take part. There are not other smaller-scale religious feasts that concern a particular group, in the *mahala* or the marketplace. In days of old, to a lesser degree today, the merrymaking in the period of the *panigyri* took place in '*siria*, temporary shelters of matting, like a coffee shop. Each coffee shop had a band, *zournades* (shawms), *klarina* (clarinets), folk, etc.

29. It is interesting to see how a teacher in Pontismeno near Irakleia represents the Rom dance manner: "On observing their tendencies and inclinations, some of their customs and their dances they like to dance — they are drawn to the dances of the Africans and easily imitate the Indians — one can easily reach the conclusion that they must be related in some way to those down there" (Pappas 1965).

30. For "exoticizing" of the Roma, mainly in literature, see Trumpener (1995, 368).

31. Extending this, we could say that music as a profession (or along with other "traditional" professions) and in the end as a necessity, partially destructures "tradition" as a transcendental concept. See also Theodosiou (1998, 10). Cf. Deltsou (2001, 201–208).

32. The dances *Leno mome* (daughter Helen), *siarene tsourapi* (colored stockings) and *rando mirtsou* (female name) corresponded to the specific tunes, whereas several different tunes correspond to the dance *paitouska*. For the dances of the region in general see Papakostas (2000, 154–170).

33. Several informants — mainly the musicians — linked this fact with the settling in the wider region of Cretans, who were working as gendarmes or civil servants.

34. For the *tsifteteli* see Raftis (1996), Buchheld (1996), Dunin (1998, 14), Lydaki (1998, 201), and Tyrovola (1999).

35. It should be clarified here that in Northern Greece *gyftoi* are the sedentary Gypsies and *tsinganoi* are the itinerant ones. In Southern Greece the opposite is the case. *Allibekioi* is a neighborhood in Serres inhabited by *gyftoi* who are different, as they themselves say, from those in Irakleia. See Exarchos (1996) and cf. Hunt (2002, 251–270).

36. Cf. Blascoy Gay (1999, 4).

37. Cf. Ness (1992, 182).

38. See in relation Gotovos (2002, 126–127).

Bibliography

Alexakis, Eleftherios. 1992. "Xoros, ethotikes omades ke simboliki sigkrotisi sto Pogoni tis Ipiro. Meleti mias periptosis" (Dance, Ethnic Groups and Symbolic Construction at Pogoni in Epirus. Case study). *Ethnographica* 8, Nafplion, Peloponnesian Folklore Foundation.

Aslanidis, Kostas. 1997. *Istorika diasparta tis Irakleias* (Historical Miscellanea of Irakleia). Irakleia Serres, Municipal Library of Irakleia.

Avdikos, Evaggelos. 1966. "To kourbani tou Agiou Athanasiou sto Didimoteiho:I thriskeftikotita os ekfrasi kinonikis antiropisis" [The *kurban* of Aghios Athanasios at Didymoteichon: Religiosity as an expression of social counterbalancing]. In *Folk Rituals. Old forms and modern expressions* (Proceedings of 1st conference), Athens, Ministry of Culture — Directorate of Folk Culture, 39–50.

_____. 2002. "To katsiki an pidisi to mandri, tha vri na faei poli. Zontas stin odo Avantos, sto horo ekeithen tis gramis" (If the kid jumps over the wall, it will find lots to eat. Living in Avantos Street, on the other side of the tracks). In *The Roma in Greece*. Athens: Elliniki Ethnologiki Etaireia, 185–229.

Balamaci, Nicolas. 1995. "The Balkan Vlachs: Born to Assimilate?" *Cultural Survival Quarterly* 19(2), 50–53.

Blau, Dick, and Charles and Angeliki Vellou Keil. 2002. *Bright Balkan Morning: Romani Lives and the Power of Music in Greek Macedonia*. Middletown, CT: Wesleyan University Press.

Blasco y Gay, Paloma. 1999. *Gypsies in Madrid: Sex, Gender, and the Performance of Identity*. Oxford: Berg.

Boeschoten, Ricky Van. 2000. "'When the Difference Matters: Sociopolitical Dimensions of Ethnicity in the District of Florina." In *Macedonia: The Politics of Identity and Difference*, ed. Jane Cowan. London: Sterling; Virginia: Pluto Press.

Bourdieu, Pierre. 1977. *Outline of a Theory of Practice*. Cambridge: Cambridge University Press.

Buchheld, Ulf. 1996. "Peri tou tsifteteliou proelfeseos" (On the provenance of the *tsifteteli*). *Paradosi kai Tehni* 26. Athens: International Organization of Folk Art.

Clebert, Jean-Paul. 1967. *The Gypsies*, trans. C. Duff. Harmondsworth: Penguin.

Cowan, Jane. 1990. *Dance and the Body Politic in Northern Greece*. Princeton, NJ: Princeton University Press.

Damianakos, Stathis. 1985. *Paradosi antarsias ke laikos politismos* (Tradition of Mutiny and Folk Culture). Athens: Plethron.

Deltsou, Elefteria. 2001. "Kritikes prosegiseis tis enias tis 'paradosis' ke ena ethnografiko paradeigma" (Critical approaches to the concept of "tradition" and an ethnographic example). In *Laografia kai Istoria* (Folklore and History). Proceedings of a Conference in Memory of Alki Kyriakidou-Nestoros, Thessaloniki, Paratiritis, 201–208.

Desmond, Jane. 1997. "Embodying Difference: Issues in Dance and Cultural Studies." In *Meaning in Motion. New Cultural Studies of Dance*, ed. Jane Desmond. Durham, NC: Duke University Press, 29–54.

Dunin, Elsie. 1998. *Gypsy St. George Day—Coming of Summer*. Skopje: Association of Admirers of Rom Folklore Art "Gypsy Heart."

Eriksen, Thomas Hylland. 1993. *Ethnicity and Nationalism*. London: Pluto Press.

Exarchos, Giorgis. 1996. *Afti eine I Gifti* (These Are the Gypsies). Athens: Gavriilidis.

Frith, Simon. 1996. "Music and Identity." In *Questions of Identity*, ed. S. Hall and P. du Gay. Thousand Oaks, CA: Sage, 108–127.

Giurchescu, Anca. 2000. "Gypsy Dance Style as a Marker of Ethnic Identity." In *Music, Language, and Literature of the Roma and Sinti*, ed. M.P. Baumann. Berlin: VWB.

Goffman, Erving. 1963. *Stigma: Notes on the Management of Spoiled Identity*. Englewood Cliffs, NJ: Prentice-Hall.

Gotovos, Athanasios. 2002. "Romiki tftotita stin Elliniki kinonia: prosdiorismi se sigrousi" (Rom Identity in Greek Society: Definitions in Conflict). In *The Roma in Greece*, Athens, Elliniki Ethnologiki Etaireia, 111–135.

Hall, Stuart. 1990. "Cultural Identity and Diaspora." In *Identity, Community, Culture, Difference*, ed. J. Rutherford. London: Lawrence & Wishart.

Herzfeld, Michael. 1987. *Anthropology Through the Looking Glass: Critical Ethnography in the Margins of Europe*. Cambridge: Cambridge University Press.

Hunt, Yvonne. 2002. "The Ababas: A Rom Ritual." In *The Roma in Greece*. Athens: Elliniki Etaireia Ethnologias, 251–270.

Kaftantzis, Giorgos. 1973. *I istoria tis Irakleias nomou Serron* (History of Irakleia in the Prefecture of Serres), Irakleia Serres: Municipality of Irakleia.

Kavkoula, Kiki. 1990. "I idea tis Kipoupolis stin Elliniki poleodomia tou mesopolemou" (The Idea of the Garden City in Greek Urban Planning of the Interwar Years). Unpublished doctoral dissertation, Thessaloniki, School of Architecture at the Aristotle University of Thessaloniki.

Keil, Charles, and Angeliki Vellou Keil. 2002. *Bright Balkan Morning: Romani Lives and the Power of Music in Greek Macedonia*. Middletown, CT: Wesleyan University Press.

Koumarianou, Maria. 2000. "Mnimi, lithi ke istoria you horou. I periptosi tis polis tis Mitilinis" [Memory, Oblivion and History of Space: The Case of the Town of Mytilene]. In *The City in Later Times. Mediterranean and Balkan Aspects (19th-20th Century). Proceedings of the 2nd International Conference*. Athens: Society for the Study of Recent Hellenism, 237–249.

Koutsouba, Maria. 1999. "I dinamiki tou horou stis metashimatistikes diadikasies tis topikis politismikis taftotitas" [The Dynamic of Dance in the Transformational Processes of Forming Local Cultural Identity]. In *Melody-Word-Movement: Proceedings of the 2nd Panhellenic Conference*, ed. K. Panopoulou. Serres: TEFAA of Serres and Municipality of Serres, 205–210.

Lafazani, Dora. 1997. "Mikta horia tou kato Strimona: Ethnotita, kinotita ke entopiotita" (Mixed Villages in the Lower Strymon: Ethnicity, Community and Localness). *Sichrona Themata* 63, Athens.

Loutzaki, Rena. 1983–1985. "Marriage as a Dance Event: Case Study. Marriage among the Refugees from Eastern Rumelia in the village of Micro Monastiri, Macedonia." *Ethnographica* 4–5, Nafplion, Peloponnesian Folklore Foundation, 143–175.
Lydaki, Anna. 1998. *I Tsigani stin poli* [Tsigganes in the City]. Athens: Kastaniotis.
Matalas, Paraskevas. 2002. *Ethnos ke Orthodoxia* [Nation and Orthodoxy]. Herakleion: Crete University Press.
Mazower, Mark. 2000. *The Balkans*. New York: Random House.
Mazraki, Despina. 1984. *The Traditional Clarinet (To Laiko klarinor)*. Athens. Kedros.
Ness, Sally Ann. 1992. *Body, Movement and Culture: Kinesthetic and Visual Symbolism in a Philippine Community*. Philadelphia: University of Pennsylvania Press.
Nitsiakos, Vassilis. 2001. "O topos tou horou ke o horos tou topou" [The Place of the Dance and the Dance of the Place]. In *Melody-Word-Movement: Proceedings of the 2nd Panhellenic Conference*, ed. K. Panopoulou. Serres: TEFAA of Serres and Municipality of Serres, 21–26.
_____. 2003. "Topos ke kinotita" [Place and Community]. In *Building Space and Time*, ed. V. Nitsiakos. Athens: Odysseas, 84–96.
Okely, Judith. 1983. *Traveler-Gypsies*. Cambridge: Cambridge University Press.
Papakostas, Christos. 2000. "Simboli sti meleti you mousikoxoreftikou' repertoriou ton nomon Dramas ke Serron" [Contribution to the Study of the Music and Dance Repertoire of the Prefectures of Drama and Serres]. In *Dance and History*, ed. Alkis Raftis. Proceedings of the 14th International Conference. Athens: International Organization of Folk Art.
_____. 2001. "O horos apo tin kinotita stin skini: praktikes ke antifasis" [Dance from the Community to the Stage: Practices and Contradictions]. In *Melody-Word-Movement. Proceedings of the 2nd Panhellenic Conference*, ed. K. Panopoulou. Serres: TEFAA of Serres and Municipality of Serres, 255–272.
Papapavlou, Maria, and Eleni Koppasi-Oikonomeia. 2002. "Eisagogi. Tsigani ke tsiganologia: logi pri eterotitas" [Introduction: Tsigganes and Tsiganology: Discourse on Otherness]. In *The Roma in Greece*. Athens: Elliniki Etaireia Ethnologias, 9–24.
Pappas, Sotirios. 1965. "Laofrafika stiheia Pontismenou Serron" [Folklore Elements at Pontismeno, Serres]. Manuscript inv. no. 3151, Athens, Research Centre for Greek Folklore, Academy of Athens.
Papathanasiou, Yiannis. 1994. *I Istoria ton Vlaxon* [The History of the Vlachs, Illustrated]. Thessaloniki: Barbounakis.
Politou, Evagelia. 2001. "Reproduction and Homogenization of the 'Special' Through the Educational System." Unpublished doctoral dissertation, University of Athens, School of Philosophy, Pedagogy and Psychology, Department of Pedagogy.
Raftis, Alkis. 1996. "Mikro dikimio gia to tsifteteli" [Short Essay on the *Tsifteteli*]. *Paradosi ke Tehni* 26, Athens, International Organization of Folk Art.
Rasmussen, Lierka V. 1996. "Orientalism, Rom Gypsy and the Culture of Intersection." In *Traditionell music von minderbeiten/Ethnische gruppen. Traditional of Music of Ethnic Group Minorities*, ed. U. Hemetek and E. Lubej. Wien, Koln, Weimar: Bohlan, 247–254.
Rombou-Levidi, Marica. 1999. "Pieces of a Dance Puzzle in the Evros Region. The Past, the Present, Local Practice and Supra-Local Ideology." In *Music of Thrace — An Interdisciplinary Approach: Evros*. Athens: The Friends of Music Society, 145–192.
Royce, Anna Peterson. 1977. *The Anthropology of Dance*. Bloomington: Indiana University Press.
Sutherland, Anne. 1975. *Gypsies: The Hidden Americans*. New York: Free Press.
Teneketzis, Thomas. 1973. *Laografika Irakleias* [Folklore of Irakleia]. Irakleia Serres, Municipality of Irakleia.
Theodosiou, Aspassia. 1998. "Spatial Embodiment of Music among Gypsies in Parakalamos." Dissertation for masters degree. Manchester University, Department of Social Anthropology.
Trumpener, Katie. 1995. "The Time of the Gypsies: A People 'Without History' in the Narratives of the West." In *Identities*, ed. K. W. Appiah and H. L. Gates. Chicago: University of Chicago Press.
Tyrovola, Vassiliki. 1999. "Laikos Politismos ke kinoniki exelixi. To paradigma tou horou

tsifteteli" [Folk Culture and Social Development. The Example of the *Tsifteteli* Dance]. In *Melody-Word-Movement Proceedings of the 2nd Panhellenic Conference*, ed. K. Panopoulou. Serres: TEFAA of Serres and Municipality of Serres, 137–174.

Tzemailas, Giorgos. 1973. "Simboli is tin istoria tis Irakleias" [Contribution to the History of Irakleia]. *Serraika Hronika vol. 6*, Athens, Historical and Folklore Society of Serres-Melenikos.

Vaxevanoglou, Aliki. 2001. *Ellines tsigani, perithoriki ke ikogeniarhes* [Greek Gypsies, Drop-outs and Family Heads]. Athens: Alexandria.

Webb, Godfrey. 1975. *Gypsies*. London: Greenwood Press.

Willems, Wim. 1997. *In Search of the True Gypsy: From Enlightenment to Final Solution*. London: Frank Cass.

5

Dance as Propaganda: The Metaxas Regime's Stadium Ceremonies, 1937–1940

IRENE LOUTZAKI

The display of folk dances can reaffirm cultural style in performance usage by indicating social or historical milieus. This is readily demonstrated in the various folk dances of any country. However, when folk dance performance is displayed for national usage, apart from the entertainment and recreation that any spectacle can offer, it can also be used as a vehicle for strengthening the nation and the race, recognizing its ceremonial, educational and disciplinary value; a statement about national identity; and a way to construct, national identity as an essential symbolic stage for the perpetuation of the nation.

On the Fourth of August a type of "National Holiday" (literally known as *the Metaxas Regime Stadium Ceremonies*) became an annual event organized by the Metaxas dictatorship in the years from 1937 to 1940, in the Panathenaic Stadium in Athens. I argue that this annual ceremony is a performative event in which folk dance display, symbolically and pragmatically, occupies a central position. In this essay therefore, I will demonstrate how folk dance through its spatial arrangement represents the unity of the "nation," and, through its symbolic capacity to mobilize powerful emotions, was used by Metaxas' regime as an instrument of propaganda.

Dictatorships and ceremonies

Ceremonies and dictatorships are often seen as intricately intertwined as they "both engage the populace in rites of collective spectacle" (Berezin 2005, n.p.). These spectacles employed by Fascist Italy, Nazi Germany, Franco's Spain, the Soviet Union, and even Turkey, Bulgaria, Romania, and other countries have been analyzed by historians as encapsulating the mobilizing character of 20th-century dictatorships (Kordes 2002, Wanner 1996, Öztürkmen 2001, Giurchescu 2001, Ilieva 2001). This essay, however, rather than merely using the example of a national ceremonial event held from 1937 to 1940, views these types of ceremonies as public display representing a particular regime's ideology and culture. These perspectives overlap and intersect, each providing a helpful vantage point of a symbolic field in which a totalitarian plan was implemented based on a national discourse of promoting the ideas of religion as a "source of good," and the analogy of a State family by the promotion of the notion of the State as Motherland. Collective spectacles organized by authoritarian regimes or military and other dictatorships are analyzed in terms of their mobilizing power within this specific 20th-century dictatorship.

Established on August 4, 1936, the dictatorship of Ioannis Metaxas (1871–1941), known as "the dictatorship of the Fourth of August," was the final act in the consolidation of conservative rule in Greece. Parliament was dissolved, political parties banned, and the opponents of the regime arrested and imprisoned. Even though the Metaxas regime appeared in a similar historical context as that of Italy's and Germany's fascist regimes, Greek Fascism carried traits which were genuinely Greek and therefore unique. In fact, Metaxas and his collaborators belonged to an extreme wing of Greek conservatism that had little faith in the parliamentary political system. Consistent with his disdain for party politics was Metaxas' refusal to form his own party, as did other authoritarian movements in Southern Europe that spawned the creation of the Italian Blackshirts and the Spanish Falange (Machaira 1987, Woodhouse 1991, Clogg 1992). Instead, the "Fourth of August" regime exercised power exclusively through state mechanisms, the civil service, the military, and the police (Sarantis 1993, 147).

The main inspiration for Greek Fascism was Hellenism. Metaxas believed that Greece could retrieve its former glory only by seeking it in herself and her own unique and powerful national tradition. The ideological justification of this "New State," which represented the "Third Hellenic Civilization,"[1] was sought in Greece's classic history as Metaxas thought Hellenic nationalism was to galvanize "the pagan values of Ancient Greece, specifically those of Sparta, with the Christian values of the medieval empire of Byzantium" (Clogg 1992, 119). On each fourth of August from 1937 to 1940 the Metaxas dictatorship held an annual celebration. This started one year after Metaxas' rise to power in 1936, during which large propaganda events were organized by the state in Athens as well as in the various provinces of the country.[2] However, the principal "Feast of the Anniversaries" was held annually with full pomp from 1937 to 1940, in the Panathenaic Stadium as commemoration of the establishment of the dictatorship headed by Ioannis Metaxas.

This mass ceremony used crucial elements of Greek folk culture in which folklore represented communal ideals and populist ideologies. The holiday was one of the major performative events on the dictatorship's calendar which brought together the entire community to celebrate Metaxas' takeover in 1936. "Public ceremonies," notes Berezin, "on the one hand communicate cultural norms, and on the other, are meant to instil the regime's regulations via repetitive ritualized events" (2005, n.p.). *The Fourth of August Ceremonies* based on staging scenes and held in various settings, can be characterized as large-scale, dramatic and message-laden festive occasions that have been widely adopted by the state authorities for propaganda purposes. The meaning of this propaganda event was to employ collective memory aiming at the creation of a shared sense of community amongst peasants by combining the new with the revival on stage of scenes from Greece's glorious past to establish a sense of continuity and communitas. A wide series of acts and events took place, among which the display of folk dances was highlighted. Participation in the dancing circle brought together men and women of all ages, of different origins in various settings (theatres, squares or factories) in Athens, among which the Panathenaic Stadium was the most pre-eminent.[3] In this prestigious space more than five thousand dancers dressed in local costumes and displayed their dances in front of an enthusiastic crowd. Designed by the State and guided by the directive and norms of the Ministry of Press and Tourism (analogous to the Ministry of Propaganda in Nazi Germany), this mass dance performance was formulated in terms of "a general mobilization drawn from a return 'to the roots and sources,' an indication of the dictator's predilection for the 'beautiful Greek tradition'" (Sarantis 1993, 150). Folk dancing was a site for the dictator to make visible in a ceremonial way those traditional values and ideals representing the "bulwark of society." Metaxas idealized Greek folk life and culture as represented by its folk dances, while at the same time he attacked foreign dances and culture.

The Press: Propaganda and Censorship

Propaganda and censorship are two concepts that are inextricably linked in every dictatorial regime: "the first imposing the silences of the regime, the second organising its shouts" (Mokas 1999, n.p.). With the takeover by the dictatorship in Greece, the freedom of the press guaranteed by the constitution was suspended, first following a confidential order issued by the dictator to the services supervising the press, and subsequently by the passing of two laws that began to be enforced in 1938. On the whole, the prohibitions concerned the non-publication of information on the government's activities, unless this was favorable information on the exercise of preventive censorship and other similar matters. While censorship transformed the spoken or written word, that of propaganda endeavored to enhance and highlight key figures of the regime — the king, the dictator and the national government — with the aim to convince Greek people that the regime was necessary and useful, and to prompt them to accept and absorb its creed concerning the autocratic state by offering impressive fêtes and stirring parades.

The connection of these fêtes with similar celebratory "fiestas" organized by national-socialist governments and military regimes of the inter-war period as well as of later periods in other European countries such as Germany and Italy (Loukas 1991, 130–131) obviously constitutes the basic lens through which my readings were viewed. However, for the early 20th century, simple access to a celebration, and especially to the folk dancing as historical fact is impossible if by "fact" we understand "a live performative event," transient in nature, and for which one can only know the event through an artefact-the text. It is obvious therefore, that I cannot actually witness an early 20th-century celebration in progress, as anthropologists carry out in the field when they observe a celebration first-hand. I can only read texts about those celebrations, even though many of the reports do not attempt to describe them in full detail or impartiality. Although I cannot watch the Fourth of August celebrations, I can however, still profitably apply tools developed by the social sciences to the investigation of celebrations as presented (misrepresented/manipulated) in texts. Thus, in this essay, through the study of press clippings and film extracts of the period, I hope to demonstrate how Athens was transformed into a huge theatre — with its stage, its backstage, its audience, its actors — all devoted to the realization of the dictator's vision known as the "Third Hellenic Civilization." By examining newspapers as a source expressing the regime's political ideology, I will focus on the role played by folk dance in supporting the dictator's ideological aim as well as the general impact that the propaganda had on the public.

Benjamin has argued that during the period of a dictatorship, politics tend to be pressed into "the production of ritual values" (1973, 241). In an analogous way, folk dancing as embodied action, which can be used for the strengthening of social bonds, and even more for accomplishing the emotional needs of the performers, or just for the pleasure of the dance itself, can be easily examined as a means of production of the ritual values as portrayed in the festivities of the Fourth of August, and interpret them from a cultural distance in the period when they were formalized.

The Fourth of August Ceremony as a Performance Event

By classifying The Fourth of August ceremony under the umbrella term "performance event," I mean in accordance with Goodridge "a planned orchestration of symbolic actions with restricted, specific objectives and social functions, including among other devices, a particular location, the presence of specialists, the need for preparation, specific use of conventions, such as parades, gestures, folk dancing, folk music and singing, all performed for an audience" (1999, 19). These activities, "serving to communicate information about a culture's most cherished values" (Leach 1954, 15–38, in Goodridge 1999, 19), constitute a complex system which on the one hand can credibly transmit meaningful qualities, while promoting symbolic links among performers or between performers and the audience.

These activities, though different in structure and style, are strongly related to each other during the performative process. By focusing on folk dancing, through the use of step patterns, as well as the performers' appearance, I will argue that a sense of community was generated. Folk dance helps "to choreograph" personal, local, regional, ethnic, religious, linguistic, and national identity. In a dictator's hands folk dance adopts a new meaning, since it was used as an authoritative "ingredient" for the regeneration of dancing. The *syrtos* performance, for example, used as the closing scene in every ceremony, transformed what was recognized as a Pan-Hellenic dance[4] into a key symbol for uniting the diverse regions of the country in a synchronized circular path. Used symbolically for demonstrating the nation's unique character to the audience and through it to the whole world, this circular dance adopts a special meaning that the regime spread through political advertisement and propaganda. Further, the distribution of the various regional dancing circles at the stadium turned rural performers who participated in the events "into symbols creating spectacular mass body language" (Danó and Roubal 2001, n.p.), helping to "dramatize the relation between power and representation" (Falasca-Zamponi 1997, 3), by creating new categories of understanding.

In these mass events, on the one hand the village performers in colorful regional dress became the artists, and on the other hand Metaxas came to represent the model of a choreographer who through the display of folk dance tried to present an ideal, fulfilled in everyday life. In this sense, Metaxas' realism may be considered as a "privileged workshop" which claimed the fatherhood of a new Greek folk style, by producing a "hybrid folk dance festival culture" (Berezin 2005, n.p.) through the scenic presentation of which someone can analyze the shifts that took place in the dance, its messages, and aesthetics from 1937 to 1940.

In these performances the concept of "Greece" was reproduced because of the presence of many representative groups of villagers wearing their traditional costumes and performing their dances. This was a period during which, on the cultural plane, many communities maintained "close" bonds with tradition, while the traditional dress was showing obvious signs of falling out of use as it was rapidly being substituted, partly or wholly, by western fashion. The invitation extended by the organizers in Athens, concerned a massive public folk fête held outside the microcosm of the village, and although this may not be evident, it contained many of the elements of a theatrical performance that lent a new aspect to the concept of "folk dance" as performative art.

According to certain testimonies, in each place-village, town or island-there was a process of selection in order to find the appropriate performers. This choice was based on two criteria: (1) performance quality, relating to dancing ability and expertise, uniformity of size, youth and beauty; and (2) the political affiliation whereby only those dancers whose families supported the regime were chosen. If the latter is valid, I assume that a number of young boys and girls may have been excluded, by virtue of their family's political beliefs as the person in charge of the creation of the community delegation was someone who enjoyed the trust of the local government.[5] The criterion of social class also played a certain role in their final selection of the candidate participants. According to my older informants who had taken part in the Fourth of August celebrations, changes were made by the performance organizers in the location of the recruited performers in the dance formation. Similar criteria of social hierarchy-based on sex, age, or marital status, as would have been the case, at a *panighyri* (village celebration)–were substituted by aesthetic criteria. By aesthetic criteria I mean the capacity to produce beauty and stir human emotional responses, that is, to spectacular dancing emphasizing the viewer's reception more than the performer's engagement.

In this essay, I argue that this aestheticization of folk dancing for the needs of nationalist performance transformed ethnic delegations representing various provinces in Greece, through their scenic presentation into what Ness has termed "an ideal vehicle for objectification of [a] nationalist identity" (1992, 98), that "synchronized steps executed by thousands of folk dancers created an electrifying impact on [the] audience that is difficult to imagine for those not present or unaware of this phenomenon" (Shay 2002, 4). In this context, aesthetization of folk dancing along with framed body behavior were employed in order to bridge power and representation on the one hand, and authority and the people on the other through the mobilizing of the strong emotions of the masses.

The Fourth of August Ceremony (1937–1940)

In this imitation of Hitler's performative events, such as the Nuremberg and Munich Rallies (see *Triumph des Willens*, made by Leni Riefenstahl, in 1935), Metaxas blended ancient Greek civilization with that of medieval Byzantium as he thought that "an amalgam of the essentially contradictory values of both would enshrine and perpetuate the values of his regime" (Clogg 1992, 118). Metaxas' "Third Hellenic Civilization" vision included the implementation of populist policies expressed by the creation of mechanisms such as the establishment of cultural and social security institutions, agricultural cooperatives, workers' homes and the creation of the *Ethniki Organosi Neolaias* (National Youth Organization, EON) modeled on fascist youth groups.

The ideology of the Third Hellenic Civilization was strongly encouraged by the regeneration of rural customs while combating modernity and foreign cultural influences. The modernization of the Metaxas state, in fact, was identified with Greek tradition and came into conflict with influential types of foreign modernization. As a result what appeared that was perceived of as "Greek" was authentic and genuine, and what was deemed to be a "foreign import" was artificial and therefore non-authentic. Against these "evils" of foreign, inauthentic culture, Metaxas proposed a new concept: "National Regeneration and Unity"–the central theme for the campaign for his "New Greece." His campaign, aimed at the creation of a new national civilization, as well as such aims as the raising of the nation's morale and international respect for the country.

Metaxas further used traditional forms of popular expression such as athletic games or gymnastics displays as methods of "controlling" the masses. Styling himself in an ideological delirium as "the First Peasant," "the First Worker," "the Leader," and "the National Father," he also lent his support to other types of events of a pan–Hellenic nature, also held in the Panathenaic

Stadium, such as the *Youth Festival*, the *Festival of the Pioneers* and the *Fourth of August ceremony*, for the purpose of preserving the relationship with the glorious past of the "Greek race."

The Anatomy of the Stadium Festivities

As part of a national holiday, a day set aside for the celebration of historical events, folk dancing was connected semantically with certain forms of political practices. In a three-dimensional form-vocal, instrumental and kinetic-these practices are encountered in politics as a dynamic process, a political ceremonial performance characterized by political symbolism, or in Turner's words, "framed behavior" (1982, 28).[6] As folk dance, music, and song all constitute major dimensions of a political event, they lend themselves to promising analytical forces both in terms of a performative event and in terms of their importance as part of political propaganda. In this context, dance, song and music are not mere entertainment, but a "cultural condition of production and use" (Kavouras 1999, 173), used with the intent of displaying power through propaganda. In the Panathenaic Stadium, each ceremony makes up a sum of successive processes, constituting a sort of "scenario" demanding ritual seriousness and dictating discipline which may vary depending every year on the political and social needs, a process which Kertzer has called "the ritual construction of political reality" (1988, 77; in Herzfeld 2001, 126).

Despite the tendency of historiography to downgrade these types of displays, the Stadium ceremonies were highlighted as cultural and artistic events of great magnitude as they were given wide coverage by the propagandist press of the period.[7] Various important moments were recorded by photographs and filmed shots of contemporary newsreels. Photo material with close ups and other technical uses of the photographic lens were accompanied by a brief and spare caption, introducing the reader to the climate of the event, showing scenery, symbols, people. These photographs communicate a very broad range of meanings expressed through body postures (especially the positioning of hands), facial expressions, and groupings of people wearing local costume, uniforms, or symbols. Film on the other hand-less useful because it was perceived as straight forward propaganda-was still embryonic in that period.[8] The use of close-ups and long shots and the final editing techniques and structures of the scenario provided panoramic images that conveyed the immense scope of the proceedings, all of which aimed to turn the dictator into an object of desire and his acts into great masterpieces.

The Fourth of August Celebration was accompanied by workers' choirs, pageantry, and military bands. Parade of Athens City at Stadiou Street (1937–1940). The annually repeated event became part of the Athenian festive calendar. Photograph ©2006 by Benaki Museum Athens–Koulas Pratsika Archives.

I will next endeavor to view the Stadium festivities and the preparations for the anniversary to a certain extent through the image "constructed" by three major newspapers[9] and the camera and photographic lens, while being fully aware of the propagandistic purposes which these "images" served. Journalism of the period, perhaps due to the very propagandistic nature of the printed stories, allows us to discern some of the aims of the dictator through the purposeful highlighting of the rhetoric of the regime and the information furnished on the practices of such regimes.

It is common knowledge among dance anthropologists that the meaning of an aesthetic creation, such as that of the festivities at the Panathenaic Stadium, are part of the intangible heritage of historic nature, and cannot be grasped without being registered or transformed into some kind of material/tangible heritage. In this case, newspapers and the fragmentary extracts of newsreels may be used as sources for the reader/viewer to realize *what* happened in that particular moment of shooting, *which* groups took part, or even *how* local delegations were distributed in the various parts of the Stadium. In this material, folk dance constitutes a body of cultural and political expression that reflects the traditionalist ideology in the context of the Stadium festivities of the Metaxas' regime. By focusing on the information adopted through the study of the press, I will explore in this section, the relationship between dance and politics and, through it, I will look at dance as a form of propaganda. Further, photographic material enriched by the various propagandistic sketches and posters for the "advertisement" of the anniversary and the fête, constitutes an outstanding separated category of research material.

In the organizing committee, the leading person was Theodoulos Nikoloudis, the Minister of Tourism and the Press, whose efforts were made to enable the events to appear spontaneously organized and attended. Spontaneity was a key element in the Metaxas' propaganda as the legitimating of a regime relying on public consent.

Nikoloudis was also the leading person in the creation of the program and was responsible for the theme selected, as the festivities had a different overriding theme every year. For instance, in the 1937 festival, priority was given to the exaltation of workers and farmers with the dictator posing as the First Farmer, the First Worker. In the 1939 festivity, the performative events focused on the state, in terms of economic and social achievement of the government, such as the *Procession of Labour*, in which men and women farmers marched past carrying baskets of grapes, sheaves of wheat or tobacco leaves, fishermen carrying nets. In 1940, the main spotlight was on the representation of the youth of Greece as "the hopeful future of the nation." Other themes were the trumpet calls of the Athens Guard, the *Te Deum*, the Hymn of the 4th August, the flag-raising ceremony, and the parade of the Falangists (the boys and girls in separate battalions, in conformity with the government policy banning mixed activities). In charge of the artistic part and the staging, the choreographer Koula Pratsika was employed, while the musical direction

5. Dance as Propaganda

The Fourth of August Celebration (rehearsal). The Edessa delegation (northern Greece) accompanied by a bagpiper and tubeleki-drummer rehearsed its local dances in the Zappeion garden in Athens. Photograph ©2006 by Benaki Museum Athens–Koulas Pratsika Archives.

of the choir was entrusted to the Conservatory of Athens. All performers were coordinated centrally by an administrative body occupied by the government, an indication of the importance of the celebration.

As August 4 drew near,[10] newspapers devoted more space to material relevant to the celebration. Pages were filled with instructions, with reference to the reasons why the people should take part in the celebrations as well as various offers.[11] They also contained reports from the provinces presenting the views of those who responded favorably to the invitation by sending letters of support to the regime expressing their solidarity and allegiance. The dynamic "show" of acceptance emphasizes the assurance that the people, as a whole, were on the side of Metaxas, in whom they implicitly trusted and whom they urged to carry on his task.

I argue that these endless descriptions function merely as publicity for someone that wants to participate in a patriotic event. Moreover, the Ceremony Organizing Committee launched a competition ("the three most attractive shop-windows featuring the theme of the Fourth of August will be awarded a prize") in an obvious attempt to involve Athenians not only as spectators but also as organizers of the event.

Two days before the Stadium ceremony, press coverage on preparations allocated greater importance to photographs, in order to add a vivid effect in the "documentation" of the preparations. In these pictures we can see representatives of various peasant groups posing in their regional costumes on archaeological sites, on the steps of the Stadium, and in their encampments. Photographs taken in makeshift studios showed staged regional protagonists holding various props alluding to agricultural labor (jars, sheaves of wheat, hoes, large baskets) in front of a natural or artificial background. Further photographs portrayed children and young people posing with the dictator or his family. In these pictures, stress was not laid on regional representation indicated by young performers' local costumes.[12] The caption ignores locality to stress instead the beauty of girls and the handsome bearing of the boys, as elements constituting the "pure" Hellenic nation. Gallantry, patriotism, modesty, courage, strength and discipline were further features attributed to Greek youth in the same captions. And while the insistence on the regional variation is evident in the regime's proclamations at the moment when the entire mosaic of Greek actuality was physically present, whether because of ignorance or on purpose, the place of origin of each group was substituted by broader geographical groupings, such as "women of beautiful Thrace," "woman from the Mesogaia villages," etc.

It is worth mentioning that through the photos I investigated taken throughout the four celebrations, there is no representation of villages, minorities and ethnic groups such as Turkish-speaking groups, nomad shepherds, gypsies, and others. This absence includes names of non–Greek tunes or musical instruments, or any other symbol of cultural difference that would fragment the unified vision of the nation. By contrast, press reports stress the importance of *kalamatianos* as a key symbol expressing unity, by providing a common kinetic language to all groups (for *syrtos*, see note 4).

The Lyceum Club of Greek Women (founded in 1911), an important Athenian cultural association, participated in the celebrations with a group that numbered over 400 members dressed in reproductions of ancient Greek tunics.[13] The captions accompanying these photographs published in the newspapers alluded to the idea of cultural continuity-the underlying theme of the "Third Hellenic Civilization" by employing expressions such as "graceful tunics, graceful maidens, living Greek dolls." The way that these girls were portrayed in the photos reflected attitudes and concepts in tune with the tenet of historical continuity between Ancient Greece and the Greece of the Metaxas' regime.

More obvious expressions of the propaganda undertaken by the Lyceum

Club of Greek Women on the regime's behalf can be discerned in photographs portraying the formulation of the words "4th of August" by the bodies of young female Lyceum members. This scene was the most spectacular display shown as a ritual of synchronized mass movements and played an important role in these celebrations.

On the days following the event, newspapers contained lengthy descriptions, stressing the immense success of the celebration. The front pages were taken up by panoramic views of the stadium showing the procession, the dancing circles, the enthusiastic crowd, the arrival of the dignitaries, unreeling like a motion picture, every episode and every "scene of the drama!" The echoes continued to reverberate and incidental details continued to occupy the attention of the press until about the 8th or 10th of August, at which time they ceased, almost suddenly, only to be revived again, with even greater intensity, the following year.

In the 1938 event, an attempt was made to give the celebration a more carefully elaborated character, with professional efficiency and more expert organization. The pivotal point around which the fête revolved was once again the popular nature of the event, based on popular sentiment and popular support, both in terms of propaganda rhetoric and the practices applied. Articles of 1938 specifically mentioned individuals and groups who offered their aid and support to the government, especially names of well-known artists, merchants and businessmen. The terms "Nation" and "Government" are presented as practically synonymous.

Another element that characterized the 1939 celebration is the important presence of the National Youth Organization with its members,[14] as much in the preparation of the celebrations as in actualization. "Today, youth spoke at the Stadium" or "Youth drew the public attention, as they marched along the streets singing the praises of the dictator," is reported as having drawn attention. The performance was made up of different age groups intended to represent "youth" united and fully concentrated towards the common goal. In the 1938 newspapers, special mention was made of the creation of the *Hymn of the 4th August* (lyrics by G. Frem, music by T. Moraitinis), the result of a contest with many candidates. The hymn was to become the prelude and refrain of every public manifestation.[15]

Metaxas regime propaganda for the Third Hellenic Civilization emerged in the rhetoric describing the 1939 events. As Dounia (1999) points out, this action probably aimed toward more effective organization of the government propaganda mechanism, on the one hand, and towards more active participation of non-governmental groups on the other. In a symbolic allusion to the national renaissance, streets were set up with triumphal arches on the

The Fourth of August Celebration. Young *alkimoi* (a type of scout), forming on the floor of the stadium the five Olympic circles. Photograph ©2006 by Benaki Museum Athens–Koula Pratsika Archives.

main avenues of the city, and a specific itinerary was planned for the procession of representative local groups. Press coverage of the events resonated with the same motif. For instance, on the front page of a newspaper, dated July 30, appeared a sketch of a sturdy male, naked from the waist up, holding in one hand a hoe and in the other, in an attitude of salute, the date of the 4th of August. Another drawing portrayed a woman dressed in a long tunic and crowned with a wreath, raising high a lighted torch, against a background of the Greek flag, accompanied by the words: "Long live the 4th August."

The 1940 celebratory events,[16] although not lacking in dynamism and fervor, appear markedly reduced in form. The "Alkimoi," the group of young boys that replaced local delegates, were employed to dance the folk dances in school-like formations, to the accompaniment of municipal choral ensembles, singing songs composed in a folkloristic idiom by classical musicians. Further, four hundred women workers from the Papastratos cigarette factory for the first time took part in the "artistic" program with recitations and the performance of choreographic compositions. The preparation of these workers was incorporated in a general program of on-going education and social welfare, in which the factory, on its own initiative, had entrusted their "training" to the school of choreographer Koula Pratsika.

On the following day, the press refer in pompous terms to the "preparations, which assumed the proportions of a plebiscite in favour of the government." Newspapers carried letters of support from foreign governments, while reference was also made to the international situation and the battles taking place, as the war clouds gathered menacingly in the region. The storm finally broke with the declaration of war and the entry of Greece into the conflict on October 28, 1940.

"In the Realm of History — The 4th of August — The Third Hellenic Civilisation"

A valuable source of information on the Stadium festivities was the television series *In the realm of History—The 4th of August—The third Hellenic civilisation* (*4th cycle*), shown on State Television channel ET1, in 1993. It was based on a scenario by the director Dionysis Gregoratos, and on texts by the historian Alkis Rhigos.

This black-and-white series constituted a document that brought to life the history of Greece and the period I examine, through the critical narration of the historian. Looking at the original footage (1937–1940), especially at those related with the festivities, the use of cameras provided panoramic images which conveyed the immense scope of the proceedings while selectively focusing on certain scenes. Although folk dancing is present in this footage, the film capacity of the period, owing to the weaknesses that characterized it at that early stage, could not technically match the representational excellence of the still camera to register credibility. Moreover, there was no possibility of recording sound simultaneously. The musical accompaniment was never the correct one. It was added on as decoration or background. Thus, the musical sound ran independently of what was happening on the screen.

A second weak point of the extracts used was their quality, as they constitute fragmentary archival material, of which the film-maker selectively or repeatedly adapts the required stills to the narrative, either to visually interpret the text of his scenario or to illustrate various themes. These merely function as a visualization of the commentary, alternating with narration, interview, and musical effects. In this way, the creator of the film, instead of relying on his narrative ability and style, simply succeeds in startling the viewer.

The Fourth of August Celebration. Young women dressed as grape harvesters in a parade at the Panathenaic Stadium in Athens. Pageantry was an ideal vehicle for promoting allegiance among its participants. Photograph ©2006 by Benaki Museum Athens–Koula Pratsika Archives.

Dance in the Fourth of August Festivities: The Performance of Political Propaganda

The Fourth of August Ceremony was a public and mass event, the aesthetic presentation of which contributed to its transformation from an artistic event into an intensely political affair. The gaudy and flashy spectacular activities as they succeeded one another, a continuous mixing of classicism with romanticism, beauty with strength, discipline with youth, created a folk festival, a popular spectacle in which everything was interrupted to highlight the basic values of the regime which could lure the masses to confirm its acceptance. Using propagandistic slogans such as "a return to the genuine roots," "strengthen the bonds between society and the genuine Greek tradition," or "eschew foreign ideas." Xenophobia was encouraged and all that was Greek was lauded, and showed off as such. As a vehicle, the organizers highlighted certain moments in which the audience cheered the regime's achievements.

A further source of information on the Stadium festivities is the archive of Koula Pratsika, a choreographer and dance school director who was co-opted as coordinator for the dances and movements of all performers during the Stadium festivities. Of particular importance in this archive, which includes handouts with the printed programs of the festivities, photographs and notes, are some undated handwritten notes, which obviously concern the year 1937. They refer to that part of the program which she had been specifically invited to organize: the trumpet players, the Averof choral ensemble and the Riders of the Pontus, folk groups, the Parade of Old Men before the *Kalamatianos*, Chorus and Bands, the Lyceum Club of Greek Women and Anthem.

What struck me in these notes was the documentation of what seemed to me as a break between two concepts of tradition: regional and national. As far as dance is concerned this break was expressed in the channeling of folk ensembles into the performance of the Panhellenic dance, *Kalamatianos*, involving all the participants in the fête. This differentiation demanded special handling on the part of Pratsika, in terms of the groups' positioning in the arena of the Stadium. Between the two types of dance performance — of the local groups, and of the *kalamatianos*— was interpolated a dance of elderly men. I can only guess that the dance performed by the elderly must have been the *tsamikos*, since they wore the classic *fustanella*, thus laying stress on the stalwart veterans and bearers of tradition who embraced all that is genuine, spontaneous and true. Indicative are also the hand-written notes on the plan of the Panathenaic Stadium on which there are marked the places reserved for the various groups, or the place from which, in the form of a *tableau vivant*, individuals were to stand during the dance of the old men and from which they were to rush forth to take part in the general *kalamatianos*.

In the 1938 program, the main portion was devoted to the folk songs of Greece, performed by a choral ensemble under the direction of Simon Karras. Each song was accompanied by short notes informing the public of the name of the writer of the lyrics, the composer, the director of the orchestra and, whenever required, the name of the performers. The "profile" of the piece is complemented by simple bits of information: "Tsamikos, leaping dance" or by information regarding the rhythmic structure of the melody (i.e., choriambic ⅝ metre). Another novelty is that folk songs were now created by musically trained composers.[17]

Thus, in turn Wheat, the Olive, the Grape, Fruit, Tobacco, Forestry, Animal Husbandry, the Sea, or the Workers — especially the latter with a representative of specific groups among others: quarrymen, masons, electricians, carpenters, weavers, etc., appear in the program. Finally, in this endless parade

The Fourth of August Celebration. Local dancers were present in this spectacle as delegates and bearers of a transcendental Greek tradition and as the embodiment of cultural unity and continuity. Regional folk dance as a form of gymnastics, performed at the Panathenaic Stadium in Athens. Photograph ©2006 by Benaki Museum Athens–Koula Pratsika Archives.

the Greek Aviation Industry, Carpet-making, the Textile industry, Social Welfare and Athletes also take part. A prominent role is also played by the Greek Orthodox Church, represented by a group of priests, who entered the arena accompanied by a men's choir who chanted various ecclesiastical hymns. Particularly involved in this part of the proceedings seems to have been the Organisation of Youths, which in some ways seems to have been pulling the strings. Now the dances are Greek or national — not folk dances — and they are performed among the other choreographic creations executed by the women workers and the athletic exercises of the boys.

Throughout the material I studied — visual, textual, published and archival — what comes out in all cases despite the variation in the annual themes of the festivities and the techniques and of their realization is an attempt by the regime and its supporters to represent the idea of a unified nation headed by the dictator Metaxas, and thereby legitimize the dictatorship as a unifying force enjoying the spontaneous and massive support of the people from all Greek provinces. The idea of a temporal, transcendental

5. Dance as Propaganda

The Fourth of August Celebration. By transposing the village square to the stadium arena, the dancers transformed their dances from a *communal participatory performance* into a *spectacle*, thus opening the way to the folklorization of traditional dances. Young women from Corfu, scout carrying the sign. Photograph ©2006 by Benaki Museum Athens–Koula Pratsika Archives.

Greece permeates the thematic mosaic embodied by the massive numbers of performers ordered according to regional provenance, profession, age, sex, etc., in tune with the overarching theme of the festivity. These groupings were organized in the stadium arena in such a way as to demonstrate unity in diversity on the one hand and emphasize the massive support of the dictatorship on the other.

The commentary of the Press reveals that the delegates from the remote provinces of Greece who performed their local dances dressed in their regional festive costumes in front of thousands of spectators were not recruited to present the regional variation and richness of Greek Culture but rather to manifest the broad geographical representation of the regime's supporters. The role of the traditional circular dance in this context, especially the panhellenic *kalamatianos* dance, is to embody the Nation as the epitome of unity, and continuity, in other words as a visualization of the Third Civilization promoted by Metaxas. As the women dressed in ancient tunics at the tail of the dance, joined hands with the regional dancers, the group of the elderly, the

Fourth of August Celebration. Ioannis Metaxas. Photograph ©2006 by Benaki Museum Athens–Koula Pratsika Archives.

workers, the peasants and the young *Alkimoi* (a type of scout), who occupied the head of the circle, the bodies of the dancers were transformed into the constitutive parts of the Metaxas propaganda. As the dancers proceeded in the homogenized movement ordained by the *syrtos* (dragging, slow) steps of the *kalamatianos* dance they were thus transformed into an embodiment of the Nation throughout the centuries. This process of transformation had some unexpected implications that exceeded the here and now of the festivities, however: a fact which I will discuss in the following concluding section.

Conclusion: The Transformation of Traditional Dance from Local Performance to National Spectacle

The stadium celebrations of the Fourth of August represented an enormous mobilization on behalf of the fascist regime of Metaxas with the aim of demonstrating and further ensuring public consent and active support of the dictatorship and its policies. Whether the propaganda goals were achieved is an open question. What is more easy to demonstrate, however, are the consequences that the massive transportation of local dances from the village square to stadium arena had on regional festive practices and the nature of dance as a traditional performative event.

What happened in the Stadium in the four consecutive annual celebrations of the fourth of August was unprecedented, as far as regional dances and dancers were concerned. Traditional dances had never before been performed outside the borders of local communities for an urban, alien, and unfamiliar public. By transposing the village square to the stadium arena, the traveling dancers transformed their dances from a communal participatory performance into a spectacle, thus opening the way to the folklorization of traditional dances.

Local dancers were present in this spectacle as delegates and bearers of a transcendental Greek tradition, and embodiments of cultural unity and continuity. Moreover the journey itself may have led to the adoption of novel attitudes and reclassifications. Metaxas relied on other fascist models[18] to attract the people from the provinces into the Stadium and to obtain their consent to participate in the festivities, where he used tradition selectively and persistently as a vehicle by which to approach the "pure soul" of the people. How far the participating people realized the extent of their use as instruments of propaganda in the innocent guise of the display of local tradition is a matter of investigation, which transcends the scope of this paper, whose scope to interpret intentions and agency is limited by the extant material so far (press, visual imagery in the form of photos and film, archival material belonging to a key figure in the stage setting).

In this essay I have attempted to describe the way in which traditional dance becomes a constitutive element of nationalist propaganda and to discuss the consequences of this process, in terms of the creation of close bonds between dance and nation. Music and dance, especially folk dance, may constitute powerful vehicles for the effective exercise of power and propaganda.

Folk dance empowers the group to reach out towards a wide range of people and as a mechanism of conventions, bring together dominant forces that lend support to a national ideology and express a popular policy. Through the exploitation of these specific cultural symbols those who hold power may imbue the performative event-be it a fiesta, a spectacle or a common folk dance performance-with a strong and dynamic political character. "Viewed as a symbol and medium of power in politics, folk dance can denote a wide range of polysemy. Ideologically, it constitutes the link between the bearer's ideology (dictator) and its object (the crowd, the audience, the performers), politically, it is transformed into the seeking of the final target, socially it dis-

The Fourth of August Celebration. Performance of workers. An example of "marching festivities" taking place at the Panathenaic Stadium in Athens. Photograph ©2006 by Benaki Museum Athens–Koula Pratsika Archives.

tinguishes itself as a differentiating element between a particular social group, a part of which expresses itself through this symbol, and the others who, in accordance to their own ideology and beliefs, protest against having other symbols (Loutzaki 2001, 136).[19]

By dealing with questions of the way political leaders transform a folk practice into a political statement I focus in effect on the mechanisms of the production and reproduction of power and national identity. The Greek State had already used traditional cultural practices since the establishment of Greece in the context of a nationalist discourse promoting a sense of national identity based on the cultural continuity between Ancient and modern Greece. Dance had occupied a peripheral role in this discourse until the Stadium festivities of the 4th of August, where it was used to mobilize great numbers of people of different origins in their various roles as performers and audience of a major public spectacle for the representation of the Nation. Dance played a key role in the creation of a sense of national communitas by creating a hierarchy of identities where the fragmenting identities based on traditional social markers such as local origin, age, sex, and class were diminished in favor of a grandiose all-encompassing national identity.

The Fourth of August Celebration. The dictatorship's notion of community was symbolized showing the ornamentation of the masses, the costumes of the dancers and the choreographic patterns. Photograph ©2006 by Benaki Museum Athens–Koula Pratsika Archives.

The Fourth of August Celebration. As the dancers proceeded in the homogenized movement ordained by the *syrtos* (dragging, slow) steps of the *kalamatianos* dance they were thus transformed into an embodiment of the Nation throughout the centuries. Photograph ©2006 by Benaki Museum Athens–Koula Pratsika Archives.

Borrowing from sociologist George Simmel, I argue that these celebratory events are the "play-form" of politics because they use theatricality, a form of politics, to communicate political legitimacy, through political interventions in *local practice* such as dance performances, and these are transformed into *national performance*. From the time folk dances became part of the Fourth of August celebration, it gave bodily presence to ideologies of youth, and even a certain kind of Greek nationalism. At the same time, however, the process of "folklorization" of dance deployed cultural representations for a broad range of ideological ends.

Notes

1. Metaxas followed Mussolini's tradition (Third Roman Empire) and that of Hitler (Third Reich) and claimed a "Third Hellenic Civilization" that embraced the values and ideals of the ancient Greeks and of the Christian-Byzantine Empire.

2. Metaxas' belief in the importance of local communities and the role these could play as economic cells provided the inspiration for the most important novelty in the regime's socio-economic policy, a plan for decentralization to ensure the viability of the various communities spread in the Greek periphery (Sarantis 1993, 156).

3. The Panathenaic Stadium, with a seating capacity of 65,000 people, was renovated at the expense of the public benefactor G. Averoff, on plans designed by the architect A. Metaxas, in order to serve as the venue for the 1896 Olympic Games regeneration. From that time on, the Stadium has hosted national and international events, such as school gymnastics displays or official basket-ball tournaments. Besides athletic events, various artistic and cultural performances have had the Stadium as their venue, such as the *Anthesteria* (Flower Festival), in 1914, the *Festival of the Children's Happiness* in 1939, the festivals of the Metaxas period from 1937 to 1940, the corresponding spectacles known as the *Military Virtue of the Hellenes* of the Colonels' Junta from 1968 to 1973, the Song Festival, music concerts, as well as more recent events such as the official opening and closure ceremonies of athletic games such as the European Field and Track Championship in 1999 (Papanikolou-Kristensen 2003).

4. The Peloponnesus, a geographical department in the southern part of Greece, was the oldest part of modern Greece where in 1821 the struggle against the Ottoman rule began. Its main dance was a slow dance in ⅞ rhythm, called *syrtos* (or kalamatianos), that, with the rise of the War of Independence in 1821, emerged as a key symbol of Greece. Being disseminated through educational channels, *syrtos* on the one hand became *the* dance of pan-Hellenic validity, and on the other its long history, along with its manipulation by the state, contributed to a large extent to the aesthetization of the folk dance in Greece.

5. "This man was the one in power. He chose us one by one. In our group were only girls, however none of them came from the villages. We were all from the town of Mytilini. The only possible explanation I know is that the organizer knew our families, one by one, and even though many of them were not supporters of the regime, he relied on our family names" (a.m., personal communication, Lesvos, April 2002).

6. According to Turner, the concepts of "frame" and "framing" are used by anthropologists "to identify demarcated times and places for a particular use, such as ritual or play, by enclosing them literally or figuratively in a border (a temple, theater, playground, or court), and so creating a set of expectations about the kind of behavior or conduct that should fill the encased space-time" (1982, 28).

7. For a month (mid–June to mid–August) newspapers used phrases such as "the festive celebration of the commemoration of the 4th of August in the capital and the provincial towns"

5. Dance as Propaganda

(*Proia* newspaper, 1/8/37); "Yesterday's solemn commemoration of the 4th of August. The entire Greek Nation celebrated the event with unbridled enthusiasm and spontaneous manifestations. At the Panathenaic Stadium, among masses of people the Entire Tradition of the Race was triumphantly revived" (*Kathimerini* newspaper, 5/8/37).

8. As films of the period had no sound, music was added after the editing. Further, film quality affected the rapidity of motion on the screen, owing to the various fluctuations of speed.

9. My main source of information was derived from three major newspapers circulated in that period — *I Proia* (morning daily; editor S. I. Pesmazoglou), *I Kathimerini* (morning daily; editor G. A. Vlachos), and the *Eleftheron Vima* (morning daily; owned by D. Lambrakis; editor G. Syriotis) — and housed in the form of microfilm in the archives of the Laboratory of History, Department of Social Anthropology, Aegean University. The collection and the first classification of the material was carried out by Eleni Dounia, Ioannis Hassiotis and Michalis Mokas, respectively, as part of the seminar on *Dance and Politics* (summer semester 1998), under the guidance of I. Loutzaki.

10. Propagandist efforts of the 4th August began to increase towards the middle of July, when the first references to the forthcoming fête appeared, and reached a peak three or four days after the anniversary celebrations, at which time the main topic in the pages of all the newspapers was the enthusiastic response of the public and its "spontaneous" manifestations of delight and approval. A lull followed, a few days later, as the belated congratulatory telegrams of supporters came in and finally, like a distant echo, the noise died down, to begin again the following year.

11. Newspapers report during the preparatory period that "the transportation of the groups from the provinces will be offered by public subsidy of travel expenses. Tickets at special low prices for buses, trains and ships, will be available for all participants, while the members of large families will travel entirely free..." or "gifts of food and drink for the guests, distribution of free tickets to spectacles and athletic meetings..." Offers were also advertised by the hotels of Athens which, together with the schools and other public buildings, were to house the "participants from the ' provinces" or other guests. Finally, entrance to the historic Stadium also was free, as it was ceded free of charge by the Olympic Committee.

12. Apart from certain specific cases in which the regional costume was worn on a regular basis, from 1937 to 1940 traditional dress had adopted particular significance and symbolic function as it was mainly used as "theatrical costume" by most of its wearers (Loutzaki 1999, 225).

13. A caption of the newspaper *Hestia* of 4/8/1937 reads: "From yesterday's rehearsal. Maidens in classical Greek dress." The photograph portrayed girls dressed in long tunics and crowned with laurel wreaths. "Girls of the Lyceum club of Greek women, forming on the floor of the Stadium on the historic date of the 4th August" (*I Ethniki* newspaper, 5/8/37).

14. The *Ethniki Organosi Neolaias* (National Youth Organization, EON) was created at the end of 1936. The objectives of this organization were the union of the youth, regardless of their background, under a common set of values. These values included the love to the Fatherland, bravery, solidarity and a rock-solid belief in the "continuity of the holy Hellenic blood." The EON was successful in bringing together youths of all economic and social strata into one single body. Boys' education emphasized discipline and physical training while girls were taught to become supportive wives and caring mothers to breed a stronger, healthier new generation. The EON published a fortnightly magazine called *Neolaia* (Greek for "Youth"), which had much influence both in schoolhouses and in higher education.

15. A brochure had already circulated with a full-size photograph of Metaxas and the words of the *Hymn of the 4th August*, and thousands of copies had been distributed to the public. In the years that followed, other pamphlets were published containing songs, outstanding among which were the *Hymn of the 4th August*, the National Anthem, the Hymn to Labour and a series of selected traditional songs (K.P., personal archives).

16. The 1940 Fourth of August celebration was organized nine days before the sinking of "Elli" and it also preceded the declaration of war by Italy, on October 28.

17. A short footnote indicates that the above songs were registered by the choral ensem-

ble of the Society for the *Foundation for the Diffusion of Greek National Music*, under the direction of Simon Karas (see ODEON No.G.A.7133).

18. See festivals and celebrations, such as the *Kraft durch Freude* and *Musik und Tanz der Volker* (Berlin, August 1936), the *Internationales Volkstanztreffen* (Berlin, 1937), the *Fêtes de Folklore* (Menton, August 1938), or the *Festive Nuremberg* (Nuremberg 1936, 1937).

19. In the case of Metaxas, there are his supporters who sing the Hymn of the 4th August, who deck their balconies with flags and send letters of support, while, in the opposite camp, the songs that are sung are the banned *rebetika*, a certain number of folk songs, the writing of texts and letters that are distributed as propaganda resistance leaflets or published in the underground press (Holst-Warhaft 1998, 113).

Bibliography

Benjamin, Walter. 1973. "The Work of Art in the Age of Mechanical Reproduction." http://www.marxists.org/reference/subject/philosophy/works/ge/benjamin.htm. (accessed 15 October 2006)

Berezin, Mabel. 2005. "The Festival State: Celebration and Commemoration in Fascist Italy." *http://www.soc.cornell.edu/faculty/berezin/FestivalDictatorship-new21.pdf*. (accessed 16 June 2006)

Clogg, Richard. 1992. *A Concise History of Greece*. Cambridge: Cambridge University Press.

Danó, Orsolya, and Roubal, Petr, eds. 2001. *Bodies in Formation. Mass Gymnastics under Communism. Testformációk. Tömegjelenetek a kommunizmusból* [bilingual edition]. Budapest: Open Society Archives at Central European University. http://www.osa.ceu.hu/galeria/spartakiad/online/. (accessed 15 September 2006)

Dounia, Helen. 1999. "I Ghiortes tis 4 Avgoustou" [Fourth of August Celebrations]. Unpublished paper presented at the seminar titled "Dance and Politics" held at the Dept. of Social Anthropology (University of the Aegean).

Falasca-Zamponi, Simonetta. 1997. Fascist Spectacle: The Aesthetics of Power in Mussolini's Italy. Berkeley: University of California Press.

Giurchescu, Anca. 2001. "The Power of Dance and Its Social and Political Use." *Yearbook for Traditional Music* 33, 107–122.

Goodridge, Janet. 1999. *Rhythm and Timing of Movement in Performance*. London: Jessica Kingsley Publishers.

Hassiotis, Ioannis. 1999. "Xoros kai Politiki 1936–1940" [Dance and Politics 1936–1940]. Unpublished essay presented at the seminar titled "Dance and Politics" held at the Dept. of Social Anthropology (University of the Aegean).

Herzfeld, Michael. 2001. *Anthropology: Theoretical Practice in Culture and Society*. Malden, Mass.: Blackwell Publishing Limited.

Holst-Warhaft, Gail. 1998. "Rebetika: The Double-descended Deep Songs of Greece." In *The Passion of Music and Dance: Body Gender and Sexuality*, ed. William Washabaugh. Oxford: Berg, 111–126.

Ilieva, Anna. 2001. "Bulgarian Folk Dance during the Socialist Era, 1944–1989." *Yearbook for Traditional Music* 33, 123–126.

Kavouras, Pavlos. 1999. "To glendi" [*The merry-making*]. In *Mousika stavrodromia sto Aigaio. Lesvos (19th–20th c.)*, ed. Sotiris Chtouris. Athens: Ministry of the Aegean — University of the Aegean, 173–241.

Kordes, Gesa. 2002. "Darmstadt, Postwar Experimentation, and the West German Search for a New Musical Identity." In *Music & German National Identity*, ed. Celia Applegate and Pamela Potter. Chicago: University of Chicago Press.

Leach E. 1954. "Aesthetics." In *The Institutions of Primitive Society*, ed. E.E. Evans-Pritchard. Oxford: Clarendon.

Loukas, Ioannis. 1991. *Ethnososialismos kai Ellinismos* [Ethnosocialism and Hellenism]. Athina: Ekdoseis Grigori.
Loutzaki, Irene. 1999. "The Association as Milieu for Dance Activity." In *Music of Thrace. An Interdisciplinary Approach: Evros*. Athens: The Friends of Music-Research Programme "Thrace," 193–247.
_____. 2001. "Folk Dance in Political Rhythms." *Yearbook for Traditional Music* 33, 127–138.
Martinez, Iveris, Luz. 2002. "Danzas nacionalistas: The Representation of History through Folkloric Dance in Venezuela." *Critique of Anthropology* 22(3), 257–282.
Machaira, Heleni. 1987. *I Neolaia tis 4 Augoustou. Photographies* [La jeunesse du 4 Aout. Photo Ectitures]. Athens: I.A.E.N. Geniki Grammateia Neas Genias.
Mokas, Michael. 1999. "Xoros kai politiki" [Dance and Politics]. Unpublished essay presented at the seminar titled "Dance and Politics" held at the Department of Social Anthropology (University of the Aegean).
Ness, Sally. 1992. *Body, Movement, and Culture: Kinesthetic and Visual Symbolism in a Philippine Community*. Philadelphia: University of Pennsylvania Press.
Öztürkmen, Arzu. 2001. "Politics of National Dance in Turkey: A Historical Reappraisal." *Yearbook for Traditional Music* 33, 139–143.
Papanikolou-Kristensen, Aristea. 2003. *To Panathinaikon Stadion. I istoria tou mesa stous aiones* [The Panatheinaic Stadium. Its History through Centuries]. Athens: Ypourgeio Politismou-Geniki Grammateia Olympiakon Agonon — Istoriki kai Ethnologiki Etaireia tis Ellados.
Sarantis, Constantine. 1993. "The Ideology and Character of the Metaxas Regime." In *Aspects of Greece 1936–1940: The Metaxas Dictatorship*, ed. Robin Higham and Thanos Veremis. Athens: ELIAMEP — Vryonis Center, 147–169.
Shay, Anthony. 2002. *Choreographic Politics: State Folk Dance Companies, Representation and Power*. Middletown, CT: Wesleyan University Press.
Turner, Victor. 1982. "Introduction." In *Celebration: Studies in Festivity and Ritual*, ed. Victor Turner. Washington, DC: Smithsonian Institution Press, 11–30.
Wanner, Catherine. 1996. "Nationalism on Stage. Music and Change in Soviet Ukraine." In *Retuning Culture: Central and Eastern Europe*, ed. M. Slobin. London: Duke University Press, 36–155.
Woodhouse, C. M. 1991. *Modern Greece: A Short History*. London: Faber and Faber.

6

Nationalism and Scholarship in Transylvanian Ethnochoreology

Colin Quigley

The Study of traditional dance in Transylvania and throughout the Carpathian basin generally is among the most thorough in the field of ethnochoreology. It is also among the most troubled by a legacy of ethno-nationalist perspectives that persist despite the momentum towards a more unified post-national New Europe. The research of scholars and their theorization of traditional dance in Transylvania has been caught between competing nationalizing ideologies and institutions based in Budapest and Bucharest, respectively. Research design, practice, and publication from these two perspectives remain disjunctive, sometimes at odds, and inadequate to an understanding of the processes of identity configuration and representation occurring there today. Transylvania remains a contested terrain and its dances a domain of dispute.

Today the Transylvanian territory is shared by three major groups: Romanians, Hungarians and Roma. These identities have been both configured and contested in folklore performance, thus offering the opportunity to examine interethnic processes of exchange, differentiation, and representation, in relation to competing national ideologies. Discussion of national identity formations in folklore in general has examined single nationality contexts. The Transylvanian situation of two nation-states and three ethno-linguistic groups is both more complicated and more typical of the current destabilization of European identities.

This essay addresses the legacy of ethnochoreology in both Hungarian and Romanian scientific literatures. Perforce, I make reference to my own observations in the field. The bulk of my field research was conducted in central Transylvania over an 18 month period during 1997 and 1998. My work there, however, began in 1995 and continues to the present. I base my assessments of what the scientists have to say on this experience. Dance-folklore is a category of expressive behavior that not only serves to construct its object, but is itself constructed within ideological frameworks. By taking this view, I treat the work of scholars and other specialists as part of the discourses contributing to these formations. This is a reflexive perspective not much in evidence until very recently in research into the music and dance folklore of this region.[1] I also view the expressive behavior that is folklore, as performance (Schechner 2002). This notion of folklore performance encompasses both traditional vernacular practice embedded in the ongoing social life of communities as well as the wide variety of presentational transformations, some of which are referred to as folklorism, to which these are subject (Bendix 1988). These two closely intertwined phenomena, linked by processes such as the appropriation of folklore forms by elites and a consequent feedback that affects vernacular practice, need to be considered together in an examination of folklore performance ideologies.[2]

Folklore Performance in Romania

The manipulation of folklore by centralized state institutions was especially significant in Romania during its totalitarian socialist regime. Anca Giurchescu has written briefly about the national system of competition and folkloric display called *Cantarea Romaniei*. Paul Nixon wrote in more detail about the institutions of cultural management in Valea Giurgului (Giurchescu 1993; Nixon 1998). The results of this pervasive, coercive system of mandated folklorism permeated popular conceptions of folk music and dance, affected their vernacular practice, and imposed models for their presentation.

Since the collapse of this system in 1989, the struggle of what is generally called "transition" to more democratic political and free-market economic systems has had profound reverberations throughout society, including the domain of folklore and its performance. The opening of this formerly closed society has evoked a variety of responses. Some forms of folklore performance, cut off from their formerly state-infused meaning, have persisted through a kind of inertia. Many people expressed a kind of "allergy" to this folklorism and a radical rejection of anything remotely associated with it. A possible re-emergence, however, is now evident in the *Ethno* music-video channel that broadcasts old and new programs of the classic socialist type, featuring professional performers in idealized peasant costumes singing in pastoral settings synchronized with orchestral musical arrangements. These forms seem to hold appeal for an older generation, who sometimes express nostalgia for the certainties of the earlier time.

At the same time, new responses are taking shape. New patronage networks are emerging, among them the international Hungarian *tánchák* revival movement that has existed since the early 1980s, the more recently arrived world music industry, and the beginnings of cultural tourism (Buckley 1994). Identities that were formerly erased or repressed are seeking means of self-representation, namely among Roma peoples. Music/dance professionals are working to re-invent their repertoire recasting its presentation for the present circumstances, often in seemingly small ways but sometimes more dramatically.

Inter-Ethnic Relations in Transylvania

Why should national identity be so dominant a theme in Transylvania? Katherine Verdery goes a long way to answering this in the first of her many influential works of historically informed anthropology, *Transylvanian Villagers* (1983). She argues convincingly that in very broad terms, "Changing political and economic relations [in the 19th and 20th centuries] produced what became the paramount issue in Transylvania, namely differences in nationality" and goes on to examine this history as experienced in one village of mixed population (Verdery 1983, 19). In *The Remote Borderland* (2001), László Kürti has examined in more detail the important place of Transylvania in the national imaginary of intellectuals in Hungary, arguing that they located referents for their national identity constructions in this periphery, displacing them to a place where those at the centers of power did not have to confront the complex realities of life but were free to imagine them as they wished. Folklore was an important touchstone in this process, as of course it has been throughout the history of European nationalisms.

The Carpathian Basin region has been home to a multi-ethnic population of Magyars, Romanians, Roma, Germans, Jews, and other smaller minority groups. All have left their mark, of course, but apart from the three addressed here, the others are no longer actively contending within the public sphere. The sense of German ethnicity, while a strong presence in Transylvania, has had its own trajectory toward what Verdery calls "structural disintegration" (1983, 68,144, 348). Most Germans have now emigrated from Romania. The specter of the missing Jews haunts some parts of Transylvania, as elsewhere in Eastern Europe, but it plays little part in active public life today, although its absence, so to speak, is made apparent by outside interest, such as that emerging from the Klezmer music revival. Other international border-crossing groups who passed across this stage — Armenian, Greek, Wallachian — have left scattered monuments but no discernible cultural residue at stake today (Verdery 1983).

A striking example of the continuing debate over the ethnic and national character of musical and dance tradition in Transylvania is the recent publication of *Transylvania: Music, Ethnicities, Discord*, an issue of *European Meetings in Ethnomusicology* edited by Marin Marian Bălașa (2002). In it he offered colleagues from both countries and abroad a forum for discussion of the Hungarian-Romanian conflict in *ethnomusicology*. The contributions come from a wide variety of scholars and enthusiasts engaged with Transylvanian music. They reflect the multiplicity of contending viewpoints that continue to animate discussion of this issue.

Marin Marian-Bălașa and Zamfir Dejeu, the two Romanian contributors, can be seen as presenting positions situated in the almost inescapably nationalized context of Romanian/Hungarian scholarship (Dejeu 2002; Marian-Bălașa 2002). Bălașa reviews the *Musics and Musicologies of the Hungarian—Romanian Conflict* in the keynote article that opens the volume. He is particularly thorough in regard to Bartók (Marian-Balasa, 2002), whom, he concludes, was subject to nationalizing pressures but in the whole avoided succumbing to them. He holds up Bartók's disinterested "scientific" stance as a model to emulate. Dejeu is not concerned with the scholarship but rather the experience of inter-ethnic relations in daily life. He describes the similar living conditions and close relations of mutual assistance that often existed between Hungarian and Romanian peasants living cheek-by-jowl in the same or nearby communities and finds evidence for "borrowing," usually by Hungarian minority *from* the Romanian majority among whom they live. He advocates more detailed study of interethnic *exchange* in these terms.

Marian-Bălașa concludes the anthology with a rather harsh characterization of those researchers who did not respond as being fearful of consequences or unwilling to confront old prejudices, and faithful in obeying the state politically promoted trends for researching and explaining the facts (2002,165). László Kürti and Lynn Hooker, on the other hand, both trained in the states, offer more distanced perspectives that aim to transcend in some way the Hungarian-Romanian division (Hooker 2002; Kürti 2002). The trauma of totalitarian rule is still born by those who experienced it. The ethnomusicologist Radulescu has provided the best reflection upon this experience, but it is worth noting that she concludes with a warning to "western" scholars who had the luxury of relative intellectual freedom that our colleagues in the east will not be uncritical of the new perspectives we may offer.

My own experience of the peculiar situation that persists in dance research in particular is noted by Kürti: "Romanian scholars utilize a one-sided ethnographic map and Hungarian folklorists yet another. Hungarian ethnographers and folklorists speak of regions that are never uttered by Romanian scholars with such an awe and reverence (these are numerous: Kalotaszeg, Mezöseg, Gyimes, Háromszék, etc.). Clearly what is at the heart of this problem is that both Hungarian and Romanian intellectuals live and work in a dual positivistic tradition separated into majority and minority spheres" (Kürti 2002).

Istvan Pávai's 1993 article on interethnic relations in instrumental dance music offers the most detailed investigation into an aspect of interethnic folklore relations, despite its admittedly preliminary nature. He is writing as a Transylvanian Magyar now resettled in Hungary, and he is a prominent researcher and promoter of Transylvanian music, at the recently founded Hungarian Heritage House. He concludes that extensive sharing has rendered the repertoire of instrumental dance music in Transylvania so mixed as to defy easy distinctions or classifications along ethnic lines (Pávai 1993). This position runs counter to the strong pressure to construct differences in these terms.

To make his case, Pávai describes the complex patterns of language, religion, and declared ethnicity found among the Roma of Transylvania. This complexity alone makes it difficult to assign particular music to particular ethnic groups. He asserts that similar complexities can be found among the Bulgarians, Greek, Armenians, and Jews of Transylvania (p. 2). He notes that groups with more mobility, such as the Gypsies and Jews, generally identify with the more stabile ethnicities of Romanian, Hungarian, and, more so in former times, the Saxon, and that this complicates the interethnic musical relationships. But even this observation provides an inadequate account of the complex situation. Saxons coming from different locales, for example, settled in various parts of Romania at various historical periods, thus bringing different music/dance repertoires with them. Melodies and dances most likely introduced by Saxons have now been so assimilated by Romanian and Hungarian communities that they have lost their earlier ethnic association. And even the Romanian-Hungarian ethnic boundary is not inviolate. There are examples of communities in which ethnicity, language, and religion have undergone complex historical mixing that defies easy categorization. Moreover, he notes, music fashions spread quite widely throughout Europe without much regard for ethnic national boundaries. As elsewhere, melodies can be found that may be traced through manuscript evidence to much earlier times and more distant sites. The issue that remains *unexamined* by Pávai is that despite the thorough and pervasive mixing that he describes, the ethnic construction of music and its use to configure ethnicity, is ever present, and even his expert exposition is framed within the terms of these processes.

Dance tradition, I would argue, as practiced among different ethnic communities in central Transylvania is similarly mixed and difficult, if not impossible to disentangle. Ethnic distinctions that can be made and that are used to mark ethnic difference are usually only relevant in local contexts. This is particularly so in the Mezöség/Cămpie Transylvaniei central region. Perhaps because of this ambiguity, Csilla Könczei, found that regional differences in dance and music style may be seen in terms of ethnic national differentiation by the communities of practice themselves. Hungarians from both Kalotaszeg and Mezöség, for example, on hearing each other's music, described their regional differences as ethnic. That is, each thought the other's music was really Romanian (Könczei 2000)!

Romanian Ethnochoreology

Transylvania, burdened though it may be with a complex history of political control, is today part of Romania and was throughout the socialist period. Romanian state institutions largely controlled its cultural life during that period. The legacies of their policies persist and continue to exert a strong influence. Moreover the majority population in Transylvania is Romanian. Their folk performance traditions, however, are far from homogeneous among themselves or in comparison to those found among Romanians in other regions of the country. The persistent force of a Romanian national cultural ideology continues to construe this variety within a national narrative.

Folkloristic ethnology was, in its inception in European romanticism, a veritable science of the nation. This perspective lingered anachronistically in Eastern Europe, taking particular form in different states and nations. In Romania, we might quote Ion Vladutiu, who writes the following in the "Introduction" to his major work on Romanian ethnography [1973].

> We shall attempt to appreciate those aspects of life and culture which emphasize the strong originality and the extremely creative and fecund spirit of the Romanian people, his love for beauty, his permanent endeavor to make the work and the life more and more beautiful.... The popular Romanian creation transmitted itself

from generation to generation as accumulated life experience that reflected the aspirations, the hopes for a better life, and the struggle of our people for a better existence [7].

This perspective was particularly prominent in Romanian dance study. Indeed, one of the primary goals of Romanian dance scholarship was long a search to demonstrate a deeper unity amongst its great variety. We find Andrei Bucsan asserting, that Romanian choreographic folklore is

> unsurpassed in the *richness* and *variety* of its forms, its typological categories, morphological aspects and stylistic nuance. But, there is also a powerful *unity*, and *differentiation* in front of that of our neighbors, in consequence of which there is the precise and distinctive *specifically* national contour in the Romanian folk dance [emphasis in original]; that "reveals itself among the most authentic and valued creations of our spiritual culture, maintaining a uninterrupted chain of autochthonous tradition [1971, 85–86].

This kind of argument and language is part and parcel of the indigenist academic discourse analyzed by Verdery in her 1991 *National Ideology under Socialism* as arising in interwar Romania and resuscitated in the 1970s when "many ... disciplines found the Nation and its values a handy rhetorical arena for waging competitive struggles" (62–63). This was particularly the case for ethnography.

While this character of Romanian ethnology was noted by a number of Western researchers who worked there in the socialist period (Halpern and Kideckel 1983; Porter 1997), only now are a new generation of Romanian scholars engaged in a more thorough critique of the ethnological scientific discourse as a contributor to Romanian ethnonationalist identity, what Serban Vaetisi, a student who spoke at a small conference on post-socialist identity held at the Babes-Bolyai University in Cluj, has called a meta-ethnography of traditional Romanian ethnology (Vaetisi 2003).

In consequence, research attention to *inter-ethnic* phenomena in dance was underdeveloped in Romanian scholarship, a state of affairs that has continued up to the present. Even when interethnic processes have been addressed, they continue to be analyzed as if the ethnicities at stake were essential identities rather than historically configured and situationally deployed.

We can follow the trajectory of Romanian national ideology into the post-socialist environment in Verdery's 1993 paper on nationalism and national sentiment in post-socialist Romania. In this essay she argues that a variety of factors have overdetermined the "salience of national sentiment in Romania" today. The attitude toward Hungarians in Transylvania in particular, she argues, have "come to represent the loss of a feeling of wholeness.... The [so-called] 'Hungarian problem' symbolizes the fragmentation, the feeling of flying apart, of chaos and loss of control, that accompanies the only thing that held Romanians together: party rule and their opposition to it.... Anti-Hungarianism consolidates self and wholeness against the newly deepened fragmentation of social life, which is both a legacy of socialism and a product of the transition itself" (200).

This oppositional strategy extends into the domain of folk cultural contestation, in which national claims to "tradition" became so pervasive an issue. Why should Bălaşa have launched what he called his "bomb" with the special issue of EME on Hungarian-Romanian conflict at this time? In light of Verdery's observations it is clearer why Transylvanian folk performance remains a contested domain.

The Romanian scholar Anca Giurchescu, who emigrated to Denmark as a refugee in 1979, has since brought a new perspective to Romanian dance study. She is less concerned with demonstrating the '*unity*' of Romanian dance even in the compendium of her earlier scholarship (Giurchescu and Bloland 1995). This comprehensive study builds upon earlier Romanian research in ethnochoreology, but is less beholden to its rationales. This is therefore the most useful Romanian study that identifies and describes dance occasions, the form and structure of differing dance types, and dance dialect regions.

Her Central Transylvanian ethnochoreographic zone (which largely comprises the Mezoseg/Campie ethnographic region), she asserts, is itself "comprised of three distinct subzones which reflect the region's complex historical and cultural evolution and the consequent diversification of its basic dance categories.... The older strata of dances ... reveal a strong underlying unity throughout the zone." She adds: "There is a great deal of intermingling of Romanian and Hungarian dances belonging to the old style due to the coexistence of these communities in certain Transylvanian villages and the fact that the same musicians play for both groups" (275).

One can see here an effort to bridge the basic article of faith of Romanian scholarship, the distinctiveness and unity within diversity of Romanian dance, with a recognition of and greater acknowledgment of the ethnic intermingling characteristic of the whole Carpathian basin region. If the heat of the national rhetoric is toned-down and absent for much of the text, the whole project nevertheless remains predicated on a notion of Romanian dance the specific character of which is to be uncovered. The conclusions remain primarily concerned with an account of these characteristics. These are determined by "analyzing the features of dance types belonging to the old, indigenous cultural stratum and the relationships between those of different (sometimes widely separated) areas" (1995, 270).

The shift that is needed now, I propose, is to move from trying to characterize Romanian dance to examining how the characterization of Romanianness has been configured in folklore dance and how this identification is situationally deployed.

Hungarian Ethnochoreology

Hungarians have been a presence in Transylvania since the Magyar Conquest a thousand years ago. The contemporary Hungarian sense of "nationness" took shape in the late 19th century in the context of evolving Austro-Hungarian political relations and the emergence of national movements among the elite of minorities in the region (Lendvai 2003). Changing configurations of Hungarian state administration held sway in different parts of Transylvania from that time.

The Transylvanian Magyar sense of Hungarian belonging has itself been contingent and somewhat problematic. The representational uses of folklore, custom, music, and dance by Magyars in Transylvania today are thus inescapably suspended within the web of meaning created by this history of contingent relations.

Hungarian investigators have, of course, analyzed music/dance culture of Transylvania with emphasis on the Magyar population in great depth. Thanks to such extensive research and publication, many features of the music/dance tradition of Hungarians throughout the full extent of historical greater Hungary are now well established. Comparison of dance-specific criteria within the framework of established ethnographic zones has produced a detailed mapping of dance dialects, and Transylvania is home to many subdivisions (Felföldi and Pesovár 1997).

The broad Hungarian view of the interethnic dimensions of dance tradition is most completely summarized in Martin's *Hungarian and Romanian Dance Relations in European Context*. In the Hungarian scientific discourse the Carpathian basin is seen as a cultural area of mixed and interacting ethnicities with a largely shared music/dance culture, reflecting different historical layers, preserved among the different ethnicities in various degrees and configurations. In other words, researchers also have not much examined inter-ethnic processes of identity construction [with the exception of Kürti who has focused less and less on dance and music in his recent work]. A move that tends not to sufficiently acknowledge the continuing importance of these processes and the place of research within them.

There are also of course Transylvanian Magyar researchers who have contributed mightily to our knowledge of Transylvanian music/dance and its formulation and dissemination. Zoltán Kallós is prominent among them, but like many others in the more polarized context of majority-minority relations there, he often articulates a more partisan perspective — one that is more prominently manifest (in word and performance) in the presentational and participatory modes of music/dance revival.

It is this movement, so called, that has widely disseminated certain examples of the music/dance repertoire of Hungarians in Transylvania through the teaching of tánchaz revival practitioners. These have become familiar as a folkdance idiom worldwide wherever the "international folk dancing," in which Dick Crum was so involved, has reached. These standardized versions of dance cycles, promulgated by tánchaz teaching, are now popularly thought of as "the" dance of a named region, such as Szék, Kalotaszeg, Mezöség, Kisküküllö, Székelyföld, Gyimes. All of this study, concomitant objectification, ensemble adaptation, and revivalist dissemination has penetrated the awareness and profoundly affected the practice of traditional dance/music among the Magyars of Transylvania.

Occasions for traditional performance *outside* the influence of this cultural force field are not so common today. When I did at times encounter Hungarian practice that escaped enclosure in these boundaries, it seemed clear that without this discipline vernacular music/dance was a much more open system which had little place for its specialized self-consciously traditional repertoire.

The Roma

The Roma of Transylvania are a very diverse group. Some have been settled for generations; others remain relatively nomadic. Some are primarily Magyar speakers while others use Romanian and a large percentage, though not all, speak Romani at home, They engage in a wide variety of occupations that are traditional among extended families, including that of professional musician, or lăutar. Under the socialist regime they were not accorded the status of a national minority, rather they were viewed as a social class and subject to a policy of assimilation. This resulted in their residence in newly built apartment blocks, and their employment in factories of all kinds.

"Gypsy music" is an elusive category, and largely an exoteric one. In both Hungarian and Romanian specialist publications one can find this question discussed — what is Gypsy music and what is its relation to the music of their host societies? Sarosi, for example, has repeatedly been moved to address this topic (Sarosi 1986, 1997). He concludes that the folk music proper of

Gypsies living in Hungary is vocal and non-professional. A characteristic feature is the vocal imitation of instrumental figures and of a rhythmic accompaniment, both types of mouth music (Sarosi 1986). But this is so for only one group of Roma in the region. Rather than trying to isolate a Gypsy music, Katalin Kovalcsik (1996) examines the choice among minority identities that face Roma musicians in Hungary. In Romanian studies, Rădulescu's 2004 "Chats about Gypsy Music" is where one finds the question reframed and answered from a more processual perspective. She uses excerpts from conversations with Roma musicians about the music(s) they play to explore their varied and sometimes contradictory characterizations of "gypsy music."

The instrumental music of the Gypsy bands in Transylvania is a varied and completely mixed repertoire representing the tastes of their patrons, be they Romanian, Hungarian, Roma, or world music marketers. It is a repertoire of melodies and harmonic accompaniment enriched by its variety of sources and periods of changing musical fashion. Some melodies are of wide distribution and popular as accompaniment for the dancing of both Hungarians, Romanians, and Roma. Other pieces remain closely held in small localities, perhaps linked to particular dances (i.e., rhythms, not so common). Radalescu's recordings of the Ardeal Ensemble from Gherla, in central Transylvania, is perhaps the only single place to find this full range examined in its own terms, or at least in those of the musicians themselves (CD #006, *Gypsy Music from Transylvania* and #007, *Romanian and Hungarian Music from Central Transylvania*, Ethnophonie, Romania 2003).

The dancing of Gypsies in central Transylvania is part and parcel of the same idiom used by Magyars and Romanians, and Gypsies almost always dance the same repertoire as that of their host communities. As in their music making, a manner of performance that is generally characterized as freer and more ornamented may sometimes serve as a distinguishing feature. In addition to this shared repertoire, some groups danced an unconnected couple dance form to faster tempos that suggest Balkan parallels. This *cingoriță* or *cingorálás* is what has come to be seen as Gypsy dance in central Transylvania, and it is undergoing a moment of newfound prestige and popularity. *Cingoriță*, as yet, however, has donned this burden only in local contexts, where it now stands alongside the well-established Hungarian and Romanian stereotypes.

While still subject to pervasive discrimination Roma have achieved a much more visible official presence and acknowledgment. One effect has been the more prominent and acknowledged inclusion of Roma ensembles in public presentations (Giurchescu 1998). These ensembles are constructing a current representation of Gypsy-ness in dance, music, and costume. In central

Transylvania, with its large population of rural-dwelling Roma, this new distillation continues to reflect the dance idiom of the Hungarians and Romanians among whom they live, but features the *cingorálás* or *cingortiă* form. The dance has steadily become more popular among young people of all ethnicities, for whom it provides some continuity with tradition while challenging its conservatism. It is also finding its way into Hungarian táncház dancing, where it seems part of the broader western "world music" fashion for things Roma. It is occasionally seen in Romanian groups now as well, brought there by the Gypsy dancers who have been given a place in these presentations.

Other dance idioms compete with this for pride of place as a Roma representation. *Mahala*, danced to the music identified with the city outskirts as once played by the professional *lăutari*, can be encountered. It is more solo in character and dancers employ more of the hip and shoulder isolations. More likely to be presented as Roma than *mahala*, however, is an exaggerated form danced by the girls and young women using "Turkish" stereotypes clearly suggestive of "belly dance." This form of dance asserts an "easternness," a key link in the emerging national narrative of a pan-European Roma identity. The results of ideologically potent research into the Romani language and the history of Roma peoples are clearly present here in a way that echoes the most heavily manipulated of the Hungarian and Romanian dance representations. Roma dance scholarship in Transylvania is so slight as to not have had much impact on either vernacular or presentational dancing.

Conclusion

Hungarian and Romanian scholarship is clearly moving out of the confines of ethno-nationalist discourse and some critique and revision of previous work have been undertaken. But, more importantly perhaps, new research questions are driving new research perspectives. In Hungary ethnochoreology is well established and institutionalized in the Dance section [Tanc Osztaly] of the Music Research Institute [Zene Tudomanyi Intezet] of the Hungarian Academy of Sciences [Magyar Tudomanyos Akademia]. They have begun a new initiative aimed at analyzing creative processes in the dance idioms of the Carpathian Basin by focusing on the "dancing-personality." With their large archive of data they are in an enviable position to do this. The Romanian Folklore and Ethnololgy Institute, home to the extensive work of the previous generation of scholars, has been poorly funded since 1989 and is unable to capitalize upon this rich resource. The Museum of the Romanian Peasant which has to some extent taken over the role of leading folklore research institution, does not have a full-time dance specialist on staff, and dance has, until now at least, taken a back seat to material culture and music research and exhibition. Both countries, blessed with such rich archival resources and continuing vitality of folkore-dance practice, offer fertile ground for a future generation.

Notes

1. While related to Moser's classic concept of Rucklauf (Moser 1962), which identifies the influence of specialist studies on tradition bearers' conscious knowledge (Bendix 1988, 12), the notion of folklore-folklorism relationship I propose goes further, I think, to view both as constitutive of the same discursive frame.

2. German folklorists developed the term "folklorism" in the 1960s (Moser 1962). It was subsequently explored in relation to eastern European contexts, in which the state was explicitly involved in these cultural domains. Investigations by Hungarian folklorists—in particular Vilmos Voight who is probably the most prolific writer on folklorism (Bendix 1988, 10)—provide background important for understanding the current situation in Transylvania.

Bibliography

Bendix, R. 1988. "Folklorism: The Challenge of a Concept." *International Folklore Review* 6, 5–15.

Buckley, A. 1994. "Professional Musicians, Dancing, and Patronage: Continuity and Change in a Transylvanian Valley." *The World of Music* 36, 31–48.

Bucsan, A. 1971. *Specificul Dansului Popular Romanesc.* Bucharest: Academiei Republicii Socialiste Romana.

Dejeu, Z. 2002. "Cultural Connections within Traditional Music and Dance in Transylvania." *European Meetings in Ethnomusicology* 9, 114–148.

Felföldi, L., and E. Pesovár, ed. 1997. *A magyar nép és nemzetiségeinek tánchagyomanya. Jelenlévœ Múlt.* Budapest: Planetás Kiadó.

Giurchescu, A. 1993. "Folklore in the Service of the State Ideology, Romania: A Case Study." *Symposium on the Balkans: Folklore and National Symbols.* Institute for European Studies, Cornell University, 1993.

———. 1998. "Gypsy Dance Style as a marker of Ethnic Identity." In *Dance, Style, Youth, Identities,* ed. T. B. a. G. Gore, Straznice, Czech Republic: Institute for Folk Culture; international Council for Traditional Music, 80–87.

Giurchescu, A., and S. Bloland. 1995. *Romanian Traditional Dance: A Contextual and Structural Approach.* Mill Valley, CA: Wild Flower Press.

Halpern, J. M., and D. A. Kideckel. 1983. "Anthropology in Eastern Europe." *Annual Review of Anthropology* 12.

Hooker, L. 2002. "Transylvania and the Politics of Musical Imagination." *European Meetings in Ethnomusicology* 9, 45–76

Kovalcsik, K. 1996. "Roma or Boyash Identity? The music of 'Ard'elan' Boyashes in Hungary." *The World of Music* 39, 77–93.

Könczei, C. 2000. "Traditional Music in Communist and Post-Communist Romania: Beyond the Battlefield of Representations." *Musiques orales et migrations musicales. Questions esthetiques, questions ethiques, Abbazes de Rozaumont, France, 2000.*

Kürti, L. 2002. "Ethnomusicology, Folk Tradition, and Responsibility: Romanian-Hungarian Intellectual Perspectives. *European Meetings in Ethnomusicology* 9, 77–97.
Lendvai, P. 2003. *The Hungarians: A Thousand Years of Victory in Defeat.* Princeton, NJ: Princeton University Press.
Marian-Bălaşa, M. 2002, "Musics and Musicologies of the 'Hungarian-Romanian conflict.'" *European Meetings in Ethnomusicology.* 9, 4–44.
Moser, H. 1962. "Vom Folklorismus in unserer Zeit." *Zeitschrift für Volkskunde* 58, 177–209.
Nixon, P. 1998. *Sociality—Music—Dance.* Vol. 34. *Skrifter fran Institutionen for musikvetenskap.* Goteborg, Sweden: Goteborgs universitet.
Pávai, I. 1993. "Interetnikus Kapcsolatok as Erdelyi Nepi Tanczeneben" [Interethnic Relations in the Folk Dance Music of Transylvania]. *Neprajzi latohatar* 4, 1–20.
Porter, J., ed. 1997. *Folklore and Traditional Music in the Former Soviet Union and Eastern Europe.* Los Angeles: Department of Ethnomusicology, University of California.
Sarosi, B. 1986. *Folk Music: Hungarian Folk Musical Idiom.* Budapest: Corvina.
_____. 1997. "Hungarian Gypsy Music: Whose Heritage?" *The Hungarian Quarterly* 38, 133–139.
Schechner, R. 2002. *Performance Studies: An Introduction.* New York: Routledge.
Vaetisi, S. 2003. "Ethnonationalist Identity in New Europe: The Romanina Culture Case. A Critical Essay on Ethno-folkloric Traditionalist Discourse." Cluj Conference on Negotiating Identities, Cluj, Romania, 2003.
Verdery, K. 1983. *Transylvanian Villagers: Three Centuries of Political, Economic, and Ethnic Change.* Berkeley: University of California Press.
_____. 1991. *National Ideology under Socialism: Identity and Cultural Politics in Ceausescu's Romania. Societies and Culture in East-Centeral Europe.* Berkeley: University of California Press.
_____. 1993. *Nationalism and National Sentiment in Post-socialist Romania. Global Forum Series, Occasioanl Paper no. 93-1.3. Third in a series on Nationalism, National Identity and Interethnic Identity.* Durham: Center for International Studies, Duke University.
Vladutiu, I. 1973. *Etnografia romaneasca.* Bucharest: Stiintifica.

7

Bulgarian Dance Culture: From Censorship to Chalga

ERICA NIELSEN

Cultural borrowing is not a new phenomenon. However, largely because of new technologies facilitating knowledge transfer, globalization is a major concern in academia today. In fact, most people involved in academia within the past decade are more than familiar with the following debate — will the world become increasingly homogeneous, or will each society retain its cultural uniqueness? Or more bluntly — is globalization a good thing? Is an influx of external cultural stimuli sabotaging Bulgarians' sense of national identity? Is this why Bulgarians' interest in *folklor i folklorni tanĉi*, the official version of folklore and folk dance supported and carefully monitored by the Bulgarian Communist Party (BCP) from 1950 to 1989, has declined?

Dance is a dynamic bodily discourse that reflects and represents society and culture. As a representational medium, it holds the power to influence perceptions and to either uphold or challenge cultural truths. The manipulation of dance under the pretense of nationalism, as in the case of state-sponsored folk song and dance ensembles, has identifiable social and political implications. National folk ensembles are often viewed as "true" or "authentic" representatives of their nation's people and culture. However, a closer investigation of Bulgarian folk ensembles, and the political and social atmosphere during their peak era from the early 1950s to late 1980s, reveals that they were perhaps more accurate in representing their sponsor, the BCP.

Opening a discussion about "Bulgarian dance" among Bulgarians generally leads to reflections on national pride, connection to the past, intricate folk costumes, unique folk instruments, complicated rhythms, and highly trained professional folk dancers. However, only a small percentage of Bulgaria's population actually pursues a career in folk dance. Those who do not spend years training in *folklor i folklorni tanĉi* often feel apprehensive when asked about how and when *they* dance. When something becomes a recognized profession, especially with a long history and expansive body of research to support it, its corresponding essence in people's daily lives often seems less important.

This apprehension to deal with dance in all contexts, including non-professional dance in daily life, was one of the challenges I faced while conducting fieldwork with my research collaborator Veselin Atanasov.[1] Although many informants were initially confused about why we were interviewing them — for wouldn't it make more sense to speak with an artistic director or professional dancer?— many eventually opened up and revealed that Bulgarian dance culture is not limited to professional folk dance. In fact, Bulgarian dance culture is a matrix that includes all dances in all contexts, collectively practiced by (or at least known to) Bulgarians. And although we would not know it from most Bulgarian souvenir shops or tourism websites — which makes us think that Bulgaria is a country where girls always sing in *a cappella* dissonance and meet boys in the village square to dance elaborate sequences which they instinctually know by birthright — there are some very sexy dance improvisations going on within today's mainstream music scene.

Dance cultural knowledge is organized schematically; that is, some dance forms are viewed as superior to others, just as there are proper and improper ways to perform most dances. This is related to cultural perceptions of aesthetics. Perhaps the most notable example in Western dance culture is classical ballet, which is often viewed as superior to other dance forms with its "high art" reputation and its physical requirements that are nearly impossible to achieve except by the less-than-one-percent blessed with the "balletbody." Just as classical ballet is presently reputed for its tastefulness and morality, and celebrated as one of the greatest artistic assets of Western European and American culture, Bulgarian *folklor i folklorni tanĉi* is thought to embody the true essence of Bulgarianness.

The decline of *folklor i folklorni tanĉi* after 1989, combined with the exponential growth of the pub-sprung, controversial music genres *chalga* and *pop folk*, is propelling many Bulgarians to a state of despair concerning the preservation of their cultural heritage and national identity. Whereas *folklore i folk tanĉi* is believed to promote good family values, modesty, proper social behavior, and national pride, *chalga* and *pop folk* are known for instigating abusive behavior and advertising sex through explicit lyrics and siliconed "role models" in music videos. This is not to say that all Bulgarians crudely dismiss *chalga* and *pop folk;* for if this were the case, most discos and at least two major television stations would be out of business.

Dance culture is dynamic and contingent; trends come and go, but always reflect the society of a given time period. We often hear that in this era of downloading, the amount of cross-cultural exchange is greater. *Chalga* and *pop folk* exemplify cultural borrowing through their mélange of Serbian, Greek, Bulgarian, Gypsy, Turkish, Arab, and American instruments, rhythms, and melodies. The improvised dance called *kuchek* which accompanies *chalga* and *pop folk* is also a combination of belly-dance styles. In addition, hip-hop moves sometimes make their way into *chalga* and *pop folk* music videos and onto dance floors.

As long as societies have valued their traditions, there has been concern about preserving them for future generations. The 21st century tug-of-war to preserve Bulgarian folklore in the face of an increasingly untraditional Bulgarian presence in pop culture is just one chapter of a larger story. The story actually begins in the 19th century, when a national revival in Bulgarian culture ignited within a weakening Ottoman Empire. This movement, led by members of Bulgaria's *intelligentsia,* began in the 1840s with the standardization of the Bulgarian language and spread of public education to teach Bulgarians about their own people and history. After the liberation of Bulgaria by Russia in 1878, Western European influences quickly swept into the region. Europeanization enabled Bulgarian women to hold new professions, raised the marriage age, reduced the birthrate, and introduced the idea of a companionate marriage. It influenced architecture, culinary practices, mannerisms, and the arts. Fearful that Bulgarians would lose touch with the knowledge and traits that bonded them together as a modern nation, the *intelligentsia* sponsored ethnographic projects and formal instruction in folklore.

Bulgarian folklorist Todor Zhivkov defines *folklore* as the artistic and creative traditions associated with the agrarian era of a society; these traditions include songs, dances, embroidery, stone work, wood-carving, bread designs, and oral traditions such as popular tales and proverbs (2006). This is what the Bulgarian *intelligentsia* intended to capture: the "old" ways of life in rural communities before they disappeared. In the mid–19th century, ethnographer brothers Dimitar and Kostadin Miladinov traveled throughout the country in an attempt to describe and regionally categorize customs and traditions. The Miladinovs published a significant collection entitled *Bulgarian Folk Songs* in 1861. In 1889, the expansive *Collection of Folklore and Ethnography*, now published in over 60 volumes, was founded by scholar Ivan D. Shishmanov. The documentation of folklore, including thousands of folk songs and their scores, was collected through the 1930s in the work of Raina Katsarova and others. Bulgarian ethnographers were not alone in their quest to preserve the rich cultural heritage of their people, especially in the field of music. Many foreign scholars and hobbyists like Yves Moreau routinely visited Bulgaria to record and document songs and dances; such collections can be found in most U.S. libraries and international folk dance archives today.

Most research on Bulgarian folklore has been conducted for the purpose of archival preservation and physical re-creation, but little attention has been paid to situating traditions in larger contexts. This oversight follows the trend in folklore scholarship from the 1800s and early 1900s, and most of 20th-century dance scholarship. Books about folk music and folk dance often appear as step-by-step maunals or cookbooks, since musical notation and Labanotation, among other notation forms, have facilitated the pure documentation of sound and movement devoid of context.

Bulgarian folklore scholarship tends to reflect common devolutionary perceptions about folklore: it either exists in the past, or presently in remote villages where elderly people still remember customs from the past. During my trips to Bulgaria, I was told that if I wanted to see authentic folklore, I had to visit small mountain villages where people still washed clothes by hand, traveled by horsecart, and raised their own animals. Western travel documentaries like Rick Steves' *Eastern Europe* cater to such nonthreateningly quaint characteristics of the country.

Oftentimes, there is a great deal of denial that folklore belongs to city folk, for it is assumed that once people become industrialized they lose touch with folklore in their everyday life. However, what most Bulgarians mean by folklore today is different than what ethnographers sought one century ago. Dance researcher Anna Ilieva concurs that ethnographers originally studied folklore as "knowledge of the people." Then, at the end of the 19th century and beginning in the 20th century, the term "folklore" gained aesthetic repute when standardized folk music using western classical music theories and techniques emerged in choirs, community chorales, military wind bands, and conservatories. Western European influences in music not only promoted Bulgaria as a "modernized" nation, but also appealed to tourists and international audiences who enjoyed the unique Bulgarian sound that was based on western aesthetics.

The shaping of folklore into a professional art genre intensified in the 1940s with the spread of national arts activities sponsored by the BCP. Since city dwellers were thought to be immune to folklore, the national arts activities brought them back to their roots and were supposed to inspire nationalistic pride. Community culture centers were established in the most remote locations of Bulgaria — even in the small mountain villages — to unite the Bulgarian people by encouraging their involvement in organized folk music and folk dance. These organized activities stripped folk customs of much of their original "in the field" context. Communism promoted industrialization and denounced religious practices, as well as anything else that did not uphold the socialist cause. Since folk traditions were originally tied to agrarian ways of life and Christian Orthodox religious customs, they declined in the field but were reborn in a new context through the national arts activities.

The first professional Bulgarian national folk music and dance ensemble founded by artistic director Philip Koutev in 1951 marked the end of folklore as common knowledge of the people. From this point on, in addition to considering folklore as something that existed in the past, it also became something performed onstage by professionals who studied music, dance, and ethnography (the regional distinctions of folk traditions) at state choreography high schools and the Academy for the Arts in Plovdiv. This dualistic notion of folklore, with its suggested continuity between spontaneous traditions in the past and structured art in the present, led to a misperception that what happened onstage was a replication of pre-industrialized times. The proscenium stage became a portal to the past, to a time where life was simpler and peasants were happy, skillful, hardworking, and held the key to natural wisdom that has since been forgotten by today's corrupt, materialistic society.

In everyday conversation in contemporary Bulgaria, the term "folklore" usually implies highly stylized folk song and dance performance evoking nationalistic sentiments among performers and spectators alike. Bulgaria's 20th-century folk ensembles were based on the model established by the former USSR's Igor Moiseyev's Dance Company, founded in 1934. The Moiseyev Dance Company depicted the former USSR through song and dance compositions containing carefully selected regional elements, but ultimately it attempted to show that all regions were happily united under a pro-Russian communist culture. The Moiseyev repertoire during communism emphasized social sameness — an important Soviet ideology — through elaborate matching costumes designed to imitate and glorify the traditional wear of each region, and intricate choreography performed in unison that was meant to show off the skillfulness and high morale of the Soviet people. Classical ballet technique and choreographic theories were implemented as a foundation for transforming dances in the field to their second existence onstage, similar to how western classical music influenced professional folk music.

The Moiseyev Dance Company encountered profound success within the USSR and abroad, and directly or indirectly inspired the creation of countless national folk music and dance ensembles around the world. It is believed that Philip Koutev decided to create a professional Bulgarian folk ensemble after seeing a former USSR ensemble based on the Moiseyev model. The Philip Koutev Ensemble attempted to represent Bulgaria's six ethnographic regions: North Bulgaria, Dobruja, Thrace, Rhodope, Shope, and Pirin. An all-male orchestra played the most traditional Bulgarian melodies and instruments—*kaval, gadulka, tambura, gaida,* and *tupan*—and variations of these instruments commissioned by Philip Koutev to expand the range of the instrumental spectrum. A female folk choir trained in a unique style called the "Bulgarian voice" developed by Philip Koutev in the 1950s (but typically perceived as ancient) accompanied the orchestra. Dozens of male and female folk dancers, trained in classical ballet and highly stylized Bulgarian folk dance, held hands and weaved in kaleidoscopic patterns with highly coordinated, virtuosic footwork. Over the next decades, the creation of more ensembles fostered friendly competition to be the best and rhythms and steps became even more complex, further distancing professionalized folklore from its origin in the field. By the 1980s, there were over a dozen professional national folk music and dance ensembles and hundreds of local amateur groups.

The mass appeal of the newly developed professional *folklor i folklorni tanči,* combined with the decline of religious folk traditions in people's daily lives, encouraged a new way of thinking about folklore in the 20th century. The folklore did not come instinctually from the people, as it was perceived during Bulgaria's 19th-century National Revival. It became a spectacle that showed off a romanticized past and encouraged Bulgarians to think, "This is how we used to celebrate; this is how we used to dance."

Under communism, folk music and folk dance were reinvented in a way that vaguely resembled the forms "in the field" they claimed to imitate. Hobsbawm and Ranger describe this type of creation, in which repetition certifies continuity with the past and authenticity, as an "invented tradition" (1992). Bulgaria's folk ensembles, with their virtuosic choreography, have been advertised as authentic for over fifty years. Since they hardly changed, preserved by the strict rules of communist censorship over the arts, they undoubtedly advocated the myth that folklore resists change. Modifications made to artistically "enhance" professional folk music and folk dance such as the implementation of western classical theories as techniques were not formally acknowledged. This gave the impression that the professional folk music, based on the philharmonic scale and performed by classically trained musicians, developed directly from pure Bulgarian influences and was unquestionably rooted in the distant past. The same could be said about professional folk dance, which was performed by dancers who warmed up with *pliés* at

Peter Petrov and dance group. Kodiak, Alaska. Photograph by Erica Neilsen.

the *barre*, and were required to learn the "folk dance" standing positions that strikingly resemble first through fifth in ballet.

Professional folk music and folk dance were the most mainstream components of Bulgarian dance culture from the 1950s through the late 1980s, mainly for three reasons. First, communist censorship over the arts suppressed the creation or practice of anything that did not follow the Stalinist formula: national in form, socialist in content. Every composer had to submit his work to a special committee to determine whether it was nationalist and socialist enough to be published. Second, the Bulgarian Communists Party's implicit ban on religion led to a decline in religious practices, and folk dances in the field were part of such customs. Third, the spread of amateur art activities made standardized folk music and folk dance available for free to everyone, so nearly everyone was able to relate to, and had a similar idea about, the new kind of folklore.

After the BCP relinquished power in 1989, funding to the arts was severely cut and most of the ensembles were dissolved. Today, the few remaining ensembles rely on lesson fees, private donations, and ticket sales for subsistence. In the past, lessons were free and professional dancers and musicians were paid equally well as doctors and lawyers. This is no longer the case. Today, the number of young people pursuing a career in folk music or folk dance is diminishing, and professional folklore has fallen from its dominant place in Bulgarian dance culture. Instead, *chalga* and *pop folk* saturate the airwaves.

Chalga and *pop folk* reflect contemporary Bulgarian culture, but paradoxically, they are also blamed for making young people lose touch with their cultural heritage. To understand why *chalga* and *pop folk* are upsetting so many people, we must consider what came before: a dance culture that celebrated the quintessential National Revival Bulgarian. This thick-skinned Bulgarian was proud, modest, worked for the welfare of the community, and was not distracted by religion or sex. Men and women were able to work the same jobs, and although most 19th-century vocational folk songs were about men, the 20th century saw a rise in songs about working women. The lightskinned Bulgarian speaker was a pure national model, untainted by Ottoman or Gypsy[2] influence.

In the amateur arts activities and professional ensembles, there were no references to Turks or Gypsies — the two largest minority groups (and most vulnerable to discrimination) in Bulgaria. Although Turkish instruments like the *oud* and Gypsy violins had been components of 19th-and early 20th-century Bulgarian folk music in the field, these elements were eliminated from professional training and venues. Dark-skinned Gypsy soloists were almost always hired to play at village celebrations until the late 19th century, but then they were replaced by professionally trained light-skinned Bulgarians of Slavic origin. The professional folk music and dance ensembles never included dark-skinned Gypsies, but on the other hand, the Gypsy groups had their own songs and dances and generally did not aspire to assimilate to the Bulgarian ethnos.

The BCP tried several times to force cultural assimilation upon the Gypsies by imposing Bulgarian names, building new neighborhoods for them in major towns and cities, and Bulgarizing their children through formal education. But Gypsy lifestyle was a far stretch from more Slavic ways, and the efforts to Bulgarize Gypsies did not result in assimilation as the BCP intended, but instead in their adaptation of traditional ways to new circumstances. For example, many Gypsies preferred not to live in their government-granted apartments, but to instead dismantle them to sell the parts.

In addition to Gypsies, the BCP also pushed to Bulgarize Turkish groups, which included Turkish immigrants from Turkey, Turkish-speaking Christian Bulgarians called *Gagauzi*, and Turkish-speaking Muslim Bulgarians labeled as *Pomak* in vernacular, or formally known as *Bulgaro-mohamedani*. The BCP's policy on Bulgarization was especially aimed at the groups of supposed "pure" Bulgarian origin, which were thought to have been forcibly converted to Islam during the Ottoman Empire. The BCP's goal was to de-islamify these people and to reclaim them as Bulgarians, so Islam was denounced (like all other religions), Turkish newspapers and speaking Turkish in public were forbidden, Turkish names were Bulgarized, and history textbooks were rewritten to avoid the words "Turkish" and "Turk." Although some Turks did attempt to assimilate, it was a modest win for the BCP considering the thousands of emigrants who showed up at the Bulgarian-Turkish border virtually overnight, straining Bulgaria's relationship with its neighbor.

In the mid–1980s, the BCP, like other communist governments, was beginning to lose ground as the gap widened increasingly between the people's lived reality and the communist ideals they had expected to achieve. The southeastern corner of Bulgaria was saturated with increasingly discontented Turkish people, and the BCP feared they would secede and form their own republic, just as the Cypriot Turks had done a decade earlier. So the BCP sought to keep the country united, and to reinforce its own ideologies, by promoting social sameness through stronger efforts to Bulgarize the Turks. This time, though, it was met with greater resistance than ever, and in 1984 bombs were set off by a Turkish resistance group in an airport and in a train station.

During communism, minority voices, religion, and sexuality were suppressed by the ideologies of BCP. This repression was reflected in the mainstream art of the time, which advocated that all citizens were the same: all were happy, hard-working, light-skinned, Bulgarian-speaking communists. They shared a past corrupted by Turks, and their present was polluted by Gypsies and the remnants of the Ottoman Empire. For this reason, Turkish and Gypsy cultural influences were excluded from Bulgaria's national arts. The only cultural diversity portrayed through the national arts was among Bulgaria's six ethnographic regions, and each of these was equally celebrated for its uniqueness within a spectrum of pure Bulgarianness.

After democracy began in 1989, *chalga* enabled Gypsy and Turkish singers a voice in mainstream Bulgarian culture, and it thereby challenged the homogeneous pro-Slavic identity which had dominated the stages and airways during communism. The term *chalga* is derived from the Turkish *çalgï* which refers to "music" or "musical instrument." *Chalga* developed underground in Bulgaria's pubs in the 1980s, but its source of inspiration is actually the *chalgazhia* musicians, usually Gypsy, who played for festivals and weddings. *Chalga* gained mainstream attention in the early 1990s with the emergence of an MTV-like culture in Bulgaria. *Chalga* singers popped up left and right, from all ethnic groups and both genders, competing for attention in what many Bulgarians perceived as a shocking display of vulgarity and sexuality. Their visual appeal was based on hyper-sexuality with little clothing, curves in all the right places, and heavy make-up. Lyrics were shallow, and careers were short-lived. But for the first decade of *chalga,* the "boob tube" lived up to its name like never before.

Around the late 1990s, after the initial *chalga* shock wore off, a new genre called *pop folk* emerged in response to a growing demand for better music, without so much cursing and explicit sexual references. Some Bulgarians consider *chalga* and *pop folk* as separate genres, whereas others believe they are one and the same. The physical appearance of most *pop folk* singers is almost identical to *chalga* singers, and music videos for both genres emphasize sexuality; more conservative viewers might even label them as "soft porn." However, *pop folk* lyrics are considered more complex and deep than *chalga* lyrics, and usually refer to love and relationships. *Chalga* songs generally employ more Gypsy instruments, staccato beats, and scat-like refrains. Although some pop singers are classified with one genre, *chalga* or *pop folk,* others transcend strict categorization with a wide variety of songs. Today, many Bulgarians acknowledge that *chalga* is toning down and merging with *pop folk,* making it even more difficult to classify singers.

Bulgarian *kuchek* and (less frequently) western hip-hop moves accompany both *chalga* and *pop folk* songs in discos and on music videos, with the excep-

Nightclub dancing to *chalga* music. Photograph by Erica Neilsen.

tion of *pop folk* ballads which generally substitute exaggerated gestures for more obvious dance moves. Two of the most popular scenarios in Bulgarian *chalga* and *pop folk* music videos are stories about relationships (both hooking up and breaking up), and references to parties and sex without any particular story. Common settings include mansion homes and fancy cars (to demonstrate wealth), cafés (good for meeting people), beaches and pools (good for showing off skin), and nightclubs (good for demonstrating wealth, meeting people, and showing off skin). There are also vague but interesting locations, like a room filled with glittering streamers, inside a glass elevator, or a staircase lined with masked men. Normally the setting changes every three to five seconds, and there are four or more different settings per video. Alternating between settings allows the video producers to blend spectacle with story-telling.

The production of *chalga* and *pop folk* videos is a huge industry which has developed considerably since the early 1990s. The original *chalga* videos were low-budget, and were more concerned with showing blatant sexuality than with story-telling and well-thought artistry. As *chalga* gained popularity, the producers of Bulgaria's main music video station called *Planeta* were accused of making young people crazy. Violent outbursts that erupted in discothèques were often attributed to *chalga* lyrics. The demand for better music videos, and better music in general, eventually led to the split-off of *pop folk* from *chalga* in the late 1990s. It also encouraged the addition of another kind of music video to *Planeta*'s repertoire: *folklor* videos.

Folk music videos existed during communism but were a far stretch from the videos of today. Originally, the folk-costume adorned musicians and choir were recorded in a plain room; no attention was given to setting. Today, just as *chalga* and *pop folk* soloists have emerged, the *folklor* soloist has largely replaced the choir. In other words, in an everyone-for-oneself democratic attitude, there is now greater emphasis on the individual than on the group; the reverse was the case during communism. The content of folk songs has not changed much — topics include village life, the seaside, courting, and *haidouti*, or the Bulgarian revolutionaries who fought against the Ottomans — but the video settings now match the lyrics. There are preserved Bulgarian villages like the renowned Old Town of Plovdiv (evoking National Revival times), the seaside (revered for its natural beauty and majesty), the forest (where the *haidouti* hid and fought for Bulgaria's freedom), and the open grassy field (symbolic of freedom and attunement with nature). Folk singers, dancers, and musicians all wear traditional, regional costumes, but they rarely appear in the same camera shot. Settings alternate just as they do in *chalga* and *pop folk* videos, but emphasis is always on nature and peasant life. Although *folklor* performers may wear heavy make-up, they are not meant to be sexy or flashy like those associated with *chalga* and *pop folk*.

In addition to *chalga, pop folk,* and *folklor,* a few young Bulgarian rock-n-roll bands and children's songs have made their way onto *Planeta,* and occasionally videos by western pop stars like Madonna and the Pussycat Dolls can be seen as well.

Conclusion

Bulgarian folk music and dance ensembles represented the six recognized regions of Bulgaria: Shope, Thrace, Rhodope, North Bulgaria, Dobrudja, and Pirin. Although folk dances in the field were tied to religion, gestures like making the sign of the cross and religious accessories were purposefully excluded, as communism did not endorse religious practices or any other activities which did not advance the socialist cause. Furthermore, although Gypsy and Turkish instruments were played during village folk celebrations, they were purposefully filtered out during the creation of Bulgaria's professional folk ensembles. Now these have reappeared in *chalga*.

In the cultural performance of state-sponsored song and dance ensembles, the ideologies of the state were upheld through the realization of performances that glorified one cultural group, the Bulgarian ethnos of Slavic origin, and discredited minorities, namely Gypsies and Turks. Although these groups played a significant role as contributors to Bulgaria's cultural diversity, heritage and history, they were deemed pollutants to Bulgarian culture. Communism did not tolerate cultural diversity, and the state's respective cultural performances advocated that all nationals were the same.

The assumption that folklore and folk dance remains unchanged through time has enabled the professional folklore man (or woman) to represent Bulgaria's "authentic" past in a similar manner for over five decades, unchallenged by other kinds of performance arts. Dwindling interest in professional folk ensembles by some is met with growing despair from others, over perceived loss of cultural heritage and national identity. However, in this essay I have attempted to deconstruct the essentialized communist character embedded in professional folk performances and to show that dance is both culturally relative and historically particular.

Amateur and professional folk ensembles are very much a product of Bulgaria's communist era, and they reflect the ideologies of the BCP. Young peoples' disinterest in folklore and folk dance is largely a function of the outdated ideologies still embedded in folk ensembles. The social "truths" relative to Bulgarian youth are those of a democratic system which embraces individualism and cultural diversity. These ideologies manifest themselves in newer kinds of artistic expressions like *chalga* and *pop folk*. Virtually anyone with the proper means (appearance, talent, money) can potentially become a singer, and minority groups are making their previously muffled voices heard.

Interestingly, the notion of individualism is also beginning to impact folk ensembles. During communism, their cultural performances emphasized large groups of dancers, musicians, and singers. Today, the majority of folk music videos show a soloist rather than an entire choir, and even folk concerts might juxtapose a soloist with an orchestra and group of dancers. Although folk ensembles are highly resistant to change, they are not static either; they are undeniably influenced by Bulgaria's current social and political situation.

It is not necessary for folk dance to remain exactly the same for preservation to occur, if preservation refers to its essence. People dance in ways that are culturally meaningful to them, and their dance choices might be very different than those of their forbearers. The Bulgarian spirit, the heart of Bulgarian national consciousness, is passed from generation to generation through the vehicles of folklore and folk dance. As the media of transmission, these must be relevant to contemporary contexts or else people will not accept them. Folklore and folk dance do not seem outdated because they are supposedly rooted in the past; they seem outdated when they are no longer relevant. Little is being done to redefine *folklor i folklorni tanĉi* for the 21st century, aside from new music videos that viewers sometimes regard as commercial breaks between *chalga* and *pop folk* videos. That being the case, Bulgarians concerned that appreciation for *folklor i folklorni tanĉi* (and Bulgarianness) is diminishing might want to think twice before holding *chalga* and *pop folk* entirely accountable. Dance culture is continuously creating itself, and dance forms that are meaningful to society will persevere over time through the efforts of innovative artists with fresh perspectives. Once Bulgarian artists get over the hurdle that *folklor i folklorni tanĉi* does not change, it can be brought into the 21st century, redefined in more meaningful contexts.

Notes

1. Fieldwork took place during three separate visits for a total of eleven weeks between 2004 and 2006. The first two trips (totaling eight weeks) were sponsored by Arizona State University's Herberger College, Department of Dance, and Graduate College as part of my work toward a Master of Fine Arts degree in Dance.
2. The label "Roma" is generally preferred over "Gypsy"; however, not all Bulgarian Gypsies are Roma. Some belong to another ethnic group called "Vlache."

Bibliography

Boneva, Bonka. 1995. "Ethnic Identities in the Making: The Case of Bulgaria." *Cultural Survival Quarterly* 19(2), 76–78.
Buchanan, Donna A. 1995. "Metaphors of Power, Metaphors of Truth: The Politics of Music Professionalism in Bulgarian Folk Orchestras." *Ethnomusicology* 39(3), 381–416.
Crampton, R. J. 1997. *Concise History of Bulgaria*. Cambridge: Cambridge University Press.

Egbert, Donald D. 1967. "Politics and the Arts in Communist Bulgaria." *Slavic Review* 26(2), 204–216.

Hobsbawm, Eric, and Terrence Ranger, eds. 1992 [1983]. *Invention of Tradition.* Cambridge: Cambridge University Press.

Hoerburger, Felix. 1968. "Once Again: On the Concept of 'Folk Dance.' " *Journal of the International Folk Music Council* 20, 30–31.

Ilieva, Anna. 1992. "Bulgarian Folk Dance in the Past 45 Years." *Proceedings. 17th Symposium of the Study Group on Ethnochoreology.* Nafplion, Greece, July 2–10, 35–38.

Keali'inohomoku, Joann W. 2002. "Folk Dance." http://gme.grolier.com. (accessed March 18, 2005)

———. 1997 [1969–1970]. "An Anthropologist Looks at Ballet as a Form of Ethnic Dance." In *Anthropology and Movement: The Study of Dances*, ed. Drid Williams. Lanham, MD: Scarecrow Press, 15–36.

———. 1990. "Angst over Ethnic Dance." *Cross-Cultural Dance Resources Newsletter* 10(1–6).

———. 1972a. "Dance Culture as a Microcosm of Holistic Culture." In *CORD Research Annual* 6, ed. T. Comstock. New York: Congress on Research in Dance, 99–106.

———. 1972b. "Folk Dance." In *Folklore and Folklife: An Introduction*, ed. Richard Dorson. Chicago: University of Chicago Press, 381–404.

Shay, Anthony. 2002. *Choreographic Politics: State Folk Dance Companies, Representation, and Power.* Middletown, CT: Wesleyan University Press.

Zhivkov, Todor. 2006. "Bulgarian Folklore." http://www.omda.bg/ENGL/ethnography/folklor.html. (accessed June 1, 2006)

8

Clapping for Serbs: Nationalism and Performance in Bosnia and Herzegovina

LYNN D. MANERS

This essay examines the role of the amateur folk ensemble in the political, moral, and symbolic economy of Bosnia and Herzegovina in the Yugoslav era, from roughly 1942 to 1992. A postscript updates the situation of these folklore ensembles during the period of the Serbian war of aggression against Bosnia and Herzegovina and the current state of uneasy peace in the post–Dayton Peace Accords environment. The folklore performances considered in this work, at first glance epiphenomenal, are seen as actually being part and parcel of ideological considerations, and as such, are subject to transformation and reinterpretation.

Originally intended as living examples of the unity of all the Yugoslav peoples, in the late 1980s both amateur or professional folklore ensembles became sites of contested meanings as the Yugoslav national model began to wane and ethno-nationalism to wax, especially in Serbia and Croatia. Bosnia and Herzegovina, the only republic of now former Yugoslavia without an eponymous ethnic majority, became a critical cultural, and later, actual, battleground for aggressive ethno-nationalism.

In the decade following the death of Tito, cracks began to appear in the elaborate structure of cultural symbols (Hammel 1993, 36) of "Yugoslav" nationality. These had been developed by the Yugoslav state both during and after World War II. An important feature of this endeavor to create a Yugoslav national identity, composed of approved diverse identities, was to find expression through folklore ensembles, both professional, semi-professional/seasonal, and amateur. Modeled on Soviet institutions and formally sponsored by state institutions such as universities and workers' organizations, Cultural Art Societies *(Kulturno Umjetnicko Drustvo,* or KUDs) functioned in all the republics and autonomous provinces of the country. They were established in both urban and rural areas and almost no village was too small to have a KUD. Villages too small or too mono-ethnic (at least in Bosnia) had village folk ensembles, which lacked state support. In the KUDs, traditional dance, music, and song folklore were arranged into suites and adapted for presentation on stage at numerous public events as part of the transformation and recontextualization of traditional music and dance into the new socialist context. In some cases this created a very odd performance. In his dissertation on folklore performance in Slavonia, Dubinskas (1983) notes the incongruity of older KUD members, dressed as youths and performing ritually associated folklore from the period of their young adulthood.

As contrasted with the re-creation of youthful experience, one of the goals of the KUD was to liberally create for its performers and audiences the symbolic experience of being a "new" Yugoslav. KUD members performed folklore from all parts of the reconstituted Yugoslavia regardless of the members' individual ethnic backgrounds. This was considered to be an especially important goal in multi-ethnic BiH (as Bosnia and Herzegovina is frequently abbreviated). As one "veteran" of the *Pokret* KUD in the late 1940s and early 1950s told me: "KUDs were intended to inoculate us [literally *pelcovan od*] against nationalism." Pre-World War II ethno-nationalism was thus analogized as a virus whose harmful effects could be prevented by socialist progress.

KUDs were fully incorporated into the political economy of Tito's Yugoslavia. Until 1966 and the extension of worker self-management to cultural activities, control came from the federal center. After 1966 it devolved to the republics. In Bosnia, this meant that the *Savez KUD BiH* (KUD Committee of Bosnia and Herzegovina) was responsible for administering and distributing funding to the more than 400 KUDs in the republic. A *Gradski Savez KUD* (City KUD Committee) supported the KUDs in a particular area and its suburbs. For example, some three dozen city and suburban KUDs came under the purview of the *Gradski Savez-Sarajevo.* Other *gradski savez* tasks included ranking KUD performances for budgetary purposes, sponsoring some performances, and storing costumes and archives, especially for KUDs too small or new to have their own dedicated institutional space. Individual KUDs were administered by a committee made up of representatives of the sponsoring institution, the group's choreographer/artistic director, its orchestral/musical director and interested volunteers. It should be mentioned that unlike Serbia *(Kolo)*, Croatia *(Lado)*, and Macedonia *(Tanec)*, Bosnia never had a professional folklore ensemble; thus the highest ranked KUD in Sarajevo was generally regarded as the functional equivalent of a professional ensemble.

KUDs were categorized as either *izvorni* (traditional) or *stilizatsia* (stage-oriented, and the vast majority). *Stilizatsia* KUDs were organized internally into A, B, C, and *Pioniri* (children's) sections and ranked among other KUDs as to whether and how well they could present a complete evening program of Yugoslav folklore. This *komplet* meant the satisfactory performance of at least one suite from each of the Yugoslav republics and autonomous provinces, although this political requirement was disguised as a requirement to represent all of Yugoslavia's ethnographic zones. This material was conveyed to aspiring choreographers at a three-summer-long course, the *Ljetna Skola Folklora* (the Summer Folklore School), administered by an institute in Zagreb, Croatia.

The idea of a *komplet* suite was the dominant model and was even found outside the country among, for example, folk ensembles of Yugoslav emigrant groups in Sweden (Ronstrom 1991). In the United States, a *komplet* performance was generally seen only in the performances of university-sponsored folklore ensembles such as those of the Duquesne University *Tamburitzans* who perform not just a pan-Yugoslav program like a first-class *stilizatsia* KUD, but add the music and dance folklore of other Balkan countries into their performances. Ethnically oriented community folklore ensembles from Serbian and Croatian communities in the United States tended to perform only the folklore of their home republic. To the best of my knowledge, before the dissolution of Tito's Yugoslavia there were no specifically Bosnian community folklore ensembles in the United States, though a number have now appeared in Bosnian refugee communities.

The raw material for *stilizatsia* KUDs and professional ensembles alike was traditional folk performance, recorded ethnographically, and then transformed and recontextualized to fit the stage. (Bosnia in particular was considered to be a "*sehara*—a treasure chest of folklore.") Both *stilizatsia* KUDs and professional ensembles were expected to specialize in a wide range of folklore from their own republic, while competently presenting the material of the other republics and autonomous provinces. This rapidly resulted in some suites becoming iconic for their republic/province (i.e., a Sumadjia suite for Serbia, a Posavina suite for Croatia, a wedding suite for Kosovo). The village folklore ensembles, the source of much of this material, where villagers actually performed their own local folklore, were excluded from the KUD system since they could not perform a pan-Yugoslav program, and, of even greater concern from an ideological point of view, might have represented only a single ethnic group. These village ensembles were generally only seen in events known as *Smotra Folklora* (Folklore Review), where the emphasis was on traditional authenticity of performance. The first *Smotra Folklora BiH* in 1985 featured just such performances by village ensembles and KUDs. However, by the next year, KUDs dominated the event.

In the pre-socialist era, and even before World War I during Austrian rule in Bosnia (1878–1914), cultural performances tended to be mono-ethnic in nature. In that era many festivals were sponsored by nationalist organizations causing the Austrian administration to closely monitor them (Besarovi_ 1968). In the post–World War II era of socialist Yugoslavia, folklore performances became not so much a celebration of one ethnic identity as a highlight about the cultural diversity within the unity of the new Yugoslav nation. A major symbol of this new ideological emphasis appeared in June 1950 when the first national folklore festival *(Smotra Jugoslavije)* was held in Belgrade. Through amateur performance, this event celebrated the many regions and republics of the new Yugoslavia. Folklore groups from Bosnia and Herzegovina performed multiple couple dances such as *Staro Bosansko Kolo* (see Dunin 1966) and *Lindjo,* soon to be elevated to the level of icon for the republic. Nationwide, these state-sponsored performance ensembles came to represent an important aesthetic locus in Yugoslav culture.

The transformations and recontextualizations of folklore for national purposes were ideological in nature and ultimately based on Gorky's maxim that folklore was the creative activity of the working class. The raw stuff of quotidian folk practice was transformed into a superstructural commodity in service to the state. In part this was achieved by shifting the audience for these performances from a traditional intimate one experienced directly by participants, to a mass approach in which the majority of the audience watched but did not participate. Unlike village performance where audiences produced the performance through their participation, the new national folklore alienated the audience from folklore production and turned participants into consumers. This certainly marked an odd inversion of the traditional Marxist proletariat-production relationship under socialism. Though most people, as audiences, were divorced from folklore production, we shall see that they were not necessarily passive or neutral.

As noted earlier, most KUDs were deliberately multi-ethnic in their membership and multi-regional in their repertoire. The few examples of mono-ethnic KUDs in Bosnia were generally composed of an ethnic minority *(narodnosti)* such as the Ukrainian KUD *Taras Sevchenko* or the Rom KUD *Veseli Brijeg* in Banja Luka. This system attempted to build, brick by brick, a Yugoslav identity that embraced a pan-Yugoslav vision of *narod* (nation) and *narodnosti* in happy co-existence and rejected the radical ethno-nationalisms of the pre–World War II era. KUDs, along with other institutions, contributed to the creation of a multi-ethnic whole. The amateur folklore organizations were deliberately created to foster just this sense of ethnic integration and, in this way, were considered equally as important as economic development. One of my *prava raja* (slang for a real Sarajevo native) friends remembers a meeting held right after the war in which a Communist Party cadre "practically foamed at the mouth while insisting that having a first-class KUD was as important as having a factory"!

However, just as *bricolage* can build something out of individual pieces, cementing them into a perceived coherent whole through experience and interpretation, so too can the pieces be vulnerable to disassembly through *demontaza* and reinterpretation. In the post–Tito era after 1980, it was this latter process which began to take hold. Furthermore, the process of disassembly only accelerated after Communism lost its credibility as a viable ideology through which to balance the centrifugal and centripetal forces of then-Yugoslavia. This conflict was played out on stages both large and small, in both literal and figurative senses.

As political and economic events transpired through the 1980s and as stresses accumulated in the system, some of the consumers of various cultural performances began to deconstruct them. They removed themselves from the experience the state had designed for them as Yugoslavs and reinterpreted their experience of these performances as ethno-nationalistic. For example, friends told me of audiences in Zagreb walking out of performances of the Wedding Dance Suite from Kosovo in protest against the Serbian policies of severe repression occurring in that province.[1]

In Tone Bringa's remarkable documentary film on the advent of hell in a very small place, *We Are All Neighbours* (1993), there is a scene which aptly illustrates the moral confusion put into motion by the start of this deconstruction. Set in the town of Kiseljak near Sarajevo, the film depicts events both before and after the ethnic cleansing of Muslim families through systematic terror and intimidation by Croatian militias. One scene in particular emphasizes the seemingly unstoppable creep of radical nationalism that resulted in the first so-called white stage of ethnic cleansing. The camera focuses on two young women involved in the typical Bosnian hospitality ritual of coffee grinding. Their comments concern the irrationality of it all. The same people who are their enemies now had been their friends in the town folklore group. In those days, no one in the group seemed to know or care what another's ethnicity was. The unspoken question is how this could have happened to friends who previously had no concern about each other's pedigree. Poignantly, what had happened to brotherhood and unity?

It is not possible to emphasize enough the importance of both the symbolic and actual role of Bosnia and Herzegovina within the post–World War II Yugoslav state. After the war of Yugoslav dissolution engulfed Bosnia, I was reminded by Bosnian friends that Sarajevo, then under Serb bombardment, had been proposed in the immediate post–Liberation era as the capital of the new state. Yet at the same time, BiH held an anomalous position as the one republic of post–World War II Yugoslavia in which no ethnic group was dominant. Serbs were a majority in Serbia, Croats in Croatia, Slovenes in Slovenia, Macedonians in Macedonia, and Montenegrins in Montenegro. In the Republic of Bosnia and Herzegovina in socialist Yugoslavia, however, no ethnic group was in a majority, though the Muslim population held a plurality of 43 percent in the 1981 census. While Serbian (and later Croatian) war propaganda attempted to rewrite the ethnicity and nationality of Bosnia's Muslim population as "Turks," it should be remembered that Bosnian Muslims are of Slavic ancestry and the descendants of those who accepted Islam as a result of the Ottoman conquest.

First mentioned in Constantine Porphyrogenitous' "De Administrando Imperio" in the 10th century, Bosnia lay on the periphery of Europe. Occupied by autochthonous Illyrian peoples, then colonized by the Roman Empire and superseded by the great movement of Slavic peoples in the 6th and 7th centuries, Bosnia began to take on its qualities as a contact zone between east and west. Its isolation as a periphery is seen in the development of Bogomilism, a set of Christian religious practices divergent from Catholicism and Orthodoxy and condemned as heretical. As Bosnia and Serbia emerged from the Middle Ages as classic feudal states, the nobility fell to the advancing Ottoman Turks at the battle of Kosovo on Vidovdan, June 28, 1389. Within the next century, the native Serbs and Croats of BiH found themselves under Turkish domination. Incorporated into the Turkish *millet* system of self-administering confessional communities, many Bosnian Christians found that it was more to their advantage to convert to Islam. These conversions thus mark the beginning of the modern Bosnian Muslim population.

The next four centuries comprise the period of Turkish Bosnia, an outpost standing against a Europe looking down on the newly Turkish lands from across the Sava. In Bosnia itself, as Turkey went from threatening the walls of Vienna to being the sick man of Europe, conditions gradually worsened, especially for Christian peasants. Tax farming elites reduced useful production and by the middle of the 19th century peasant revolts were common.

In 1878, at the Congress of Berlin, the Ottoman Empire ceded control over Bosnia to Hapsburg Austro-Hungary. Acting as the colonial power, Austria set out to make Bosnia into an ideal though primarily self-sufficient colony. The Austrian period, 1878 to 1917, saw attempts to rationalize agriculture, develop industry, and create a modern administrative infrastructure. At the same time, under Baron Kallay's administration, an attempt was made to foment a uniquely Bosnian interconfessional identity, the so-called *Bosniak*. Austro-Hungary hoped this would act as a counterweight to perceived ethnic agitation from Serb and Croatian sources.

Much of this ethnic and nationalist agitation took folkloric forms. This emphasis on performance and ethnicity was especially apparent in various ethnic-based cultural, educational, and benevolent organizations which, banned from direct political expression, sponsored a range of other activities. The first specifically Muslim festival in Bosnia was held in Tesanj in 1895 and included lectures, plays, and dramatic presentations (Kemura 1986, 135). *Gajret,* an organization for "Serb Muslims," was also an active sponsor of cultural events, beginning in 1905. Croatian performance groups, such as *tamburitza* orchestras and choruses, appeared in this period as did Serbian (Ekmećić n.d) and Croatian (Alilović 1980) elementary schools.

The armistice of World War I brought the end of Hapsburg Bosnia as the region was incorporated into the new Kingdom of Serbs, Croats, and Slovenes. Although ethnic agitation was particularly rancorous in much of the new kingdom, Bosnia remained a predominantly rural backwater. Even so, in a state-wide attempt at dealing with ethno-nationalism, the entire country was divided up into *banovine,* or regional governorships, which deliberately cut across traditional ethnic borders.

The beginning of World War II triggered a reign of terror in much of what is now ex-Yugoslavia. The war had an especially strong impact in Bosnia as its mountainous terrain was especially amenable to small-unit, guerrilla-type tactics. Bosnia thus took on a central role in the communist-named National Liberation Struggle (NOB). Bosnia was in fact so central to Yugoslav identity that it was from the Bosnian town of Jajce in 1942 that the country's new existence was proclaimed in a meeting of the Anti-Fascist Council for the Liberation of Yugoslavia, or AVNOJ. Despite its centrality to the Yugoslav concept, Bosnia's unique multi-ethnic composition allowed for continued creation and exploitation of grievances, both perceived and actual. Thus, much of the slaughter in Bosnia took on an inter-communal aspect. Ramet (1992, 255) notes, for example, that approximately 328,000 people lost their lives in Bosnia in the NOB. This inter-communal violence has come back to haunt Bosnia. World War II grievances are still fresh enough in memory to be exploited for ethno-nationalist purposes.

The National Liberation Struggle also marked the beginning of the use of cultural performances by the socialist Yugoslav proto-state as an aid in nation building. The 1942 statutes of the Proletarian National Liberation Brigades required every Partizan unit to have a culture team (Dedić 1981, 123). Along with agitprop theater, members of these cultural teams were responsible for the creation of an invented tradition of "Partizan Kolos." These circle dances were either choreographed *de novo* or transformed from an existing ethnic-associated dance into non- or multi-ethnic "Yugoslav" forms of folk dance. Until the breakup of modern Yugoslavia, festivals where these wartime Partizan dances and their post-war descendants were performed were a regular feature of the choreographer's calendar. At the same time that Partizan kolos were being created as a step to defuse ethnic differences, the choreographed "folk" dances of the urban bourgeois, known as "Ballroom Kolos" *(Radikal, Salonsko Kolo, Trgovacko Kolo,* etc.), popular in the interwar period, disappeared from the repertoire of both quotidian and symbolic performance. This resulted from a coordinated state campaign to erase class distinctions.

In the post-war era, national unity as represented in performance by the creation of a pan-Yugoslav standard repertoire became an important goal. After 1948 and Tito's break with Stalin, Yugoslavia began to develop an independent third way between East and West.[2] The Muslim population in Tito's Yugoslavia, especially the relatively well-educated one of urbanizing Bosnia, was thus seen as an asset, especially in facilitating relations with Muslim countries. After the first "oil shock" of the 1970s, and continuing into the 1980s, many a nominally Muslim Bosnian engineer was found working on projects in Iraq or Saudi Arabia. Foreign projects with large numbers of Yugoslav workers had culture workers, such as folk dance choreographers, assigned to them, as indeed happened to a Sarajevo KUD director of my acquaintance. Showing off a suite of Muslim dances from Sarajevo was a useful propaganda tool when performing for visiting foreign dignitaries from countries hosting Yugoslav guest workers.

However, this recognition of Muslim ethnicity was fairly late in coming and the result of some negotiation at the national level. The position of the Muslims of Bosnia and Herzegovina was an anomalous one in the early years of Tito's Yugoslavia; in fact, the original 1948 census allowed for categories of "Serb-Muslim," "Croatian-Muslim," and "Undefined Muslim" (Velat 1988, 139), while the 1953 census only allowed for a category of "Yugoslav unidentified." Following that experiment, a new category emerged, that of *Muslimani (etnicki pripadnost)*—Muslim by ethnic belonging—which eventually led to the descriptor *Muslimani u smislu narodnosti*—Muslim in the sense of a national ethnic group. Bosnian Muslims, though, in no way resembled a unified group. Individuals of my acquaintance ranged in their self-descriptions from *mahala* Muslim (highly devout, living in an Old Town *komsiluk*, or neighborhood) to "suburban" Muslim (non-religious intellectual of Muslim family) to "Communist" Muslim (officially atheist, from a strong Party family).

As might be expected in a multi-ethnic environment, where mobility between groups was allowed, intermarriage was not uncommon. These intermarriages also created the all-important *veze*, or connections, across ethnic lines. As in many socialist/Communist states, individuals perceived and often expressed to me that in their experience, connections were often far more important than any other factor in obtaining access to scarce resources. Urban folklore ensembles, such as KUD *Slobodan Princip Seljo* of Sarajevo, were one of the venues of inter-ethnic structural integration in Bosnia; many of the members of the *Veterani* section had met their future other-ethnic spouse at a rehearsal. Crossing all ethnic lines, many young KUD members told me that they had chosen "Yugoslav" as a descriptor in the most recent census.

The republic itself was also in an anomalous position vis-à-vis the federal state. Bosnia was not of the rich north (Slovenia, Croatia, Serbian Vojvodina), and it was not an obvious part of the poor south (Macedonia, Montenegro, parts of Serbia, and Kosovo). As tax monies flowed from the richer north to the LDRs (less developed regions), Bosnia found itself betwixt and between. According to Plestina (1987, 200) Bosnia was considered an LDR in the first five-year plan, only to be dropped from that status in the second and then subsequently reinstated. Traditionally rich in natural resources, its uneven development contributed to its being seen from the federal center as neither one nor the other. Thus, in some calculations, Bosnia was part of the north, in others part of the south. As an example of its "northern" developed status, in interviews with Bosnian KUD members in their early twenties, many remembered "Pennies for Kosovo" days in their elementary schools when pocket change was collected to be sent south.

Bosnia's position as neither developed nor undeveloped became even more untenable in the Yugoslav economic decline. The oil shock of the 1970s exposed many of the weaknesses in the Yugoslav version of a managed economy, and Bosnia suffered accordingly. Through the 1970s and 1980s workers in various industries, through their BOALs (Basic Organization of Associated Labor), voted themselves pay raises to be paid for by loans from banks controlled by the industries in which they worked. Thus was inflation pushed ever higher. By the middle and late 1980s, classic hyper-inflation had set in, exacerbating rising tensions between republics. Magnusson (1987, 76) notes that by the early and middle 1980s "almost every aspect of ideology [was] under fire: revolutionary history, the actual practice of 'brotherhood and unity,' self-management and the functioning of the political system." The disintegration of the Soviet Union and the subsequent public revulsion at the exposure of the Potemkin village unreality of applied Marxist ideologies after the fall of the Berlin Wall further fractured the dissolving relationship between the Yugoslav republics. A substitute for Communism as ideology was sought and found by some in radical ethno-nationalism. This ideological shift was to show up in the ways in which audiences experienced and reacted to folklore performances.

Recall that during the Tito era, KUDs and professional folklore ensembles were required to perform pan-Yugoslav programs. Only occasionally were exceptions allowed, primarily if the group represented a national minority. The following example illustrates the intensity of audience response to a predominantly Albanian program presented by *Shota*, and it illuminates the stakes for the states in managing folklore performances.

The affective potential of these kinds of cultural performances and their potential power to mobilize ethnicity were made stunningly clear to me one evening. A sophisticated Bosnian friend and I sat in the audience at the Djuro Djakovic Worker's University Theater in Sarajevo waiting for a group from Kosovo to perform. Looking around at the sold-out auditorium before the program began, he commented that "there must not be a sweet shop open in Sarajevo tonight!"—a reference to one of the economic specializations of Yugoslav Albanians. As the performance began, even he was surprised at the power of the program to move the audience emotionally. An almost electric hush fell over the audience as familiar songs began to evoke affective responses. In one moment of seemingly heightened perception, I looked around and saw something which until then I had only associated with Western charismatic Christianity. Many men in the audience had stood up, their eyes closed, and were swaying to the beat with their arms and hands held up towards the stage as if basking in the sun. Although I had seen positive audience response before, the intensity of this moment was unprecedented in my experience with folklore performance.

What was not so apparent in viewing these public performances was that they were the result of a sophisticated process of negotiation of identities between the Yugoslav state and its constituent nations and national minorities. Engaged in a complicated minuet of coercion and control over cultural performances, Yugoslavia as the most multi-national state in Eastern Europe and Bosnia and Herzegovina, the most multi-ethnic republic within the Yugoslav state, presented a unique set of circumstances. What may have seemed to the average viewer to be simply a folklore show romanticizing a primarily rural past was really the result of a complex discourse about symbolic national identity with aspects of negotiation and resistance and with roots antedating the Marxist model and extending back well into the last century. In my view, this negotiation of identity between ethnicity and the state was highly visible in what I have come to call the social lives of dances, a concept I have adapted from ideas presented by Appadurai (1986) and Maquet (1971).

By the social lives of dances, I mean that dances, or indeed other classes of aesthetic goods, objects, and behaviors, act as complex types of symbolic and actual commodities as they circulate in and out of various levels of involvement with the types of political economies in which they find themselves embedded (Maners 1995). It is not so much the social formation of these types of aesthetic production which concern me as it is the role of political economies in their selection and reproduction. While aesthetic objects were certainly valued goods, especially in the former socialist states of Eastern Europe, their worth was often determined by the needs of party ideology (Giurchescu 1987). Through the lens of a particular folklore performance that I witnessed near the end of the Yugoslav era one can see the explicit linkage between dance and political economy in former Yugoslavia and, by extension, to most of pre-1989 Eastern Europe. This linkage of folkloric performance and politics continues today, now harnessed to the new post–Communist ideologies of ethno-nationalism in the other ex-Yugoslav republics.

In the fall of 1987, in the seemingly innocuous confines of the performance space of KUD *Slobodan Princip-Seljo* in Sarajevo, I witnessed a moment of *parakrousis* into which then-Yugoslavia was falling. *Parakrousis,* as the Greeks defined it, is that one discordant element in an otherwise harmonious presentation which may reveal its underlying conflict. In this case, that discordant, telling note came not from the performers or their performance, but from the audience, the consumers of this manifestation of the state's ideology.

In retrospect, it is not so unusual that this drama would unfold in a realm seemingly so far removed from the political and ideological as folk dance and music adapted to the stage as entertainment. It was just this very aspect of what the Yugoslavs called *folklor* which played a powerful ideological role in the founding of the post–World War II Yugoslav state. *Folklor,* composed of many disparate national elements, was almost by definition ripe for reappropriation and conversion from Yugoslav polysemy to ethnic monosemy.

Having witnessed hundreds of performances of Yugoslav folk material since the 1960s, and specializing in the aesthetic anthropologies of dance and music, I came to the performance that evening with a set of expectations about what I might see. A typical *Gradski Smotra* (City Folklore Review) such as this one would normally feature a number of performances of dance suites by the sponsoring amateur group as well as a number of suites by visiting amateur groups from elsewhere in the city. Each would strive to put on the best possible presentation. The quality of a given KUD was often judged by its performances, and budgetary allotments from the *porez kultura* (culture tax) would be adjusted accordingly. It was not at all unknown for a KUD to decline in status and even cease to function if its performances consistently fell below the judges' standards. The substantive aesthetic requirement was that a suite must be *komplet* (i.e., appropriate in music, dance, and costuming for the republic or province it was representing). Furthermore, KUDs were not only judged formally. As audiences were often composed of the dancers' friends and families as well as members of other amateur ensembles, informal judgments were rendered throughout via the traditional method of audience response.

This night, however, there was an odd and disharmonious affect to the program. It began with a suite of dances from Croatia with the usual colorful dances from Posavina and Slavonia. Following the Croatian suite, an even more colorful and lively set of urban Muslim dances from Sarajevo appeared with the women dressed in *dimije* (wide satin pantaloons) and *papuce* (backless slippers), while the men held forth in fez, vest, and baggy trousers.

Everything seemed to proceed according to expectation. However, I was puzzled at the audience reaction to the next suite as it began to unfold. This was of a Serbian dance from the Sumadija region. (Bosnian groups would often alternate this suite with one of the Serbian dances called *okolina Sarajeva*, dances from the Sarajevo region, immediately recognizable by the women's black *dimija*.) I had seen the Sumadija suite, a classic of its genre, choreographed by Branko Markovic, performed by *Kolo* in Belgrade on more than one occasion. The immediately recognizable aspect of the choreography is its initial appearance as a line of dancers, to a lively tune, move in a diagonal line downstage then pass across the foot of the stage before curving back at another diagonal and eventually resolving to lines at the sides of the stage. What struck me as odd was nothing about the dance suite per se, but rather the audience's reaction to it. As the suite proceeded, I began to sense a very unusual display of affect by the audience. To my ear, boisterous noticeable pockets of applause were interspersed in the theater with pockets of silence. Many audience members had what appeared to be a nominal response. They neither hissed nor booed, but passively responded by "sitting on their hands."

Struck by something I had never before witnessed at a KUD performance, I turned to a friend seated next to me and asked if she had noticed something strange and if she could explain it. At the conclusion of the suite, she affirmed my perception of the audience's affect. Her interpretation was that only Serbs in the audience were clapping for Serbs and, in fact, that they were over-reacting. Non-Serbs, though, politely applauded as they had for the other suites. Later that evening when we met with some KUD members in the smoky environs of a local small café, this opinion was confirmed: Serbs were only clapping for Serbs. Something had changed in the way in which Serbs related to the presentation of Serbian cultural performances, a change not apparent among non–Serbs.

My friends laid much of the blame for this state of affairs informally on the doorstep of the Serbian Academy of Arts and Sciences (SANU) in Belgrade. The year before it had published an infamous memorandum attempting to reposition Serbia as a victim of Federal Yugoslavia. Thus, had this moment of *parakrousis* occurred in a previous year, it might have been interpreted as simply friends clapping for friends. Now, however, it served as a harbinger of the coming crisis. As much as the state had invested in presenting an image of unified Yugoslavia through an elaborate system of folklore performance, that same system which had conveyed the polysemy of the state was now in the process of being deconstructed before our eyes into ethnic monosemy.

In retrospect then, folk music and dance in Bosnia and Herzegovina was a part of not just a critical aesthetic locus, but of a critical symbolic focus within the political economy. The main purpose of amateurism in the performance of folklore groups, replicating that of the professional ensembles, was to emphasize the fundamental equality of the Yugoslav nations and nationalities. While KUDs in the other republics and autonomous provinces may have found it hard even to have ethnically mixed ensembles, in Bosnia and Herzegovina this was a given based simply on the demographics of the republic. Bosnia and Herzegovina, as the one non-ethnically based republic in Yugoslavia, always had the most to lose in any potential reinterpretation of these cultural performances.

After Communism lost its legitimacy as an organizing principle, ethnonationalism replaced nationalism so that, bringing us full circle, people could clap for their own just as I had witnessed that evening in Sarajevo. Thus *bricolage* was replaced by *demontaza* as audiences began to deconstruct symbols of Yugoslav national identity into narrower ethnic ones.

At the time of the Dayton Accords, the KUDs of Sarajevo (and at least one in Tuzla and in Mostar) had survived the war. Reflecting the bitter emotions of being shelled by former Serbian neighbors and radical *chetniks* alike, the surviving KUDs of the capital had "ethnically cleansed" their repertoires of Serbian material, including such traditional favorites as those from Serb villages *okolina Sarajeva*.

In the first folklore festival held in post–Yugoslav, but still under siege in Sarajevo, a new National Folklore Ensemble performed suites of Bosnian Croatian and Bosnian Muslim traditional dances, Croatian *lindjos*, traditional dances from Herzegovina *(trampas)* and Bosnian oriental dances reflecting Bosnia's Turkish/Ottoman heritage. The mayor of Sarajevo was quoted as saying that the folklore festival was "another way to fight and to resist." Thus these kinds of cultural performances took on yet another new meaning in a changed political, symbolic, and moral economy.

In the summer of 1997, I revisited the now independent state of BiH. Met at the airport by an old friend from the *Veterani* of KUD *Slobodan Princip Seljo*, I soon found myself whisked off to a *teferic* (picnic) at the weekend cabin high on a mountainside. Common to such picnics, we dined on roast goat, drank homemade *rakija*, chatted, sang, and danced kolos until dusk. As we talked, I asked about the KUDs in the post–Yugoslav era. One Veteran told me that while it was politically correct to dismantle things from the old Communist days, the KUDs hadn't been. He reminded me that new KUDs had appeared during the war and that at least a semi-professional ensemble had been established. This is in interesting contrast to the situation reported by Rice (1996, 186) for Bulgaria, where the former state folklore ensembles were seen as part of the decay of the system and are today in parlous straits.

KUDs had continued to rehearse and perform throughout the war, though in much reduced circumstances. The *Gradski Savez-Sarajevo* had lost its archives and costume collection to shelling and the head of the Savez KUD-BiH, Svetan Ninkovic (a Serb), had been murdered in his home during a particularly dark period during the siege. Some choreographers had also felt the siren song of ethnicity and decamped to Croatia or Montenegro, while male dancers and musicians were drafted into the army and both males and females fled the country as refugees. In the new Bosnia, some KUDs still reflect the sponsorship of various institutions and one KUD successor, *Kolo Bosansko*, sponsored by the Bosnian Cultural Center, aspires to be a professional ensemble while the others soldier on in the spirit of amateurism.

The next morning, while out for a walk, I came across another pre-war acquaintance, the eminent choreographer Hajrudin Hadzic. He encouraged me to attend an event on June 7th honoring the 125th anniversary of the Bosnian railways. KUD *Zeljeznicar*, sponsored by the railway association in the old days, would be performing a suite of dances he had choreographed which he assured me I would find interesting.

Arriving at the theatre that evening, I found myself in a well-dressed crowd of foreign and local dignitaries and interested spectators. After a few speeches (which were translated into English), a chorus performed and I noticed the dancers of KUD *Zeljeznicar* beginning to line up at the back of the stage. Before the war, dressed as they were in the traditional garb of Bosnian Serbs, Croats, and Muslims, nothing would have struck me as unusual. Clearly they were going to perform *Sarajevo Zavrazlama* (Sarajevo Medley), a suite composed of Serb, Croat, and Muslim dances. Pre–1992, the performance of this suite would have been unremarkable, though in the late 1980s it would have become subject to reinterpretation. During the war years of 1992 to 1995, presenting Serbian material would have been unthinkable and now, in 1997, reflecting the Bosnian government's official policy of cultural diversity (Laušević 1996, 130) in which Muslims and non–Muslims alike were to be equals, such a performance was again, unremarkable.

Thus, folklore ensembles and their repertoires become like palimpsests upon which layers of meaning, of nationalism and ethno-nationalism, of construction and deconstruction and reconstruction, shimmer through one another upon the page.

Notes

1. The Wedding Dance Suite had become so iconic of Kosovo, that, according to Reineck (1986) parts of its choreography began to appear at Kosovo Albanian wedding celebrations as a "traditional" folk dance.

2. Tito, of course, along with Nehru of India, Nasser of Egypt, and Sukarno of Indonesia, together spearheaded the development of the non-aligned movement, given life at the Bandung (Indonesia) conference in 1955.

Bibliography

Alilovic, Ivan. 1980. *Tragom Hrvatske Kulturne Bastine u Hercegovini*. Zagreb: Hrvatsko Knjizeno Drustvo.
Appadurai, Arjun, (ed.) 1986. *The Social Life of Things*. Cambridge: Cambridge University Press.
Besarovic, R., (ed.) 1968. *Kultura i Umjetnost u Bosni i Hercegovini Pod Austrougarskom Upravom*. Sarajevo: Arhiv BiH.
Bringa, Tone. 1993. *We are Are All Neighbours*. Granada Video. Disappearing World Series.
Dedic, Milutin. 1981. "Cultural-Artistic Amateurism." *Yugoslav Survey*, May , 1981, :121–140.
Dubinskas, Frank. 1983. "Performing Slavonian Folklore: The Politics of Reminiscence and Recreating the Past." Unpublished Ph.D. dissertation, Stanford University.
Dunin, Elsie. 1966. "Silent Dance of the Dinaric Mountain Area. Analysis of Purpose, Form and Style of Selected Dances." Unpublished Master's master's thesis, University of California, Los Angeles..

Ekmecic, Milorad. n.d. "The Advance of Civilization and National Politics in Bosnia and Hercegovina in the XIX Century." Unpublished m.smanuscript.

Giurchescu, Anca. 1987. "The National Festival 'Song to Romania': Manipulation of Symbols in the Political Discourse." in In *Symbols of Power: The Esthetics of Political Legitimation in the Soviet Union and Eastern Europe*, ed. Claes. Arvidsson, Claes and Lars Erik Blomqvist, eds. Pp. 163–171. Stockholm: Almqvist and Wiksell International, 163–171.

Hammel, E. A. 1993. "The Yugoslav Labyrinth." *Anthropology of East Europe Review*, vol. 11. (1–2), :35–42.

Kemura, Ibrahim. 1986. *Uloga "Gareta" u Drustvenom Zivotu Muslimana Bosne i Hercegovine (1903–1941)*. Sarajevo: Veselin Maslesa.

Lausevic, Mirjana. 1996. "The 'Ilahiya' as a Symbol of Bosnian Muslim National Identity." In *Retuning Culture: Musical Changes in Central and Eastern Europe*, ed. Mark. Slobin, ed. Durham, NC: Duke University Press.

Magnusson, Kjell. 1987. The Secularization of Ideology: Tthe Yugoslav Case." In *Symbols of Power: The Esthetics of Political Legitimation in the Soviet Union and Eastern Europe*, ed.. Claes Arvidsson and Lars Erik Blomqvist, eds. Pp. 73–84. . Stockholm: Almqvist and Wiskell International, 73–84.

Maners, Lynn. 1995. "The Social Lives of Dances in Bosnia and Herzegovina: Cultural Performance and the Anthropology of Aesthetic Phenomena." Unpublished Ph.D. dissertation, University of California, Los Angeles.

Maquet, Jacques. 1971. *Introduction to Aesthetic Anthropology*. Reading, MA: Addison Wesley: McCabe Module in Anthropology.

Plestina, Dijana M. 1987. "Politics and Inequality: A Study of Regional Disparities in Yugoslavia." Unpublished Ph.D. dissertation, University of California, Berkeley.

Ramet, Sabrina. 1992. *Nationalism and Federalism in Yugoslavia, 1962–1991*. (second edition). 2nd ed. Bloomington:, Indiana University Press.

Reinceck, Janet. 1986. "The Place of the Dance Event in Social Organization and Social Change Among Albanians in Kosovo, Yugoslavia." *UCLA Journal of Dance Ethnology* 10, 27–38.

Rice, Timothy. 1996. "The Dialectics of Economics and Aesthetics in Bulgarian Music." In *Retuning Culture, Musical Changes in Central and Eastern Europe*, ed. Mark. Slobin, ed. Durham, NC: Duke University Press.

Ronstrom, Owe. 1991. *Folklor: Staged Folk Music and Dance Performances of Yugoslavs in Stockholm. Yearbook for Traditional Music*,: 69–77.

Velat, Dubravka. 1988. *Stanovnistvo Jugoslavije u Posleratom Periodu: Graficki Prikaz Statisticke Stanovnistvo*. Beograd: Savezni Zavod za Statisticku.

9

Choreographing the Other: The Serbian State Folk Dance Ensemble, Gypsies, Muslims, and Albanians

ANTHONY SHAY

Kolo, the Serbian State Folk Dance Ensemble, has produced several choreographic productions that feature the dances, music, costumes, and, to some degree, the customs of three of the largest and most unpopular minority groups: the Gypsies (*Roma*), the Muslims of the Sandjak of Novi Pazar (*Muslimani*), and the Albanians of Kosovo-Metohija (*Shiptari*), which also constitutes a large Muslim presence. Dance, of all of the forms of cultural production, possesses polysemic means of communication, and because it is embodied and immediate, dance carries a unique capacity to create iconic and stereotypical images. I will argue, through close readings of the choreographies found over the years in the Kolo repertoire in two videos (see the videolog) and live performances in America and Beograd, that these depictions, which can range from the quaint and primitive, to negative, dismissive portrayals of these ethnic minorities, contributed to the violence and hatred that ensued with the breakup of the former Yugoslavia through the reinforcement of already extant stereotypes. In fact these portrayals constitute choreographic creations of the "Other" in Serbian society.

I argue that the power to represent is not only power in a theoretical Foucauldian sense, but the power of representation, especially of those powerless to resist the field of representation provided by state-supported national dance ensembles, is a very real power. Dance scholars have begun to look at issues of representation and dance and human rights within fascist (Kant 2004; Manning and Benson 2001; von Bibra 1987) and communist (Maners 2005; Shay 2002; Zemtsovsky and Kunanbaeva 1997) contexts of the past, as well as questioning the stances toward dance taken by theocratic regimes like that of the Islamic Republic and Iran and the former Taliban regime of Afghanistan (Shay 1999, 2005). I also suggest that the actual content of the dances, as well as their context, needs to be interrogated to provide details of the ways in which dance can be utilized by specific regimes to choreographically denigrate and erase the presence of unwanted and unpopular ethnic and minority groups.

Dance and Anthropology

Anthropologists over the past two decades have begun to give dance and other movement activities increased attention as forms of cultural expression that, like social organization and kinship, have the potential to provide lenses through which to observe issues of identity formation, ethnic difference, and culturally learned aesthetic viewpoints, and other pertinent information regarding human behavior. But this attitude has been late in coming.

In 1974, I gave a paper at the American Anthropological Association meeting in Mexico City in a session of four papers that was the first full session devoted to dance ever organized by that august body. In "...And Then They Danced," I described the way in which anthropological fieldwork typically slighted the role of dance by giving intricate descriptions of feasts and banquets and other societal celebratory events, including what such events could tell us about particular societies such as kinship networks, social organization, food ways and economic structure. Upon finishing these elaborate descriptions, the typical anthropologist would add: "...and then they danced." American studies scholar Jane C. Desmond notes that:

> The academy's aversion to the material body, as well as its fictive separation of mental and physical productions, has rendered humanities scholarship that investigates the mute dancing body nearly invisible. That dancing — in a Euro-American context at least — is regarded as a pastime (social dancing) or as entertainment (Broadway shows), or, when elevated to the status of an "art form," is often performed mainly by women (ballet) or by "folk" dancers or nonwhites (often dubbed "native" dances, etc.) also surely contributes to the position of dance scholarship [1997, 30].

However, the "meaning" of dance and how it is employed and regarded in various human societies can form a central vehicle for research, particularly in those societies in which dance and related forms of movement occupy a central role in group activities. As Desmond notes: "So ubiquitous, so 'naturalized' as to be nearly unnoticed as a symbolic system, movement is a primary not secondary social 'text'— complex, polysemous, always already meaningful, yet continuously changing. Its articulation signals group affiliation and group differences, whether consciously performed or not. Movement serves as a marker for the production of gender, racial, ethnic, class, and national identities" (1997, 31). Thus, as this case study of the Serbian State Folk Ensemble demonstrates, movement and performances of movement can serve as powerful ethnic markers of the most basic kind and demand close readings by anthropologists in order to understand the political, ethnic, and social dynamics present in the former Yugoslavia and other Eastern European states.

Dancing for the State: The Art of the State

Throughout history abundant evidence exists that once large states existed, the arts were pressed into service to create powerful and positive images of elite elements of the ruling classes. For example, Iranian dynasties utilized architecture, architectural ornament, sculpture, clothing and other decorative elements to give a dynasty such as the Timurid dynasty (1380–1506) a specific and unique image. The *kitabkhana*, the government atelier in which large groups of artists and craftsmen produced manuscripts of epic poetry like the *Shahnama* (the epic history of Persia with intricate calligraphy and fabulous miniature paintings, highly prized objects for royal eyes only), also designed more public aspects of image for the regime like architectural edifices such as palaces and mosques, outdoor pavilions and elaborate tents, and tiles and clothing. Islamic art historians Thomas W. Lentz and Glenn D. Lowry note:

> Out of this newly emerged, literary-based Timurid vision came the constituent visual elements that fueled the dynasty's cultural aspirations and established the basis of its art. Through the kings, heroes, and lovers from traditional works like the *Shahnama* of Firdawsi or the *Khamsa* of Nizami, Timurid myths and fantasies were repeatedly played out in an idealized setting. The perceived glory of Timurid destiny was presented in scenes that through repetition assumed their own distinct and visionary qualities.... This imaginary world was portrayed with a perfection of form and purity of color heretofore unseen in Islamic painting; its iconlike compositions were painted with ever-increasing precision and lyricism, as if to assure [*sic*], like sympathetic magic, its certainty and existence. The dynasty's consistent pictorial re-creation of a princely world cast it in Timurid guise, as contemporary

court fashion, architecture, and inscription in these pictures strengthened the linkage.... The key to the creation of the Timurids' art lies in the methods and objectives of the kitabkhana staff, those artists and craftsmen responsible for visualizing princely aspiration [1989, 162–163].

Dancers appear in central positions (after the shah) in Timurid and Safavid (1501–1725) miniatures in festive scenes that suggest that the symbol of the dancer indicates a joyful, carefree life in which the rulers were at ease and not concerned about barbarians at the gate, which constituted an essential aspect of royal propaganda. However, the miniatures depicted an idealized world; the real world was, in fact, filled with danger: barbarians were frequently at the gates. Troupes of dancers actually performed at court festivities, but there is no evidence to suggest that dance was any formal aspect of the court image per se, as it did at the court of Louis XIV.

It is important to grasp that the public performance of dance by professional performers in the Islamic Middle East and Central Asia, while serving as a form of cultural expression, has always been linked to prostitution for both male and female performers. In addition, public female dancers are widely viewed as invading male, that is, public space and in an Islamic context they have the potential to produce *fitnah*, or social chaos, a tearing apart of the social fabric. Thus, dance per se is not reviled by any but the most zealous, such as the Taliban of Afghanistan; rather it is the public performance of it that can frequently bring down clerical ire for threatening societal order.[1]

One of the most spectacular early uses of dance employed for the purposes of exalting the king, his court, and his nation was the case of Louis XIV, the Sun King. Louis himself appeared in these elaborate and expensive productions in which he played the role of Apollo and other mythological figures to represent his glory and brilliance as a ruler.[2] He was, by all accounts, a brilliant dancer in his youth. Baroque dance scholar Wendy Hilton observes: "In a seventeenth-century ballet, Louis XIV was usually the central figure of the performance, his roles reflecting his deification; the King's most famous identification was with the Greek sun-god Apollo, a role he danced many times" (1981, 7). Hilton adds the important point that the prime minister, Jules Mazarin, specifically sought visual means to glorify the crown: "When peace reigned once more in Paris [after the Fronde], Mazarin sought ways to reestablish confidence in his government and in the person of the King, who was then fourteen years old, beautiful to behold, and talented as a dancer. In the ballet de cour, Mazarin found an ideal vehicle for the achievement of this latter purpose" (1981, 7).

A potent later example of the state use and control of dance and movement in Nazi Germany is described by dance historians Manning and Benson:

> In the Third Reich dance came under the authority of Josef Goebbels' Ministry of Culture, which issued a stream of directives setting standards for prospective dancers, including proof of Aryan origin. The Ministry sponsored large-scale dance festivals in Berlin in 1934, 1935, and 1936.... The Nazis staged immense spectacles by enlarging the scale of the movement choir ... with thousands of Berlin schoolchildren, who executed precision patterns on the field of the Olympic stadium. Moving in unison ranks, the boys and girls glorified the presence of the F(hrer, who reviewed them from the stands. The movement choir had become the basis for mass propaganda [2001, 223–223].

Anne von Bibra, in her study of folk dances of the Lower Franconian region of Germany, indicates that folk dance was frequently utilized by the National Socialist Party in the same way as the movement choirs described by Manning and Benson: "Organized by the NSDAP [National Socialist Party], these huge gatherings of villagers in *Trachten* [traditional dress] were held in Nuremberg" (von Bibra 1987, 57). Following the strong eighteenth- and nineteenth-century Enlightenment models, the rural populations, the folk, embodied the "purist" ethnic elements of each state — an idea that David Shoenbaum put succinctly: "the practicing German farmer was a superior individual and the city with all it represented was a moral swamp" (quoted in von Bibra 1987, 379).

The Soviet Union, and later several of its satellite states, also utilized productions featuring masses of folk dancers and others. "Thirty-five pompous Ten-Day Festivals of 'national arts' were staged in Moscow from 1936 to 1960, merely for show and propaganda" (Zemtsovsky and Kunanbaeva 1997, 8). These festivals, as in the case of Nazi Germany, were to symbolize mass support for the regime. In the case of the Soviet Union, "the folk" in whose name the regime had been established were smiling peasant folk dancers. The Soviet ruling elite were so impressed with the effects that these festivals produced that in 1937 they directed Igor Moiseyev to found a professional company of folk dancers, which came to bear his name in the West after World War II.

Such mass demonstrations, especially the huge 1952 and 1956 Moscow Festivals, which received coverage in the American media, sent chills through much of the American public who were unused to such flagrant political manifestations of thousands of people demonstrating for the state. But when the Moiseyev Dance Company finally arrived in the United States in 1958, premiering before millions on the *Ed Sullivan Show*, and appearing in every major city, the one hundred performers, all smiling all the time, completely captivated American audiences, destroying the carefully crafted American government image of the "evil empire" (Shay 2002, 57–60).

The Characteristics of State Folk Dance Ensembles

I suggest that for purposes of this presentation that state-sponsored national folk dance ensembles come in two general types: (1) those that represent single ethnic nation-states such as Mazowsze of Poland; the Turkish State Folk Dance Company; the Armenian State Folk Dance; LADO, the Croatian State Ensemble of Folk Dances and Songs; and the Dora Stratou Greek Dances Theatre, and (2) those that represent multi-ethnic nation-states and attempt to include a pan-ethnic representation in their programs such as Bayanihan of the Philippines, Ballet Folklorico of Mexico, the Moiseyev Dance Company, and the former Iranian State Folk Dance Ensemble (known as the Mahalli Dancers when abroad).

There are typically four types of representation found in the repertoires of state-sponsored dance companies. The first type is positive representation. For example, LADO, the Croatian State Ensemble, shows Croatian peasants in a positive light through the dancers' elegant, noble bearing, modest costumes; by extension, the Croatian people are shown to be a fine nation. Mexico's Ballet Folklorico creates a similar positive image of its represented groups. For example, to look at the noble bearing of the Aztecs through Amalia Hernandez's choreography one would never suspect that their ancestors slaughtered thousands of victims at the Great Temple of Tenochtitlan, ripping open their chests and pulling out their still beating hearts before casting their corpses down the bloodied stairways of the sacred site.

It is perhaps the most typical of the fields of representation that we find in the repertoires of these state-sponsored ensembles. This positive representation, such as the Russians in the Moiseyev company, most frequently characterizes the titular majority group that the particular ensemble represents.

A second type of representation is the "quaint," "exotic," or "primitive" representation of a minority ethnic group that enables the state, through the choreographic lens of the state ensemble, to portray specific ethnic groups as "less" than the majority population by depicting a specific group as "noble" (or not so noble) savages. Thus, the Yaqui Deer Dance depicts the Yaquis as primitive, in contrast to the festive Mestizo dances that constitute representations of Jalisco or Vera Cruz. Moiseyev's depictions of the Baltic peoples fall under the "quaint" category as they execute droll polkas with often doll-like movements.

A third representation is negative or pernicious choreographic images frequently used to reinforce majority prejudices toward unpopular ethnic groups. Such openly negative representation tends to be infrequent, but the negative portrayal of Gypsies by Kolo, the Serbian State Folk Dance Ensemble, in this paper demonstrates how such stereotyping can produce and promote corrosive interethnic relations.

The last is no representation: in other words significant minorities are not represented in the repertoires of particular dance companies. The Bulgarian State Ensemble of Folk Songs and Dances (known as the Philip Koutev Ensemble outside of Bulgaria) never represented the Turkish population, which constituted over 10 percent of the total population of Bulgaria. This lack of representation echoes the governmental erasure of Turkish identity to the point that all those of Turkish ethnicity were required to adopt Bulgarian surnames. Gypsies, too, were absent from the Bulgarian representational field. The Turkish State Folk Dance Ensemble, reflecting the official government's political stance, has never represented the Kurdish population, estimated at between 20 and 30 percent of the total. The Turkish government has steadfastly maintained that Kurds do not exist in Turkey; instead they are designated as "Mountain Turks," or some other such fictional identity.

The Moiseyev Company, despite Moiseyev's Jewish origins, never produced a suite depicting Jewish life until after the Soviet Union collapsed. Many observers find Moiseyev's "Fiddler on the Roof" images of Jewish stereotypical behavior less than compelling as an authentic depiction of shtetl life.

It should be pointed out that in many repertoires the urban population is almost completely missing. This, of course, underscores the romanticism of the eighteenth- and nineteenth-century intellectual preoccupation with the concept that the peasant constituted the "pure" repository of all that is good and authentic in the national ethos. The urban population, on the other hand, were perceived as somehow corrupted and open to "alien" and "foreign" traits; therefore, they display negative behavior. In the former Soviet Union, the term "cosmopolitan" became a code word for the politically suspect. Ironically, it is largely for the upper and middle urban classes that these repertoires were created, for their support is crucial to the financial well-being of these dance ensembles. Among such audiences there is frequently a desire to see their respective peasantries shown in a positive, naïve, and above all hygienic light with all traces of bodily functions erased.

Also, the second and third modes of choreographic representation, the "quaint/exotic/primitive" and the "negative" are often presented to contrast the positive depictions of the majority population. Thus, in the Moiseyev Company concerts the Russians are noble, proud, and elegant, while the Lithuanians or Latvians are quaint peasants.

Lynn Maners, in his study of government-supported and amateur dance companies in Bosnia (2005), introduces a useful concept in the manner in which the state recontextualized dance for the stage: "authenticity of intent and authenticity of content":

> These two divergent types are seen as anchoring a continuum, whose end points are authenticity of content and authenticity of intent. From the state's perspective, authenticity of intent is far more important than the idea that the content of a performance be true to its performance in its original context. As an ideological production, folk dance performances are important for what they symbolize about the state: its hegemonistic or idealized self-image and its projection of that image to others. The state cares less about the recontextualization of a dance to the stage than it does about the message the performance sends to its audience(s). The transformed and recontextualized dance performance becomes an important part of state level political symbolism, and states invest in creating or converting both amateur and professional ensembles. Authenticity of content (steps, costumes, music, props, and instruments) may, in fact, be an important goal for a group's choreographer or artistic director. When this aligns with the state's interest in authenticity of intent, i.e., when the ideological message is appropriately conveyed through content, then intent and content fuse.

Thus, as far as the state is concerned, authenticity of intent, which frequently characterizes choreographic productions like those of Moiseyev and Kolo, take precedence over authenticity of content.

The Establishment of State Folk Ensembles in the Former Yugoslavia

The Soviet Union, tolerating no deviations from their own practices, directed the founding of state-sponsored dance companies in all of the Soviet republics and autonomous regions, and in the countries of the soviet bloc, which in that period included Yugoslavia (before Tito's break in 1947–48). Modeled after the Moiseyev Dance Company, local companies adjusted their repertoires and choreographic strategies to local conditions. Even after the break with Moscow, Tito's Yugoslavia continued to support the burgeoning world of folk dance and song. Josip Broz Tito himself benefited from the appearances of these companies since several panegyric songs and dances were composed in his honor, reminding their audiences of Tito's role as leader of the partisans who freed Yugoslavia from the fascists and civic and ferocious ethnic strife that characterized wartime Yugoslavia.

Immediately after World War II, throughout Yugoslavia, partly in response to the fear that a precious folkloric tradition would be lost, and partly to provide urban youth with wholesome physical activity, a huge movement of amateur folk dance companies rose. These amateur activities generated genuine interest among large portions of the urban population, which to a large extent continues today (*Folklor Naroda Jugoslavije* 1963, n.p.).

Kolo was the first of the dance ensembles of the former Yugoslavia to be established on a professional level in May 1948 under the title of the "State Ensemble of Folk Dances of the People's Republic of Serbia"; it took the name Kolo (after the most popular genre of Serbian folk dance) in 1953 (*Folklor Naroda Jugoslavije* 1963, n.p.; *Kolo, Beograd-Yugoslavia* n.d.). Kolo was designed to show the happy rainbow of ethnicity and ethnic coexistence of the Yugoslav Republic through the choreographic strategies of providing a dance from each of the republics, as well as Vojvodina and Kosovo, the two autonomous regions of Serbia. The ensemble also maintained an all-Serbian repertoire for special occasions. Kolo, under the title of Yugoslav Folk Ballet, performing "Slavonic Rhapsody," which first toured the United States in 1956, created considerable interest in the concert world as the first cultural representatives of the communist world. The publicity never featured the word "Serbian."

The original plan was to have a professional ensemble in each of the six constituent republics, but Bosnia-Herzegovina, Montenegro, and Slovenia, while having considerable amateur dance activity, never established professional companies. Croatia and Macedonia established their professional companies LADO and Tanec from pre-existing amateur companies (Jožo Vlahović and Koco Racin, respectively), which had won significant prizes in major Eastern European festivals (*Folklor Naroda Jugoslavije* 1963, n.p.).

The Yugoslav government, as the Soviet government before them, found that Yugoslav folk dance was both a terrific propaganda tool, reminding the world of Tito's independence from the USSR and Yugoslavia's existence between East and West, and a profitable economic venture since the tours to the West garnered much-needed Western currency. All three of the professional ensembles had intensive touring schedules, and Yugoslav folk dance concerts became a popular concert staple throughout Europe, the United States, Australia, and Asia during the next four decades.

All of the dance companies came under considerable state management, especially when on tour abroad, and in the first years, government agents accompanied the dance companies to prevent defections to the West (Shay 2002, 116–117). All of the companies, invariably titled "Yugoslav Folk Ballet" when on tour outside of Yugoslavia, featured folk dances from the various republics and autonomous regions. The three professional ensembles maintained two distinct identities: that of a pan Yugoslav dance company as well as of a specific republic identity. For example, LADO, the Ensemble of Folk Dances and Songs of Croatia, performed both all Croatian and pan Yugoslav evenings in their annual appearances in the Dubrovnik Summer Festival.[3]

Serbian Identity

Serbia and Montenegro have a combined population of over 10 million, of whom 2 million, almost entirely Albanian, live in the autonomous area of Kosovo, and so, although officially still a part of Serbia, this population essentially lies outside of Serbian control. I need to stress that to be identified as a Serb an individual must be a speaker of Serbo-Croatian, and most importantly, be a member of the Serbian Orthodox faith. This does not imply that a particular Serb is a believer in Orthodoxy, but that his or her family is identified as Serbian Orthodox. Also, one does not have to reside in Serbia to be a Serb. Prior to the disintegration of the former Yugoslavia, fully 12 percent of the population of Croatia was Serbian. It is important to grasp that even during the communist era, when religion was cast in a negative light in social life, religion remained a major marker of ethnic identity. Many Serbs have little or no faith, but if Serbian Orthodoxy was an integral element in their heritage, they are still considered to be Serbian. Thus, it is these ethnic requirements — Serbo-Croatian as one's native language and being born in a family whose origins lie in the Serbian Orthodox faith — that determine an individual's "Serbianness"; that means that Gypsies, Slavic Muslims, Albanians, and other minority groups residing in Serbia can never be Serbian.

I need not reiterate for anyone that Serbs, often with the tacit or explicit support of the Serbian government, have been shown to have engaged in ethnic cleansing in Croatia, Bosnia, and Kosovo in the worst atrocities that Europeans had seen since World War II. They targeted Croatians (who are Roman Catholic), Slavic Moslems, and later in Kosovo they attacked the Albanians. Thus, ethnic representation of these minorities in a state-sponsored dance company assumes a crucial significance in national life.

It is important to stress, as I describe the way in which ethnic minorities are represented in Kolo's repertoire, that no state directive existed to deliberately denigrate any specific group and individual choreographers did not harbor evil notions of hatred toward any specific group. In fact, to be represented in the repertoire of the state-sponsored dance ensemble was often considered an honor for one's ethnic group (Shay 2002, 23). Rather, I suggest that individual choreographers, in undertaking the state imperative to represent the various ethnicities within their repertoires, turned to unmediated, pre-existing ethnic stereotypes that already floated freely in Serbian society to create the choreographic images that ultimately appeared in their programs.

I turn now to a close reading of four choreographic depictions from the repertoire of Kolo, the State Folk Dance Ensemble of Serbia. In the opening sequences (prologue) of the video *Kolo* (1987), dancers' faces are shown in what I call the "Heroic Young Serbia" representational mode juxtapositioned with Serbian Orthodox icons of saints, inviting the viewer to see how the Serbs resemble the chaste and the martyred saints — that they are, in fact, the same. The opening dance sequences, Dances of Serbia (#1), reinforces these images with the Serbian dancers from Šumadija (Central Serbian region) modestly dressed. The music is tastefully, almost classically played by a "folk" orchestra whose instrumentation is perhaps more suited to playing Mozart's chamber music, always a hallmark of Kolo's productions.[4] The dances display moderation rather than vigor; the demeanor of the dancers is elegant and dignified. The choreography of lines and circles characterizing these kolo dances are ordered. Thus, this depiction of the Serbian peasant, and by inference the Serbian nation, constitutes a positive depiction, described as my first category of modes of representation.

In the second depiction that I describe (#9), the Albanians (Shiptari) are represented in the "primitive" mode. The Albanian population, largely but not entirely located in the Kosovo-Metohija region of what is officially South Serbia, numbers over 2 million. The austere costumes, the noble demeanor of the dancers, and the solo drum, all highlighted by dramatic lighting, show the Albanians as noble savages. They are, of course, performing as primitive men with the prehistoric cave men fighting over a woman, and their dance represents death and resurrection, a primitive folk belief. The staging suggests a hypermasculine and primitive, dangerous environment. All is one-dimensional and spare. The two dancers (Serbs), brandishing their swords, have been chosen for their hawklike, and therefore, warlike facial features, dramatically lighted to emphasize these martial characteristics.

In the third dance (#3), the Muslims of the Sandjak, a small group of Slavic Muslims who, like the Muslims of Bosnia, are depicted as exotic. The women wear gauzy veils never seen in this region, but that are very much a part of the orientalist depictions found in Hollywood and Broadway musical productions like *Kismet*. Here the women go to fetch the water (because obviously they have no piped water in their primitive houses). The emphasis of the dance with languorous hip movements, devoid of energy, choreographically produces the orientalist notion of harem women as slothful creatures used to sitting around all day in their luxurious abodes. This is a feminine and "feminized" culture.

Each of these choreographed ethnic portraits of the "other" in Serbian society varied according to the ethnic group being portrayed. The Gypsies (#10) are shown as childlike, indolent, over-sexed and therefore worthless people. The choreographies featured stereotypical props as a Gypsy wagon, a camp fire and the clothes were covered with patches. They are shown in high relief in the programs of the Serbian State Ensemble in comparison with the Serbs. In the Serbian folk dances, the women are portrayed as demure and the costumes cover the entire body except the lower arms, while the hair is arranged in "proper" braids. The Gypsies on the other hand have their hair free and disordered to signify "sexual looseness," and the blouses are off the shoulder and they show bare legs (none of this is what actual Gypsies would do). At the end of the dance, a man runs his hand up the woman's leg under her skirt until the lights fade out, indicating an evening of unbridled passion ahead.[5] Most of the viewers of these images in the conference presentation in which I gave the original version of this paper were shocked by the overtly negative images of Gypsies contained in the choreography.

It is perhaps useful to mention that Roma have always played important roles in both café and village musical life in Serbia, and they are widely perceived as having an "innate" musical talent, much in the same way that African Americans were perceived as having "natural rhythm." Currently, Roma have taken a prominent role in turbo music, which is wildly popular with Serbian youth. I suggest that this popularity also parallels the experience of African Americans in rock 'n' roll in which white youth flocked to rock music, which was the despair of the older generations and the American establishment. Turbo music, like rock 'n' roll, contains the elements of generational rebellion that challenges established attitudes toward ethnicity and proper behavior in Serbian society.

The Albanians fare only slightly better: they are depicted as "primitive" and "warlike." Like the Gypsies, the choreography shows the Albanians fighting over a woman. The Muslims of the Sandjak of Novi Pazar are depicted as exotic, dreamlike creatures from the *Thousand and One Nights*. It must be grasped that the Muslims of Bosnia, who were slaughtered, raped, and tortured in the thousands, are essentially the same as those of Serbia — that is, the process of Islamicization of the two populations was historically similar.

As social scientist Craig Calhoun notes: "Underlying much of the pressure towards repressive sameness and essentialist identities is a tendency to think in terms of what Harrison White (1992) has called categorical identities. The abstractness of categories encourages framing claims about them as though they offered a kind of trump card over the other identities of individuals" (1994, 26).

I argue that, in fact, these choreographies visually establish these ethnic groups as lower "Others" in Serbian society. To what degree can such negative, disparaging depictions of the "Other" permit and encourage the excesses of ethnic cleansing that characterized Serbian civil life during the breakup of the former Yugoslavia?

The representations of state-sponsored dance companies come with all of the panoply and authority of the financial and political support of a national government and create little space for resistance. The examples of representation that are provided through video images for this essay beg the question of how the represented peoples might have represented themselves.

By using the examples from the Kolo repertoire, I by no means wish to suggest that the practice of choreographically depicting the Other exists only in the Serbian company. There also exist other examples in Ballet Folklorico, in which the rebellious and poverty stricken peasants of Chiapas are depicted in a never-never land in which the dancers wear lacy, embroidered black dresses and dance to the mellifluous strains of the giant Isthmus marimba and the sizeable African Mexican population is choreographically totally absent except for giant Black Sambo images in the Vera Cruz carnival scene. The Bayanihan ensemble of the Philippines depicts its Muslim population as cold, distant and haughty.

This then poses the question: What are the responsibilities of choreographers in the depictions of the Other? My conclusion is that the choreographer who represents the Other bears responsibility when creating and reinforcing negative, dehumanizing images. On the most serious level of evaluation they can aid the state and the individual to participate in crimes against humanity such as those perpetrated in the former Yugoslavia by regarding minority groups as "lesser others" and perpetuating negative popular images through their artistic production. The burden lies on the choreographer, and the ensemble for whom they create choreographic works, to represent all ethnic groups in an ethically responsible manner.

Notes

1. In this discussion of dance in the Middle East, it is solo improvised dance performed by professional dancers, rather than communal, regional folk dances, that are widely held in ill repute. In Afghanistan, all forms of dance were banned by the Taliban.
2. Other monarchs, notably Henry VIII and his daughter, Elizabeth I, were highly lauded as excellent dancers and several paintings depict them performing at court. There was, however, no conscious effort to turn their performances into public propagandistic displays as was the case for Louis XIV.
3. One evening in 1974 in Poreč, a Slovenian resort town on the Adriatic coast, I saw a joint concert of Kolo, LADO, and Tanec. Each of the ensembles performed four dance suites representative of its specific republic. Kolo performed the "Serbian Suite," "Dances of Vranje," "Banat Dances," and "Dances of Eastern Serbia."
4. Although Yugoslavia has a wide variety of untempered folk instruments (that is, instruments with uneven tunings not compatible to the piano), the policy in Kolo seemed to be to avoid the use of these instruments in favor of an orchestra of violins, flute, oboe, and clarinet, which created sounds more congenial to the Western listener. The oboe, for example, replaced

the *zurna*, a double reed instrument with a piercing sound. By contrast, the Croatian ensemble, LADO, utilized a wide range of authentic folk instruments in their pursuit of "authenticity of content" in Maners's terms.

    5. One might contrast the use of stereotypical images of Gypsies found in the 1947 film "*Golden Earrings*" starring Marlene Dietrich with the pernicious images projected by Kolo. In the depiction in "*Golden Earrings*," the Gypsies are shown with all of the stereotypical elements of Gypsy life known to Americans at that time. Unlike the Serbian version of childlike, lustful, oversexed, and indolent characteristics found in the two choreographies of Kolo, "*Golden Earrings*" depicts the Gypsies as a freedom-loving, romantic, and colorful people living a simple, pleasure-filled life, shorn of any negative characteristics.

Bibliography

Calhoun, Craig. 1994. "Social Theory and the Politics of Identity." In *Social Theory and the Politics of Identity*, ed. Craig Calhoun." Oxford: Blackwell, 9–36.

Desmond, Jane C. 1997. "Embodying Difference: Issues in Dance and Cultural Studies." In *Meaning in Motion: New Cultural Studies of Dance*, ed. Jane C. Desmond. Durham, NC: Duke University Press, 29–54.

Folklor Naroda Jugoslavije (Folklore of the Yugoslav Peoples). 1963. Zagreb: Graficki Zavod Hrvatske.

Hilton, Wendy. 1981. *Dance of Court and Theater: The French Noble Style, 1690–1725*. Hightstown, NJ: Princeton Book Company.

Kant, Marion. 2004. "German Dance and Modernity: Don't Mention the Nazis." In *Rethinking Dance History: A Reader*, ed. Alexandra Carter. New York: Routledge, 107–118.

Kolo: Ansambl Narodnih Igara Serbije (Ensemble of Folk Dances of Serbia). Program for summer and fall. www.kolo.co.yu.

Kolo, Beograd-Jugoslavija (prospectus). n.d. Beograd: Novi Dani.

Kolo: Jugoslvenski Nacionalni Balet. (Yugoslav National Ballet). n.d. Programs (from the 1950s, 1960s, and 1970s).

Lentz, Thomas W., and Glenn D. Lowry. 1989. *Timur and the Princely Vision: Persian Art and Culture in the Fifteenth Century*. Washington, DC: Smithsonian Institution Press.

Maners, Lynn. 2005. "To Dance Is (Not a) Human (Right): Public Performance and Political Economy in the Balkans." Paper given at Annual Conference of Congress on Research in Dance (Dance and Human Rights). Montreal, November 10–13.

Manning, Susan Allene, and Melissa Benson. 2001. "Interrupted Continuities: Modern Dance in Germany." In *Moving History/Dancing Cultures: a Dance History Reader*, ed. Ann Dils and Ann Cooper Albright. Middletown, CT: Wesleyan University Press, 218–227.

Shay, Anthony. 1974. "...And Then They Danced." Paper presented at the 73rd annual meeting of the American Anthropological Association, Mexico City, November 19–24.

_____. 1999. *Choreophobia: Solo Improvised Dance in the Iranian World*. Costa Mesa, CA: Mazda Publishers.

_____. 2002. *Choreographic Politics: State Folk Dance Companies, Representation, and Power*. Middletown, CT: Wesleyan University Press.

_____. 2005. "Dance and Jurisprudence in the Islamic Middle East." In *Belly Dance: Orientalism, Transnationalism, and Harem Fantasy*, ed. Anthony Shay and Barbara Sellers-Young. Costa Mesa, CA: Mazda Publishers, 51–84.

von Bibra, Anne Louise. 1987. "Continuity and Change in the Dance Events of the Two Lower Franconian Villages During the Twentieth Century." Masters thesis, University of California, Los Angeles.

Yugoslav Folk Dances. 1950(?) Beograd: Jugoslavia.

Zemtsovsky, Izaly, and Alma Kunanbaeva. 1997. "Communism and Folklore." In *Folklore and*

Traditional Music in the Former Soviet Union and Eastern Europe, ed. James Porter. Los Angeles: UCLA Department of Ethnomusicology, 3–23.

Videolog

Jugoslavije u Pesmi i Igre. n.d. Beograd: Televizija Beograd.
Kolo: Yugoslavian National Ballet. 1987. Radio-Televizija Beograd.

Balkan Dance in America

10

"Inside, Outside, Upside-Down": The Role of Mainstream Society Participants in the Ethnic Dance Movement

ROBIN J. EVANCHUK

In the spring of 1956 Dr. Mary Bran, a successful West Coast entrepreneur, brought a performing group called Tanec to seven major cities in the United States. Though the Macedonia-based group performed music and dance from Yugoslavia, it is doubtful that Dr. Bran was at all interested in ethnicity. Dr. Bran should, however, be credited with bringing one of the first performing groups from eastern Europe to the United States after the thaw in the Cold War.

Bran took advantage of the interest such a group would bring to those who were curious about people from that part of the world, despite the prejudices of the McCarthy era that were still prevalent. Many openly objected to a "Communist" group in their midst and performances were only moderately attended in Los Angeles with the bulk of the audience for Tanec being Yugoslavian Americans, college students, and folk dance enthusiasts.

The 1950s had opened an ethnic revival movement, especially in music and dance, promoted by prestigious coffee houses such as the "Ash Grove" in Los Angeles and the "Hungry I" in San Francisco. This new interest did much to promote the recognition and appreciation of ethnic groups and their customs. Ethnic activities and events recurrently became a fashionable part of the public domain. To be considered culturally literate, many Americans felt the need to learn about the histories and cultures of American nationality groups, and to sample their folklore as well. Indeed, the ethnic movement could only have been sustained with support from Americans of all backgrounds and creeds.

Though most Americans responded in what could be termed a rather conventional manner to the interest in cultural traditions, some individuals behaved quite differently. Many who did not claim membership in any particular ethnic group periodically "adopted" single cultural communities, participating enthusiastically in their unique cultural activities. In the book *Assimilation in American Life*, Milton Gordon (1964) attempts to explain this need to associate with an ethnic group:

> ... the sense of ethnicity has proved to be hardy. As though with a wily cunning of its own, as though there were some essential element in man's nature that demanded it-something that compelled him to merge his lonely individual identity in some ancestral group of fellows smaller by far than the whole human race, smaller often than the nation-the sense of ethnic belonging has survived [24–25].

Why did some individuals who were not members of a particular ethnic group participate so enthusiastically in certain cultural activities of minority groups? How did they react and respond to being both outside and inside participants in a culture different from their own? How did they assess their contributions to the ethnic group and to the revival movement? The proposed ethnic revival of the 1950s has generated studies involving groups of precise ethnic descent. Researchers such as Robert B. Klymasz (1973) and Beatrice S. Weinreich (1960) have initiated exhaustive discussion on revivals and survivals of immigrant and ethnic folklore. An analysis of the diverse approaches to many of these studies has been written by Robert A. Georges. Less understood and rarely addressed, however, is the impact of this revival on the majority culture. I will discuss this aspect as well as the previous questions by examining individuals who felt they had no unique ethnic ancestry themselves, but who took part in the ethnic folk dance revival of the period.

Folk and square dancing had been a popular hobby and pastime in the United States since the early part of the 20th century. Books such as *The Country Dance Book* (1937) by Beth Tolman and Ralph Page were popular, particularly at colleges and universities on both coasts. In Doris Hering's "Twenty Five Years of American Dance" (1954), Michael Herman, director of the Community Folk Dance Center in New York in the 1950s, reported:

> Just about twenty-five years ago Dr. Elizabeth Burchenal said in one of her folk dance books, "A very general appreciation of folk dancing as it may apply to the everyday life of American people is yet to come. It is still a kingdom around the corner, just waiting to be discovered." Well, the kingdom has not only been dis-

covered, it is occupied by well over a million people who participate in some sort of folk dance activity every day. And the population is steadily growing!

These folk dance enthusiasts had formed loose federations which held regular social meetings once a week, and organized festivals on various weekends. At such meetings dancers donned ethnic costumes and executed dances from a large assortment of countries, usually with short performances by member groups in the form of "exhibitions" or "demonstrations" which were placed in the middle of the folk dance program.

Considerable emphasis was placed on the international aspects of the program. For example, in the summer of 1956, a festival in Long Beach, California, listed more than one hundred different dances. About thirty countries were represented with an average of two dances per country. In the Long Beach program no single dance form or country as yet dominated the festival. The emphasis at this time was on couple dances in the "intermediate" range of difficulty, leaning toward a preference for Scandinavian dances. Only four selections were from Balkan countries, a fact which suggests that this area was not yet accorded any special privilege.

During this period personal preferences of dancers covered a wide range of countries including the Balkans, but most participants followed the belief stated by numerous federation members which promoted the concept that doing dances from a variety of countries promoted one's deeper understanding of peoples of the world. This exemplified for them "the American way" of doing things. On the other hand, I can recall from personal experience that these dance events were regularly visited by members of the FBI or CIA. Why these visits occurred was never explained, but apparently Cold War fears aroused suspicion of those interested in dances of other countries, particularly those that were associated in any way with the Soviet Union. However, the strong international flavor of the program, as well as the much appreciated advocacy of international dance by the Vice President at the time, Richard Nixon, allowed participants to enjoy an eastern European dance or two without being looked upon with suspicion by fellow dancers or visitors to these events.

The tour of the Macedonian group Tanec was followed the same year by the unprecedented arrival of another Balkan troupe, Kolo. Acquiring its name from the national dance form of Yugoslavia, this second performing group (this time from Beograd) not only changed the lives of many individuals in the United States, but also irreversibly altered the nature of international folk dancing and the personal lives of many of its participants. A new level of enthusiasm emerged. Some folk dancers in the audience returned night after night to the theater to see every performance of Tanec and Kolo.

Some followed the groups to other cities and by the time the performers left the area these devoted individuals had acquired a strong familiarity with the dances, music and style of the companies and had begun to pattern their own dance styles after what they had seen on the stage. Contacts were then made with local members of the Balkan-American community with whom the dancers met and from whom they could obtain useful information on the Balkan Culture. In time, these devotees became strong supporters of this ethnic culture and wished to become a part of such a culture locally.

Since participation in Balkan folk dances eventually out-shadowed all other dance cultures for these people the impact of these visiting dance troupes requires some evaluation in order to explain the rationale for their unique choice.

Why the Balkans?

Using the recollections of those that had been involved, interview sessions were set up with folk dancers who had been active during the period as well as with Yugoslavian Americans who were also connected with folk dancing. Those interviewed were chosen from participants in the Los Angeles and San Francisco areas who were willing to spend time recalling events of what is termed by them as "the Balkan years" of the folk dance movement. Though the real names of the informants will be easily recognized by those who were involved in folk dancing, pseudonyms created by the interviewees will be used throughout to protect the privacy of those who consented to take part in this study.

At that first Tanec concert in 1956, as the lights were lowered and the curtain rose, few had any idea of what to expect or what would be contained in an evening of folk dance "in concert." It would have been difficult to predict the impact the next two hours would have on the individuals attending.

"It was so different from anything I had ever seen before," stated Joanna, who was eighteen years of age at the time of the Tanec performance. "Different" was a word used by many of those interviewed and yet, by the very nature of their folk dance experience, which was promoted by an active Folk Dance Federation, they had often been exposed to cultures that could be termed "different" from their own. Some explanations are supplied by the interviewees themselves. "These were real people," said Pavo who had been folk dancing since the 1940s. "Looking down at them from the balcony, their singing, the color in the darkened audience, looking down at these people from another world, they were spotlighted, and we warmed to them." The "realness" noticed by Pavo seemed to center around the fact that standards set by those managing the Yugoslavian companies did not seem to be concerned with models of how an "ideal" performer should look but only whether or not he or she could sing, play an instrument or dance. Unlike the American stereotypical idea of what a performer should look like-handsome, thin, meticulously outfitted-these performers came in a multitude of sizes, shapes and costumes. Sizes ranged from thin and willowy to frankly fat which was quite unlike the stamped-out wallpaper pattern demeanor of a theater chorus line. It is possible that what the audience saw was not "difference" but similarity, a marked similarity to themselves. Indeed, some in the audience noted resemblances between their own friends and the Yugoslavian performers. Recalls one informant, "It was weird, the guy leading one dance looked just like Tom Wagner [a prominent Los Angeles folk dancer]. The female singer looked like Mary Wagner when she would sing at different functions. We sat mesmerized through the whole performance."

They did look "real," they looked like the folk dancers, and yet the lookalike performers were "spotlighted." They were set apart and presented in an exciting way to the Los Angeles audience. Noting these similarities between Yugoslavian performers and their own friends and acquaintances appears to have been one of the first major steps in the bonding process between the primarily non–Yugoslavian folk dancers and the ethnic culture itself.

For the first time, folk dance enthusiasts felt they could model their own behavior on that of the members of the dance troupes. By so doing they could earn the right to be considered Balkan dancers even though they were not Yugoslavians.

Familiarity with a few of the music or dance selections presented also helped to create a sense of identity with the Yugoslavian troupe. When questioned on what they remembered about the program in retrospect, most mentioned the dance "Nebesko kolo." Though only a few Yugoslavian dances were done at each Federation-sponsored festival, this selection was one of them. (One wonders what the members of Tanec must have thought when this small dance, amid so many others on their program, received such an enthusiastic response by the Los Angeles audience.)

Audience members were attracted to what they perceived to be simpler examples of the dance and musical repertoire than would be presented by professional dance troupes who performed ballet and modern dance. The kolo dance form itself further unravels the mystery of why the preference for Balkan dance examples developed as rapidly as it did. The majority of Yugoslavian dance customs were executed in circles and lines. Though not unique to Yugoslavia or the Balkan countries alone, this style of dance allowed a greater degree of participation for less skilled dancers, which made these participants feel comfortable joining in. "People were captivated by dancing in lines," stated Pavo. "It helped with the imbalance of the sexes. I think that could partly explain the interest in line dances." Social situations were remarkably easier when one did not have to depend constantly on a partner of the opposite sex in order to participate. Phyllida, who was also caught up in the movement, recalls, "Coming from the majority culture where couple dancing was the thing to do, if you happened to be shy, or not such a good dancer, here was a form of dance that you could be responsible for yourself." Mark, one of the leaders of the Balkan movement, echoed Phyllida's sentiments, "I was always an introvert. Suddenly this unlocked doors for me, and when I found out I had a certain amount of flair for it, it was like wildfire!"

A final reason for the reverence for Balkan dance may lie in the common desire of many people to perform for others in some way. In the past, the local dancers had participated in demonstrations or exhibitions for the regional Federation festivals but their performances were usually on a gym floor with other folk dance enthusiasts sitting on the same floor around them. The music that served the dancers came from the now outdated 78rpm records or reel-to-reel tape recorders which were not always in the best of condition. The dancers from Tanec and Kolo, however, were elevated and "spotlighted," rendering a completely new kind of "exhibition" with "real"—not homemade–costumes and live music played with the proper instruments. "The phrase 'we can do that' was on everyone's lips or on their mind," recalled one interviewee after seeing the performances. Certainly, the irresistible desire to perform as Tanec and Kolo had done was present, and the time was right for the Balkan boosters to get ready to do just that.

Get ready they did! An impressive number of people (the exact count has never been attempted) departed in the summer of 1957 for Yugoslavia and other parts of the Balkans. This was the first contact for most of these Americans with the supposed origin and source of the Balkan culture that had become their passion. Many of these people made the journey as a pilgrimage to the "wellspring" of the culture to find and purchase items of "authentic" Balkan folklore. This group of people went into towns and cities expropriating costumes, folk art, instruments and dance directions from entire neighborhoods, purchasing and bargaining for anything the local population was willing to sell or trade. By late fall of that year, everyone had returned, bringing back a profusion of costumes, records, books, artifacts, music, songs, and dances for those who had remained at home. Now began their attempted transformation from partial to perfect participation in Balkan ethnicity.

In order to be properly outfitted, dancers visiting the Balkans gleaned every bit of information they could find on ethnic clothing. Costume descriptions from the Balkans were meticulously copied into carefully detailed reconstructions. During this process it became obvious that Balkan women often wore long thick braids, not permanent, under their elaborate headdresses. This style was readily adopted in the United States. Recalls one dancer I will call Lidya, "We searched every store asking for false hair. A lot of us went to the same stores without knowing it. All asking the same questions. I swear we started the wig fashions in the sixties!" Rose, another dancer whose major interest was Balkan dress, agreed. "Christian Dior had less influence on Los Angeles fashion than the folk dancers had! I believe firmly that [we could] start a fashion. I could go from store to store asking for a weird and funny piece of yardage and they couldn't produce it. Six months later I would walk into the same store and they would have it." Rose believes merchants noticed the interest in the unusual materials and misinterpreted it as a fashion trend.

Followers of the Balkan folk dance movement searched for other apparel pieces as well, such as embroidered ribbon, braid, ethnic jewelry, and footwear. Stated Victor, "There were two places you could get dance boots [common in many ethnic costumes]. One was in New York and the other in Mexico. I actually drove down to Tijuana, to the Atlas Shoe Shop with my pocket full of boot orders, then drove down again six weeks later to pick them up!" Dancers were ordering constantly from the New York store they had found and often they would wear their "treasures" to school and to work. It is conceivable that the highly sensitive fashion industry was influenced by the demands for wigs and all folk-related items such as boots, coin necklaces and embroidered trim from eastern Europe, for as those of us who were not exactly of "hippie age" can recall, these articles were highly popular among many age groups in the 1960s.

By the end of fall in 1957, interested individuals had already established a program of learning and performing Balkan dances. Consider Mark's recollections of a typical week during this period: "Monday after work was Serbo-Croatian language practice; Tuesday night, the singing group met; Wednesday, the dance group practiced; Thursday was usually a night at a Yugoslav café, eating, dancing, practicing the language and listening to the orchestra; Friday was dancing, and Saturday and Sunday more of the same with sewing of costumes, attending an ethnic picnic or seeing a Yugoslavian movie if there was one around."

Another informant recalls the initial efforts of the devotees to learn Serbo-Croatian at a time when texts and guides in that language were scarce in the Los Angeles area. The group finally obtained the only language aids available, distributed by the United States Armed Forces. The dancers recalled working with such irrelevant and unsuitable sentences as "Do you have a gun?" "Raise your hands above your head," and "Take me to the railroad station." Despite the obvious inappropriateness of such phrasing in the handbooks, the group was able to use them to advantage by learning proper grammar and sentence construction, then adding vocabulary from other sources later on. By the beginning of the New Year these committed persons had already made contact with members of ethnic Balkan communities in the Los Angeles area and were able to communicate with them with some proficiency in their native language. They had thoroughly memorized the entire programs of dances, songs and music that both Kolo and Tanec had offered. Three long-playing records of the performance had mysteriously emerged and were being sold at a local folk dance record store as well as at festivals all over the state. Books and magazines with instructions on the making of Balkan costumes and dance directions flourished and old issues of *National Geographic* (with *any* section devoted to the Balkans) became precious possessions.

Reaction by the local Balkan communities was on the whole positive. Local members of Yugoslav and Bulgarian communities began to request these devotees to teach them the dances of their particular region or country. "They begged us to teach at the Serbian Hall in San Pedro, and the ethnics came to learn," stated Mary Wagner. In truth, the folk dancers helped to make Balkan dance an object of appreciation for the ethnic communities, instilling in those members a more positive sense of their own Balkan ethnic identities. Because of the lack of support from the Folk Dance Federation, in general these Balkanophiles turned more and more to the ethnic communities to reinforce and justify their own commitment to Balkan culture. (Some informants have even stated that a few of these groups are still in operation; one of them located in San Pedro is still supposedly being taught from time to time by one of the original converts to the culture.) As ethnic groups gained recognition and visibility in the 1960s, the folk dance enthusiasts could feel that they had contributed to, and become a legitimate part of, this ethnic reawakening, learning from and contributing to its strength and maintenance.

As identity with Yugoslavia and other Balkan countries grew stronger, its influence became the fundamental force in the dancer's lives. Professed Mark, "I had a reverence for those people. The hero of my life was the president of the local Bulgarian club." The folk dancers used Balkan folklore to shape a new identity of sorts for themselves. Unlike some people of no particular ethnic descent who might have had some feelings of disappointment in not being part of the ethnic revival, the folk dancers (when ethnicity became the rage in the 1960s) took advantage of their involvement in Balkan dance to adopt a surrogate ethnic identity. In describing further how they felt about devoting themselves to Balkan culture in the early 1960s Phyllida remarked, "It was like the opening out of some wonderfully colored flower in a grey world. It was like the flower children. All you need is love." Stated another interviewee, "Somehow you have a purpose."

It is not surprising then that after visualizing and comparing their supposedly dull, lifeless mainstream culture to that of the Balkan one, the need to "adopt" an ethnic culture as their own seemed very compelling. Because of the strong influence that Balkan culture had on these individuals they began to lead a double existence, with job, home and family on one side and their Balkan world on the other. After a while it became apparent to some that even this compartmentalization of ethnic and mainstream identities wasn't sufficiently satisfying, and the Balkan identity began to project itself into other aspects of their lives. This varied collection of people began to form a unique group and to think of themselves as distinct from the rest of the recreational folk dance community as well as from those "non–Balkan" people whom they encountered in their everyday lives. A single person behaving in this unique way would have gone virtually unnoticed but as a group their strong influence began to be felt by the folk dance community in general.

In time, the West Coast movement of Balkan dance became one of the most enthusiastic in the country, setting itself apart from the general Federation membership. In imitation of the Tanec and Kolo troupes, semi-professional performing groups began to surface in the late 1950s and early 1960s, particularly in Los Angeles and San Francisco. At first, these were exactly patterned after the two original touring companies. One dancer noted, "We had learned their program and we followed it. Hell, we even made the same mistakes they did." Later in the period, as confidence grew, these American performing troupes began to explore new programs, adding new music and dance ideas of their own.

Tension often resulted between the West and East Coast branches of the movement. For example, the West Coast groups favored "kolo" dancing over other dance forms. Mr. V. F. Beliajus (1957) writes in an article entitled "Dance Situation–1957" that

> kolo dancing out East, tho [sic] popular, is not the craze. Nore [sic] does it share the West Coast enthusiasm within any reach of proportions. The best kolo dancers and in greatest numbers are nearly all on the West Coast. On a whole and for the most part the East Coaster and all Central States take kolo on an equal footing as a part of international dancing which is by far healthier and should be highly commended. For kolo seems to be a mania which also inspires tendencies of selfishness.

Beliajus explained that the "kolomaniacs" are often aloof and exclusive and attempt to dominate the floor (17). Kolo dancers thought of themselves

Members of Yosemite Workshop (dance ensemble) in Macedonian dances from the Skopje region 1957. Courtesy Robin Evanchuk.

as the elite of folk dancers. As Phyllida observes, "There was definitely an elite. At Gandy's [a distinguished Southern California folk dance group] they would always play the men's show-off Balkan dances and everyone sat and watched in disgust or awe." Those watching in "disgust" appear to be those who were not as interested in Balkan dance and preferred a more general folk dance program. Those who did not count themselves as part of the Balkan movement were often dismissed and ignored by those involved in the Balkan section. Thus, the kolo enthusiasts were able to influence the folk dance world in significant ways.

Some critics went so far as to say that kolo enthusiasts might wish to form their own Federation, which would be the first major break with the folk dance movement. The dominance of kolo dancing was also evident in San Francisco's popular Kolo Festival, which took place always on Thanksgiving weekend and which presented only Balkan music and dance. Newsletters appeared that were devoted solely to Balkan interests, and another popular folk dance magazine, *Let's Dance*, created a Balkan section in its publication. Festival programs of this later period of the mid-sixties list many more Balkan dances than were evident before the arrival of Tanec. As new folk dancers appeared, many were swiftly absorbed into the kolo movement section of folk dancing. Folk dance coffee houses emerged in various parts of southern California that were devoted mostly to line dances. The anti-kolo people felt, in the words of Pavo, then president of the Southern California Folk Dance Federation, that "they were letting things get away from them."

The Balkan movement asserted its primacy as a result of the leadership of two individuals whom I have called Mark and Alice. Both had entered folk dance organizations years earlier and had become devoted members of various Federation-sponsored groups. They were recognized for their skills, contagious enthusiasm, and ability to charm and captivate others in the group. A frequent statement was that Alice "is perfect." "If Mark hadn't been there we wouldn't have done as much" was another. "People were intrigued by Mark and Alice. Each had a mystery about them" was a third comment. Working together both appeared to have the ability to draw a multitude of different types of people into what they were doing. Though they played a prominent role in keeping this group together, these two charismatic leaders may have also been partially responsible for its collapse. For almost all interviewees cited "too many people" as one of the reasons for the dissolution of the Balkan movement.

As the movement became larger first on the West Coast and ultimately on the East Coast, in large cities such as Boston and New York, the crusade began to lose its tightly knit unity and control. Those describing the end of the Balkan era could cite no one incident or time that marked it. The word used most often by interviewees was "dilution." "There were too many new people," said one person. Another stated, "New people changed the quality of the groups, and people began to compete against each other." To be sure, as new enthusiasts were drawn into the movement by Balkan dance classes generally taught by the charismatic Mark and Alice as well as by others proficient in Balkan dance, and by the exciting new performances given by the entire core group the Balkan crusade became too large to control. This seems to be reflected in the coffee houses that had originally dedicated themselves to Balkan dance. "They added Persian, Armenian, Israeli and Greek to their programs. The Balkan aspect was diluted by similar line-dance cultures."

By the end of the 1960s most of the original group had become separated joining and forming new affiliations, though they still remained connected on a smaller scale. More frequently, members of ethnic cultures were excluding some non-ethics interested in Balkan activities from fully participating with them probably due to the larger numbers of non–Balkan participants attending their functions and the non-membership of that bloc in Balkan belief systems. Churches and church halls often provided the loca-

Members of Yosemite Workshop in Posavina (Croatia) costumes. Courtesy Robin Evanchuk.

tions where dancing and dance teaching took place and congregants and clergy may have wished these activities to be reserved for members of their faith exclusively. "We would and could not be in any way authentic Yugoslavs," commented one informant. "We were still just Americans playing at it. We couldn't step over and into the skin of a Yugoslav. We couldn't go any further."

This period of decline was further marked by the untimely death of Alice who died in an auto accident north of Beograd in Serbia. She is buried in a small cemetery in Westwood, California, and her grave is still visited occasionally by those who knew her and danced with her.

In conclusion, enthusiastic participation of these mainstream Americans in the Balkan ethnic experience seems to have been due to the initial contact with featured and highlighted performers from a Balkan country, the physical similarity facilitating the ability to identify with the ethnic performers, the ease in accomplishment of the dances, and a dissatisfaction with the supposed dullness of their own majority culture. The added intrigue of these entertainers providing Americans with what was then a rare opportunity to make contact with individuals from a Soviet country also seems to have given

10. "Inside, Outside, Upside-Down"

Members of Yosemite Workshop performing Vrličko Kolo (Croatia). Courtesy Robin Evanchuk.

the activity the added excitement of being regarded as a bit dangerous. For young people of the 1950s who would soon witness a very different and freer decade, this risk was enough to make the Balkans their first culture choice.

It has been more than fifty years since this dedicated group of American folk dancers were sitting in the balcony of a Los Angeles theater watching the performance that inspired them. Many are now retired and some have passed away. The country that so forcefully influenced them recently disappeared entirely from world maps. Six fresh countries — Bosnia and Herzegovina, Croatia, Montenegro, the Republic of Macedonia, Serbia, and Slovenia — were created from Yugoslavia's former parts.

Today some of these devotees still participate in folk dance events and some retain their Balkan interests but don't do any dancing. Others are no longer able to dance but still attend some dance events. Most of the interviewees feel they contributed a great deal to Americans of Yugoslavian descent as well as to mainstream Americans. First, they gave confirmation to Balkan ethnic communities by their positive, enthusiastic reinforcement of Balkan culture. Appreciation of Yugoslavian ethnic identities was demonstrated by growing members of the non–Balkan mainstream American society that visited them. Second, by the formation of American performing groups specializing in Balkan art forms, they contributed to the growth, acceptance, and visibility of ethnic cultures in the United States.

Although many of the performance groups have ceased to exist some others still prosper. The performing company Avaz is a notable example of a self-supporting group that still has a high profile in both the ethnic and non-ethnic communities featuring not only Balkan material but selections from other areas of the world as well. Aman, the first Balkan-based company to achieve professional status- after over forty-four years-closed its doors in 2006. Balkan material in these groups as well as others have expanded knowledge about this area of the world and its traditions. For example, in 1979 the Aman company made its New York debut at the Brooklyn Academy of Music, and both Aman and Avaz have also toured outside the United States. During 1981 and 1982 Aman gave more than seventy performances in fifteen states. The company was the featured entertainment attraction during the opening months of the Walt Disney World Epcot Center World Showcase in Florida. During its residency at Epcot Center, Aman appeared on a CBS network television special. Aman's twentieth season, 1983–84, began with the company's first international tour. The United States Information Agency sponsored a seven-country tour to North Africa and the Middle East. Though both of these groups did add presentations from countries other than the Balkans to their repertoires, the Balkan presentations are considered to be their specialty by critics and audiences alike, attesting to the continued popularity of Balkan music and dance.

The dominant American culture frequently has been characterized by researchers and informants as a rather dull but dangerous behemoth with an aptitude for smothering the ethnic identity of the smaller subcultures. Consider, for example, Phyllida's description of her life before the Balkan contact as a "grey world." Or, the argument of Herbert J. Gans (1979) that, "there has been no revival, ... acculturation and assimilation continue to take place."

In Robert A. Georges's "Research Perspectives in Ethnic Folklore Studies" (1983), one of his models is based on the assumptions of researchers that "regard immigrant and ethnic groups as indivisible wholes and ... as group members who are indistinguishable culturally from one another." Not only is homogeneity assumed in ethnic groups, but in the American dominant culture as well. This assumption can, at least, be partially disproved by the evaluation of the activities of these unique individuals of the mainstream in the 1950s and 60s. Members of the host culture such as the Balkan enthusiasts have contributed in their own exceptional way to changing these assumptions.

The era of Balkan dance left a profound impression on all of its partic-

Members of Yosemite Workshop singing Macedonian song. Courtesy Robin Evanchuk.

ipants. The San Francisco Kolo Festival still survives, drawing hundreds of people each Thanksgiving weekend and the California Folkdance Federation now lists 129 dancers on its Internet site. More than 30 percent of those are from the Balkans. Most of those interviewed referred enthusiastically to their experiences. Tom Wagner maintained that Balkan culture in general had given his wife and himself endless pleasure. "We feel very special, as though we got into something most people couldn't. And it did something to our family. I tell you [if] a social worker could design an activity to be safe and good, you couldn't do much better." Tom continued to perpetuate that tradition, teaching Balkan culture to his children. Added Joanna, "They [the Balkan years] were some of the happiest years of my life. Now, at the concerts I am the one with the tears streaming down my face because I can't [participate]." Pavo admitted that one half of his music and books are still Balkan. "Four or five of my ten favorite songs are Balkan. I still enjoy cooking and creating a Yugoslavian dinner." Others have become immensely interested in travel, not just to the Balkans but to other areas such as China, India, and Australia in order to explore customs and culture patterns different from their own. Another informant confessed the influence the Balkan dance movement had on his life: "By God," he declared, "when I die I hope I have a heart-attack while dancing Ushest kolo!"

Notes

*The beginning portion of the title of this article was taken from Stan and Jan Berenstain's *The Berenstain Bears Inside Outside Upside Down* (New York: Random House, 1997). This paper is an extended version of an essay that appeared in *Folklore and Mythology Studies*, 11/12, 115–129 (1987/88). I also wish to express my appreciation to Professor Michael Owen Jones for his encouragement and advice on this essay.

Bibliography

Beliajus, V. F. 1957. "Dance Situation-1957." In *Viltus* XVI, 15, 17.
Gans, Herbert J., Nathan Glazer, and Joseph R. Gusfield, eds. 1979. *On the Making of Americans: Essays in Honor of David Kiesman*. Philadelphia: University of Pennsylvania Press.
Georges, Robert A. 1983. "Research Perspectives in Ethnic Folklore Studies," *Folklore and Mythology Studies* 7, 1–23.
Gordon, Milton. 1964. *Assimilation in American Life: The Role of Race, Religion and National Origins*. New York: Oxford University Press.
Hering, Doris, ed. 1954. "*Twenty Five Years of American Dance.*" New York: *Dance Magazine*, 172.
Klymasz, Robert G. 1973. "From Immigrant to Ethnic Folklore: A Canadian View of Process and Transition." *Journal of the Folklore Institute* 10, 131–139.
Tolman, Beth, and Ralph Page. 1937. *Country Dance Book*. New York: Barnes.
Weinreich, Beatrice S. 1960. "The Americanization of Passover." In *Studies in Biblical and Jewish Folklore*, ed. Raphael Patai, Francis Lee Utley, and Dov Noy. Indiana University Folklore Series. No. 13. Bloomington: Indiana University Press, 329–366.

11

Balkan Tradition, American Alternative: Dance, Community, and the People of the Pines*

JUNE ADLER VAIL

When you dance *Ličko Kolo* you sense a dozen people's interconnected hands and synchronized steps. The dance begins in silence. To the rhythm of deliberate footfalls, one voice keens and is echoed plaintively by the whole group: "Sing to me, O Falcon, beneath my love's window. She fell asleep; cold was the stone beneath her head. I took away the stone and there I placed my hand." As the dancers follow a curved path, the line expands and contracts, breathing as a single body. The challenge is to adjust your movements to an unspoken common denominator: not to do what "feels right," or dance as brilliantly as possible, but to move in harmony with the group. The ensemble becomes greater than the sum of its parts, a visible embodiment of sensuality and cohesion.

Ličko Kolo is a line dance from the former Yugoslavia's Dalmatian coast and part of the repertory of Borovčani Balkan Dance and Music, a performing group I belonged to from 1978 to 1982.[1] Over time, as a participant and observer, I realized that Borovčani could be interpreted as a community of dancers with its own culture, history, structure, and import. Looking back, the group's staged choreographies and social processes seem to illuminate facets of America's fragmented society in the late seventies and early eighties.

Anthropologists, cultural critics, and dance theorists have carried on lively debates about the relationship between art and society, dance and cul-

*This essay appeared previously in Morris Gay, ed., Moving Words: Rewriting Dance, New York: Routledge, 1996.

ture. Should society, or history, be considered as "background" to art (Clark 1984, 250)? Does dancing, as a cultural form, "reflect" social values?

Sociologist Janet Woolf maintains that a mechanistic model of the relationship between cultural forms and social process implied by the word "reflection" is

> ... no longer a notion which theories of representation will allow. Cultural forms, like dance, do not just directly represent the social in some unmediated way. Rather, they *re*-present it in the codes and processes — of signification — the language of dance. Moreover, far from reflecting the already-given social world, dance and other cultural forms participate in the production of that world [1992, 707].

Similarly, anthropologist Cynthia Novack has articulated dancing's dual process:

> Culture is embodied. A primary means of understanding, knowing, making sense of the world comes through shared conceptions of our bodies and selves and through the movement experience society offers us. Movement constitutes an ever-present reality in which we constantly participate. We perform movement, invent it, interpret it, and reinterpret it, on conscious and unconscious levels. In these actions, we participate in and reinforce culture, and we also create it [1990, 8].

Detailed description of specific communities of dancers can document ways in which this mutually constitutive process occurs. Folk dances are often assumed to express the participants' shared identity, reflecting an already defined social world. Anthropologist Clifford Geertz suggests that art "materialize[s] a way of experiencing, bring[s] a particular cast of mind out into the world of objects where men can look at it" (1983, 99). Reciprocally, folk dancing also induces casts of mind and creates ways of experiencing and behaving. We dance the dances, and the dances, in turn, "dance" us.

In this interpretive analysis of Borovčani, my professional interests as a dance critic and researcher intersect with my personal history as a dancer and participant.[2] The justification for writing about a now-defunct amateur troupe, at the margins of American culture and the edge of a continent, lies in Borovčani's value as an example of a community of dancers that reinvented Balkan dance and movement for its own purposes, representing an American "cast of mind" and creating its own subculture.

I associate Balkan dancing with an embroidery sampler of Bulgarian patterns I began in 1980 and worked on for more than a year. I now marvel at the tiny cross-stitches, delicate in some designs, dense in others. Red, blue, yellow, olive green, and brown threads dance in intricate, repetitive patterns across the bleached linen. If you turn the sampler over, the reverse of the precise, lively stitching is a mishmash of knots and thread-ends where the bright colors overlap, begin, and end. On the back, the band with the densest pattern is a thick mat of floss, with brown predominant, although on the front brown appears only as minute outline stitches.

The sampler's front and back suggest Borovčani's two interwoven sides: polished, staged performances and casual, rather messy social organization. On the flip-side, tensions surrounded issues of authority and democracy, individual and collective goals, mainstream and counterculture values, professionalism and amateurism, dancing skills and interpersonal relations, and discipline and spontaneity. The fabric of the group tended to unravel into separate strands: long-time members and newer ones, expert dancers and novices, men and women, dancers and musicians. But like the embroidery, the group's intertwined aspects together created colorful, textured, energetic designs.

Performance: Balkan Dances, American Alternatives

Borovčani's performances often began with a processional dance through the audience and into a space or onto a stage, signaling the continuities between performance and everyday life and the similarities between performers and viewers. On stage, one musician or dancer would greet the audience and announce three or four dances at a time: she might offer commentaries on the dances' origins, costumes, music, or choreographic details between sets. Before an instrumental interlude or vocal segment a musician would speak briefly about Balkan music or the singers' distinctive open-throat style.

Our musical accompaniment included accordion, fiddles, recorder, and drums (a small and large handmade Macedonian *tupan*). These corresponded fairly accurately to contemporary, if not traditional, Slavic instruments. Instrumental sounds, such as the Bulgarian *gaida* (bagpipe), were mimicked on the accordion but without any pretense of historical or scholarly authenticity. The musicians learned tunes by imitating records and tapes or playing with other musicians. The accordionist played for all performances and nearly all rehearsals, although she often would have preferred to dance.

Wandering line dances usually skirted the edges of the stage or performance area, close to viewers who often surrounded us on three sides and at the same level. Straight line dances tended to occupy the center of the stage, facing the audience, cutting across on a horizontal plane or moving forward and back, towards and then away from the spectators. Borovčani's stylistic "signature" communicated down-to-earth energy, focused clarity, disciplined dexterity, and responsiveness among the performers and to the audience.

Unison movement is the most powerful stylistic element in Balkan dance, implying solidarity of purpose. Emphatic rhythms and overall group spatial configurations — open and closed circles and lines — also convey a sense of cohesion. Line dancing requires constant body contact: dancers are entwined by hand-, belt-, shoulder-, or waist-holds. The body of the group as a whole reveals important spatial forms. The dancers' individual body shapes are less significant: dancers can be any size, if they are strong and quick-footed.

Balkan rhythms are often complex and irregular: $7/16$, $11/16$, and $15/16$ times are common. Dance phrases do not always coincide exactly with musical phrasing. But most dances reproduce the structure of their musical accompaniment. In performance the dancers sometimes had the sense of being immersed in music and supported, even intoxicated, by its potent rhythms and insistent nasal sonorities.

The musicians placed themselves near the dancers or were enclosed within their circle to communicate visual cues and keep a common tempo: moving musicians and singing dancers. We dancers usually faced the music, and often interacted with the musicians, smiling and calling out to them. They also actively acknowledged remarks from dancers or applause from the audience. Facial expressions, off-hand jokes, and improvised yips or hollers were part of the performance. "Good dancers" could smile, talk with a neighbor, or call out while keeping up with intricate steps and holding proper spacing.

By 1982 the group had accumulated a repertory of over thirty dances, learned entirely through the imitation and repetition of step sequences, taught by a core group of experienced dancers who had mastered them. The repertory was composed principally of dances from Serbia, Croatia, and other provinces of the former Yugoslavia; Bulgaria; and a few East European countries, including Hungary and Poland.[3]

Stylistically, in most Balkan and East European dance the body is held erect but not rigid, and the trunk tends to move as a single unit. The most active parts of the body are the legs and feet, and arms and hands, coordinated with the orientation of the head. Often the upper body rotates contrapposto to the lower. Occasional jumps and hops, leaps, turns, and kneeling movements occur in men's dances, but the basic vocabulary consists of well-grounded, resilient walking and running.

The steps of Balkan dances are named and codified and can be taught relatively efficiently as the minimal units of choreographed sequences. These sequences are learned in sections, usually determined by the structure and rhythm of the music. The sections are then organized into dances or suites, with reiterated refrains or whole sequences repeated twice through. Sometimes a leader spontaneously calls the next section on the spot from among alternative variations. The overall organization of steps into sections, sections into dances, and dances into suites is intimately bound to rhythmic and spatial patterns.

For dramatic effect there are whole body vibrations, heel bounces, quick pas de basque, swooping Yemenite steps, zippy scissors kicks, reel steps, prances with high knees, and military heel clicks. Though most of the step combinations require rhythmic subtlety and intricate footwork, the women's feet are kept carefully close to the ground, and the upper torso is restrained. The men's style is flashier, with low squats and heel slaps, though the actual steps may be the same as the women's. Differences in male and female dance styles portray the male as physically more powerful, aggressive, and airborne, and the female as comparatively modest, stable, and earthy.

In Laban Movement Analysis terms, Balkan dances embody direct focus and sudden, forceful, "bound" energy. These movement characteristics can be interpreted as indicating assertiveness, clear thinking, pride, and vitality. The vigorous dances often accelerate from a slow, controlled beginning, growing in speed, complexity, and excitement. The endings of many dances are climactic and exuberant. Our bows were quick, with a running exit, like a circus act, we joked.

One way Borovčani represented "the social" through its codes and processes of signification — its language of dance — was hinted at by a dancer who commented, "Performing brings joy to the audience, but really, I like costumes and being someone else."

The women's costumes were a refinement of the funky peasant aesthetic that prevailed in everyday wardrobes and rehearsal clothing. For performances each of us wore an embroidered white peasant blouse, mid-calf-length white cotton skirt with red and black trim, based on Croatian prototypes, white stockings gartered at the knee with red ribbons, Serbian *opanke* (light woven leather shoes with turned-up toes), a woven sash and a green, blue, black, or red flowered challis shawl, usually tied like an apron around the waist. The typical hairstyle was braids, usually pinned up and entwined with red ribbon. The men wore white Croatian shirts (made from a commercial pattern), black pants, red sash, multi-colored hand-knit wool socks, Macedonian *opanke*, and black vests with red, yellow, and blue piping.

In its costumed references to the world beyond the stage, Borovčani's principal mode of representation was *imitative*, or *metonymic*, to use a literary trope often employed to describe a dance's relationship to worldly events. According to dance theorist Susan Foster, this mode "improves upon, as it replaces, the world to which it refers. The body substitutes for the subject, offering the best version of the subject it can" (1986, 66).

What world was impersonated, what subject improved upon and offered up for scrutiny? Who was the "someone else" one dancer enjoyed becoming? There seemed to be a double, and equivocal, possibility: an exotic "old country" world of modest, marriageable women and strong, energetic men, and simultaneously, an idealized contemporary vision of a homogeneous, egalitarian community "living the good life" in Maine.[4]

The imitative mode "leaves little doubt about the referent" (Foster 1986, 66) and Borovčani theatrically cued the audience to recognize the dancers as a band of exotic yet familiar rustics. In accordance with this category, we also tacitly invited viewers to evaluate how believably we impersonated peasants and how capably we portrayed aspects of our contemporary selves.

Because Borovčani's choreography also displayed virtuoso movement skills, the repertory combined what Foster terms the *reflective* mode with the *imitative*. "Reflective representation makes exclusive reference to the performance of movement itself" (ibid.), and only incidentally to other events in the world. Like the "pure dance" sections of narrative ballets or Indian classical dances, Balkan dancing's *reflective* representation was framed by *imitative* costumes and characteristic Balkan music, but it invited appreciation of the dances' intrinsic physicality and complexity and the performers' charisma and skill.

Finally, in the representation of mutual affection and group cohesion, Borovčani's dances can also be considered *metaphoric*, according to Foster's model. Above all, line and circle dances depicted the quality of harmony, translating shared experience into motion and design. The physical closeness of the dancers, their unison movement and common focus evoked analogies to — family circles? close-knit community? participatory democracy? political alliances? lines of defense? The dancers, although exotically costumed, metaphorically suggested synchrony with one another and their surroundings.

These modes of representation conveyed meanings on different levels simultaneously: traditional Balkan peasantry through colorful costumes and commentaries; virtuosic dance display through exciting energy, unfamiliar rhythms and sonorities; and contemporary community through the dances' inclusive forms, the focus of the performers' gaze and their proximity to the audience.

Borovčani performances seemed to embody the latent utopian tendency in American culture. Unlike indigenous, or professional, Balkan troupes which intentionally represent "the national," the group could more accurately be said to have represented "like-minded, racially homogeneous community" or "back-to-the-land values." As one member put it, "We are authentic Americans dancing in the style of the Balkans."

The People of the Pines

As a loosely woven community of dancers and musicians, Borovčani became a Maine institution during its five-year history. The group's most significant behind-the-scenes processes included how members were chosen; how the group structured itself; how it conducted rehearsals and meetings; how it assigned women's and men's responsibilities; what dancing meant as a physical, aesthetic and social activity; and how dancing helped create a culture.

In 1977, the group was christened Borovčani, Serbo-Croatian for "people of the pines." By 1982, when it dispersed, six members remained from the original "clan" of fifteen. Nine had left, and over time nine others had replaced them. Membership fluctuated as some people went back to school, had children, or moved away, but new recruits — several already expert in Balkan dance — always seemed to turn up.

The original group was self-selected, but, after a year, when I joined, the audition process required attendance at weekly rehearsals for a month or two, during which members evaluated a prospect's dancing abilities and social compatibility. The candidate could then ask to be voted in. Voting was usually a formality, since most who stuck it out for the trial period could sense they would be admitted. In five years just one aspirant was actually rejected by vote. Though its dances embodied inclusiveness, Borovčani limited membership to a relatively exclusive few.

The twelve respondents to the questionnaire I administered in 1982 were all white Americans, but within that category there was some diversity in age, education, and occupation. Seven women ranged in age from 24 to 38 and five men from 23 to 37. Nine were single or separated, and three were married — of these, two were parents. The levels of education ranged from college drop-outs (three) to master's degree recipients (two). Seven had an undergraduate B.A. or B.S. degree.

Members included a co-op warehouse worker, a musician, three teachers, a draughtsperson/graduate student, a pharmaceutical salesman, a graphic artist, a carpenter, a greenhouse worker, two odd-jobbers, and one self-styled *bon vivant*. The data records a Quaker, a Catholic convert and seven vegetarians. All had opposed the war in Vietnam, but otherwise we held diverse political views. Most had moved to Maine during the great immigration of the seventies.

Our mongrel ethnic backgrounds, going back two or more generations, included various combinations of Italian, Scottish, Polish, French, Belgian, English, Lithuanian, German, Lebanese, Dutch, Swedish, Irish, and Swiss, but there was not a Balkan among us. Despite variations in height, weight, and coloring, our physical appearances suggested essential similarities rather than differences.

Most of us actively participated in social, folk, and theater dance forms besides Balkan dancing. Members listed ballroom, boogie, and disco; New England contra dancing, Morris dance, English country dance, international folk dance, and Appalachian clogging; and contact improvisation and modern dance. Two dancers played recorder and penny whistle, and one each piano, violin, pipe and tabor, acoustic bass and squeezebox. Three were singers.

It is difficult to characterize Borovčani's internal organization and relationships. There was no single elected, or even informally acknowledged, leader. Most decisions about where or when to perform, and for what fee, were made during lengthy, often disorganized meetings held after weekly practices. Borovčani performed several times a year in Maine and elsewhere in New England — often at arts centers, elderhostels, schools and colleges, resort hotels, weddings, folk clubs, in self-produced concerts, and annually at the Maine Festival.[5] Fees ranged from gratis programs to $350 for roughly an hour's performance. Revenues covered transportation costs to performances and miscellaneous expenses for publicity, costumes, and rent for rehearsal space at a local church. There was no profit or income to individuals.

Despite its collective ethos, Borovčani exhibited some aspects of a meritocracy: those who executed dances best were the ones most likely to lead, when it was necessary. The ability to direct in a non-threatening way was also important. One member commented: "The better dancers or organizers usually take over and make good leaders. Those that can't dance well but try to be leaders just annoy the rest of the group."

Because we were ideologically committed to participatory decision making and consensual action, meetings sometimes became chaotic. A despot or two usually rose to the occasion. One dancer observed ironically that "Borovčani is run by temporary dictators who assume command (usually in a fit of pique), only to be softened, modified, and eventually reassimilated by the group. Thus things get done in a truly [?] democratic way."

Still another important structural factor was seniority. Most of the original, and older, members agreed that "leaders seemed to emerge when needed" and that the group "has a loose structure, but a shared sense of values." In spite of "personal differences" and "too much gab and gossip" they felt Borovčani were "dear people." In contrast, several newer, younger members thought there was "little communication," because the group was "a bit scattered" and "too anarchistic." In their view, there was "too much time spent talking and not enough dancing." They would have preferred more efficient, centralized leadership, taken on by senior members.

Members of Borovčani Dance Ensemble in performance. Photograph by David Vail.

Rehearsals often demonstrated the dilemma of leaderlessness. Endless joking and teasing, small talk and gossip created a familiar, familial intimacy. We chose a particular dance, performed it, discussed it, repeated parts, then ran the entire dance again. Then we milled around, drank some water, and broke into groups. Finally a weary musician or self-appointed director would loudly call everyone together for another dance.

In preparation for a performance, someone (usually the person who taught the dance) would volunteer constructive criticism and suggest who should perform publicly. Although this was sometimes a source of tension, everyone agreed that the goal was the best possible performance. Dancers themselves often opted out of a particular dance to give others a chance. Line dances were led and called by those who knew or performed them best. By 1982 the repertory's most complex dances were taught and led by one male expert.

Apart from teaching, however, most of Borovčani's off-stage tasks were undertaken by women. Several men in the group cultivated a devil-may-care nonchalance about the details of governance. We women sensed that if we didn't do it, no one would. Ad hoc female committees took on financial decision-making, booking arrangements, publicity, program design and execution, and often choreography and staging for a particular event. But we never called it "artistic direction" or "administration."

Women also sewed costumes, partly of necessity and partly because of pride in "women's work." Departing members passed along skirts or vests, which were collectively owned; but new articles, including the more elaborate men's shirts, were often needed.

The roles of men and women as members of the group diverged from their danced representations. While aspects of male dominance and female submissiveness were dramatized choreographically, most members, men and women, would have insisted that they personally rejected traditional roles.

Whatever individuals' contradictory motivations or behavior, the central focus of the group was dancing. Most members cited the physical discipline and challenge of dancing as their prime reasons for belonging. However, a few mentioned social, spiritual, or aesthetic motives, with comments such as, "I love people, and any activity that brings people together in a holistic and spiritual way is very attractive to me," and, "Dance and music are a necessary part of living — we express cooperatively the love of movement and beauty. I like doing ethnic dance because it is what people have been doing for centuries." Others cited changing considerations: "First, I became a member because I loved the dance and music but also needed to be with people who were like me in some ways. Then, because I mainly needed the people. Now, because I mainly love to dance."

But most saw the group essentially as yet another way to dance:

"I love to dance and Boston is too far away."

"I like to be active, wear costumes, have the chance to really learn a dance — the only way you can get people to work hard to learn something perfectly is if they have performance as a goal."

"I like to dance with good dancers. If the group's level of dancing went down I would probably quit. I also like the people involved and there is an opportunity to socialize."

Even for those who emphasized technical challenges as their motivation, social experiences became integrated with the physical and aesthetic. Dancing with the goal of eventual public display modeled particular patterns of interpersonal relations. Researchers of folk and social dance forms have commented on the "instant community" and "intimate anonymity" that dancing creates in voluntary associations, in contrast to groupings based on long-shared values or primary relationships, such as family, neighborhood, ethnicity, or religion (Abbott 1987, 164–65; Ronström 1992, 259; Hast 1993, 21).

An example of "instant community" is described in Owe Ronström's study of Yugoslav immigrants in Stockholm, Sweden, between 1983 and 1988. Before the civil wars and disintegration of the Yugoslav Republic, dances and parties in Stockholm included Serbs, Croatians, Bosnians and others to learn common dances and define a "Yugoslav" community in an alien setting:

As they perform, the musicians and dancers ... tune their bodies and minds into communication with each other, with previous performers, and with the other people present in a social relation based on living through several temporal dimensions at the same time. Yet one neither can nor need suppose that the coordination of bodies and minds in time and space leads to the integration of values, experiences, or meaning. This is probably an important explanation for the fact that Serbs, Croats, Macedonians, Montenegrins, Bosnians and Hungarians — people who in other contexts perhaps regard themselves as dissimilar rather then alike — so easily can interact as Yugoslavs in the contexts I have studied. (Ronström 1992, 259)

As a performing group Borovčani differed in obvious ways from an immigrant association defining itself in relation to a foreign host society. But in both groups Balkan dance created, for a time, a sense of community among dancers without a profound or articulated "integration of values, experiences, and meanings."

Dancing, particularly in unison with others, can structure a confluence of self and situation that corresponds to what Victor Turner calls the shared flow of *communitas*, "the holistic sensation when we act with total involvement, when action and awareness are one (one ceases to flow if one becomes aware that one is doing it)" (1986, 133).

This perception is similar to what Gestalt therapists term "spontaneous engagement," in which emotion, perception and movement are unified. As a "person-in-action," the individual experiences a sensation of actualizing and losing the self at the same time: "there is no sense of oneself or of other things other than one's experience of the situation. The feeling is immediate, concrete and present, and integrally involves perception, muscularity and excitation" (Perls et al. 1951, 377). For some Borovčani members, rehearsing and performing offered this kind of personal liberation and social integration: "When the chemistry is right," one male dancer confided, "the music, dancers, mood and all, it's an ecstatic moment for me. It's experiencing the now."

The sensation of *communitas* was strongest in performance, but also developed at weekly rehearsals, which were closer to "folk dancing" or just folks dancing. We rehearsed year-round, from six to eight on Wednesday evenings in a local church social hall, a large empty room with a hardwood floor. Only two dancers lived in town: the rest came from up to fifty miles away in all directions. Most members were full-time workers for whom the evening trip was a labor of love, especially in winter.

Members described the way dancing felt in vivid terms that help explain this commitment:

> "[Balkan dance is] lots of fun and intense action. Different from any other type of dancing I know."
> "I find Balkan dancing very sexy, stimulating, exciting, and seductive."
> "It's a rich meaty type of dance good for flirting, showing off, working up a sweat—the music is great ... you can put your soul into it."
> "I think the music creates a big part of the feel. There's a proud feeling that comes with the music and Balkan steps."
> "It's ordered—the steps are very interesting and controlled, not crazy, but balanced—contra dancing is more social, boogie more individual."
> "Balkan is a very primal, yet highly precise and sophisticated form of dance, probably the most of any folk dances."

These comments point out Balkan dancing's physical pleasures, emotional resonances, aesthetic challenges, erotic possibilities, and social constraints. They suggest that dancing participates in the production of social worlds in part by reshaping individual understanding and collective behavior through biological and psychological means. Gratifying dance experiences move us physically and emotionally in particular ways that can influence behavior on and off the dance floor. Kinesthetic memories of Bulgarian line dances, no doubt adrenaline-assisted and neuro-chemically transmitted, arouse for me an intense response: intellectual appreciation, aesthetic satisfaction, physical animation, emotional warmth.[6] Dancing channeled a powerful group energy flow and modeled collective effort.

But despite powerful shared experiences, Balkan dancing was clearly not an integral part of members' ethnic heritage or social worlds. One dancer said dryly, "Sometimes it's very alien. I can tell my ancestors were not Balkan." Although several of us had visited Eastern Europe and the Balkan countries and one was a graduate student in Slavic studies, most knew almost nothing about the origins of the dances and songs we performed. The focus was on learning dances with attention to traditional style, but without scholarly regard for the circumstances that engendered them.

Borovčani reinterpreted the Balkan tradition for American purposes. The goals of the performers suited the spirit of the times and delighted enthusiastic audiences.

In appropriating Balkan dances, Borovčani posed American alternatives:

"What if..." (the staged representations of happy peasants and communal harmony suggested) bodies could be channels for communication without manipulation or violence? What if individuals could experience elusive feelings of shared identity and fellowship in concerted action: a disciplined, joyous, sensuous and complex sense of belonging?

And, "What if..." (the troupe's behind-the-scenes life implied) adult Americans could dance together; share physical closeness and trust (with or without personal entanglements); become exasperated, vent their anger, and reconcile their differences; take turns as leaders and followers; and accommodate one another in the interest of a community greater than the sum of its parts?

"Sell the Horse, Sell the House: Only Dance"[7]

However, between 1978 and 1982 the social and political mood of the United States was changing, and while Borovčani "performed" communalism and collaboration, the dominant ideology of the Reagan era celebrated individualism and competition. Following the 1980 election many Maine people, particularly transplants "from away" in their twenties and thirties, either focused on careers or retreated further upcountry.

Within our group, new opportunities and pressures from families and jobs affected individuals' levels of energy and commitment. Obvious rifts opened along old fault lines. While some members pushed for more professionalism, others took a more relaxed attitude. Before the group's final concert, one dancer successfully lobbied for the inclusion of her boyfriend, an inexperienced dancer, and the quality of dancing suffered.

As a performing ensemble on the margins of the dominant culture, Borovčani embodied attitudes characteristic of a particular time and place. We danced small-is-beautiful rural ideals, traditional gender roles, physical discipline, and individuals' strong connections to the group. The dancing had brought "a particular cast of mind out into the world" (Geertz 1983, 99). And the dances had danced us, inducing a cast of mind in members and audiences, suggesting ways of experiencing and behaving that are still with me. Offstage, Borovčani earnestly if untidily enacted egalitarianism, non-commercialism, and collective responsibility. Unlike a living folk dance tradition on native ground, often integral to maintaining social identities and achieving political goals, Balkan dance in Maine had only a transitory capacity to create a world for its members and communicate with its viewers. By 1982, Borovčani's moment had passed.

To several of us the "public images of sentiment" (Geertz 1983, 82) the group had represented began to seem naive. And contradictions had become apparent: we were an exclusive group performing inclusivity; our public displays of feminine modesty and male charisma belied the organization's realities. Though we imagined ourselves opponents to mainstream values we sometimes catered to mainstream audiences, offering them a slice of feel-good utopianism; and while the choreography signaled a larger solidarity, as a group we lacked purposeful intent beyond perfecting and performing the dances.

This version of Borovčani's story circles back to the dance and song that began it. At the 1982 Maine Festival performance, jazz dancers waited in the wings with a Devo soundtrack, wearing leopardskin leotards and fleshcolored tights, black jazz shoes and little white socks, black lipstick and pointy fifties shades. On stage, we concluded the vocal for *Ličko Kolo*. The dancers held hands and followed the leader, creating staccato rhythms of increasing speed and force with our footfalls. The line snaked in S-curves that doubled back on themselves. In passing, we wordlessly, warmly acknowledged each other. At last, the leader began a circle that coiled into a tight spiral, faster and closer, until there was nowhere to go. We stamped together and stopped, in silence.

Notes

1. In 1982 I surveyed the Borovčani membership as part of a research project on dance and culture. I also wrote and narrated a half-hour video documentary on the group, broadcast by Maine Public Television.

2. This narrative approach can be loosely categorized as processual analysis, a position in anthropology which "stresses the case history method; it shows how ideas, events, and institutions interact and change through time" (Rosaldo 1989, 92–93).

3. New dances were learned at dance festival workshops, dance camps, or during visits from visiting professionals.

4. *Living the Good Life: How to Live Sanely and Simply in a Troubled World* (1970) by Helen and Scott Nearing of Harborside, Maine, inspired a generation of Maine homesteaders.

5. The Maine Festival, founded in 1977, was conceived as a celebration of Maine arts, crafts, music, performance and folk traditions. It expanded to include nationally and internationally recognized performers.

6. For a book on chemically based kinesthetic, emotional and intellectual response, see *Descartes' Error: Emotion, Reason, and the Human Brain* (1994) by Antonio R. Demasio (New York: G. P. Putnam's Sons).

7. The Serbian song "Ajde v̄ano" goes: "Come, v̄ana, dance the Kolo! Sell the horse, sell the house: only dance" (Graetz et al. 1977, 6–7).

Bibliography

Abbott, P. 1987. *Seeking Many Inventions*. Knoxville: University of Tennessee Press.
Blacking, J. 1982. "Movement and Meaning: Dance in Social Anthropological Perspective." *Dance Research Journal* (Spring) 1(1), 89–99.

DMC Library. 1975. *Bulgarian Embroideries*. The Rev. ed. Mulhouse, France: Editions Th. de Dillmont.
Foster, S. L. 1986. *Reading Dancing: Bodies and Subjects in Contemporary American Dance*. Berkeley: University of California Press.
Geertz, C. 1973. *The Interpretation of Cultures*. London: Hutchinson.
_____. 1983. *Local Knowledge: Further Essays in Interpretive Anthropology*. New York: Basic Books.
Graetz, A., Buchholz, J., and Peppler, J., eds. 1977. *The Laduvane Songbook*. Cambridge, MA: Myxomop Publications.
Hast, D. E. 1993. "Performance, Transformation, and Community: Contra Dance in New England." *Dance Research Journal* (Spring) 25(1), 21–32.
Nearing, H., and Nearing. S. 1987 [1970]. *Living the Good Life: How to Live Sanely and Simply in a Troubled World*. New York: Schocken Books.
Novack, C. 1990. *Sharing the Dance: Contact Improvisation and American Culture*. Madison: University of Wisconsin Press.
_____. 1993. "Ballet, Gender and Cultural Power." In *Dance, Gender and Culture*, ed. H. Thomas. New York: St. Martins Press.
Perls, F., Hefferline, R. F., and Goodman. P. 1951. *Gestalt Therapy*. New York: Dell Publishing.
Ronström, O. 1989. "The Dance Event—A Terminological and Methodological Discussion of the Concept." In *The Dance Event: A Complex Cultural Phenomenon*, ed. L Torp. Proceedings from the Fifteenth Symposium of the ITCM Study Group on Ethnochoreology. Copenhagen: ICTM Study Group on Ethnochoreology.
_____. 1992. *Att Gestalta ett Ursprung*. Stockholm: Stockholm University, Institutet för folklivsforskning.
Rosaldo, R. 1989. *Culture and Truth: The Remaking of Social Analysis*. Boston: Beacon Press.
Turner, V. 1986. *The Anthropology of Performance*. New York: PAJ Publications.
Wolff, J. 1992. "Excess and Inhibition: Interdisciplinarity in the Study of Art." In *Cultural Studies*, ed. L. Grossberg, C. Nelson, and P. Treichler. New York: Routledge.

Morphology of Balkan Dance and Music

12

Hai la Joc! Periodicity at Play in Romanian Dance Music

JAMIE L. WEBSTER

In Romanian, the noun *joc* and accompanying verb *joaca* are used interchangeably to mean *play* and *dance*.[1] Associations with this play of meanings suggest that dance and dance music are both *recreational* and *creatively malleable*. When dancers and singers *play* with dance music in either a recreational or a concert context, musical groupings and *periodicity* are created in the performance that could not be experienced from listening to the normative melody and harmony structures out of context. In other words, relations between musical components and musical sections are perceived differently, in ways that affect perceptions of overall form, when dance music is experienced in context.

Perceived structures of folk music change with the addition of dance and improvised text. This study focuses on one performance of a dance song with instrumental accompaniment called *"Jocul de-a Lungal"* from Transylvania, Romania. Using audio and video recordings as source material, this project includes transcriptions of (a) the instrumental accompaniment, (b) extemporaneous rhymes (*strigături*) that are called out over the accompaniment, and (c) rhythmic elements that are explicitly and implicitly expressed through the dancers' movements and body percussion. Additionally, transcriptions distinguish between the movements of the video-recorded dancers and body percussion already present in their prerecorded musical accompaniment. Furthermore, I compare interactions of musical periods between instrumental, vocal, and choreographic (both visual and aural) components.

This study shows how the normative musical element (melody, rhythm, and harmony played by musical instruments) provides an isoperiodic foundation (that might initially be perceived as simply "repetitive") that allows for spontaneous participation from dancers and *strigături* (extemporaneous octosyllabic rhymes) callers that interacts with the isoperiodic foundation in non-isoperiodic ways. In other words, although some musical layers remain constant, others change throughout the performance, allowing for different musical relationships. While each layer (instrumental, vocal, choreographic) consists of a unique hierarchical structure of periodicity, each *aligns* and *misaligns* (or is displaced) with other layers' hierarchical structures at important musical moments — therefore creating both periodic *play* in the ways the elements alternate with one another and suggesting a larger musical form when all layers are combined. The product of all musical elements combined is more complex than the representation of any element on its own. I suggest that analysis of the synthesized musical elements is valuable because first, it reveals unsuspected complexity in the performance and second, it clarifies the complex interaction of participating musical elements that may help observers understand cultural aspects of the music. Following a summary of recent scholarship on Romanian dance music, sections will analyze each of the musical elements: instrumental, vocal, and choreographic, as well as their combination.

Eastern Europe and its folk music traditions have been relatively unexplored in North American and West European scholarship (Maners 2004, 5). Maners posits that Eastern Europe's historical absence from the western consciousness is due to the close geographic and cultural proximity of Eastern Europe to West European globalized and economically developed societies (ibid.). Others have suggested that there is little to study as East European folk culture has declined since the Second World War (Kraft 2004; Rice 1994). While ethnomusicological studies of the Balkans seem to have increased in recent decades, perhaps motivated by the notion that this region is at a crossroads between European and Middle Eastern culture and history, I suspect that less scholarship has resulted for Romania because its geographical/cultural history is perceived more as an intermediary between the Balkans and Western Europe rather than between Europe and a Saidian Other. Likewise, Romania has not received the media's ethnographic attention as other Balkan countries, especially those directly involved with the wars of the 1990s, have experienced in the years following the fall of Socialism. Furthermore, the Romanian language is Latin based, and is considered by some to be the closest living language to early Latin (although others note the influence of Slavic languages), thus blurring imagined distinctions *from* and kinships *with* Slavic speaking geographic neighbors and historical empires (Roman, Ottoman, and Austro-Hungarian) that are often associated with either Balkan *or* West European cultures, but rarely both. In conversations with colleagues, I have often encountered the perception that Romania is not *Ottoman* enough to be Balkan, not *Slavic* enough to be East European, yet also not *modern* enough to be European. Perhaps the perceptions that complicate categorization also play into Romania's short shrift in scholarship of artistic culture. Conversely, these perceptions could suggest Romanian culture is unique and valuable for its combination of Ottoman, Slavic, and West European influences.

Little scholarship regarding Romanian dance music from Transylvania is available to English readers. Perhaps the most well-known scholarship focusing on Romania stems from Bela Bartok's transcriptions and recordings from Transylvania. However, Bartok focused on the musical practices of ethnic Hungarians living in Transylvania, and generally did not pursue Romanian idioms in detail. Similarly, while composer Georges Enescu used Romanian melodies and ethnic markers in his works for orchestra, these compositions were institutionally driven and are more representative of music from northern, eastern and southern regions of Romania, but less representative of Transylvania. Likewise, contemporary western folkloric scholarship on either Romanian musical *or* choreographic practices (typically not both) has not garnered a critical mass of research concerning *dance music*, often focusing instead on recent anthropological trends regarding music as cultural currency, and performance events as reflections of ethnic identity and social values (Buckley 1994; Freedman 1990; Frigyesi 1996; Kligman 1988; Kürti 2004; Mills 2004; Smith 2004). This study is unique in that it focuses on (a) ethnically *Romanian* music from Transylvania, (b) dance music from the *folk* repertoire (*musica populara*) rather than classicized style, and (c) musical elements unique to the *performance* event.[2]

Jocul de-a Lungal

Source Materials

In the summer of 1997, after recognizing a strong personal attraction to music and dance styles from Transylvania through my involvement in International Folk Dancing in the United States, I embarked on a self-fashioned tour of Romania for which I arranged music and dance lessons with conservatory teachers, ensemble leaders and performers, and well-regarded independent performers. In addition to formal lessons, I observed several folkloric performances by professional and semiprofessional ensembles, and attended participatory events such as evening social dances and a night-long wedding celebration. Through these experiences of watching musicians, dancers, and vocalists interact, I discovered for myself that it is *the experience* itself that shapes Transylvanian music and dance more than the recorded music and dance note artifacts I had encountered at home. Dance music is not complete without the dance, and the vocalizations of dancers and musicians both invite participants and bind their activities together.

Audio and video recordings of "Jocul de-a Lungal" provide an opportunity to hear and see how instrumental music, dance, and vocalizations interact in performance events. I chose this particular example for study because first, the audio recording is readily available through local folk dance collections; second, a visual interpretation of the dance as demonstrated by the well-known Romanian dance teacher Mihai David and his female dance partner Giorgiana Wenzel is also accessible in the United States and clearly shows the dancers' movements without obstruction. Third, I have familiarity with this dance type and learned a similar set of dance patterns accompanied by a different melody while in Bucharest, studying from David's colleagues, Prof. Giurgiu-Remus, Prof. Dolcu Constantin, and Prof. Mihai Muche.[3]

An unfortunate aspect of the International Folk Dance movement in the United States is that many recordings are disseminated without crediting performers. As such, I have neither been able to discover who the performers are in the audio recording of "Jocul de-a Lungal" nor do I know whether the performance took place at a social gathering or as part of staged performance. Similarly, while the video demonstration of the dance steps clearly articulates movement patterns, it also necessarily (and ironically for the purposes of this paper) separates the dancers from an interactive event represented in the audio recording (although David frequently vocalizes along with the audio-recorded performers). In other words, although these source materials provide some audio and visual clarity that more informal videography, such as my own field recordings, does not, they cannot provide all the dynamic interactions involved in a live, single event performance. The analysis garnered from these materials, though not all inclusive, nevertheless *highlights* the ways that instrumental music, dance and vocalizations interact in Romanian dance music from Transylvania.

Historical and Cultural Contexts

Dance melodies (*melodii de joc*) comprise a large portion of living music traditions in Romania (Cosma 2006). These melodies accompany dancing at events held for weddings, saints' days, family celebrations, and on many Sundays (ibid.). Although each region in Romania exhibits stylistic diversity and specificity of genres, general musical elements often include "closely stepped modes; a narrow melodic range; a limited number of motifs, phrases and movements; and a pronounced variability in the production of melodic figures" (Cosma 2006).

Dance music is typically played for social occasions by professional male musicians called *lăutari* (of either Romanian or Romani ethnicity) in ensembles known as *tarafs* (Cosma 2006). Music is typically transmitted orally, and, while improvisation is often an important element, musicians work with a mentally held model of basic melodies and contemporary harmonizations (ibid.). In Transylvania, tarafs often consist of two to eight instruments including violin, clarinet, *cobză* (lute), a second violin, viola and double bass (ibid.). This recording of "Jocul de-a Lungal" includes violins, a *țambal mic* (small dulcimer), and a double bass. Many recordings accessible to Americans feature professional and semi-professional performers from national ensembles. It is unknown whether this recording was made by a taraf or state ensemble. Additionally, the audio recording includes men's voices calling strigături (extemporaneous octosyllabic rhymes), and commenting on the experience of the dance with vocables and commands. These calls, which are typically spontaneous and dynamic, function as invitations to the dance, markers of synchronization for steps, and markers for progressions of patterns ("Strigăturile"). Additionally, callers might make comments indirectly about or directed toward village girls present at the event (Cosma 2006). Correlated musical rhythms and syllable counts allow vocalizers to interchange texts between melodies and/or improvise on the spot. Percussive sounds created by improvisational slapping, stomping and clapping are often part of men's dancing figures in Transylvania and play prominently in individuals' expression.[4] In this recording, dancers add snapping, slapping and stomping. I address instrumental roles, body percussion and a few of the vocalizations in the following section on instrumental music, and explore the vocalized strigături in greater detail in the section regarding text.

While most dance music is purely instrumental, pieces including vocal roles are thought to be remnants of dance forms popular in Europe during the Middle Ages. "Jocul de-a Lungal" belongs to the De-a lungal ("along the way") category from northern Transylvania that is also historically far reaching. The De-a lungal genre is a subcategory of Purtata dances (couple dances with walking steps performed counterclockwise in a circular promenade) that developed from courtly walking dances. (Cosma 2006; Mellish and Green 2006).[5] According to Mellish and Green (2006), Romanian walking dances likely came from the ethnically Hungarian Transylvanian nobility and were predominantly distributed in the northern areas of Hungarian feudal rule in Transylvania. Purtata dances are common throughout Transylvania, but De-a lungal dances, often with slightly stretched ¾ time, are specific to northern Transylvania, specifically to the Someș and Năsăud areas to the North and East of the capital city, Cluj-Napoca (Mellish and Green).

Instrumental Melody and Harmony

A full transcription of "Jocul de-a Lungal" in its entirety is included in the main body of the essay (Scores 1–6). The instrumental piece, "Jocul de-a Lungal" includes a clear hierarchy of sections. The violin melody of Jocul de-a Lungal alternates between two eight-measure sections or themes (A, B), each of which is repeated. Furthermore, each theme is divided into four-measure antecedent and consequent phrases. Thus, if the first theme antecedent is labeled *a*, and if its consequent is labeled *b*, and the second theme antecedent and consequent are likewise labeled *c* and *d*, then the overall form of the instrumental piece is as follows:

Instrumental Music

Themes:	A	B	A	B
Phrases:	*a b a b*	*c d c d*	*a b a b*	*c d c d*

Theme A is recognizable by its consistent pattern of four sixteenth notes most often followed by four eighth notes. The repetition of this pattern, the dynamic accent heard in the string players' performance emphasizing the pitch "F," and the harmonic cadences at measures 8, 16, 24, and 32 supports a triple feel to this music and justifies the choice to assign ¾ as the meter of this piece. While some European compositions employ sixteenth notes in an upbeat figure preceding a downbeat, the choreographic movements discussed later (in greater detail) also suggest that the sixteenth note groupings align with the literal downbeat of the dancers' feet.

Further analysis of rhythmic groupings in the repeated melody provides some evidence of play inherent in the musical form. While the sixteenth notes followed by eighth notes pattern provides a rhythmic motor to the melody, it is interrupted in phrase *a* by an agogic pause on pitch "A" at the end of the second measure. Unlike the first half of the phrase *a*, the end of phrase *a* elides into the consequent phrase by continuing the standard sixteenth notes followed by eighth notes pattern through the end of phrase *b* in measure eight. Therefore, although each phrase has four measures, the experience of the rhythm may be felt as a shorter motive (measures 1–2) followed by an extended phrase (measures 3–8).

Melodically, accidentals may show play with tonal expectations. Most prominently, the fourth scale degree (B/Bb) alternates between flat and natural nearly every measure, and sometimes within the same measure. Traditional Romanian music has two dominant modes: anhemitonic pentatonic and elliptical pentatonic modes, and an "uncertain mode," with flexible third,

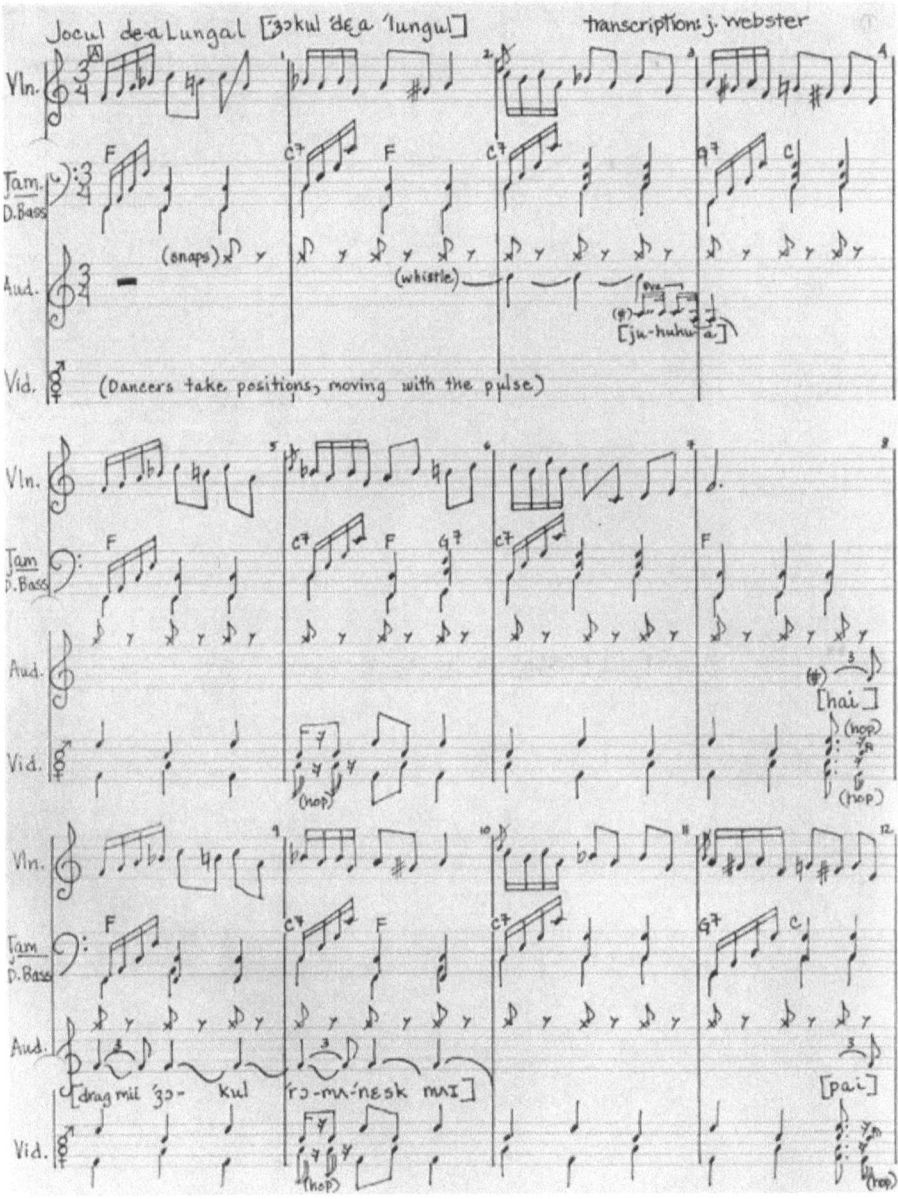

Score 1

fourth and seventh (and sometimes second and sixth) scale degrees (Cosma 2006). The uncertain mode is commonly used in dance melodies (which were historically monophonic), but is often modified to accommodate harmony practiced by the *Tarafuri*. "Jocul de-a Lungal" seems to fit this model in that it includes many chromatic neighbors, and also uses harmony that can be

Score 2

notated and understood in western European notation. Although natural and flat "Bs" are used in near equal numbers, the placement of Bb on stronger beats and the fact that all B naturals seem to resolve to C suggests that Bb is basic and that B natural facilitates the use of secondary dominants realized through the double bass and *ţambul mic* parts. Similarly, sequences of descending notes show melodic play with chromatic lower neighbor tones, thus alternating between G natural and G#, and between F and F#.

12. Hai la Joc!

Score 3

The *țambal mic* and the double bass provide rhythmic and harmonic support to the violin melody. Both parts seem to follow the same harmonic structure, though each player improvises to some degree throughout the piece. The harmonic model that the accompanying instruments follows is:

Score 4

Measures	1	.	.	2	.	.	3	.	.	4	.	.
Theme A:												
phrase *a*	F			C7		F		C7		G7	C	
phrase *b*	F			C7	F		G7		C7			F

Theme B:

Score 5

phrase *c*	F	Bb	G7C7	F
phrase *d*	F	Bb	G7C7	F

Harmonies in Theme A emphasize tonic to dominant relationships and extend to secondary dominants in the last measure of phrase *a* and the second measure of phrase *b*. Harmonic relationships for Theme B are identical between

Vln. = Violins   Ţam. = Ţambal mic (small dulcimer)   D. Bass = Double Bass

Aud. = Sounds (voices, body percussion and whistles) from audio recording

Vid. = notated dance steps from video recording

Score 6

phrases c and d, cadencing relatively quickly from tonic to subdominant, secondary dominant, dominant and back to tonic. Harmonic progressions for both Themes A and B, while set in a basic model, may play with listeners' expectations by deceptively extending to secondary dominant harmonies.

While rhythmically, the melody of Theme A might be experienced as a shorter phrase followed by a longer phrase, or alternatively as two shorter phrases (measures 1–2, 3–4) followed by a four measure phrase (measures 5–8), this pattern reverses in the harmonic form when considering both themes. In other words, Theme A accomplishes an asymmetry at the micro level that is reversed in the macro level of Themes A and B combined, in which Theme A is extended, while Theme B is composed of shorter, four measure units.

The sparseness of *ţambal mic* and double bass notes in the full transcription located at the end of the paper reflects difficulties with recording audibility. As a rule, the ţambal player in this recording extrapolates sixteenth note arpeggios, blocked chords and other rhythmic figures using the harmonies listed above in root position. The first page of full transcription provides an example of the ţambal part (stems up) with ascending arpeggios followed by either open fifths or blocked chords. As the piece progresses and themes are repeated, the tambal player improvises upon the harmonic structure by playing different rhythms consisting of quarter, eighth and sixteenth note values. These patterns increase slightly in rhythmic density from beginning to end.

The double bass player improvises by exchanging harmonic roots with other chord tones and by using neighbor and passing tones. For instance, on the first repetition of phrase *a* in measure nine, the player plays the pitch "A" on beat two (stem down) while still supporting a tonic harmony. Similarly, the player uses pitch "G" as a passing tone in the first measure of each Theme B phrase starting at measure forty-nine. Whether because of tuning issues or memory lapses in harmonic form, the double bass occasionally plays some unexpected tones that do not seem to match either the melody or the harmony provided by the ţambal. I have indicated these occurrences (found in beat three of measure 14, beat two of measure 38, and beat three of measure 44) by "normalizing" the written pitch and including the actual pitch in parentheses. Additionally, the bass player occasionally varies his rhythmic pattern (e.g., measures 13, 20, 37, 40 and 61).

Extramusical percussion is created by audio-recorded dancers/musicians who either snap, slap and/or stomp and creatively play with the expectations and experiences of the instrumental music. Finger snaps from at least two hands are heard from the beginning of the third beat of the very first measure. These snaps continue for each beat of the piece through the third beat of the last measure of three. These snaps are shown as non-pitched rhythms on the third staff down of each grand staff (labeled "Aud." for Audio recording). While two or more snaps at any given time do not always arrive at the same moment of the beat, it is reasonable to believe that they are intended to be heard on the beat.[6] A sharply articulated whistle that occurs on each beat of the third measure seems to accentuate the metric confines of the three-beat measure, while a call from a separate performer, "[ju-hu-hu-a]," blurs the boundaries of measures three and four through syncopation.[7]

At moments of transition, such as between phrases *b* and *c* (measure 15), body percussion presumably made by a dancer's slaps[8] similarly blurs boundaries between measures and between the Themes themselves. In measure 15, as well as at similar transitions in measures 23, 31, 39, 47, 55 and 63, percussive sounds begin on the second beat in the following pattern.

This pattern resembles the rhythmic motive of the melodic themes in that a number of events with close rhythmic proximity are followed by the same number of events at greater distances from one another. It is curious that this percussive statement begins on beat two, thus displacing the rhythmic figure of three subdivided beats into the next measure, and, in so doing, blurring metric distinctions and perhaps expectations regarding the metric beginning of the next phrase. The first time this happens as an event, it creates a relatively long period (measures 1⁵⁄₁₆). After measure 15, the same event occurs every eight measures. Curiously, it is reasonable to believe that for every slap of a leg in mid air, the same leg/foot comes down on a rebound beat. We can't see or hear this, but it is likely happening in the original performance. At the very end of the piece, a final slapping figure (that also seems to include stomping) similarly blurs boundaries between the final two measures by grouping notes into three sets of three-note periods, each equaling a dotted quarter note in length.

In summary, instrumental parts remain constant from beginning to end, following a mostly hierarchical structure of isoperiodic patterns that seem to include only small amounts of rhythmic and harmonic play. The piece is divided into two Themes, each with two phrases of four measures. Although the violins do not improvise in this piece, the violin melody subtly plays with agogic rhythm by pausing at the end of the second measure in phrase *a*. Both double bass and *țambal mic* parts follow a harmonic model directly related to the melodic hierarchy, but tend to vary rhythmic elements and bass line pitches. Furthermore, cadential figures in harmonic progressions may play with the listeners' expectations by extending to secondary dominants. Additional body percussion heard in the audio recording serves to blur metric and phrase boundaries at transition points.

Vocalized Text

A lexical transcription and translation appear in the following example (Ex. 1). In an effort to capture the Transylvanian dialect, I have chosen in most cases to transcribe words (with language assistance from K. Kirilov, A. Petruța and R. Westra) as they are pronounced by the callers in the recording, even when this is in conflict with standard Romanian grammar and/or pronunciation. However, because the goal of my fully notated transcription located at the end of the paper is to capture sound elements of the music, the text in that location is transcribed using the International Phonetic Alphabet system indicated by brackets. Since these rhymes are called rather than sung, I have assigned an approximate pitch for the rhythmic events, and have indicated fluctuations in pitch through contoured lines. Although other participants are heard interjecting vocables such as [ju-ha-hah] and invitations/commands such as "hop" (meaning "jump") I include only lexical and nonlexical sounds that directly and/or immediately relate to the strigături in this section.

In order to clarify periodic structures in the text, I categorize elements through a filter of performance grouping (e.g., location of entrances, distinctions between performers), sound (e.g., beginning and ending rhymes), and textual meaning (e.g., lexical and implied). Similar to instrumental elements

Jocul de-a Lungal
Dance in a row
(Transylvania, Romania)

Text and Translation

Hai drag mi-i jocul Românesc, măi	Hey I like the Romanian dance
Păi dar mă tem ca să-l pornesc, măi	Still, I'm afraid to start up
Că de nu l-oi porni bine	If I don't start right
Păi zău m-oi face de rușine	I'm really going to make a fool of myself
Pă du-te dor și iară vină	Longing, go and come again
Pă pe la mîndra prin grădină	Through my darling's garden
Pă du-te dor și vină iară	Longing, come and go again
Către nori pînă pă sară (hop)	Toward the clouds 'till nightfall (jump)
Pă draga mea floare de munte	My darling, flower of the mountains
Pă eu că tine nu văd unde	I can't see someone like you anywhere else
Pă draga mea floare de șes, măi	My darling, flower of the plains
Pă eu că tine nu găsesc, măi (hop, hop).	I won't find anyone else like you (jump, jump)

Example 1

of the performance, the text is organized in hierarchical ways. The vocalized text or strigături in this version of "Jocul de-a Lungal" includes twelve lines of speech-like prosody shouted by two men in alternation and together. Each line of strigături contains eight or nine syllables over six strong (trochaic) beats, and is performed during the first two measures of an instrumental phrase.[9] Each pair of lines ends with a rhyming word or syllable. Each set of four lines relates to a shared meaning or perspective. Other aspects of the text reveal less hierarchical and/or non-isoperiodic elements.

Although strigături are typically octosyllabic, many include prefix invitations or interjections such as "hai" meaning "hey" or "păi" meaning "but/well/still." Each phrase has eight syllables plus the possible addition of the onset rhyming word *hai* or *păi/pă*. Likewise, when phrases fall short of eight syllables, callers typically add the stock vocable "*măi.*" Lines 1, 2, 11 and 12 only have seven syllables following *Hai/Păi/Pă*, so *măi* is added at the end. According to Adriana Petruța and Roxanne Westra, strigături need not be

Text Rhyme and Framing Events

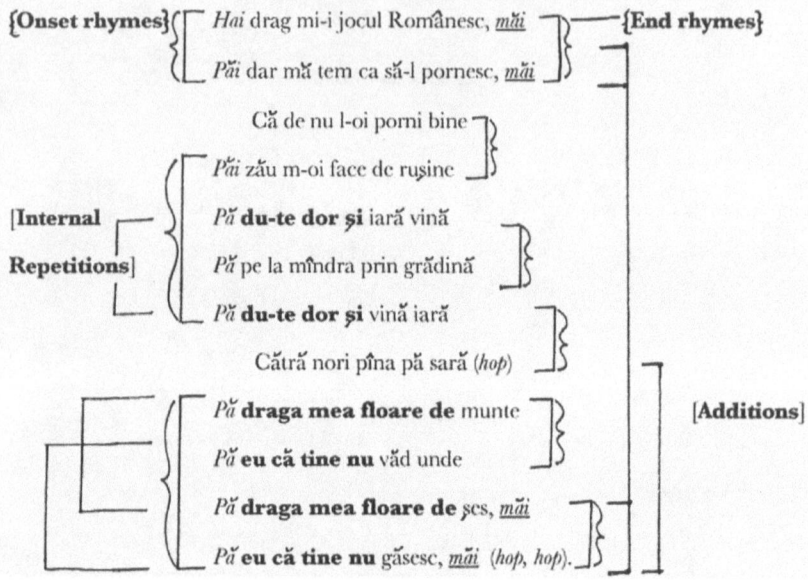

Example 2

grammatically correct, and in fact, may strive to sound colloquial. Petruța related how grammar teachers scolded her class for beginning sentences with *păi* (or the Transylvanian pronunciation "pă"), yet nearly every sentence in this sample of shouts begins with this word.

Although the choice to add *hai*, *păi* and/or *măi* might be made unconsciously by some performers, it still constitutes a performance *choice* rather than necessity as none of the latter words positively or adversely affect grammar or meaning. Furthermore, the absence of the onset word changes the rhythm performed by the caller from beginning his verse on an upbeat to beginning on a downbeat. An analysis found in the above example (Ex. 2) shows groupings formed by rhyme and textual frames such as *hai* and *măi*. While groupings created by ending rhyme schemes are in regularly occurring pairs, groupings created by the onset rhymes *hai*, *păi* and *pă* are syncopated against this structure. After two lines with an onset rhyme, the same caller delivers one line without one, followed by another line with an onset rhyme. The second caller delivers three lines with the Transylvania-ized word *pă*, followed by a fourth line without an onset rhyme. The last quatrain includes onset rhymes for each line.

The end rhyme additive *măi* is located in the first two lines and last two lines, thus framing the set of three quatrains. Additional dance commands such as "*hop*" and internal repetitions of text increase as the text progresses. In the first quatrain, no lines repeat text. In the second complete quatrain,

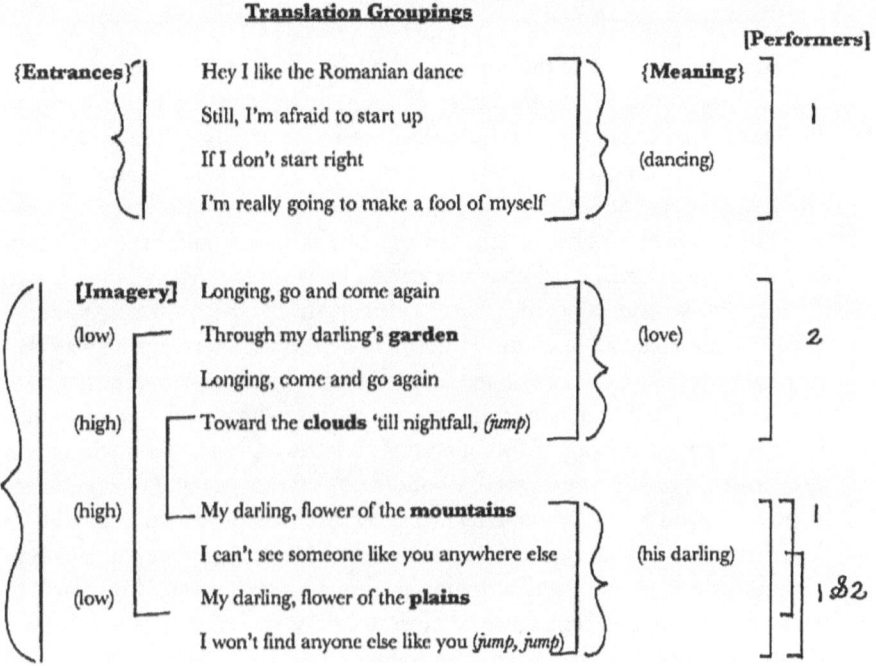

Example 3

two lines include nearly identical texts. In the third complete quatrain two sets of two lines include nearly identical texts. Similarly, the first full quatrain does not include any additional dance commands. The second quatrain includes one "*hop*," and the third quatrain ends with "*hop, hop.*"

According to Petruța, the first caller uses standardized Romanian pronunciation, while the second caller uses Transylvanian dialect, thus accounting for pronunciation differences between the quatrains, and the non-literal rhyme between *hai, păi* and *pă*. Although *hai* and *păi/pă* do not literally rhyme, they are experienced as rhymes. Similarly, meanings in strigături are implied where grammar falls short. For example, in the third quatrain the callers more literally state "I can't see like you anywhere else," although it is understood that they mean that they "can't see anyone like" or "won't find another gal like" their darling anywhere else. An analysis of groupings based on translation (meanings and imagery) and performers' entrances is above (Ex. 3).

Groupings by textual imagery are emphasized through the location of quatrains against the instrumental music (indicated to the left of the text) while groupings by overall meaning are emphasized through the division of lines between the two men performing calls (indicated to the right of the text). The first caller begins the first quatrain after the instrumentalists have completed half of Theme A (one pair of *a* and *b* phrases). Grouping phrases as quatrains is supported by the close proximity of the first four lines within the instrumental form, the performance of the four lines by a single caller, and the shared meaning of the four lines referring to Romanian dancing. The second caller waits for the last two phrases of Theme B to pass (phrases *c* and *d*) before beginning the second quatrain, the lines of which also share a meaning of love and/or longing for his darling. The third quatrain begins without an instrumental break with lines alternating between the first caller and both the first and second caller together. In this quatrain, the speaker(s) speak(s) to the female object of affection rather than about her. Notably, the way that the callers alternate between one and both performers parallels the ways that inner texts repeat in the third quatrain as shown in the preceding graph. As mentioned above, the large grouping of two quatrains performed in succession without an instrumental break is emphasized by both the shift in subject matter from dance to romance, and by palindromic textual imagery between the two quatrains. In these latter two quatrains, the caller speaks of his darling's garden,[10] the clouds, the mountains and the plains, bringing the listener's imagination from earth to sky to the horizon and back down to earth. In this way, the imagery moves from low to high, and then from high back to low.

A combined analysis showing groupings based on ending and onset rhymes, additive framing events and dance commands, entrances, performers, internal repetitions, meanings and imagery is summarized in the following example (Ex. 4). This graph synthesizes the other two graphs in that it shows how some elements (such as ending rhymes, meanings and performers) relate in hierarchical ways based on pairs and quatrains of lines, while other elements (such as onset rhymes) are syncopated against the former regularity, while still other elements (such as additive endings, internal repetitions and palindromic images) increase in density as the text progresses from beginning to end. The relationship between text and instrumental melody, while discussed earlier and shown on a later graph, is not shown on this diagram. In summary, the first quatrain of text is syncopated against the first iterations of Themes A and B, while the second and third quatrains of text are performed along with the reiterations of Themes A and B.

Dance

According to metaphor theory, music is often conceptualized as motion through space (Johnson and Larson 2003, 66). Dance, though, provides concrete motion through space, and is an artistic element that makes music visible. Conversely, for clarity in analysis, I have transferred patterns of dance steps into the less concrete idiom of staff notation. A transcription of chore-

Combined Sound, Meaning and Performer's Text Groupings

```
    OR    E                                         M  ER  A    P
    ⎡    ⎡  Hai drag mi-i jocul Românesc, măi          ⎤  ⎤    ⎤
    ⎣    ⎣  Păi dar mă tem ca să-l pornesc, măi        ⎦  ⎦    ⎥
                                                                ⎥
            Că de nu l-oi porni bine                 ⎤         ⎥
         ⎣  Păi zău m-oi face de rușine              ⎦         ⎥
    ⎡    ⎡  Pă du-te dor și iară vină                ⎤         ⎥
    IR   I                                                      ⎥
    ⎢    ⎣  Pă pe la mîndra prin grădină              ⎦         ⎥
    ⎢    ⎡  Pă du-te dor și vină iară                ⎤         ⎥
    ⎢                                                    A      ⎥
    ⎢    ⎣  Cătră nori pînă pă sară (hop)            ⎦         ⎥
    ⎡ ⎡  ⎡  Pă draga mea floare de munte             ⎤         ⎥
    ⎢ ⎢                                                          ⎥
    ⎢ ⎣  ⎣  Pă eu că tine nu văd unde                ⎦         ⎥
    ⎢ ⎡  ⎡  Pă draga mea floare de scs, măi          ⎤         ⎥
    ⎣ ⎣  ⎣  Pă eu că tine nu găsesc, măi (hop, hop). ⎦         ⎦
```

KEY

IR = internal repetitions
OR = onset rhyme
I = imagery
E = entrances
M = meaning
ER = end rhyme
A = additives
P = performers

Example 4

ographic figures performed by Mihai David and Giorgiana Wenzel follows (Score 7).

Measures of dance and instrumental transcription are of equal length and each four-measure figure of dance transcription corresponds with the thematic order of the instrumental music. Thus, figure I accompanies Theme A, figure II accompanies Theme B, figure III accompanies the repetition of Theme A,

Score 7

and figure IV accompanies the repetition of Theme B. The top staff of every pair shows the man's/leader's choreographic movements while the bottom staff of every pair shows the woman's/follower's choreographic movements. Male and female dance parts are transcribed in this way in order to represent the respective positions of partners as their dance figures progress through time (e.g., women typically dance at the man's right in these patterns). A clock symbol at the beginning of each pair of staves indicates whether the couple traverses a counterclockwise or clockwise trajectory.

In order to clarify periodic structures in the dance, I have chosen to categorize elements through a filter of rhythm as sound (e.g., stepping and/or slapping as musical events) and direction of movements (e.g., forward and backward, clockwise and counterclockwise). As such, dancers' steps are transcribed as musical beats and represent steps as events with duration. Rests are notated when dancers' feet leave the ground in the case of hops or leaps. In a further effort to visually represent the respective movements of both the male and female dancer, different spaces are used for their respective feet. In both staves, the left foot is represented by a higher note with stem pointing down, and the right foot is represented by a lower note with stem pointing up. If the reader were to turn the transcription ninety degrees counterclockwise, the placement of the notes would more literally represent the steps of the dancers moving from left to right feet while moving forward. Additionally, arrows above each staff indicate whether each particular dancer is moving forward, backward, to one side, or in place. Up and down movements are minimal in this dance, though ends of phrases are often emphasized by either a plié and/or a hopping step leading into the next phrase. This notation format is condensed to one staff in the full transcription located at the end of the paper.

Conceptually similar to the text element of this "Jocul de-a Lungal" performance, the choreographic movements follow both strong hierarchical *and* non-isoperiodic structures, though they align more closely with the instrumental framework of the piece. For example, this dance shows a strong hierarchical structure in the ways that one couple made up of two dancers with a total of four feet fit movements to four choreographic phrases, each with four measures of three beats. The choreographic and instrumental phrase lengths are equal, thus allowing for parallel alignment between dance figures and instrumental themes/phrases. This alignment is not perfect, however, as the instrumental themes repeat while the dance figures progress. Contrarily, each instrumental theme consists of two alternating/progressing phrases, while each dance figure repeats only one phrase. Thus, at the level that instrumental themes show isoperiodicity, the choreographic movements do not and vice versa. Furthermore, the contrast between musical phrases is more intense than that between dance phrases, as shown below:

Instrumental Themes:	A	B	A	B
Choreographic Figures:	I	II	III	IV
Instrumental Phrases:	a b a b	c d c d	a b a b	c d c d
Choreographic Phrases:	x a a a	b b b b	a' a' a' a'	b' b' b' b'

While each of the four dance figures shares common rhythmic and/or directional elements that distinguish the patterns as De-a Lungal, the dance shows non-isoperiodicity in the way that each successive figure differs from its predecessor. Figures I and III share *rhythmic* patterns, but not *direction* or *footwork* (the dancers move oppositionally in the first figure, and in parallel in the third). Similarly, figures II and IV share rhythmic patterns but not direction. Figures I and II do *not* share rhythmic patterns, but are *closely* related regarding the dancers' large and small scale direction. Both of these figures travel in *counterclockwise* motion, beginning with *forward* movements on the downbeat of the first measure, and heading *backward* on the downbeat of the third measure. Likewise, figures III and IV travel *clockwise*, and head *forward* on downbeats of both the first and third measures. In assigning the letters *a'* and *b'* as the phrase indicators for figures III and IV, it is clear that I have a preference for rhythmic similarity over directional disparity. This decision is based on my experience of the dance as an observer, and my experience of the movements as I imitated them along with the video recording.

Brackets under the dance notation also reflect observational and kinesthetic experiences of movement groupings. When dancers use pairs of feet to move along with music in triple meter, hemiola is nearly unavoidable. Tactus-preserving hemiola is emphasized in the first dance figure by alternating directional movements forward and back throughout the four-measure phrase. Footwork is bracketed in two-beat increments for both dancers, reflecting alternating feet and alternating directions. With the exception of the second measure, footwork changes with every beat, on the beat. In the second measure, dancers pause on beat one, then hop toward a rhythmically faster figure beginning on beat two. As an observer of this step, I nearly omitted the second eighth-note hop in this second measure, and realized my mistake only in learning the steps in my own feet. However, while my foot literally touched ground on the second eighth note, the rhythmic movement *experience* for both figures I and figure III is as follows (Ex. 5). Similarly, the movement experience for both figures II and IV is as follows (Ex. 6).

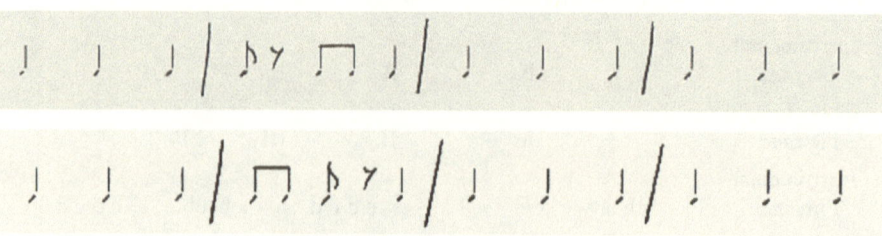

Top: Example 5. *Bottom:* Example 6.

Notice that the main difference between the two figures (that seem so different through observation and imitation) is the exchange of one eighth note for a virtual rest. I have indicated alternative observational and experiential groupings for figures II and IV based on direction and footwork. In notational observation more so than experience, the female movements for measure two allow for many different interpretations. Could faster rhythms indicate a new grouping? Should it be a beginning or an ending when both feet are on the floor? In experience, the larger patterns based on direction seem to dictate groupings, and therefore the preferred groupings for figure II parallel groupings indicated for figure IV.

Although the repetition of each figure to fit the lengths of instrumental themes tends to blur direct connections between figures, I posit that the hops present at the ends of figures I and III facilitate elisions between these figures and figures II and IV respectively, in antecedent to consequent fashion. While these hops literally fall at the ends of phrases, the physics of movement dictates that a hop on one leg with the other extended nearly guarantees some sort of landing on or near the next downbeat. Through these ending hops then, the new phrases have already begun. Furthermore, the sideways movements exhibited in figures II and IV create antecedent and consequent relationships between the repeated dance phrases as dancers exchange locations in one phrase, and change back in the next. Incidentally, David tends to perform the figure slightly differently when he returns to Wenzel's left. Perhaps unconsciously, or due to some physical imbalance, David adds a hop in between the slap and the step backwards in the second and fourth phrases of figure IV. Thus, in more detailed form in which hops are indicated by an asterisk and changes in direction are indicated by one and two apostrophes, the order of dance phrases might be represented as:

x   a* a* a*   b b' b b'   a'*a'*a'*a'*   b' b"*b' b"*

Finally, it is curious that the faster rhythms of the couples' movements always occur during the first and second beats of the second measure of each phrase, often including a two eighth note rhythmic figure, while in the audio recording, the audible two eighth note figure always occurs on the third beat of the third measure. Whether this observation reveals continuity or disparity, and/or regional or performer variation between the seen and unseen dance is unclear, yet it can show an aspect of rhythmic play experienced by the observer of the combined audio and video performance.

In summary, there are several observable hierarchical elements in the structural foundation of choreographic movement that facilitates alignment with other musical elements, yet the choreographic choices of the performers allows for variability that creates non-isoperiodicity either independently or in conjunction with the instrumental phrases. For instance, entrances of the different dance figures align with instrumental theme entrances, but contrarily, variations between dance figures create new period patterns with each combination of choreographic and other musical element.

The following representation of the overall form shows how, much like each individual musical element, the piece as a whole is divided into halves, with each half reflecting an element of surprise, asymmetry and/or *play*. A binary subdivision is supported by the instrumental break between strigă-turi entrances, the symmetrical reiteration of the instrumental Theme A, and the change in direction from counterclockwise to clockwise in the dance figures.

Overall form:

	a	b	c	
Text:	*a a' b b'*	*c c' d d'*	*e e' f f'*	
	A	B	A	B
Instruments:	*a b a b*	*c d c d*	*a b a b*	*c d c d*
	I	II	III	IV
Dance:	*x a a a*	*b b b b*	*a'a'a'a'*	*b'b'b'b'*

In the first half of the piece, the vocalized text (quatrain a) is displaced over Themes A and B. In the second half, the text realigns with the instrumental themes. Choreographically, dance figures align with instrumental themes throughout the piece, but continue to evolve (along with the text) through variation in rhythm and direction from beginning to end. Differences between the two halves also allow for symmetrical similarities. For instance, texts, though more densely delivered in the second half, are evenly divided in general meaning between the two halves — the subject of the first half is dance, while the subject of the second half is romance. Additionally, this binary grouping is nuanced by the absence of one "păi" in the first text, and the similar absence of one "pă" in the second grouping. Furthermore, because the dancers progress counterclockwise for the first half, and then answer this movement in the latter two figures with clockwise direction, it is as if the two sets of dance figures are in a symmetrical antecedent consequent relation despite the progression of variable figures.

Conclusion

This paper has explored the ways that perceived structures of folk music change with the synthesis of dance and improvised text. This study of the dance tune, "Jocul de-a Lungal" from Transylvania, Romania, along with vocalized dance calls and dance demonstration provided source material for analysis of cooperative instrumental, vocal and choreographic elements of performance. Analysis of individual elements clarified unique hierarchical systems of structure and periodicity, while subsequent analysis revealed levels at which elements interacted in periodic ways. Analysis of the synthesized musical elements showed how Romanian music makers and dancers creatively shaped the structure of the piece through play with periodicity.

Notes

1. "Hai la Joc!" means "Come to play/dance!"
2. Following Tenzer's suggestions, musical analysis need not supplant cultural study, but rather, complements it through the provision of musical context (2006, 6).
3. I also learned an alternate melody and text for De-a Lungal, called "Mîndra me-a de la Ciugud" from the Professors Haplea in Cluj-Napoca.
4. At a 2006 dance workshop in Portland, Oregon, Romanian dance teacher Christian Florescu explained that improvisational slapping and stomping in Romanian men's dance is derived from Bavarian practices that spread to the South and East. According to Mr. Florescu, young Bavarian men witnessed a type of forest bird beating his wings against his body during courtship, and decided to adopt the bird's practice into their own wooing by using their hands, legs and feet to create rhythmic patterns.
5. According to Mellish and Green (2006), purtata dances developed in parallel, but somewhat prior to western European dances such as the *pavane, allemande,* and *basse danse.* Contemporary walking dances exist along the northern and eastern edges of Europe, in Norway, Sweden, former Czechoslovakia, Poland, Hungary and Romania.
6. Demonstration dancer Mihai David also delivers an extemporaneous vocable call at the beginning of the video performance which similarly blurs measure distinctions, but was not added to the transcription in order to foster clarity between staves.
7. Romanian dance sometimes includes finger snaps in alternation with various walking steps (e.g., side to side). It is possible, though unknown at this time, whether the snaps heard in the recording indicate unheard dance steps in the spaces between snaps.
8. While it is possible that these sounds are made by stomping feet, it is more likely made by slapping based on the quality/timbre of the sound and the background knowledge that Transylvanian men's footwear was historically softer than that of their Hungarian counterparts, thus lending itself less to percussive sounds.
9. The scansion of syllables to beats also provides opportunity for play. For instance, the word "*porni*" in the first quatrain should have an accent on the second syllable, but is pronounced as 'por-ni' instead in order to fit the rhythm. Ironically and playfully, this incorrectly emphasized set of syllables occurs in the line of text in which the caller frets that he may not be able to start the dance correctly. The play with words thus implies that his rhythm might not be accurate.
10. Gardens can have several symbolic meanings in folk poetry. Many folk texts use the courtyard or garden as a location for courtship in marriage, while others speak of the garden as a metaphor for a young woman who has been morally protected and attended to like a rose tree in blossom, but not yet plucked.

Bibliography

Buckley, Ann. 1994. "Professional Musicians, Dancing and Patronage: Continuity and Change in a Transylvanian Community." *World of Music: Journal of the International Institute for Traditional Music* 36(3), 31–48.

Cosma, Octavian, Adriana Sirli, Speranta Radulescu, and Anca Giurchescu. 2006. "Romania," ed. L. Macy, http://www.grovemusic.com. (accessed 6 June 2006)

Freedman, Diane C. 1990. "Gender Identity and Dance Style in Rural Transylvania." *East European Quarterly* 23(4), 419–430.

Frigyesi, Judit. 1996. "Aesthetic of the Hungarian Revival Movement." In *Returning Culture: Musical Changes in Central and Eastern Europe*, ed. Mark Slobin. Durham, NC: Duke University Press, 54–75.

Johnson, Mark L., and Steve Larson. 2003. " 'Something in the Way She Moves'— Metaphors of Musical Motion." *Metaphor and Symbol*, 18(2), 63–84 .

Kligman, Gail. 1988. *Wedding of the Dead: Ritual, Politics and Popular Culture in Transylvania*. Berkeley: University of California Press.

Kraft, Wayne B. 2004. "Transylvanian Dancing in the Final Hour." *Anthropology of East Europe Review* 22(1), 51–60.

Kürti, Laszlo. 2001. *Remote Borderland: Transylvania in the Hungarian Imagination*. Albany: State University of New York Press.

_____. 2004. "The Last Dance." *Anthropology of East Europe Review* 22(1), 7–24.

Maners, Lynn. 2004. "Introduction." *Anthropology of East Europe Review* 22(1) , 5–6.

Mellish, Liz, and Nick Green. "Eliznik." http://www.eliznik.org.uk/RomaniaDance/purtata.htm. (accessed 6 June 2006)

Mills, Amy. 2004. "Dancing Yourself, Dancing for Others." *Anthropology of East Europe Review* 22(1), 37–49.

Rice, Timothy. 1994. *May It Fill Your Soul: Experiencing Bulgarian Music*. Chicago: University of Chicago Press.

Smith, Jeffrey Alyn. 2004. "From Banning to Commodity Incorporation: Binding, Bonding, and Banding in Eastern European Music." *Anthropology of East Europe Review* 22(1), 25–36.

Tenzer, Michael. 2006. "Introduction: Analysis, Categorization and Theory of Musics of the World." In *Analytical Studies in World Music*, ed. Michael Tenzer. New York: Oxford University Press, 3–38.

Website

"Strigăturile." http://www.cnaa.acad.md/nomenclature/philology/100109/exam.
Interviews/Language Assistance
Kalin Kirilov (May 2006), Adriana Petruța (May 2006), and Roxanne Westra (May/June 2006).

CD/DVD

"Jocul de-a Lungal." *Romanian Dances*. Vol. 6 (couple dances), taught by Mihai David.

13

Dvoransko Kolo: *From the 1840s to the Twentieth Century*

Nancy Lee Chalfa Ruyter

In the early 19th century, the area that eventually became unified as Yugoslavia — and later broke up into separate nations — was still occupied by foreign powers. Parts of what would eventually become the Republic of Croatia had variously been under the control of the Venetians, the Austrians, the Hungarians, and the Ottoman Turks. In the 1830s and 1840s, a strong nationalist movement began to develop in the major urban center of Zagreb. The movement's leaders wanted to bring together Croatians and other Slavs in a united effort to promote Slavic language, culture, and identity — and eventually independence. The nationalists worked through various media to further their cause: writings, speeches, clothing colors and style, music, theater — and dance, the subject of this essay. While the full story of dance and South Slavic nationalism in 19th-century Croatia would include developments in the theatrical art of ballet as well as in social dance, here I focus on a ballroom dance — the *dvoransko kolo*— that was introduced in the 1840s and became one of the rallying symbols for the Croatian nationalists. It went through various developments and survived into the 20th century. One of the sources of our knowledge about this dance was Dick Crum who learned a version of it in the 1950s and later taught it in the United States. This chapter, dedicated to his work and many contributions, begins with the context in which the *dvoransko kolo* was developed and then traces its history into the 20th century and what we know about the dance itself.[1]

The initial nationalistic period during which the *dvoransko kolo* was introduced (ca. 1835–1850) is known as the *Ilirski Pokret* (Illyrian Revival).

This refers to the ancient and supposedly original inhabitants of the area — the Illyrians — and followed the example of Napoleon in harking back to that time. He had had some power in the area from 1809 to 1814 and called the region he controlled the "Illyrian Provinces."[2]

The nationalist leaders faced a difficult task. The majority of the Croatian population was rural, and as one would expect, they were separated from the urban communities by social and economic conditions, education and life style. There was little specifically Croatian about cultural life in Zagreb. The city's public language, dress, manners, architecture, literature, art, music, and dance all followed German, Italian, or other Western European models. The German language was used in publications and on the stage. The Croatian country folk, in contrast, possessed their own rich culture that included language, unwritten poetry and stories, architecture, crafts, dress, beliefs, customs, music, and dance. And it was with such local traditions that the nationalists wished to identify — despite the fact that they themselves were members of the urban classes.

The promoters of the Illyrian vision worked on many fronts to bring all elements of the Croatian population together and create a commitment to South Slavic unity. In addition to political activism, their program included the publication of periodicals in the Croatian language; promotion of that language in education, politics and literature; the foundation of institutions to further South Slavic culture; and the promotion of national music, literature, drama, art, and dance.

The Illyrian idea had found expression in the performing arts from the beginning. By the late 1830s, songs were being composed and sung in Croatian, and Illyrian musical societies had been organized. In 1840, the citizens of Zagreb attended the first original play written in the Croatian language, and in 1846, the first opera. Special efforts were made to introduce examples of native Croatian — which meant peasant — artistic expression to the urban society. The Illyrians were working toward two objectives: that the city dwellers should develop respect and love for the native culture; and that the peasants should feel more unity of spirit with the city by seeing their own culture accepted there. The nationalist leaders knew, however, that the traditional rural music and dance would never find acceptance in the city without adaptation. Therefore, carefully arranged versions of peasant songs were performed by classically trained singers; traditional folk melodies were arranged in urban musical forms and played on urban instruments; and village dance motifs were brought into and adapted to the ballroom dance setting.

According to the Croatian cultural historian Nada Premerl, the first records of balls in Zagreb date from the mid–18th century. They were held in locations such as the homes of wealthy Zagreb families, the governor's courtyard, or the archbishop's palace. One of the most famous ballrooms in Zagreb was built in 1796 as part of a grand new palace, and in 1797, it began to be used for theatrical performances as well as for balls. The building, which was purchased by Count Antun Amadé in 1807 and became the center of Zagreb's cultural life, was known as the *Amadeov Teatar* (Amadé's Theater). Balls, musical presentations and drama were presented there until the building of a public theater in 1834. Eventually, this building was purchased by the pro–Hungarian political faction who were diametrically opposed to the Illyrians, and the building served as their headquarters and social center. There they held lavish pro-Hungarian balls as well as other events (Premerl 1974, 139; Dobronić 1983, 237–238).

During the 19th century, organizing and attending balls was a major social and recreational activity for the Zagreb middle and upper classes, and the number of ballrooms attests to the importance of this activity. In 1834, with completion of a new theater on what became *Markov Trg* (Mark's Square), Zagreb obtained also its first public ballroom — in the theater's foyer (Premerl 1974, 139; Dobronić 1983, 13–14). Also completed in 1834 was the *Streljana* (literally, "rifle range"), a building with a ballroom owned by the *Granjansko Streljačko Društvo* (Citizen Riflemen's Society), a Zagreb organization dating from 1786. Not only was the *Streljana* the center of Zagreb social life for decades; it also became one of the centers of the nationalist movement. Many of the Illyrian leaders belonged to the Society, and under their influence it sponsored patriotic meetings, entertainments, and celebrations (Ladović 1974, 127–129; Kampuš and Karaman 1978, 140).

In the 19th century, Zagreb ballrooms also included one in the palace of Count Karlo Drašković, a prominent supporter of the Illyrians and their cause who eventually sold the building to them for a small price. After it had been converted into a nationalist center, its official title was *Narodni Dom* (People's Home), but it was familiarly referred to as the *Dvorana* (Ballroom) because of the large ballroom that took up the entire first floor. The rest of the building was used for meeting rooms and offices for the various Illyrian activities (Dobronić 1983, 132–137; Premerl 1974, 139; Kampuš and Karaman 1978, 146–147).

Throughout the 19th century, Zagreb was the site of a rich and varied ball season during carnival time. From New Year's Day to Ash Wednesday, members of this urban society vied with each other in the presentation of elaborate and brilliant balls — just as did their counterparts in Vienna. Balls would be organized by individuals; by professional groups such as doctors, lawyers, or pharmacists; or by political factions such as the Illyrians or the pro-Hungarians. According to Premerl, the stately and complex dances such as the minuet, cotillion, and quadrille, which had been popular during the 18th century, began to lose their appeal, and simpler and livelier dances such as the waltz, Slavic polka, gallop, and mazurka gradually replaced them. Not only were the new dances less formal and presumably more enjoyable, but they also seemed to embody a more democratic spirit — which was appealing to the growing middle class of merchants and businessmen. Apparently in Croatia, there was the same initial disapproval of the waltz that accompanied it wherever it had been introduced, but the Illyrians found a way to quell the objections. Count Jurica Orsić, leader of the Riflemen's Society, suggested that Croatian native melodies be adapted from their normal duple to triple meter and played for the waltzes. In this way, "patriotism was satisfied, and the waltz — was still danced."[3]

Traditionally in Zagreb, the currently fashionable international ball repertoire determined the program, but at the Illyrian balls in the 1840s, a new dance was added. Termed *dvoransko kolo* (ballroom kolo), or by other names, it merged elements of the traditional South Slavic kolo (a communal dance form) with patterns of the quadrille, one of the internationally popular ballroom dances. The term *kolo* and the dance type to which it refers have deep roots throughout the Slavic world. It is believed to have come into the Balkans with the first Slavic migration in the 5th century A.D. Today, the term is still in widespread use in many parts of the former Yugoslavia and may refer to a variety of circle dances, other kinds of dances, and other aspects of a dance event (Mladenović 1980, 56–57). Kolos were — and still are — danced by South Slavic populations in connection with significant social and religious events. The Illyrians' concern that their balls lacked any native elements led to their interest in the kolo. As the quintessential South Slavic dance, it could be a powerful and stirring instrument in the service of their cause. They realized, however, that the city elite would never join in a peasant dance in its natural state, or even consider it worthy of attention. Therefore, the kolo, just as the folk music and songs, would have to be "refined" and adapted to fit the urban context. Thus was born the *dvoransko kolo*.

Franjo Kuhač (1834–1911), Croatian composer, music historian, and pioneering ethnomusicologist, wrote extensively on Croatian music and dance and paid particular attention to the ballroom kolo. In a report written some years before 1864 and published in 1872, he provides both historical background and a detailed description of the actual dance — perhaps in its original version or in a later one. He credits its creation to a group of patriotic naval officers who were concerned about national life and culture. They decided to create a dance for the ballroom that would combine the known with the unknown — the already accepted with the seemingly foreign. They chose the *četvorka* (quadrille) as the basic form, because this dance had a history of popularity throughout Croatia and Slavonia. Within this form, they incorporated steps and figures from folk dances of various South Slavic regions. Toward the end of 1841, one of the officers, Marko Bogunović, introduced the dance and taught it to a group of young patriotic ladies and gentlemen in Zagreb. It was first danced in public, under the name *Slavonsko kolo*, on January 27, 1842, at a ball that will be discussed below.

As Kuhač describes the dance, it was done in sets of even numbers of couples — at least four, but optimally no more than eight (although he includes diagrams that show up to 14 couples in a set). The couples stood in a square formation that could also function as a circle. The dance was composed in rondo form with seven sections: AB, AC, AD, AE, AF, AG, AH. The A part of each section was the "kolo," a relatively slow pattern which was performed in circular formation. The second parts of the sections were faster and danced in couples. These figures, with approximate English translations, were *Osmica* (figure of eight), *Karika* (chain or ring), *Zvezda* or *Zviezda* (star), *Tociljalka* (sliding or skating), *Oklajia* (rolling-pin), *Prolaz* (passing through), and finally, *Zmija* (snake), which was sometimes called *Veliko kolo* (great kolo), and which lasted longer than any of the other figures. Sometimes the middle figures would be in a slightly different order (Kuhač 1872; archival materials), and the version Dick Crum learned had only six figures — some the same as those of Kuhač and some different.

The term *dvoransko kolo* became the general name for this type of dance, along with the less frequent *salonsko kolo* (salon kolo). In printed programs, announcements, and musical scores, however, it was variously named *Slavonsko kolo* (Slavonian kolo), *Hrvatsko kolo* (Croatian kolo), *Hrvatsko Salonsko kolo, Narodno kolo* (national or folk kolo), and later in the century, simply *Kolo* (archival materials). As with so much of dance terminology, sometimes different names were used for what was presumably the same dance, and sometimes the same name for different versions of the dance (see Kuhač 1872, 4 [4]: 60–61).

According to Kuhač, the first music for the ballroom kolo was put together by the officers from bits and pieces of folk melodies that they could hum or whistle. In 1841, Vatroslav Lisinski, the first major Croatian composer, completed a piano score for the dance using the officers' tunes for the first section and other folk melodies for the following sections. An orchestral arrangement of this piece was first played at the January 27, 1842, ball. After that, at least six Croatian composers — including Kuhač himself — and two

Serbian composers created subsequent versions of accompaniment for the ballroom kolo (Kuhač 1872, 4[4]:61).

The ball referred to above was the first of many Illyrian balls that would be held during the 1840s. This one took place at the *Streljana*, a favorite site along with the *Dvorana* for Illyrian entertainments. The nationalist theme was carried out in the red and white colors of the decorations and the ladies' gowns; in the use of the Croatian language for announcements; in the incorporation of Croatian folk melodies in music for the usual ball dances (such as the waltz, polka, mazurka, and the traditional quadrille); and in the introduction of the ballroom kolo. In addition to his composition for this dance, Lisinski had also provided a "*Hrvatsko kolo*" in ¾ time and a suite of waltzes — with an introduction, five figures, and a finale — which was called "*Valceri za narodnu večeru zabavu*" (Waltzes for a national evening entertainment) (Vukotinovič 1842, 23–24; Kuhač 1904, 158).

It was quite daring in 1842 to perform anything that had connections with the peasantry, even if it had been "refined" and placed in the context of a society ball. Among the first group of young people to dance the ballroom kolo was the beautiful Countess Sidonija Erdödy (1819–1884), daughter of old and distinguished Zagreb nobility, albeit with Hungarian forebearers. Her participation gave the dance prestige and ensured that it would be taken up by other members of the society. In a glowing report on the ball, the fervent Illyrian writer and politician Ljudevit Vukotinovič (1842) wrote that she

> deserves our congratulations that she deigned to step into this kolo and lead it. Many think that the countess thereby lowered herself; I feel like she raised herself. What the countess deserved in thanks, so also did the other ladies who danced the kolo; because, for a native matter, they made the same contribution [23–24; translation by Hans C. Ruyter].

Vukotinovič also mentioned the contempt that some ladies at the ball expressed toward the kolo, one of them going so far as to call it a "bear dance" (ibid., 24).

In 1843, Sidonija married one Antun Rubido, but this did not prevent her continued activity as both a leading Illyrian and a prominent figure in the Zagreb musical scene. She had an outstanding soprano voice and sang the leading role in the first Croatian opera, Lisinski's *Ljubav i Zloba* (Love and Malice), as well as singing patriotic and folk-inspired songs at Illyrian events. In addition, she herself composed some music for dancing (Kuhač 1893a, 252–266).

Many of the Illyrian objectives had been accomplished by the end of the 1840s, but the 1850s saw the imposition of an absolutist and repressive regime throughout the Austrian Empire, and the march toward South Slav nationalism and eventual autonomy was interrupted for about a decade. When it re-emerged, it naturally took on new configurations and purposes.

The next stage in the development of the ballroom kolo, and the dance form's continuing existence into the 20th century, involved the work of Pietro Coronelli (1825–1902), a leading Italian ballet dancer who spent the last 43 years of his life as a social dance master in Croatia.

Coronelli was born in Venice on December 3, 1825, into a respected and well-situated family who lived a few blocks from the grand opera house of the city — La Fenice. His father, Lauro Carlo Coronelli, was a highly placed government official, and his mother, Anna Pasqualino, had been born a countess.[4] When Coronelli was 13, his father entered him into the competition for admittance to the La Fenice ballet school. He was accepted and quickly rose to the status of soloist and then *primo ballerino* (Premerl 1974, 144n; La Fenice documents). During his professional ballet years, he was under contract to La Fenice, but also appeared in Milan, Rome, Florence, and other Italian and European cities. He danced leading roles and partnered notable ballerinas such as Fanny Elssler, Sofia Fuoco, and the American Augusta Maywood.[5]

One wonders what led to the dramatic change of direction that Coronelli's life took in 1857. He performed during the 1856–57 ballet season, but after that, his professional life was almost totally devoted to social dance. In October 1857, he began working as a social dance teacher — or dance master — in and around Rijeka (known then by its Italian name, Fiume) where the Austrian Imperial Navy was based. He had a regular position at the naval academy and also traveled to other cities to teach (Radović 1974, 1556). In February 1859 he moved to Zagreb where he spent the rest of his life. Whatever his preparation for this new role as dance master, he would become highly successful in the work.

Coronelli apparently came to Zagreb at the invitation of a wealthy merchant and Croatian nationalist, Baron Ambroz Vranyczany, who wanted a dance master for his daughter and her friends. From all accounts, Zagreb had had no dance master prior to this time. Coronelli began teaching at the Vranyczany palace, but soon decided to establish his own independent school, and on October 15th, he was granted a permit from the Zagreb government (Cindrić 1974; Premerl 1974, 144; Radović 1974, 1556).

The main location of the Coronelli school from its beginning until 1914 was the Streljana, discussed above as one of the major centers of South Slavic nationalism in the 1840s (Radović 1974, 1558; Ladović 1974, 127–129). In addition to teaching there, Coronelli followed the usual practice of dance masters by teaching at other institutions in Zagreb and traveling to at least eight other Croatian cities and also to the Slovenian Maribor (Radović 1974,

1558–1559). In addition to teaching and arranging dance parties for his students, Coronelli arranged and led the dancing that frequently followed musical concerts and officiated at grand balls that commemorated special events (Radović 1974, 1557–1558; archival materials). He offered instruction in currently popular ballroom dances on the international circuit, dances of the recent past, and local favorites. There are records of his teaching the polonaise, minuet, Viennese waltz, mazurka, fast polka, French polka and quadrille (Cindrić 1974; archival materials).

In 1861, Coronelli added something new to his teaching repertoire — a revived and revised version of the *dvoransko kolo*. Croatian nationalism had been repressed during the absolutist period of the 1850s, and the ballroom kolo had disappeared from the social scene. The freedoms that began to return to Croatian social and political life in the 1860s permitted, among other things, the return to Croatian language and the revival of Croatian culture (Andreis 1974, 186–187). Alberto Štriga, an ardent Illyrian who had promoted Croatian music in the 1840s, renewed his nationalist activity in the new era. As part of this effort, he and his fellow patriots decided it would be good to rework the old ballroom kolo and reintroduce it. Štriga contacted Coronelli as a respected dance master who might help with this endeavor. According to Coronelli's daughter Bianca, her father took great interest in the project and embarked on a serious study of Croatian folk dances in order to use authentic steps in his new version of the ballroom kolo (Andreis 1974, 146–49; archival materials). Franjo Kuhač has written that in 1864, Coronelli spoke to him, claiming to have "corrected" the ballroom kolo, extracting foreign elements from it, and replacing them with new figures that he had invented (1872 4[4]: 60). One wonders how much Coronelli might have learned about the original *dvoransko kolo*, since it had died out during the 1850s. Perhaps the Illyrians who were eager to revive it remembered it and taught it to him or performed it for him. Since Kuhač was a child during the 1840s, it is unlikely that he knew much about the early version or versions.

The program format that had been introduced at the Illyrian balls in the 1840s and revived in the 1860s continued to be used well into the 20th century. The ballroom kolo became a popular dance that would be included once or twice in any social dance given in Croatia or Serbia — even though the dance events were no longer political. An array of internationally popular social dances were included along with the kolo. Through the years, new versions of ballroom kolo were choreographed and new music written for them. Ballroom kolos can be found on dance programs up to World War I.

In 1897, in his 70s, Coronelli became too ill to continue teaching, and his daughter Elvira took over the school. She ran it independently until 1915 when her sister Bianca joined her. In addition to having studied with her father, Elvira had earned a diploma in 1903 from a dance academy in Berlin. I have seen that proudly displayed in the home of Coronelli's grandson and great grandson in Šestine on the outskirts of Zagreb. Coronelli's two sons, Carlo and Umberto, had no interest in becoming dance masters.

In 1954, Dick Crum met with Elvira, who was still teaching dance in Zagreb, to learn the ballroom kolo as taught by her father. If she was born in 1879 as stated by Radović (1974, 1554), Elvira would have been 75 years old at this time; and if, indeed, the popularity of the ballroom kolo had faded around the time of the First World War, some 35 to 40 years would have passed since the dance had been done. One wonders how Elvira remembered it. Perhaps she had notes from her father, or from her own earlier teaching. Or perhaps she used the Kuhač description, although that differs from what she taught Dick Crum.

In June 1984, Dick Crum reconstructed the ballroom kolo he had learned from Elvira at the University of California, Irvine (UCI). The dancers who participated included both UCI undergraduate and graduate dance majors and some members of the Southern California international folk dance community. The dance was performed to its piano score. A video was made which includes the six separate sections identified by captions on the screen and verbally by Crum in the film. Then the dancers perform all six sections continuously. The sections in this version are (1) *Osmica* (figure 8); (2) *Promjena* (exchange); (3) *Zvjezda* (star); (4) *Maleni cruzi* (little circles); (5) *Vijenac* (wreath or garland); and (6) *Veselo za zmije* (merrily with serpent or snake).

The video is a document of a dance that has gone through time and who knows what changes. This dance form began with the ballroom kolo of the 1840s; re-appeared in the Coronelli revision of the 1860s; was passed from Coronelli to Elvira — probably in the late 19th century; and then, in the 1950s from Elvira to Dick Crum; and finally, some thirty years after that, from Dick Crum to dancers at UC Irvine. We can ask to what extent the dance performed in this latest version is similar to the original, but at the same time be very grateful that we have at least some record of the tradition.

It should be noted that over the years many versions of "ballroom kolos" developed, some of which are still in the repertoires of international recreational folk dance groups in the United States and perhaps beyond (see, for example, Crum 1954; Maners 1995, 98–99). Also, while the form disappeared from its original home, it has been carried abroad to at least one area in the Croatian diaspora. In studying the dance culture of third and fourth generation Croatian immigrants in Antofagasta, Chile, dance ethnologist Elsie Ivancich Dunin discovered that one of the dances they still perform is the

Salonsko kolo. She saw this initially in her first visits to the community in 1985 and 1986, and then again in another visit in 1996, and, most recently, danced by a folklore group from Antofagasta that performed in the 2000 international folklore festival in Zagreb which featured groups of Croatians living in other countries (Dunin 1988, 2002).

Thus, the tradition continues...

Notes

1. Most of this material was originally presented in Ruyter 1984, 1985, and 1989. For each of those works, I am grateful to my late husband, Hans C. Ruyter, for his collaboration.
2. Information on the Illyrian Revival has been taken from Kampuš and Karaman (1978, 121–149); Andreis (1974, 140–149); and Kuhač (1893a, 1893b).
3. Premerl (1974, 140), quoting from Antonija Kasowitz-Cvijić, "Nekoć na svečanom balu," *Jutarnji List* (November 20, 1927). Translation by Hans C. Ruyter. Information has also been drawn from the archival materials (see below).
4. Baptismal certificate in the archive of the Gran Teatro La Fenice, dated May 28, 1839; Coronelli gravestone in Mirogoj cemetery in Zagreb; and Radović (1974). The latter obtained information on Coronelli's pre–Zagreb life from Coronelli's daughter Bianca and from Marija Reich, the Coronelli housekeeper from 1922 (20 years after Pietro Coronelli's death) until Bianca's death in 1974 — so it is all secondary. The La Fenice archive unfortunately did not survive a disastrous fire that destroyed this historic theater and everything in it. I did research in that archive in 1984 before its disappearance.
5. Premerl (1974, 144n); Radović (1974, 1556); Ruyter (1985, 69); La Fenice archive; Music Library of the Giorgio Cini Foundation, Venice; Dance Collection of the New York City Library for the Performing Arts.

Bibliography

Archival materials. Dance and ball announcements and programs in the collections of the *Muzej Grada Zagreba* (Zagreb City Museum) and the *Hrvatski Glazbeni Zavod* (Croatian Music Society).
Andreis, Josip. 1974. *Music in Croatia*, trans. Vladimir Ivir. Zagreb: Institute of Musicology — Academy of Music.
Cindrić, P. 1974. "Zagrebački vremeplov: Generacije su plesale..." *Vjesnik* (Zagreb, February 23).
Crum, Dick. 1954. "Some Background on the Kolo in the United States." *Viltis* 13/45 (October/November), 4–5.
Dobronić, Lelja. 1983. *Zagrebački Gornji Grad, Nekad i Danas*. Zagreb: Školska Knjiga (first published 1967).
Dunin, Elsie Ivancich. 1988. "Salonsko Kolo as Cultural Identity in a Chilean Yugoslav Community (1917–1986)." *Narodna Umjetnost*, special issue 2. Zagreb: Institute of Ethnology and Folklore.
_____. 2002. "Chileans of Croatian Descent in Zagreb." *CCDR Newsletter* 20 (Autumn), 1, 3.
Kampuš, Ivan, and Igor Karaman. 1978. *Zagreb through a Thousand Years*, trans. Karla Cizelj and Nikica Jovanović. Zagreb: Školska Knjiga.
Kuhač, Franjo. 1872. "Dvoransko Kolo." *Vienac Zabavi i Pouci* (Zagreb) series: 4 (4):58–61; 4 (7):106–107; 4 (8):123–124; 4 (9):138–140; 4 (10):154–155; 4 (11):170–173.

_____. 1893a. *Ilirski Glazbenici.* Zagreb: Tisak Karla Albrechta.
_____. 1893b. *Ples i Plesovna Glazba.* Zagreb: Naklada Tiskare Anton Scholz.
_____. 1904. *Vatroslav Lisinski i Njegova Doba.* 2nd rev. and enl. ed. Zagreb: Izdala "Matica Hrvatska" (first published 1887).
Ladović, Vanda. 1974. "Oslikani ciljevi gradanskog streljačkog društva u Zagrebu." *Iz Starog i Novog Zagreba* V (Zagreb), 127–138.
Maners, Lynn D. 1995. "The Social Lives of Dances in Bosnia and Hercegovina: Cultural Performance and the Anthropology of Aesthetic Phenomena." Ph.D. thesis, University of California, Los Angeles.
Mladenović, Olivera. 1973. *Kolo u Južnih Slovena* (Kolo among the Southern Slavs). Belgrade: Serbian Academy of Sciences.
_____. 1980. "Forms and Types of Serbian Folk Dances." *Dance Studies* (Jersey, Channel Islands) 4, 53–85.
Premerl, Nada. 1974. "Ples kao oblik društvenog života u prošlosti Zagreba." *Iz Starog i Novog Zagreba* V (Zagreb), 139–150, followed by 18 photographs.
Radović, Milivoj. 1974. "Pietro Coronelli." *Povijest Sporta: Grada i Prilozi* 5 (March), 1554–1560.
Ruyter, Nancy Lee Chalfa, with Hans C. Ruyter. 1984. "Dvoransko Kolo: Dance and South Slavic Nationalism in Nineteenth-Century Croatia." *Proceedings: Society of Dance History Scholars: Seventh Annual Conference* (Goucher College, Towson, MD, 17–19 February, 1984), 101–108.
_____. 1985. "Pietro Coronelli: Dance Master of Zagreb." Paper presented at Congress of Research in Dance (CORD) Annual Conference, Ohio State University, November 8–11.
_____. 1989. "Pietro Coronelli: Dance Master of Zagreb." *Dance Research* (London) 7/1 (Spring), 78–83 (shorter version of 1985).
Vukotinović, Ljudevit. 1842. "Salon u Zagrebu." *Danica Ilirska* 8(6), 23–24.

14

Dance Structure and Its Application to the Understanding of Macedonian "Cross" Dances

ROBERT HENRY LEIBMAN

Dance is often described as culturally patterned movements of the human body through time and space. To further distinguish dance from other forms of human behavior, authors add that these movements must be artistic, expressive, stylized, rhythmic and/or purposefully selected and that they heighten, subdue, elaborate or transform the repertoire of everyday kinetic activities.[1] If dance is culturally patterned movement, not only does the style of movement vary from culture to culture, but so does the focus of this movement. Different traditions may focus on the arms, the central torso, the feet, or the whole body[2]; or, for example, as in American square dance, the focus becomes the larger spatial forms created by all the dancers together.[3] In the case of the Balkans, it is generally the footwork, the sometimes complicated patterns of successive steps, hops, slaps, stamps, etc., which is the focus of dance as culturally-patterned movement.[4]

Balkan dances, for the most part, consist of relatively short sequences of movements defined, primarily, by the patterned movement of the legs and feet. Dancing consists of the repeated performance (with variations) of one or more such movement sequences by all of the participants moving in unison. Many dances consist of a single such sequence, but some involve somewhat longer sequences that consist of two or more conjoined shorter subsequences. Analytically, these sequences and subsequences can be broken down into short segments of equal length that could be called *dance measures*. In most cases, these dance measures will coincide with the measures of the accompanying music, but not always. Sometimes, it will be advantageous to consider dance measures that are of a different length (frequently double or half) than the length of the corresponding musical measures. Even if dance and music measures are of the same length, it may add to our comparative understanding of different dances if we allow for a shifted articulation between dance and musical measures — i.e., where the measure boundaries for dance and music do not coincide.[5]

In most dancing in the Balkans, the dancers are positioned in an open or closed circle, a straight or curved line (or some other form) and are usually bound to one another by their arms and/or hands. If they are not in a closed circle, there will be a leader at one end (the front) of the line and a second, the "tail," perhaps, at the other. Sometimes, the leader and "tail" may be allowed or even expected to perform actions that are different than those of the other dancers in the line. In between the two ends, the dancers may or may not be ordered by age, gender, etc. Sometimes, there even are multiple lines or semi-circles dancing inside one another or following one another and participation in these different lines usually is determined by age, gender, etc.[6]

Variations

While the dancers in a single line all move in unison, they do not all dance identically. Rather, they perform "variations" on or within the framework of a basic pattern which ties all of their varied performances together into a unified whole. Clearly such "variations" must be reasonably compatible with one another so that neighboring dancers can simultaneously perform different "variations" without interfering with one another. "Variations" are not only limited by physical constraints (and these differ according to the way in which the dancers hold one another), they are also limited by cultural constraints — the local vocabulary of available movements, the local norms on proper behavior for dancers of a particular age, gender, class, etc. Moreover, and this is a point that I will return to later, these "variations" do not generally involve changes of the entire dance sequence, but rather of small segments within it. In fact, most variations only involve changes within individual dance measures which may or may not be accompanied by variations within any of the other dance measures in the sequence. Variations may simply involve performing the same movements with different levels of energy (hop vs. lift in place, leap vs. step)[7], performing different actions with the non-weight-bearing foot (close L foot to the R foot without taking weight vs. swing L foot forward slightly vs. raise the L leg high forward with knee bent and foreleg hanging down, etc.), or changing the relative placement of the feet while still taking the same number and type of steps (step on R foot, then onto the L foot across in front of the R foot, vs. step on R foot, then on L foot diagonally behind R foot, etc.).

Other common forms of variation involve actually taking a greater or fewer number of steps during that measure (a step-hop or step-lift vs. a pas-de-bas or some other type of quick three-step sequence). In fact, most "variations" are of the sort just described — they involve individual measures within the dance sequence and preserve the parity ("evenness" or "oddness") of the number of weight shifts within that measure. The step-hop (one weight shift) might be replaced by a pas-de-bas (three weight shifts), but it would not usually be replaced by a step, step (two weight shifts). Thus, there are "odd" measures which involve an odd number of weight shifts (i.e., 1, 3, or 5), and "even" measures which involve an even number of weight shifts (i.e., 0, 2, 4, or rarely 6).

Choreographic Structure

With this in mind, I have suggested that the "basic pattern" of each dance can be thought of as a more surface level manifestation of an underlying structure consisting of a linear sequence of "dance measures" each of which is characterized as being either "even" or "odd" and is represented by a "0" or "1," respectively. While much variation can be seen in the actions performed within the individual dance measures when considered from a surface level perspective, the underlying structure of all performances of a given dance is relatively invariant.

Even when variations are performed that do violate the parity of a given measure, this almost always involves a corresponding change of parity in an adjacent measure[8] — in fact, the change in parity of one measure *must* be accompanied by a change in parity of another measure somewhere in the dance sequence since *the full dance sequence must ultimately involve a total even number of weight shifts, or you would be on the wrong foot at the beginning of its next repetition.* Thus, no dance with 001 structure can exist since it would have a net odd number of weight shifts.

On the other hand, the "even" structure 011 is exceedingly common in the southern Balkans where there is a greater tendency towards asymmetric structures. In fact, among all 011 dances, there is a subclass that is ubiquitous throughout Europe and into the Middle East. (Included among these dances are the French *single branle*; the ballad dance of the Faroe Islands; the Jewish *hora*; the Greek *hasaposerviko*; the Macedonian *lesnoto, pravoto,* or *ramnoto*; *ličko kolo,* and similar dances from western Bosnia and western Croatia; the Arabic *dabke*, etc.)[9]

While "odd" structures like 01, 001, 0001 cannot exist as complete dance phrases, their repetitions (0101, 001001, 0001001) can and do. In such cases, the repetition often mirrors the original sub-phrase and is performed with reverse footwork and direction of motion. Direction of motion is, however, a somewhat independent aspect of dance structure and reverse footwork is not always accompanied by reverse direction of motion.[10] To indicate it we can add arrows beneath the sequence of 0's and 1's as well as a "/" as a separator between segments which go in opposite directions. Thus, several dances from northern Macedonia and southern Kosovo with 001001 structure could be better represented as *001>/<001*.[11]

While the concept of underlying dance structure presented here arose from my investigation of the nature of variation within the performances of given dances by all of the dancers in the dance, it also proves useful in comparing and classifying different dances. I have found that most of the extremely large number of dances which do or did exist in this area of the world are based on a fairly limited number of underlying structures, particularly symmetric structures such as 01/01, 001/001, 0001/0001, etc., 1101/1101, 0111/0111, 00111/00111 and asymmetric structures such as 01111 and 0011 (as well as the ubiquitous 011).[12] In some cases, particularly in the north (Croatia and Serbia), dances are often composed of the alternation of two or three subsequences, each of which is built on one of these simple underlying structures. Thus:

Šumadinka[13]   *1101>/ 11<01 / 0001>/<0001*
                           A   B

Milanovo kolo[14]   *1101>/<1101 / 01 / 01 / 01 / 01*
                               A   B   B

Železničko kolo[15]   *0001>/<0001 / 01 / 01 / 01 / 01*
                                  A   B   B

the Croatian dance *Dere*[16]   *<01 / 01> / <0001 / 0001> / <0001 / 0001>*
                                              A   B   B

and a dance which is well-known throughout Yugoslavia:

Seljančica[17]   *01>/<01 / 01>/<01 / 1/1 / 1/1 / 0001>/<0001*
                          A   A   B   B   C

Differences between dances with the same structure often involve the same sorts of measure-specific differences within the pattern as exist between the different "variations" of a single dance — e.g., three quick weight-shifts instead of a step-lift, but they may also involve differences of a sort that would not be found among the simultaneous performances by different dancers within a single dance (differences in the direction of motion, meter, etc.) and often reflect regional preferences — e.g., most dances in Serbia, Macedonia, Bulgaria, and Greece begin with a step onto the R foot moving to the right (or a preparatory lift on the L foot in place before stepping to the right), but the reverse is true in Croatia, Slovenia, and much of Western Europe. Thus the basic 011 structure is generally performed as *01>/<1* or *0>*11 in the former, while it is often *<011* or *<0*11 in the latter. (Note initial leftward movement in *Dere* above.)[18]

The underlying structure (sequence of 0s and 1s) of a dance is a highly abstract representation of that dance which is arrived at by beginning with a more surface level representation which includes meter, rhythm, direction of motion, etc. In order to be able to look at and compare different performances of the same dance or performances of different dances I devised some simple, easily readable ways of graphically representing the sequence of steps (weight shifts) against a backdrop of the musical beats of the given meter. Thus, for example, in looking at *Lesnoto*, the basic Macedonian three-measure dance (011), we can represent a basic performance of this dance in 7/8

a. **diagram 1**

meter as follows:
Major beats are labeled in each measure. (All beats are labeled in measure 1.)
 Upper case letters represent steps (weight shifts) onto the indicated foot (R = right, L = left)
Direction of motion relative to line or circle is indicated by an arrow.
 ← to left, CW; → to right, CCW; ↑ into center, ↓ backing out of center
 o non-weight-shift at a major beat. Does not indicate action of the nonweight-bearing foot.
 ô is a lift (non-weight-shift) on the weight-bearing foot.
 (R̦) is a touch with the non-weight-bearing foot — in this case, the R. (This co-occurs with a non-weight-shift.)

b. **diagram 2**

14. Dance Structure and Its Application

c. **diagram 3**

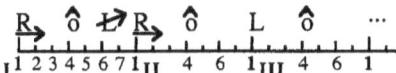

Compare the above with the following "variations":
In b) a preparatory lift on ct. 4 of measure I delays the step onto L (from count 4 to count 6).

d. **diagram 4**

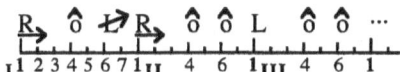

In c) this is accompanied by slight lift on the weight-bearing foot on count 4 of

e. **diagram 5**

f. **diagram 6**

measures II and III.
Some might even add a second small lift on the weight-bearing foot on count 6 of measures II and III.
Step-close or step-lift(s) in measures II and III may each be replaced by three quick crossing steps.
Crossing step in measure III may e) move in and out of circle, or f) it may back out and then in.
The step onto L on ct. 4 (g) or 6 in (h) of measure I may be behind R instead of in front.

Focusing on weight shifts only, we could represent the above examples variously as:

| RLo | Roo | Loo |, | RoL | Roo | Loo |, | RLo | RLR | LRL |, | RoL | RLR | LRL |,
| RLo | Roo | LRL |, etc. More abstractly, using X to indicate any weight shift without specifying the particular foot, we have | XXo | Xoo | Xoo |, | XoX | Xoo | Xoo |, | XXo | XXX | XXX |,
and | XXo | Xoo | XXX |. We see that they all satisfy 011 structure.

Macedonian Cross Dances
("Krstačka," "Krsteno")

There are many dances from Macedonia and South Serbia in which one (or more) measures of rightward movement alternates with an even number of "crossing" steps in place. The "crossing" step, performed while facing towards the center of the circle, is a one-measure sequence consisting of a lift (non-weight-shift) in place followed by three steps (weight-shifts) moving into and out of the circle forming the "cross." The pattern is then repeated with reverse footwork. If we imagine this pattern as consisting of four counts, we could describe it (beginning here with weight on L) as:

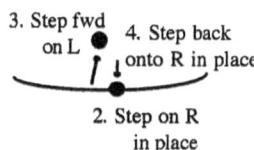

diagram 9

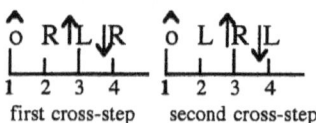

diagram 10

1. Lift in place on ball of L (can become a hop); free leg (R) may be raised forward a bit while this is done.
2. Step in place (next to L) on R.
3. Step forward into circle (on foot L).
4. Step back onto foot R in place.

Repeat with reverse footwork.

VARIATIONS: a. Sometimes, especially as the music becomes faster, the step on count 2 may be preceded by a quick lift on the weight-bearing foot. Depending on the meter of the music, this lift may be done prior to the beat or it may be done on the beat. (Infrequently, a similar quick preliminary lift may be added on count 4.) b. In some dances, the step forward into the circle on count 3 may be replaced with a step back out of the circle, especially in those measures which begin with weight on the R foot.

14. Dance Structure and Its Application

diagram 11

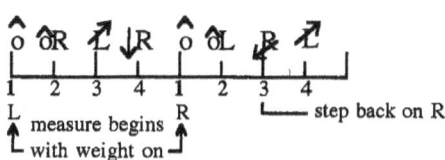

diagram 12

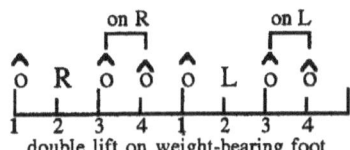

diagram 13

c. In some dances, the two steps on counts 3 and 4 (in and out of the circle) are replaced by two lifts (*čukče*) in place on the weight-bearing foot, often with the free foot raised forward, bent at the knee. This actually takes the "cross" out of the cross step.

Thus "crossing" measures can be represented as: | OR$^\uparrow$L$\downarrow$R | and | OL$^\uparrow$R$\downarrow$L | or, if we use X to indicate *any* weight shift, simply | OX$\downarrow$X$\uparrow$X | with variations of the form | OX$^\uparrow$X$\downarrow$X | and | OXOO |. Ultimately, these are all "odd" measures represented by a 1. Note that *there is no weight shift on the first count* of each crossing measure and *there is always a weight shift on the second count*.

There are two basic types of "cross dances" and they differ with respect to how the movement to the right is handled. In Type I the rightward movement occurs during a single measure which in its simplest form involves facing right of center and moving forward (CCW):

1. Lift L, 2. Step R, 3. Lift L, 4. Step R.> (Then in place.)

In Type II the rightward movement spans the first measure *plus beginning of the second*:

I. *1. Lift L, 2. Step R, 3. Step L, 4. Step R.>*

II. *1. Step L, 2. Step R>* 3. Step L into center, 4. Step R back (out of center)

For easy comparison, here is a representation of the two basic 5-measure cross dance types as they might be performed in 4/4 meter. The first is a Type I dance and the second is Type II:

diagram 14

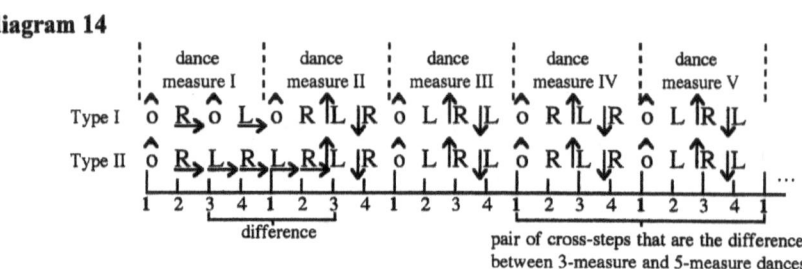

Note that the two types really only differ for a period of 4 counts (the end of measure I and beginning of measure II). This leads to a seemingly different structure, 01111 for Type I and 10111 for Type II, but when performed repeatedly this difference is minimized since the sequences are essentially the same long sequence with different starting points: 01111011110111101111... vs. 10111101110111101111... In fact, depending on the occasion, the particular leader, and local stylistic preferences, a given dance may be begun at different points in the sequence — sometimes even at a point other than the beginning of a dance measure, so I would downplay any differences in structure that are due only to the choice of starting point. Both Type I and Type II structures are found as 3-measure sequences, generally in southern Macedonia and northern Greece, as well as 5-measure sequences, primarily in northern Macedonia and Kosovo.[19] Three-measure dances consist of the first three measures of the five-measure structures above:

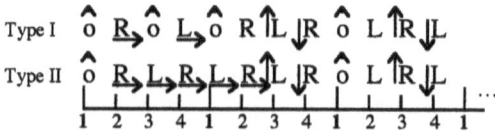

diagram 15

Now we look at a number of examples and variations of dances of both Types in various meters. Diagrams of the dance phrase will indicate both musical and dance measures and their subdivisions. We begin with *Cigansko kolo*, a 5-measure Type I dance from the village of Koretište, near Gnjilane in southeast Kosovo. The music consists of 10 measures of 2/4.[20]

diagram 16

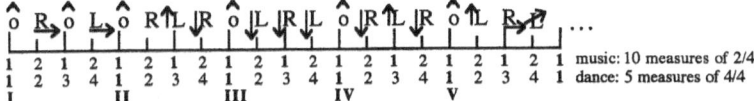

The dance often begins with measure II of the 5-measure sequence. Thus the "even," moving measure is performed at the end. Note that the three weight shifts in measures III and V don't really create the normal "crossing" pattern since they each involve movement in one direction only, not forward and back.

Sitna Lisa is a 5-measure Type I dance from the Skopje region performed to 10 measures of 7/16.[21]

a. **diagram 17**

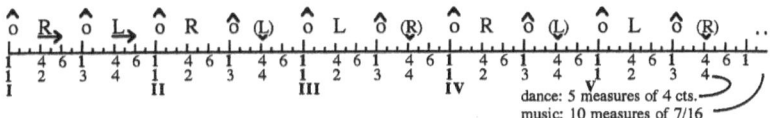

b. **diagram 18**

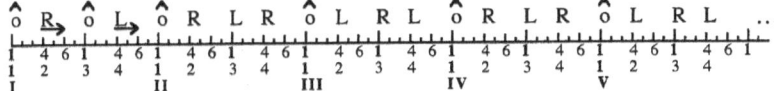

The crosses are done a) with a mere touch in place (R) and (L) or b) as the music becomes livelier, with a weight shift onto the touching foot quickly followed by a shift back to the original weight-supporting foot. As with many cross-dances, extra lifts may be added preceding the weight shift on ct. 2.

Teškoto is a 3-measure Type I dance from W. Maced, performed to 6 measures of 2/4 music.[22]

diagram 19

This is a heavy men's dance which begins with a slow section in which the dancers follow the slow improvised movements of the leader. When the leader is ready, the music gets faster and the dancers perform the regular pattern described here. Note that in cts. 3 and 4 of dance measure II, the normal "cross" is replaced by two lifts on the R foot-with the free right foot raised forward, first diagonally left and then diagonally right. Variations not shown here include squats and individual CW turns that can be done while dancing measure I.

Jeni Jol is a 3-measure Type I dance of the Turkish minority in Veles done to 6 measures of 2/4.[23]

diagram 20

A woman's dance in which lift-steps are performed as touch-steps. The parenthesized symbols—(↑R), (R↗), (↓R)—represent touches in the direction of motion with the non-weight-bearing foot.

Toska is a 5-measure Type I dance from the Radoviš area, in SE Maced, done to 10 measures of 3/8.[24]

diagram 21

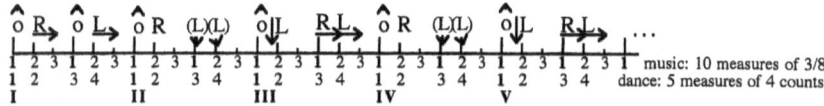

A men's dance. The "crosses" in dance measures II and IV actually involve touches with the left foot in front on counts 3 and 4 (rather than weight shifts) and in measures III and V involve movement to the right rather than in place. This is an interesting example in that the dance is sometimes performed without the moving measure (dance measure I = musical measures I and II), but it *is* done this way in some of the villages of that region.

Postupano is a 5-measure Type I dance from Skopje performed to 5 measures of 13/16.[25]

a. **diagram 22**

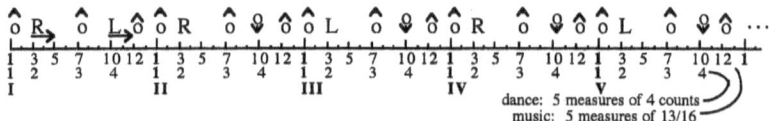

b. **diagram 23**

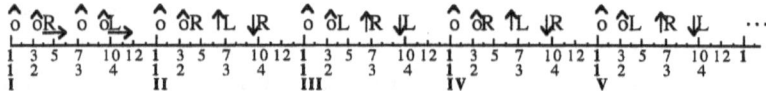

Primarily a men's dance. a) is a basic variation which involves lifts on counts 3 and 4 of dance measures II–V (rather then weight-shifts in and out); b) is one of many possible variations: cross-steps involving weight shifts on counts 3 and 4 of measures II–V. An additional lift is added prior to the weight shift on count 2 of all five measures.

Finally, *Oro (Svekrvino kolo)* is a more complicated example of a 5-measure Type I dance. It is from the village of Ranilug near Gnjilane in southern

Kosovo.[26] The complication lies in the lack of a simple concordance between the lengths of the musical measures and dance measures. Unlike those in which a dance measure exactly corresponds to one or two measures of music, in this case the dance measure is only a fraction of the musical measure in length. The music is described as consisting of alternating measures of ¹¹⁄₁₆ and ⁷⁄₁₆ (= 18/16). The four major counts per dance measure correspond to beats 1, 4, 8, 10 in measures of ¹¹⁄₁₆ and 1, 4 in measures of ⁷⁄₁₆ so the five dance measures of a dance phrase correspond to about 3⅓ measures of music and the dance phrase, therefore, alternately begins at three different points within the ¹⁸⁄₁₆ measure. All of this is shown in the three dance measures below:

diagram 24

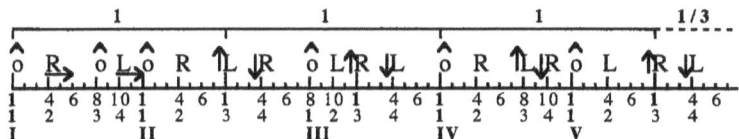

diagram 25

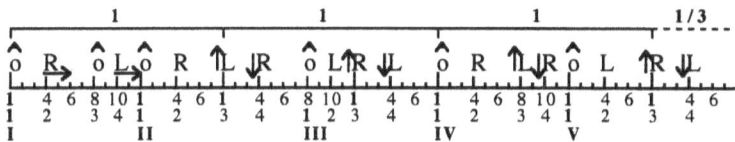

diagram 26

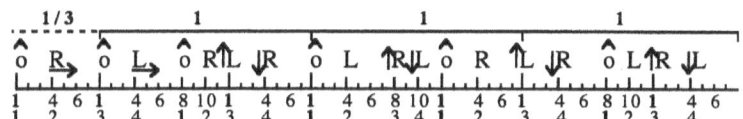

Now, we look at some examples of Type II. Here are some in three measures:

Što mi e milo is a 3-measure Type II dance from SW Macedonia in ⁹⁄₁₆.[27]

diagram 27

Berančе, Pušteno, Ne odi Džemo, are 3-measure Type II dances from SW Macedonia in ¹²⁄₁₆.[28]

diagram 28

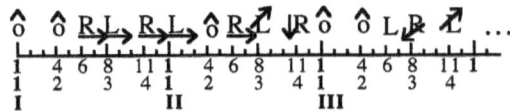

diagram 29

diagram 30

A very common dance in Southwestern Macedonia performed to a variety of names. We see a) the basic, b) added lift on ct. 2 of each dance measure, c) step backward (not forward) on R in the cross in measure III.

These dances are occasionally done as 5-measure dances by adding two additional cross-steps.

Ibrahim Odža, a 5-measure Type II dance from northern Macedonia described here in 12/16, (though it is sometimes played in 13/16 by extending the last beat from 2/16 to 3/16).[29]

Aensko krsteno is another 5-measure Type II dance from the Skopje area. Its music is in 13/16.[30]

a. **diagram 32**

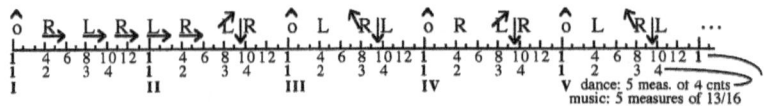

b. **diagram 33**

c. **diagram 34**

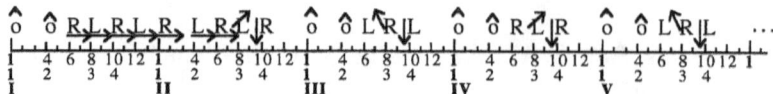

a) Basic, b) with lifts on ct. 2 of each measure, c) lift-step-step is replaced by three quick steps at end of measure 1 and beginning of measure 2. This is an example of a parity change in adjacent measures. 01000 becomes 10000.

While most cross-dances involve sequences of either 3 or 5 dance measures, this is not always the case. *Baba Đurđa* is a 7-measure Type II dance from the Skopje area in 7/8 meter.[31]

a. **diagram 35**

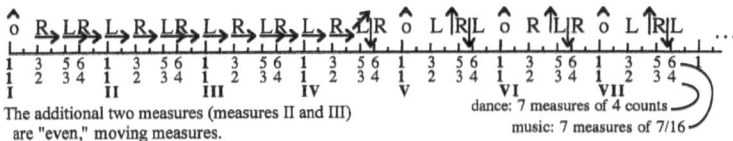

The additional two measures (measures II and III) are "even," moving measures.

dance: 7 measures of 4 counts
music: 7 measures of 7/16

b. **diagram 36**

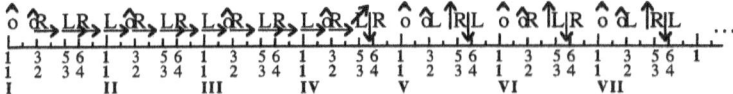

An additional preparatory lift is added to the weight-shift on ct. 2 of each measure.

diagram 37

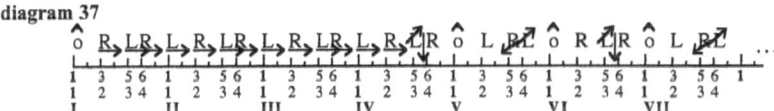

The cross-steps in measures V and VII involve a step backwards on the R, rather than forward.

c. **diagram 38**

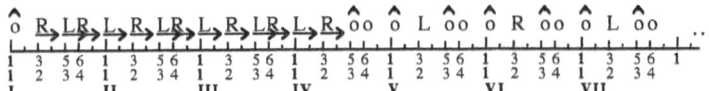

The cross-steps are done without a cross (measures IV–VII). In V–VII, weight is shifted on ct. 2 and then remains there as we lift in place on counts 3 and 4.

The dance *Čamče* in 12/16 from the village of Peštani in SW Macedonia takes this one step further. The sequence is variable in length. While the sequence is frequently 3 measures in length, it is often expanded by adding any number of additional "even" moving measures (similar to measures II and III in Baba Đurđa) and then performing an even number of "odd" crossing measures. Odd measures must be added in pairs to retain a total even number of weight of weight shifts.[32]

diagram 39

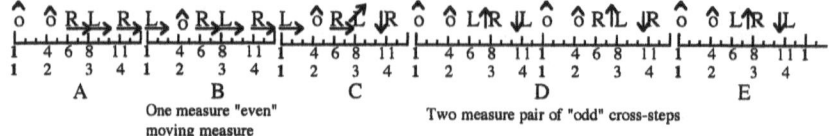

The basic 3-measure dance consists of ACE. Adding D, we get the 5-measure sequence ACDE. Now add more Bs and Ds to get sequences like ABBBCDDDE (12 measures).

Related Structures

A few dances exist which are quite similar to the basic three-measure *Berance*, but differ from it by the addition of a single modified cross-step which, because it consists of an even number of weight shifts (one weight shift is added or dropped) does not have to be added in pairs. One such dance is *Nesho*, a 4-measure Type II dance in 12/16 from Lake Prespa in SW Macedonia.[33] The dance phrase is also extendable by a one-measure "tag," usually done twice.

diagram 40

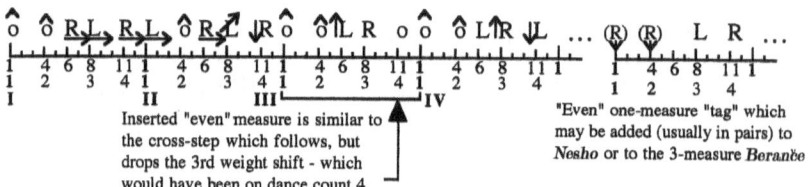

diagram 41

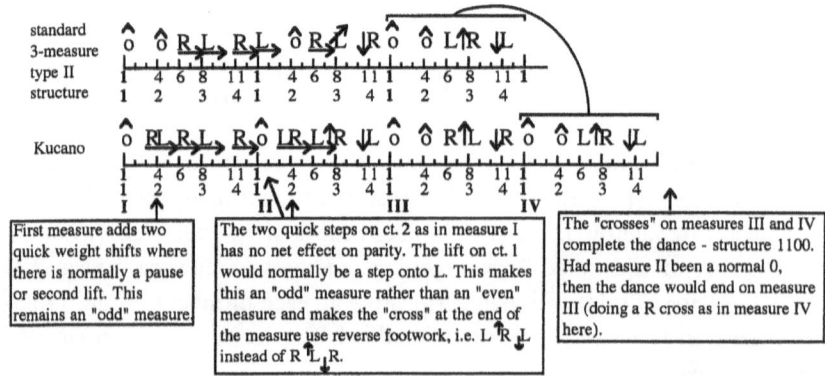

14. Dance Structure and Its Application

Another such dance is *Kucano*, a 4-measure Type II dance from near Prilep[34] (although an additional pair of cross-steps is often added as the dance becomes faster):

As already noted in the case of the dance *Toska* from the Radoviš area, dropping the single "even" measure on which the dancers move to the right, results in a never-ending sequence of pairs of even measures. Examples of this include 2-measure dances like *Sta Dhia* and *Beraçe* (no "moving" step — just pairs of crossing steps with more or less movement). Compare the 5-measure Type II dance in $^{12}/_{16}$, *Ibrahim Odža*, with a two-measure *Berançe* also in $^{12}/_{16}$.[35]

diagram 42

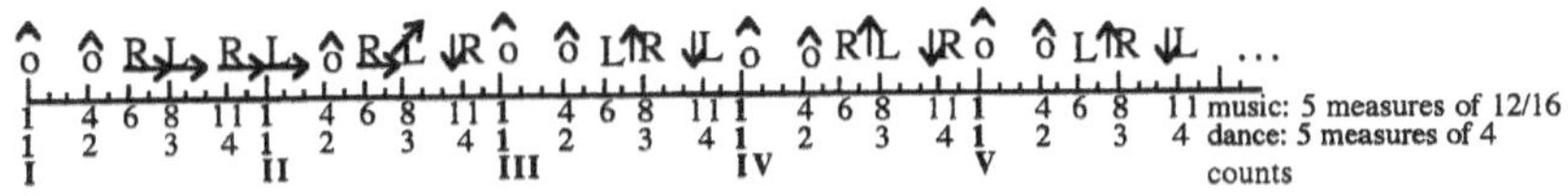

diagram 43

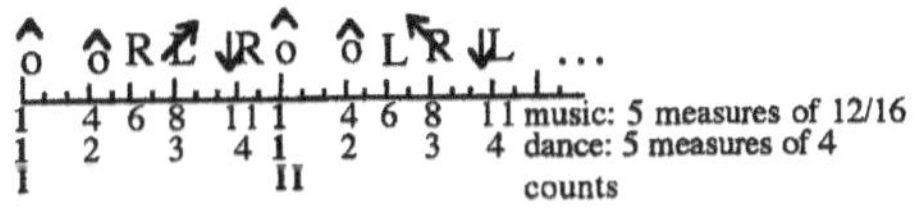

Conclusions

Hopefully, the previous examples have given some indication of the wide variety of cross-dances that exist in Macedonia which, while all having the same underlying structure, differ with respect to details. The structural perspective has not only allowed us to more closely describe the obvious similarities among such dances, but it has also helped us to be aware of relationships between dances that might not otherwise be evident.

At the same time, the structural approach has helped us to better understand the dynamics of Balkan dancing as they occurred in a traditional setting, how dancers in a line or circle could dance together without all having to dance exactly the same. The extent to which such dancers could vary in their simultaneous performance of the dance was often much greater than that which might be envisioned by those who only know these dances from having seen staged choreographies, or from having learned them in formal teaching sessions presented by folk dance teachers as a succession of sequence-length "figures," each of which is to be done identically by all of the dancers at the same time. What I have tried to show is that the dance often consists of a group of individuals each dancing their own structured improvisation on the basic dance sequence using "variations" at different points within that sequence in such a way that, while not all dancing in unison, they are all dancing compatibly.

Notes

1. "Dance consists of culturally patterned, stylized, artistic [aesthetic] bodily movement." This is a "minimal" definition of dance "not intended to tell you what 'dance' means, but allow you to recognize the labeled phenomena wherever and whenever encountered" (Waterman 1962, 48).

"[Dance is] patterned movement performed as an end in itself" (Royce 1977, 8). Also, "the body making patterns in time and space" (Royce 1977, 3).

Dance is "a transient mode of expression performed in a given form and style by the human body moving in space ... [which] occurs through purposefully selected and controlled rhythmic movements ... [such that] the resulting phenomenon is recognized as dance both by the performer and the observing members of the group" (Kealiinohomoku 1970, 28).

Dance is "human behavior composed, from the dancer's perspective, of purposeful, intentionally-rhythmical, culturally patterned sequences of non-verbal body movement and gesture which are not ordinary motor activities, the motion having inherent and 'aesthetic' value" (Hanna 1977, 211).

"Out of the ordinary motor activities dance selects, heightens or subdues, juggles gestures and steps to achieve a pattern, and does this with a purpose transcending utility" (Kurath 1970, 234).

2. See Kaeppler (1972) on Tongan dance and Ikegami (1971) on hand movements in Indian dance.

3. Casey (1976), La Vita (1983).

4. This should be clear from the fact that most descriptions of dances from the Balkans (including those written by natives) focus *primarily* on the footwork rather than on the movement of the arms, the torso, etc., though significant arm movement does occur in some regions (e.g., north Bulgaria).

5. See Leibman (1992, 325–335) for a discussion of how the family of cross-dances described later in this paper can be seen as being related to another subfamily of dances with 011 structure (including *Devetorka* and *Gankino*) by such a shifted articulation.

6. For a discussion of dance shape, connections between dancers, gender, role of the leader and "tail," etc., see Chapter 3 of Leibman 1992. See also Mladenović (1968, 1973).

7. See Leibman (1972b; 1992, 62–67, 232). Compare with Singer (1974).

8. For an example of this, consider the discussion of *Žensko krsteno* on p. XX. In particular, compare variation c with those labeled a and b. There are many Macedonian dances in which two successive even measures (hop-step-step) (= 00) might be replaced by two successive odd measures (step-step-step) (=11), e.g., measures I and II in *Crnogorka* (Dunin et. al. 1973, 99–102; Dimoski 1977, 62–66); likewise in measures I and II of *Cigančica* (Leibman 2004, 6–7).

9. Crum (1977, 21–23); Arbeau (1967, 132–133). See Ivančan (1981, 46–54, 187–196) for a thorough discussion of *Ličko kolo* and related *kolos* in the valleys of the Dinaric mountains. See Dopuđa (1986, 7–44) for an extensive discussion of *Starobosansko kolo* and others from W. Bosnia.

10. While symmetric dances in Serbia may move only slightly more to the right than to the left, there is much greater rightward movement in Macedonian dances, so that they often begin their rightward movement during the last measure or two of the second half of the dance, i.e., during that portion of the dance in which one might expect them to be moving to the left. I have seen this many times when watching and filming Macedonians do Serbian dances such as *U šest, Žikino,* and *Čačak.* See Leibman 1977–78 for more on how this feature appears in the 0111/0111 dances of eastern Macedonia (e.g., *Berovka, Ratevka*).

11. *Crnogorka* is such a dance from the Skopje area. See Dunin et al. (1973, 99–102); Dimoski (1977, 62–65). Likewise, the dances *Oj, devojce, riti ti* and *Potam, povam* are two such dances from the village of Koretište about a mile from Gnjilane in southeastern Kosovo. They are among twenty dances which I filmed with the aid of Steve Kotansky in late June 1972 as males from that village, ranging in age from late teens to their 50s and 60s, danced for us to the music of two *zurle* and a *tupan* whom we hired in Gnjilane.

12. For an extended discussion of dances with these structures, see Leibman (1992, 286–291).

13. Janković and Janković (1934, 23–24).

14. Filcich (1959, 62).

15. Janković and Janković (1964, 1111–1112).

16. Ivančan (1964, 51–54, 194).

17. Janković and Janković (1934, 60–61); Crum (1993, n.p).

18. See Leibman (1992, 221–225) for additional discussion of right-left distinctions.

19. Among examples in this paper, most five-measure dances — *Cigansko kolo, Oro, Ibraim Odža, Postupano, Žensko krsteno* — are all from Skopje (northern Macedonia) and Gnjilane (SE Kosovo), while the three-measure dances are from central and southwestern Macedonia. Many similar three-measure dances also exist in northwestern Greece (Aegean Macedonia). See Boxell (1990, 25–38, *Patrounino, Pousteno, Savlitsena, Stankino*); Burke (1974, 9, *Levendikos*), etc. Note that the three-measure dance, *Savlitsena* or *Maškoto*, becomes a five-measure dance when brought to Skopje (Leibman 1972a, 34–36).

20. *Cigansko kolo* is another dance I filmed in the village of Koretište. See note 11 above.

21. Leibman (1972a, 25).

22. Dunin and Višinski (1995, 269, Figure VIII). See also Figure IX "turns" and Figure X "squats" on p. 270. (This is a description of the 15-figure choreography by the Ensemble Tanec.) This is a dance which in its simpler village form I have watched, participated in and filmed on August 28, 1967, in the village of Gari, near Debar, Macedonia, and at the Mavroski Sobir, a festival on Lake Mavrovo near Debar, both in late June 1967 and June 1968.

23. Dunin and Višinski (1995, 160–61).

24. Taken from my films of village dance groups from around Radoviš in southeastern Macedonia. The villages of Injevo (Ilindenski denovi, Bitola 2005), Gabrevci (Ilindenski denovi, Bitola 1971) and Topolnica (Balkanski Folklor Festival in Ohrid, July 8). A slightly different variation of this dance appears in Dimoski (1974, 69–72). The truncated version from Injevo (without the moving measure) appears in Glass (1975, n.p.).

25. Dunin and Višinski (1995, 205–207). Example a) is Figure I for Men. Example b) is like Figure V for women, but includes a preparatory lift on dance ct. 2 of each measure. This is taken from my unpublished notes written for Pece Atanasovski's teaching tour of the United States in 1982.

26. Janković and Janković (1951 [v.6], 67–71).

27. Crum (1974). See also *Ne sedi, Džemo,* in Janković and Janković (1951, 74–75).

28. *Beranče* as performed on stage by Tanec is described in Dunin and Višinski (1995, 85–91). For *Pousteno (Pušteno)* see Boxell (1990, 28–29). *Ne odi Džemo* is in Holden et al. (1965b, 8).

29. Dunin et al. (1973, 79–80). Notated in 13/16 here.
30. Dunin and Višinski (1995, 298–299; especially a. and b.); Holden (1965c, 12, for variant c).
Also a film of dancers from the village of Miladinovci performing at the Beograd Sabor on September 8.
31. Holden (1965b, 4).
32. Leibman (2004, 4–5). Based on attendance, dancing, and filming others dance at many weddings in the village of Peštani in the late 60s and early 70s.
33. Leibman (1974, 17).
34. Leibman (1972a, 29–30).
35. As seen and recorded in the village of Vevčani, just north of Struga in SW Macedonia, during a wedding on July 7, 1967. See also *Beraçe*, a similar two-measure dance in 12/16 which is less symmetric in that there is a constant movement towards the right. The dance is done by Tosk Albanians living in the villages of Krani and Arvati on the eastern shore of Lake Prespa in SW Macedonia, about 10 km north of the Greek border (Leibman 1974, 17).

Bibliography

Aman. 1972. *Syllabus for Aman 3rd Annual Dance Institute, January 28–30, 1972*. Los Angeles: Aman. (Pages are unnumbered.)

———. 1973. *Syllabus for Aman 4th Annual Dance Institute, April 6–7, 1973*. Los Angeles: Aman. (Pages are unnumbered.)

Arbeau, Thoinot. 1967. *Orchesography*. Translated by Mary Stewart Evans. With a New Introduction and Notes by Julia Sutton. New York: Dover Books. [This translation was originally published in 1948 in London by Kamin Dance Publishers, Inc.; Arbeau's *Orchesographie* was originally published in 1589 at Langres by Jehan des Preyz.]

Boxell, Dennis. 1990. "Dances of Greek Macedonia." In *Syllabus for the University of Chicago Folkdancers' 28th Annual International Dance and Music Festival, 2–4 Nov. 90*. Chicago: University of Chicago.

Burke, Bill. 1974. "*Levendikos*." In *Syllabus of Dance Descriptions for the 23rd Annual Kolo Festival*. San Francisco: Kolo Festival, 9.

Casey, Betty. 1976. *The Complete Book of Square Dancing (and Round Dancing)*. Garden City, N.Y.: Doubleday.

Crum, Dick. 1974. "*Što mi e milo*." In *Syllabus of Dance Descriptions for the 23rd Annual Kolo Festival*. San Francisco: Kolo Festival, 15.

———. 1977. *Nama #2 Dance Syllabus*. Los Angeles: NAMA.

———. 1993. *Old-Tyme Kolos*. Los Angeles: 1993 Tamburitza Extravaganza.

Dimoski, Mihailo. 1974a. *Orskata tradicija vo selo Injevo (radoviško)*. Biblioteka na spisanieto Makedonski folklor, no.4. Skopje: Institut za folklor.

———. 1977. *Makedonski narodni ora od repertoarot na ansamblot za narodni igri i pesni "Tanec."* Makedonsko narodno tvorčestvo. Orska narodna tradicija. Kn. 2. Skopje: Institut za Folklor.

Dopuđa, Jelena. 1986. *Narodni Plesovi-Igre u Bosni I Hercegovini*. Zagreb: Kulturno-prosvjetnih sabor Hrvatske.

Dunin, Elsie, Mihailo Dimoski, and Stanimir Višinski. 1973. *Makedonski narodni plesovi (Macedonian Folk Dances)*. Zagreb: Prosvjetni Sabor Hrvatske. Muzička Biblioteka.

Dunin, Elsie Ivancich, and Stanimir Višinski. 1995. *Dances of Macedonia: Performance Genre-Tanec*. Skopje: Macedonia.

Filcich, John. 1952. *Igra Kolo. Dance Kolos with John Filcich*. Oakland: Slav-Art Music, Co.

———. 1959. "Milanovo kolo." In *Dance Syllabus for the 12th Annual Folk Dance Camp at the College of the Pacific, Stockton, Ca*. Stockton: Folk Dance Federation, 62.

14. Dance Structure and Its Application

Glass, Barry. 1975. "*Toska.*" In *Syllabus of Dance Descriptions for the 25th Annual Kolo Festival*. San Francisco: Kolo Festival.
Hanna, Judith Lynn. 1977. "To Dance Is Human: Some Psychobiological Bases of an 'Expressive' Form." In *The Anthropology of the Body*, ed. John Blacking. A.S.A. Monograph 15. New York: Academic Press, 211–232.
Holden, Rickey, et al. 1965a. *Macedonian Folk Dances, vol. I, LP-15*. (Dance notes for 12 Macedonian dances. This booklet came with the LP containing the music to which these dances could be performed.) Newark: Folkraft Records.
_____. 1965b. *Macedonian Folk Dances, vol. II, LP-24*. (Dance notes for 12 Macedonian dances. This booklet came with the LP containing the music to which these dances could be performed.) Newark: Folkraft Records.
_____. 1965c. *Macedonian Folk Dances, vol. III, LP-25*. (Dance notes for 11 Macedonian dances. This booklet came with the LP containing the music to which these dances could be performed.) Newark: Folkraft Records.
Ikegami, Yoshiko. 1971. "A Stratificational Analysis of the Hand Gesture in Indian Classic Dance." *Semiotica* 4(4), 365–391.
Ivančan, Ivan. 1964. *Narodni plesovi Hrvatske*. v.1, 2nd ed. Zagreb: Savez muzičkih društava Hrvatske. (Originally published in 1957.)
_____. 1981. *Narodni plesovi I igre u Lici*. Zagreb: Prosvjetni sabor Hrvatske.
Janković, Ljubica S. 1968. *Problem i teorija pojedinačne aritmičnosti u ritmičnosti celine izvođenja orske igre i melodije*. Srpski Etnografski Zbornik 82. Beograd: SANU.
Janković, Danica S., and Janković, Ljubica S. 1934, 1937, 1939. *Narodne igre* v. 1–3. Beograd: Srpske kraljevske akademije nauka u Beogradu.
_____. 1948-52. *Narodne igre* v. 4–7. Beograd: Prosveta.
_____. 1964. *Narodne igre* v. 8. Beograd: Prosveta.
Kaeppler, Adrienne L. 1972."Method and Theory in Analyzing Dance Structure with an Analysis of Tongan Dance." *Ethnomusicology*. 16 (2), 173–217.
Kealiinohomoku, Joann. 1970. "An Anthropologist Looks at Ballet as a Form of Ethnic Dance." *Impulse*.
Kremenliev, Boris. 1952. *Bulgarian-Macedonian Folk Music*. Berkeley: University of California Press.
Kurath, Gertrude Prokasch, with Antonio Garcia. 1970. *Music and Dance of the Tewa Pueblos*. Museum of New Mexico Research Records no. 8. Santa Fe: Museum of New Mexico Press, 1970.
La Vita, James. 1983. *Allemande Left With Your Left Hand: Structure and Meaning in Modern Western Square Dancing*. Unpublished masters thesis: University of California, Berkeley.
Leibman, Robert. 1972a. *Macedonian Folk Dances Presented by Pece Atanasovski*. Los Angeles: Snark Records.
_____. 1972b. "The Musical Culture of a Macedonian Village, Peštani." Unpublished paper.
_____. 1973. *Traditional Songs and Dances from the Soko Banja Area*, ed. Robert H. Leibman. (Notes for Balkan Heritage Series vol.1-accompanying Selo Records LP-1, an LP of instrumental and vocal music recorded in the Soko Banja area of Serbia by Robert H. Leibman.) San Francisco: Festival Records.
_____. 1974. "Descriptions of Dances: *Beraçe, Devolliçe, Grčkoto, Nesho*." In *Syllabus of Dance Descriptions, The 23rd Annual Kolo Festival*. San Francisco: Kolo Festival Committee.
_____. 1977-78. "Discovering Structure in Yugoslav Folk Dances." *Mixed Pickles* (Dec. 1977, Jan. 1978 and Feb. 1978).
_____. 1992. "Dancing Bears and Purple Transformations: The Structure of Dance in the Balkans." Unpublished dissertation. Philadelphia: University of Pennsylvania.
_____. 2004. Syllabus of Dance Descriptions for 57th Annual Texas Camp, November 25–28, 2004.
Mladenović, Olivera. 1968. "Jedan vid tradicionalne hijerarhije u makedonskom oru." In *Rad XIII-og kongresa SFJ u Dojranu 1966 godine*. Skopje: SUFJ, 125–130.
_____. 1971. "Neka pitanja metodologije, klasifikacije i terminologije naših narodnih igara." In

Rad XV-og kongresa SUFJ u Jajcu 12–16. septembra 1968. godine. Sarajevo: Savez udruženja folklorista Jugoslavije, 303–306.

_____. 1973. *Kolo u južnih slavena* (The "Kolo" Dance of the South Slavs). Monograph v. 14, Ethnographical Institute. Belgrade: Serbian Academy of Sciences and Arts.

Royce, Anya Peterson. 1977. *The Anthropology of Dance*. Bloomington: Indiana University Press.

Singer, Alice. 1974. "The Metrical Structure of Macedonian Dance." *Ethnomusicology* 18(3), 379–404.

Waterman, Richard. 1962. "Role of Dance in Human Society." *Focus on Dance II*, 47–55.

About the Contributors

Robin J. Evanchuk holds a Ph.D. in folklore and mythology from UCLA. She is the author (with Ysamur Flores Peña) of *Garments and Altars of Santeria: Speaking Without a Voice* (University Press of Mississippi, 1999). She has contributed several articles to the *Journal of Western Folklore* and the *Southern Folklore Journal*. She founded and directed a dance company, the Liberty Assembly, dedicated to American dance traditions. She has taught folklore at UCLA and Harvard.

Robert Henry Leibman holds an MA in folklore and mythology from UCLA and a Ph.D. in folklore from the University of Pennsylvania. He has conducted extensive research in Serbia and Macedonia, including a Fulbright research fellowship, and published a monograph on *Traditional Songs and Dances of Soka Banja Area* (San Francisco: Festival Records, 1973). He currently holds the position of professor of mathematics at Austin Community College.

Irene Loutzaki is a lecturer of the anthropology of dance at the University of Athens (Music Studies Department). She has served as a research fellow at the Peloponnesian Folklore Foundation (1974–1996), Nafplion. She currently participates in the Research Programme Thrace–Eastern Macedonia, sponsored by the Friends of Music Society, the aim of which is to create a database for cultural data. Her continuing research interests focus on such issues as gender and class relations, cultural policy and cultural practices and the political dimension of dance. She is a member of the International Council of Museums (ICOM) and the International Council for Traditional Music (ICTM). Her works have been widely published in both Greek and international journals.

Lynn D. Maners holds a Ph.D. in world arts and cultures from UCLA. He is the editor of the *Anthropology of East Europe Review*. He teaches anthropology at the University of Arizona.

Erica Nielsen earned her MFA in dance from the University of Arizona. She has conducted field work in Bulgaria in 2004 and 2006, and in France in 2001.

Christos Papakostas is a Ph.D. candidate at the University of Thessaly in the Department of History, Archeology, and Social Anthropology. He has taught and performed Greek folk dances with many local companies and taught in France, Belgium, England, and Canada. He is also a noted traditional percussionist and has performed widely as an instrumentalist.

Colin Quigley holds a Ph.D. in folklore from UCLA. His books include *Close to the Floor: Folk Dance in Newfoundland* (1985) and *Music from the Heart: Compositions of a Folk Fiddler* (1995). He has published articles in such journals as *Ethnomusicology*, the *ICTM Yearbook for Traditional Music*, and *Western Folklore*. From 1997 to 1999 he was lead researcher and curator for the Smithsonian Institution's "Gateways to Romania" Folklife Festival program. He is currently an associate professor in the Departments of World Arts and Cultures and Ethnomusicology at UCLA.

Nancy Lee Chalfa Ruyter holds a Ph.D. in history and is a dance historian, choreographer, and teacher. She has been a professor in the Dance Department of the University of California, Irvine, since 1982. She is the author of *Reformers and Visionaries: The Americanization of the Art of Dance* (1979), *The Cultivation of Body and Mind in 19th Century American Delsartism* (1999) and many articles on the Delsarte system and its uses, Spanish dance, Balkan dance, Latin American and Spanish theater, and theater movement. She is currently working on a biography of the international dance artist La Meri (Russell Meriwether Hughes, 1898–1988).

Anthony Shay holds a Ph.D. in dance history and theory from the University of California, Riverside, and has also earned MA degrees in anthropology and folklore and mythology from California State University in Los Angeles and UCLA. He is the author of the books *Choreophobia: Solo Improvised Dance in the Iranian World* (Mazda Publishers, 1999) and *Choreographic Politics* (2002) and co-editor and contributor (with Barbara Sellers-Young) of *Belly Dance: Orientalism, Transnationalism and Harem Fantasy* (Mazda Publishers, 2005). His most recent book is *Choreographing Identities: Folk Dance, Ethnicity, and Festival in the United States and Canada* (McFarland, 2006). He has published numerous articles in the *Oxford Encyclopedia of Dance*, the *Journal of Iranian Studies*, *Dance Research Journal*, the *Journal of Visual Anthropology*, the *Garland Encyclopedia of World Music*, and the *World Encyclopedia of Contemporary Theatre*.

Shay received the "Outstanding Scholarly Dance Publication" award from the Congress on Research in Dance for the year 2002 for *Choreographic Politics: State Folk Dance Companies, Representation and Power* (Wesleyan University Press), which was also singled out by the Kurt Weil Foundation for Honorable Mention.

Carol Silverman is a professor in the Anthropology and Folklore Program at the University of Oregon. She started as a folk dancer and, inspired by Dick Crum, became a scholar while continuing to sing Balkan music. Focusing on Bulgarian and Macedonian Roma, she has investigated the relationship among music, politics, ethnicity, ritual, and gender. She has contributed widely to both academic journals and collected volumes addressing ethnomusicology and anthropology. Her new book is *Performing Diaspora: Cultural Politics of Balkan Romani Music* (Oxford University Press, forthcoming).

June Adler Vail holds an MALS degree in dance from Wesleyan University and is a professor of dance in the Department of Theater and Dance, Bowdoin College. A former choreographer and performer, she was dance critic for the *Maine Times* for twenty years. Her research focuses on dancing as cultural performance and on various approaches to dance writing. Her book *Kulturella Koreografier* (Cultural Choreographies) addresses the broad range of dance forms practiced in Sweden and was published (in Swedish) in 1998.

Jamie L. Webster earned an MA in folklore at the University of Oregon and is a Ph.D. student of musicology and ethnomusicology, specializing in twentieth-century performance in East European and Euro-American music, at the School of Music and Dance at the University of Oregon, Eugene. She has recently published an article on the topic of American women performing Bulgarian songs in the *Anthropology of East Europe Review*.

Index

Aesthetics 94, 95, 98, 104, 133, 155, 157, 162, 206
Age of Aquarius (concept) *see* New Age
Agora (marketplace) 70, 71, 73, 75, 76, 77, 79, 81, 82, 83
Albania and Albanians 13, 21, 37, 42, 53, 63n12, 63n14, 64n16; in Macedonia 53; in Serbia 16–17, 29, 154, 161, 170, 171, 172
Alkimoi (Greek youth group) 102, 108
Aman Folk Ensemble 8, 32n13, 192
Amateur performing groups 28–29, 56–57, 64n25, 137, 142, 145–160, 168, 191–192, 195–208, 215; *see also* KUD
Ambler, Eric 13, 29
Americans 23, 24–26, 29, 32n12; involved in Balkan dance and music 7, 8, 14, 23–26, 179–194, 195–208
Anatov, Veselin 131
Anthropology and anthropologists 162–163, 195, 196, 215
Appropriation 58, 117, 206
Armenians 40, 119, 120
Assimilation 38, 120, 138
Athens 89–115
Austria-Hungary 10, 21, 124, 148, 150–151, 215, 239, 244–245; *see also* Hapsburg Empire
Authenticity 9, 25, 28, 95, 130, 135, 167–168, 197, 200
AVAZ International Dance Theatre 192
Azirov, Severdžan 57
Azis (Bulgarian Rom vocalist) 58

Balamoi (non-Roma) 74, 76, 78, 79, 81, 82, 84n28
Balkan Dancing (film) 25

Balkan Wars (1912; 1913) 24, 74
Balkanism 19–20
Ballet 131, 135, 183, 239
Ballet Folklorico de Mexico 166, 173
Baltic Republics 31n12, 166, 167
Bartok, Bela 119, 215
Bayanihan (State dance ensemble of the Philippines) 169, 173
Bazaar 73–74
Belgrade (Beograd) 75, 161, 169, 181, 190
Beliajus, Vyts 187–188
Belly dance 27, 28, 42, 43, 47, 52, 54, 57, 58, 59, 61, 63n14, 127
Beranče (Macedonian line dance) 47
Bitola (Macedonian town) 47
Black Lamb and Grey Falcon (book title) 26
Bogomilism 150
Borovčani Balkan Dance and Music (dance company) 195–208
Bosnia and Herzegovina 16, 21, 23, 27, 28–29, 145–160, 169, 170, 191, 205; Muslims *see* Bosniak
Bosniak (Bosnian Muslim) 18, 29, 149, 150, 151
Bran, Mary 179
Bringa, Tone 149
Broadway 20, 171
Bucharest 116
Bucsan, Andrei 122
Budapest 116
Bulgaria and Bulgarians 13, 16, 20, 21, 22, 23, 26, 27, 28, 30, 37, 53, 54, 57, 58, 59, 70, 72, 78, 90, 120, 130–144, 158, 186, 198, 206, 254
Bulgarian State Folk Dance and Song Ensemble (aka Philip Koutev Company) 26, 31n3, 134, 135, 167

275

Butler, Judith 41
Byron, Lord George Gordon 12–13, 19, 30n1
Byzantium 90, 112n1

Čalgija (Balkan musical and orchestral genre of Turkish origin) 40
Cantadhda (Greek Island vocal genre) 23
Carpathian region 118, 124, 127
Cartier, Michel 31n4
Casetta, Mario 25
Catholic Church and Catholics 150, 170
Çengi (female dancer) 40, 41, 42–43, 47, 62n5, 62n6, 63n14
Censorship 91–92, 135, 137
Chalga (also çalgi [Turkish], çalgija [Serbian and Macedonian]; Balkan musical and orchestral genre of Turkish origin) 40, 54, 58, 131–132, 137, 139–143
Chateaubriand, Vicomte Francois Rene 13
Christians 62n4, 73, 74, 75, 84n14, 150, 154
Christie, Agatha 19, 20
CIA (Central Intelligence Agency) 181
Çiftetelli (solo improvised dance) 22, 40, 42, 62; see also Kyuchek; Tsifteteli
Cingorită/cingorálás (Transylvanian Roma dance genre) 126–127
Coccharara, Giussepe 31n6
Čoček see Kyuchek
Cold War 13, 181
Commercialism 44, 54, 57, 60, 73–74, 84n28, 140–141, 207
Communist Party and Communists 28, 38, 125, 162, 179, 214; Bulgarian 130, 133–134, 135, 137, 138, 142; Romanian 117, 125, 214; Yugoslavian 149, 153, 154, 157, 158, 170
Community (concept) 195–208
Coronelli, Bianca 246, 247
Coronelli, Elvira 246–247
Coronelli, Pietro 30, 245–247
Costumes and clothing 16, 17, 18, 19, 28, 41, 42, 48, 52, 55, 56, 57, 58, 59, 63n14, 91, 94, 95, 100, 105, 107, 113n12, 126, 127, 131, 134, 141, 156, 159, 161, 165, 171, 172, 185, 197, 199, 200, 204, 244
Croatia and Croats 13, 16, 18, 19, 22, 23, 24, 25, 26, 29, 30, 31n8, 31n12, 145, 147, 149, 151, 153, 156, 158, 159, 169, 170, 191, 198, 205, 239–249, 253, 254
"Cross" dances (Macedonian) 256–266
Crum, Dick 5–11, 12, 13–14, 29, 30, 125, 239, 243, 247
Čuperlika (Macedonian Turkish and Roma dance) 52, 56

Dalmatia 23
Dance, Balkan morphology of 22–23, 29–30, 213–238, 250–270; Croatian 25, 254; Greek 69–88, 89–115, 253; Hungarian 116–129; Macedonian 25, 250–270; Roma 37–68, 69–88, 125–127; Romanian 14, 116–129, 213–238; Serbian 171, 172, 253, 254; South Serbian 256–266
Dancers: female 37–68, 135, 164, 230–236; male 37, 40, 41, 62n5, 62n8, 62n10, 63n13, 64n17, 135, 230–236
David, Mihai 216, 231, 235, 237n6
Dayton Peace Agreement 145, 157
Dejeu, Z. 119
Dictatorship 89–91, 108–109
Dora Stratou Greek Dance Theatre 18, 166
Dubinskas, Frank 146
Dunin, Elsie 45, 46, 47, 247–248
Duquesne University Tamburitzans see Tamburitzans
Durham, Edith 20
Durrell, Lawrence 20
Dvoransko Kolo (19th century Croatian ballroom dance) 29, 239–249; structure 243
Džansever (vocalist) 51

Eastern Europe 14, 15, 20, 26, 30, 31n2, 38, 39, 121, 154, 155, 163, 169, 198, 206, 214, 215
Enescu, Georges 215
Entopioi see Bulgaria and Bulgarians
Ethnic cleansing 29, 38, 149–150, 157, 170, 172
Ethnicity 15–19, 27–29, 37–68, 69–88, 116–128, 130–142, 145–160, 161–175, 179–194, 201, 215
Ethno-nationalism 145–146, 149, 151, 154, 155, 159
Evanchuk, Robin J. 25, 29
Exoticism 26, 60, 77, 85n30, 171, 172, 200

Fascism 89–115, 162, 164–165
FBI (Federal Bureau of Investigation) 181
Festivals 5, 27–28, 54, 55, 56, 89–115, 148, 151, 158, 165, 169; Romani 37, 39, 56, 57, 59–60
Filcich, John 31n4
Flaubert, Gustave 20
Folk dance camps 7; see also Recreational international folk dancing
Folk Dance Federation of California 182, 183, 188, 189, 193
Folk dance in America see Recreational international folk dancing
Folklor i Folklorni tanci (Bulgarian theatricalized folk dance genre) 130–144
Folklore 15, 16, 19, 23, 24, 28, 31n6, 91, 116, 117, 128n1, 128n2, 130, 132–135, 141, 142–143, 147, 148, 151, 154–155, 165, 168, 180, 184, 215
Folklore videos 141
Folklorism (concept) 102, 117–118, 128n1
Folklorization 109, 112
Foster, Susan 199, 200
Foucault, Michel 19, 161
Fourth of August celebrations 89–115

Index

France 21
Frula (Serbian folk dance company) 55–56

Gandy Dancers (folk dance group) 188
Garjet (Bosnian Muslim organization) 151
Geary, Patrick 17–18
Gender 26, 27, 37–68, 100, 110, 135, 163, 201, 203–204, 207, 208, 251; *see also* Sexuality
Georges, Robert A. 180
Gerika (group of old dances among Greek Roma) 70, 78, 79
Germans and Germany 118–119, 120, 240; Nazi 90, 91, 92, 164–165; *see also* Saxons
Giurchescu, Anca 117, 123
Globalization 130, 214
Golden Earrings (1947 film) 174n5
Goldsworthy, Vesna 19, 20
Great Britain 21
Greece and Greeks 8, 12, 13, 18, 21, 22, 23, 25, 27, 30, 31n7, 40, 53, 69–88, 89–115, 119, 120, 132, 254; Ancient 13, 90, 95, 100, 110, 112n1; Fascist 89–115
Gyftos see Gypsies
Gypsies 27, 28, 73, 74, 75, 80, 81, 82, 83, 100, 120, 126, 137, 139, 142, 161, 167, 171–172, 174n5; *see also* Roma

Hadžić, Hajrudin 158
Haidouti (Bulgarian freedom fighters) 141; see also *Hajduk*
Hajduk (Serbian freedom fighters) 13; see also *Haidouti*
Hapsburg Empire 10, 21, 124, 148, 150–151, 214
Harmony 23, 131, 214, 217, 218–226
Hellenism 90, 100
Henna ceremony 45, 52
Herder, Johann Gottfried 15
Herman, Maryann 7, 180–181
Herman, Michael 7, 180–181
Herodotus 17
Hip-hop 139
Hitler, Adolf 95
Hollywood 20, 171
Homosexuality 41, 58
Hope, Anthony 19
Horo (also *oro, hora*; dance genre) 22
Hungarian Academy of Sciences, Dance Section 127
Hungarians in Serbia 17
Hungary and Hungarians 28, 116–129, 198, 205, 215, 217–218, 241
"Hymn of the Fourth of August" 101, 113n15, 114n19

Identity, ethnic and national 14–16, 26, 28, 43, 71, 74, 76, 77, 83, 95, 110, 116, 118, 126, 131, 142, 186, 187; Serbian 170–172; Yugoslav 145, 149, 153, 154, 161–175, 214–215
Ideology 18, 71, 72, 91, 95, 109, 110, 117, 139, 142, 145, 148, 155

Igranka (dance event) 48–49
Ilieva, Anna 133
Illyrian Revival 239–240
Illyrians (Yugoslav political movement) 240, 242, 244–245
Immigrants 182, 186, 191, 201, 205
Improvisation 47, 81, 131, 217
Instruments, musical *see* Musical instruments
Intelligentsia 132
International folk dancing 8, 9, 31n5, 31n11, 125, 179–194, 202, 216
Irakleia (town in Greece) 69–99
Iran 162, 163–164, 166
Islam 17, 38, 40, 45, 138, 150
Istanbul 12, 42, 74
Italy and Italians 240, 245; fascist 90, 92
Izvorni KUD (authentic dance group) 147–148

Janković, Danica 24, 30, 41, 56
Janković, Ljubica 24, 30, 41, 56
Jews 31n8, 40, 118, 119, 120, 167
Jocul de-a Lungal (Romanian dance) 213–238
Jumaya (former name of Irakleia) *see* Irakleia

Kafantzis, Yorgos 73–74
Kalamatianos (Greek dance) 78, 100, 105, 107, 108, 112n4
Kallös, Zoltán 125
Karayanni, Stavros Stavrou 20
Karsilamas (also *karşlima*, solo improvised dance genre) 70; see also *Tsifteteli*; *Kyuchek*
Katsarova, Raina 133
Keil, Angeliki 73
Keil, Charles 73
Kismet (Hollywood and Broadway musical) 20, 171
Klapa (Dalmatian vocal genre) 23
Köçek (male dancer) 40, 41, 42, 58
Kolo (circle dance genre in Bosnia, Croatia, and Serbia) 7, 22, 79, 171, 179–194, 195–208, 242; Ballroom kolos 152, 239–249
Kolo (Serbian State Ensemble of Folk Dance) 13, 29, 31n3, 55, 147, 161–175, 181–182, 184, 187
Kolo Festival (annual festival held in San Francisco) 188, 192
"Kolomania" 29, 187–188
Könczei, Csilla 121
Kosovars *see* Albanians in Serbia
Kosovo 21, 29, 42, 47, 56–57, 149, 150, 153, 161, 169, 170, 171
Kosovo Polje, Battle of (1389) 31n7, 150
Koštana (Serbian play and musical production) 41, 63–64n15
Kostinick, Hugh 31n10
Koutev, Philip (also Filip Kutev) 26, 31n3, 134, 135, 167
Krstacko 256–266

Kuchek see Kyuchek
KUD (*kulturno umjetničko društvo*; amateur artistic dance companies in the former Yugoslavia) 56, 145–160
Kuhač, Franjo 242–244, 246, 247
Kürti, Laszlo 118, 119–120, 124
Kyuchek (also *kuchek, čoček* [Serbian, Macedonian, Romani]; genre of solo improvised dance) 22, 27, 37–68, 132, 139; movements 42, 47, 51, 63*n*14

Lado (State Ensemble of Folk Dance and Songs of Croatia) 26, 31*n*3, 147, 166, 173–174*n*4
Language 10, 18, 83*n*8; Albanian 23; Bosnian 16; Bulgarian 23, 38, 132; Croatian 16, 18, 23, 240, 244, 246; German 240; Greek 72; Hungarian 125; Latin 214–215; Macedonian 17, 23; Romani 37–38, 125; Romanian 23, 125, 214–215, 226–229; Serbian 16, 18, 23, 170; Serbo-Croatian 16, 170, 185–186, 201; Slavic 214–215, Slovene 23, Turkish 38
Laušević, Mirjana 13, 23, 25, 32*n*13
Lăutari (Romanian musicians) 127, 217
Le Carré, John 13
Lehar, Franz 20
Leibman, Robert Henry 23, 30
Ličko Kolo (Croatian folk dance) 195, 208
Lisinski, Vatroslav 243, 244
Louis IX 27, 164
Loutzaki, Irene 27–28
Lyceum Club of Greek Women 100–101, 105, 113*n*13

Macedonia and Macedonians 13, 17, 18, 22, 23, 24, 27, 30, 37–68, 71, 150, 153, 169, 179, 191, 205
Madonna (pop star) 141
Mahala (neighborhood; quarter; especially in Ottoman towns) 69, 70, 71, 73, 75, 76, 77, 78, 79, 80, 81, 82, 83, 84*n*12, 123, 153
Mahala (Roma solo improvised dance similar to čoček/kyuchek, meaning from the neighborhood) 54, 64*n*23, 127; movements 127
Maine 195–208
Manea (Roma solo improvised dance similar to čoček/kyuchek) 54, 64*n*23
Maners, Lynn 28–29, 167–168, 214
Manipulation (of folklore) 89–115, 117–118, 130, 146–149
Manning, Olive 20
Marian-Bălașa, Marin 119, 123
Martin, Gyorgy 124
Matchette, Vilma 31*n*4
Media 21, 58, 60, 61, 91–93, 95–97, 100, 103, 107, 109, 112*n*4, 113*n*11, 118, 132, 139, 165
Melody 217, 218–226, 240, 243
Merry Widow (comic opera) 20
Metaphor Theory 230
Metaxas, Ioannis 28, 80–115

Metaxas regime 89–115
Mexico 5, 14
Middle East 41
Miladanov, Dimitar 132
Miladanov, Konstantin 132
Millet system (also milet; Ottoman social organization based on religious affiliation) 16, 17, 69; *see also* Ottoman Empire
Minorities *see* Ethnicity
Modern dance 183, 202
Moiseyev, Igor 15, 31*n*3, 134, 165
Moiseyev Dance Company 15, 30–31*n*3, 134–135, 165, 166, 167, 168
Montenegro (Crna Gora) and Montenegrans 10, 20, 31*n*12, 150, 153, 158, 169, 170, 191, 206
Moreau, Yves 134
"Mouth" music 126
Movement, Balkan dance 47, 63*n*12, 63*n*14, 127, 198, 198–199, 208, 230–236, 250–270
MTV 139
Museum of the Romanian Peasant 127–128
Music 19, 161; Balkan 22–26, 198, 200; Bulgarian 131, 132, 135, 137–142; Croatian 239, 242; Eastern Europe 214; Greek 75–76; Hungarian 119–121; Roma 39, 75–76, 125–127, 172; Romanian 119–121, 213–238; Serbian 171, 172; Structure of 213–238; Transylvania 119–121, 126, 213–238; Turkish 40
Music videos 57–59, 65*n*30, 132, 139–141, 142–143; *see also* Media
Musical instruments 28, 45–46, 51, 69, 78, 84*n*28, 132, 135, 137, 139, 173–174*n*4, 197, 202, 214, 217, 218–226, 240, 243
Musicians 63*n*11, 127, 139; American 197, 198, 205, 216; Gypsy/Roma 38, 39, 54, 73, 75–76, 84*n*28, 126, 127, 137–138, 139, 205
Muslims 43, 62, 173; Albanian 53, 170; Balkan 43, 44, 45; Bosnian 149, 150, 151, 152–153, 156, 159, 172; in Bulgaria 53, 64*n*26, 138; in Macedonia 27, 53, 74; in Serbia 17, 29, 55, 161, 170, 171, 172
Mussolini, Benito 112*n*1
Mustafov, Ferus 51, 57

Nation and Nationalism 14, 15–16, 17–18, 23–24, 27–29, 30, 60, 89, 145–160; Bulgarian 130, 131, 134, 142; Croatian 239–249; Hungarian 116–129; Romanian 116–129; South Slavic 239, 244–245
National dance companies *see* State folk ensembles
National Geographic (magazine) 186
National Revival (Bulgarian cultural and political movement) 132, 135
National Youth Organization (EON) 95, 102, 106, 113*n*14
Neilsen, Erica 28
New Age 24–25

Index

New York City 52–53, 57, 64*n*19
Nikoloudis, Theodoulos 98
Ninković, Svetan 158
Nixon, Paul 117

Obrenović (Serbian royal family) 20
Oriental dance *see* Belly dance; *Çiftetelli*
Orientalism 19–20, 40, 58, 60
Orthodox church and Eastern Orthodox people 16, 43, 48, 53, 54, 106, 134, 150, 170, 171
Other (concept) 19, 53, 54, 56, 60, 73, 161, 171, 172–173, 214
Ottoman Empire and Ottomans 12, 16, 21, 22, 27, 31*n*7, 37, 39, 40, 42, 47, 74, 135, 137, 139, 141, 150, 158, 239; millet system in 16, 84*n*11, 150, 215

Panathenaic Stadium 89–115
Pan-Hellenic dances 93, 105, 107, 112*n*4
Papakostas, Christos 27
Papazov, Ivo 42
Parakrousis 157
Partizani (partisans of Yugoslavia) 151–152, 168
Pávai, Istvan 120–121
Peasants 15, 16, 19, 20, 24, 25, 28, 30, 39, 73, 91, 93–94, 95, 108, 118, 134, 165, 200, 207, 240, 242, 244; *see also* Villages and villagers
Peloponnesus 112*n*4
"People of the Pines" *see* Borovčani
Performance 116, 117, 145–159, 195–208, 213, 215
Periodicity 213, 214, 233, 235, 236–237
Petura, Adriana 226, 228
Phralipe (Romani amateur folk dance company) 56–57, 64*n*25
Planeta (Bulgarian television station) 141
Play 213, 214, 235, 236, 237
Polka 22, 246
Pomak (Bulgarian Muslims) 138
Pop folk (Bulgarian musical genre) 131–132, 137, 139–143
Pornography 58, 64*n*27, 139
Prastaimnaski (dance) 70, 79
Pratsika, Koula 98, 103, 105
Pravo horo (Bulgarian line dance) 47, 53
Premerl, Nada 240–241, 242
Propaganda 89, 91–93, 95, 100–103, 104, 108, 113*n*10, 169
Purtata dances (genre of Romanian dance) 217–218
Pussycat Dolls (pop vocal group) 141

Quigley, Colin 28

Race 27, 39, 69–70, 72, 89, 95, 163
Raftis, Alkis 18
Recreational international folk dancing 8, 9, 31*n*5, 31*n*11, 125, 179–194, 202; *see also* International folk dancing
Redžepova, Esma 45, 46, 50–51, 57, 59, 65*n*30
Redžepova, Usnija 64*n*15
Religion 16, 90, 134, 137, 138, 142, 150, 170
Representation 161–175
Research 28, 116–129, 162–163, 214, 215
Rhythms 23, 78, 132, 198, 213, 214, 217, 223, 227, 231, 233, 234, 235, 250–270
Rice, Tim 26, 158
Roma 27, 28, 29, 31*n*8, 37–68, 69–88, 116, 118, 125–127, 161; Macedonia 45, 69–88; Romania 116, 118, 125–127, 143*n*2; *see also* Gypsies
Romani (Roma language) 27, 127
Romania and Romanians 5, 8, 12, 18, 22, 28, 29–30, 31*n*7, 37, 38, 53, 54, 90, 116–129, 213–238
Romanian Americans 5
Romanian Folklore and Ethnology Institute 127
Rousseau, Jean Jacques 24
Ruritania (mythical Balkan country) 19
Russia and Russians 21, 31*n*2, 132, 134, 166, 167, 215
Ruyter, Nancy Lee Chalfa 29, 30

Said, Edward 19, 214
St. Paul Festival of Nations 5
Salieva, Zvezda 42
Salonsko kolo 152; see also *Dvoransko kolo*
Sarajevo 147, 149, 150, 152, 153, 157
Sarakatsani (Greek ethnic group) 72, 74, 78
Sarosi, B. 125–126
Savigliano, Marta 54
Saxons 120
Scholarship *see* Research
Secret of Chimneys (novel) 20
Serbia and Serbs 12, 13, 16–17, 18, 20, 21, 22, 23, 24, 27, 28, 29, 30, 31*n*7, 31*n*12, 53, 54, 55, 63*n*14, 75, 79, 132, 145, 147, 150, 151, 153, 156–158, 161–175, 186, 189, 191, 198, 244, 246, 253, 254, 267*n*10
Serres (region of Greek Macedonia) 69–88
Sevdah (Bosnian music genre) 23
Sexuality 27, 41, 43–47, 52, 53, 54, 58, 61, 62*n*7, 63*n*11, 131, 137, 138, 139, 141, 171, 172, 174*n*5, 207
Shame 43–44
Shay, Anthony 28–29, 41, 55
Shelley, Percy Bysshe 12
Shishmanov, Ivan D. 132
Shota (Kosovar Albanian dance company) 154
Silverman, Carol 27
Šiptari *see* Albanians in Serbia
Slavonia 146, 243

Slavs and Slavic 31*n*2, 37, 38, 43, 138, 139, 142, 150, 206, 239, 242
Slovenia and Slovenians 22, 23, 150, 153, 169, 191
Smotra Folklora (folklore festival) 148; *see also* Festivals
Socialism *see* Communists and the Communist Party
Sofia 20
Solo improvised dance 27, 28, 37–68, 173*n*1
South Slavs 43, 240, 243; *see also* Bulgarians; Croats; Macedonians; Serbs; Slovenians; Slavs
Space (concept) 71, 73, 75, 77–78
Spectacle 89, 90, 94, 104, 108–110
Stanković, Boris 41
State folk ensembles 9, 13, 18, 28, 31*n*3, 37, 54–55, 130, 134, 137, 142, 145, 161–175
Stereotypes and stereotypification 55, 56, 59, 60, 61, 65*n*30, 75–76, 127, 161, 167, 170, 171–173, 174*n*5, 183
Steves, Rick 133
Stigmatization 73, 161, 173
Stilizacija (theatricalized folk choreography or folk musical arrangement) 147–148
Strigături (extemporaneous rhymes in Romanian dance) 213, 214, 217, 226–230
Structure: dance 230–236, 250–270; music 213–238
Subculture 196, 200
Sugarman, Jane 40, 43, 53, 63*n*14
Šutka *see* Šuto Orizari
Šuto Orizari (Roma settlement in Macedonia) 46, 48, 50, 51, 53, 61*n*1
Symbols and symbolism 89, 90, 93, 95, 101, 109, 110, 112*n*4, 145, 146, 148, 150, 157
Syrtos 78, 79, 81, 93, 100, 112*n*4

Tamburica (also tamburitza; string orchestra found in Croatia and Serbia) 151
Tamburitzans (U.S. performing group based at Duquesne University) 6–7, 147
Tammies (Duquesne University Tamburitzans) *see* Tamburitzans
Tánchaz (Hungarian dance movement begun in the 1980s) 118, 125
Tanec (Macedonian State Folk Dance Ensemble) 13, 31*n*3, 56, 147, 169, 173*n*3, 179, 181–182, 183, 184, 187, 188
Tango 54, 70, 78
Taraf (Romanian orchestra) 217, 219
Television *see* Media
Third Hellenic Civilization 92, 95, 101, 103, 104, 107, 112*n*1
Thrace 78, 100
Timurids (Iranian dynasty) 163–164
Tito, Josip Broz 24, 54–55, 145, 146, 152, 154, 159*n*2, 168
Todorova, Maria 29*n*2

Tourism 91, 131
Tradition 76, 77, 85*n*3, 94, 95, 123, 132, 133, 168
Transylvania 28, 29–30, 116–129
Tsamikos (Greek dance) 78, 105
Tsifteteli (also *çifteteli*; solo improvised dance genre) 22, 40, 70, 79–81, 82; see also *Kyuchek*
Tsiganology 75, 84*n*21, 22
Tsinganiki (Greek Roma ethnic group) 69, 80, 81, 83*n*7
Turbo music 172
Turkey and Turks 13, 21, 22, 27, 28, 31*n*9, 41, 42, 43, 53, 57, 73, 78, 90, 127, 132; in Bulgaria 132, 137, 138–139, 142, 167; in Greece 70, 73, 100; in Yugoslavia 150, 158; *see also* Ottoman Empire and Ottoman
Turkish State Folk Dance Ensemble 167

Union of Soviet Socialist Republics (USSR) 15, 31*n*3, 134, 146, 154, 165, 167, 168, 169, 181
University of California, Irvine 247
USSR (Union of Soviet Socialist Republics) 15, 31*n*3, 134, 146, 154, 165, 167, 168, 169, 181
Utopia (concept) 200

Vaetsi, Serban 122
Variation (in dance) 251–252
Verdery, Katherine 118, 122
Victimization 21–22, 157
Villages and villagers 25, 93–94, 109, 131, 133, 134, 146, 147–148, 165; *see also* Peasants
Violence 22, 24, 39, 141, 161
Virginity 44, 64*n*18
Vlach (also Vlah; Romanian-speaking, semi-nomadic people found in various Balkan regions) 21, 70, 71, 72, 73, 74, 77, 84*n*11, 84*n*23
Vladutiu, Ion 121–122
Voight, Vilmos 128*n*2
Voix Bulgares (vocal group) 23
Vojvodina (formerly autonomous province of North Serbia) 169
von Bibra (Wharton), Anne 165
Voulgarika (group of Greek dances of Bulgarian origin) 78, 79

Waltz 22, 78, 242, 244, 246
We Are All Neighbors (documentary film) 149
Webster, Jamie 29–30
Weddings 45, 46, 48, 49–50, 52, 53, 57, 76, 84*n*28, 149, 159*n*1
Wenzel, Giorgiana 216, 231, 235
West, Rebecca 20, 21, 22, 25–26
Westra, Roxanne 226
Women 20, 37–68, 100–101, 105, 113*n*13, 132, 137,

World War II 38, 146, 148, 149, 150, 151, 168, 170, 214

Xenophobia 95, 104, 161

Yuftos (alternate name for Roma) 61*n*2, 69, 70
Yugoslav State Folk Ballet 31*n*3, 169

Yugoslavia (former) 7, 8, 18, 24, 27, 31*n*10, 55, 57, 145–160, 161–175, 179, 181, 182, 183, 186, 198, 205
Yunakov, Yuri 44

Zagreb 24, 29, 31*n*8, 239–249
Zhivkov, Todor 132

www.ingramcontent.com/pod-product-compliance
Lightning Source LLC
Chambersburg PA
CBHW051212300426
44116CB00006B/530